ARCHAIC STYLE IN ENGLISH LITERATURE, 1590–1674

Ranging from the works of Shakespeare, Spenser, Jonson and Milton to those of Robert Southwell and Anna Trapnel, this ground-breaking study explores the conscious use of archaic style by poets and dramatists between 1590 and 1674. It focuses on the wide-ranging, complex and self-aware uses of archaic linguistic and poetic style, analysing the uses to which writers put literary style in order to re-embody and reshape the past. Munro brings together scholarly conversations on temporality, memory and historiography, on the relationships between medieval and early modern literary cultures, on the workings of dramatic and poetic style, and on national history and identity. Neither pure anachronism nor pure nostalgia, the attempts of writers to reconstruct outmoded styles within their own works reveal a largely untold story about the workings of literary influence and tradition, the interactions between past and present, and the uncertain contours of English nationhood.

LUCY MUNRO is a lecturer in Shakespeare and Early Modern Drama Studies at King's College London. She is the author of *Children of the Queen's Revels: A Jacobean Theatre Repertory* (Cambridge, 2005), hailed by Roslyn Lander Knutson in *The Times Literary Supplement* as a book that 'redefines the template for company histories'. Her essays on early modern literature have appeared in a number of collections, including *The Oxford Handbook of Early Modern Theatre* (2009), and in journals including *Shakespeare*, *Modern Philology* and *Huntington Library Quarterly*. She has edited Sharpham's *The Fleer*, Shakespeare and Wilkins' *Pericles*, Fletcher's *The Tamer Tamed* and, for an acclaimed online edition, Brome's *The Demoiselle* and *The Queen and Concubine*.

ARCHAIC STYLE IN ENGLISH LITERATURE, 1590–1674

LUCY MUNRO

CAMBRIDGE
UNIVERSITY PRESS

CAMBRIDGE
UNIVERSITY PRESS

University Printing House, Cambridge CB2 8BS, United Kingdom

Published in the United States of America by Cambridge University Press, New York

Cambridge University Press is part of the University of Cambridge.

It furthers the University's mission by disseminating knowledge in the pursuit of education, learning and research at the highest international levels of excellence.

www.cambridge.org
Information on this title: www.cambridge.org/9781107042797

© Lucy Munro 2013

First published 2013

Printed and bound in the United Kingdom by CPI Group Ltd, Croydon CR0 4YY

A catalogue record for this publication is available from the British Library

Library of Congress Cataloging-in-Publication Data
Munro, Lucy.
Archaic style in English literature, 1590–1674 / Lucy Monro.
pages cm
Includes bibliographical references and index.
ISBN 978-1-107-04279-7 (Hardback)
1. English literature–Early modern, 1500–1700–History and criticism. 2. English language–Early modern, 1500–1700–Style. 3. English language–Archaisms. 4. English language–Style. I. Title.
PR421.M86 2013
820.9′003–dc23 2013014368

ISBN 978-1-107-04279-7 Hardback

To Matt Haynes

Contents

Illustrations

Photographs are courtesy of the Beinecke Rare Book and Manuscript Library, Yale University.

Preface

In preparing this book, I spent a good deal of time considering what procedure to follow in choosing editions for primary texts. There are no modern-spelling editions of many of the texts discussed here, notably those of Spenser, who is conventionally published in original spelling. Moreover, modernising early modern texts can obscure aspects of the ways in which they would have functioned for early modern readers. Yet to cite all texts in old spelling would not only risk jettisoning all of the valuable editorial work carried out on the works of authors such as Shakespeare, Jonson and Middleton, it would also obscure for modern readers the distinctions between words and styles which are archaic to us in the twenty-first century and those that would have registered as archaic to their original readers and spectators. In short: it seems self-defeating to modernise all quotations, yet fetishistic to cite Shakespeare and Jonson in old spelling. As a compromise, I have therefore cited a mixture of different kinds of texts and editions – sixteenth- and seventeenth-century quarto and folio texts; manuscripts; old-spelling editions; and modern-spelling editions – hoping in the process to foreground language change, and the various ways in which texts may and may not be archaic. Titles of primary texts are standardised and, in most cases, modernised in the main text, but given in their original form when early editions are cited in the notes.

Unless noted otherwise, all references to Shakespeare's works are to Stanley Wells and Gary Taylor (eds.), *The Oxford Shakespeare: The Complete Works*, 2nd edn (2005); references to Chaucer's works are to Larry D. Benson (ed.), *The Riverside Chaucer*, 3rd edn (1988); references to Milton's poems are to Gordon Campbell (ed.), *Complete English Poems, Of Education, Areopagitica* (1990); and references to Spenser's works are to *The Faerie Queene*, ed. A. C. Hamilton (1977) and *The Shorter Poems*, ed. Richard A. McCabe (1999). Latin text and modern translations of the works of Virgil are from *Virgil I (Eclogues, Georgics, Aeneid I–VI)* and *II (Aeneid 7–12, Appendix Vergiliana)*, ed. and trans. H. Rushton Fairclough;

rev. G. P. Goold, Loeb Classical Library, 2 vols. (1999). All references to the
Bible, unless noted otherwise, are from the 'King James' version (1611).

The work for this book was supported by the Leverhulme Trust, who
awarded me a Research Fellowship in 2009–10, and the Research Institute
for Humanities, Keele University, who provided me with research leave in
autumn 2010. I am especially grateful to those friends and colleagues who
read and commented on sections and chapters: Hannah Crawforth,
Julie Sanders, Clare McManus, David Matthews, Jonathan Hope
(whom I would also like to thank for shared unpublished research with
me), Scott McCracken, Ann Hughes, Christina Wald, Tripthi Pillai, Anita
Sherman, Nina Levine and Alison Findlay. My greatest debt is to Tanya
Pollard, who has read multiple drafts with unfailing good humour,
supporting and cajoling me in equal measure; any virtues that this book
may have in terms of its clarity of argument should be credited to her,
and any vices should be put down to my failure to follow her advice.

I would also like to thank the following for help, suggestions and good
questions: Gordon McMullan, James Knowles, Andrew King, Kate
Chedgzoy, Clare Kinney, Scott Black, Karen Britland, Tania Demetriou,
Will Stenhouse, Adam Smyth, Sue Wiseman, Martin Butler, Jerome De
Groot, Angus Vine, Subha Mukherji, Miriam Jacobson, Roberta Barker,
David Nicol, Paul Yachnin, Sarah Werner, Wes Folkerth, Holly
Dugan, Margreta de Grazia, Fiona Ritchie, Farah Karim-Cooper, Tiffany
Stern, Adam Zucker, Ben Robinson, Garrett Sullivan, Jeff Masten, Alan
Dessen, Ollie Jones (for document supply), Joel Swann (for Chaucerian
jokes in manuscript), Catherine Bates, Tom Rutter, Leah Scragg
(with whom I first read Spenser, Milton and Jonson as an undergraduate
at Manchester University), Christine Rees, David Lindley, Tobias Döring,
Kiernan Ryan, Susanne Greenhalgh, Jane Kingsley-Smith, Matthew
Neufeld, Jessica Dyson, Andy Kesson, Rosanna Cox, Marion O'Connor,
Catherine Richardson, Chris Jones, Alex Davis, Adam Rounce, Sharon
Ruston, Anna Barton, Patrick Spottiswoode, Richard Cust, Hugh
Adlington and Gillian Wright.

I owe a special debt to my colleagues in English at Keele, David
Amigoni, Nick Bentley, Susan Bruce, Anthony Carrigan, Beth Johnson,
Scott McCracken, Ceri Morgan, Roger Pooley, Nick Seager, Jim Sheard,
Jonathon Shears and Joe Stretch, for their consistent support and intellec-
tual drive. This book would be very different, and much poorer, without
them. For their hilarious and mostly unusable suggestions for alternative
titles I would also like to thank Pamela Allen Brown, Jerome De Groot,
Jonathan Hope, Jim Marino, Nick Seager and Alan Stewart.

I tried out draft material at a number of seminars and conferences, and would like to thank the following: the English research seminar at Nottingham University; the Centre for Reformation and Renaissance Studies, Birmingham University; the Centre for Medieval and Renaissance Studies, University of Kent; the 'Spiritual and Material Renaissance' colloquium, Sheffield Hallam University; the Renaissance and Early Modern seminar, Leeds University (special thanks to Alex Bamji); the Centre for Research in Renaissance Studies, Roehampton University; the Department of English, University College, Cork; the English work-in-progress seminar, Keele University; the London Shakespeare Seminar; the English and Drama departments of Dalhousie University; the Shakespeare and Performance Research Team, McGill University; seminar organisers and participants at the Shakespeare Association of America annual conference (especially Julie Sanders and Kate Chedgzoy for 'Sites of Memory/Sites of Performance' in Washington, DC); the Renaissance Society of America (with thanks to Robert Dulgarian); the International Shakespeare Congress; the International Medieval Congress; the Marlowe Society of America; and the International Shakespeare Conference, Stratford-on-Avon.

Many thanks are also due to Sarah Stanton for all of her support and belief in this project, and to Rebecca Taylor, Bryony Hall and Paul Smith. I would also like to thank the two anonymous readers for Cambridge University Press and two anonymous readers for the journal *Shakespeare* for their supportive and extremely productive comments, all of which have improved this book enormously. Staff at the British Library, the Folger Shakespeare Library, Senate House Library and Keele University Library have been unfailingly courteous and helpful; I am also very grateful to the Beinecke Rare Book and Manuscript Library, Yale University and the Shakespeare Birthplace Trust, for their help with the illustrations.

Part of Chapter 4 appeared in my essay 'Archaism, the "Middle Age" and the Morality Play in Shakespearean Drama', published in *Shakespeare* 8.4 (2012), 356–67. I am very grateful to the editors and Taylor and Francis for permission to reproduce that material here.

Last, but not least, I would like to thank my family: George Munro, Duncan Munro, Liz Munro, Ewan and Isla, Len and Enid Haynes, Jenni Burton and, above all, Matt Haynes, whose response to my delighted discovery of a copy of George Daniel's poems, pages uncut, in Keele University Library was 'And you're writing a *book* about this book?'. This book is for him, if he wants it.

Abbreviations

BL	British Library, London
CBJ	*The Cambridge Edition of the Works of Ben Jonson*, gen. eds. David Bevington, Martin Butler and Ian Donaldson, 7 vols. (Cambridge University Press, 2012)
CEP	John Milton, *Complete English Poems, Of Education, Areopagitica*, ed. Gordon Campbell (London: J. M. Dent, 1990)
EEBO	*Early English Books Online* (Proquest, 2003–13): eebo.chadwyck.com
FQ	Edmund Spenser, *The Faerie Queene*, ed. A. C. Hamilton (London: Longman, 1977)
LION	*Literature Online* (Proquest, 1996–2013): lion.chadwyck.co.uk
NA	National Archives, Kew, London
ODNB	*The Oxford Dictionary of National Biography*, gen. eds. H. C. G. Matthew, Brian Harrison and Lawrence Goldman (Oxford University Press, 2004–12): www.oxforddnb.com
OED	*The Oxford English Dictionary Online* (Oxford University Press): www.oed.com
SP	Edmund Spenser, *The Shorter Poems*, ed. Richard A. McCabe (London: Penguin, 1999)

Introduction: conceptualising archaism

In spring 1590, book-buyers in London were confronted with a long narrative poem, 'Disposed into twelue books, *Fashioning* XII. Morall vertues', published by William Ponsonby. If they bought the poem, or leafed through it on the stationer's stall, they encountered first a dedication 'TO THE MOST MIGHTIE AND MAGNIFICENT EMPRESSE ELIZABETH', then, on the following pages, the title and subtitle of the first book, and a four-stanza Proem. The Proem opens with the lines,

> LO I the man, whose Muse whilome did maske,
>   As time her taught, in lowly Shepheards weeds,
>   Am now enforst a far vnfitter taske,
>   For trumpets sterne to chaunge mine Oaten reeds,
>   And sing of Knights and Ladies gentle deeds;
>   Whose prayses hauing slept in silence long,
>   Me, all too meane, the sacred Muse areeds
>   To blazon broad emongst her learned throng:
> Fierce warres and faithful loues shall moralize my song.
>
> (Book 1, Proem, 1.1–9)

The style of this opening might already have struck our potential reader as odd, and this sensation would have intensified if he or she turned the page and glanced over the opening of Canto 1 (see Figure 1):

Canto I.

> *The Patron of true Holinesse,*
>   *Foule Errour doth defeate:*
>   *Hypocrisie him to entrapp,*
>   *Doth to his home entreate.*

I.

> A Gentle Knight was pricking on the plaine,
>   Y cladd in mightie armes and siluer shielde,
>   Wherein old dints of deepe wounds did remaine,
>   The cruell markes of many' a bloudy fielde;

3

Canto I.

The Patrone of true Holinesse,
Foule Errour doth defeate:
Hypocrisie him to entrappe,
Doth to his home entreate.

A Gentle Knight was pricking on the plaine,
  Ycladd in mightie armes and siluer shielde,
Wherein old dints of deepe woundes did remaine,
The cruell markes of many' a bloody fielde;
Yet armes till that time did he neuer wield:
His angry steede did chide his foming bitt,
As much disdayning to the curbe to yield:
Full iolly knight he seemd, and faire did sitt,
As one for knightly giusts and fierce encounters fitt.

And on his brest a bloodie Crosse he bore,
  The deare remembrance of his dying Lord,
For whose sweete sake that glorious badge he wore,
And dead as liuing euer him ador'd:
Vpon his shield the like was also scor'd,
For soueraine hope, which in his helpe he had:
Right faithfull true he was in deede and word,
But of his cheere did seeme too solemne sad;
Yet nothing did he dread, but euer was ydrad.

Vpon a great aduenture he was bond,
  That greatest *Gloriana* to him gaue,
That greatest Glorious Queene of *Faery* lond,
To winne him worshippe, and her grace to haue,

A 3   Which

Figure 1 The opening of Book 1, Canto 1 of Edmund Spenser's *The Faerie Queene*
(London, 1590), A3r (p. 3).

Yet armes till that time did he neuer wield:
His angry steede did chide his foming bitt,
As much disdayning to the curbe to yield:
Full iolly knight he seemd, and faire did sitt,
As one for knightly giusts and fierce encounters fitt. (1.1.1.1–9)

Skimming through Edmund Spenser's epic poem *The Faerie Queene*, our imaginary reader would have been struck by the fact that certain aspects of its vocabulary and style are archaic. Words such as 'whilome', 'areed', 'pricking' and 'Y cladd' would all have sounded old-fashioned to late-Elizabethan ears. 'Pricking' in the sense of riding or spurring one's horse seems to have been rare, if not entirely obsolete, in 1590; similarly, the past-participle 'y' prefix – derived from the Old English 'ge-' and common in medieval and early Tudor works – was becoming unusual even in poetry. He or she might also have been disconcerted by the four-line argument that precedes the first stanza of Book 1, written in the so-called 'common measure' or 'ballad measure', which by the last decade of the sixteenth century was rarely used outside ballads and translations of the Psalms. Less eye-catching than these features, but adding to the effect, are the old-fashioned inversions in Spenser's syntax, which aid the rhyme, and his emphatic use of auxiliary 'do': 'As much disdayning to the curbe to yield'; 'Yet armes till that time did he neuer wield'. An astute reader might, in addition, have realised that the Proem's allusion to the poet whose Muse formerly appeared 'in lowly Shepheards weeds' was a reference to Spenser, the archaising author of a collection of pastoral eclogues, *The Shepheardes Calender* (1579). *The Faerie Queene* has a past, in more ways than one, and the cumulative effect of these archaisms and allusions is to destabilise the reader, making him or her unsure of how to position the work temporally, how to characterise its use of English, or how to assess precisely its relationships with either contemporary or older literary texts and genres.

Spenser's *Shepheardes Calender* and *Faerie Queene* are two of the sixteenth century's best-known examples of literary archaism: the self-conscious incorporation into imaginative texts of linguistic or poetic styles that would have registered as outmoded or old-fashioned to the audiences or readers of the works in which they appear. Indeed, we are forcibly reminded of the extent to which Spenser has become synonymous with early modern archaism by our habitual use of old spelling in quoting both the text and titles of his works. Scholars and publishers do not generally, in contrast, refer to Shakespeare's *A Midsommer Nights Dreame* or Jonson's *The Divell is an Asse*, even though both of these texts contain examples of deliberate archaism. Our attention to Spenser has also blinded us to the prominence and range of the uses of outmoded styles in early modern literary culture. To look beyond Spenser is to acknowledge both the alternative forms of archaism that were available to writers between 1590 and 1674 – ranging from Old English to the conventions of the Tudor morality play – and the widely divergent uses to which they might be put.

Looking at these titles in their original spelling also forcibly reminds us of the distinction between two different categories of archaic style encountered by early modern readers and spectators: a text may survive the moment of its original production and become outmoded, or it might be deliberately written in an old-fashioned style, as a 'calculated continuity, or re-evocation'.[1] *The Faerie Queene* and select aspects of *A Midsommer Nights Dreame* and *The Divell is an Asse* appeared to be archaic to their original readers, and were intended to be so; in addition, all three works have gradually become archaic in the 400 years since their original composition and production. Quoting *The Faerie Queene* in old spelling thus blurs the distinction between these two forms of archaism, even though there are valid grounds in general for presenting Spenser's works in their original form.[2]

This book focuses on deliberate stylistic archaism in poems and plays in which its presence is a central part in their design. Its central argument is that paying close attention to the self-aware deployment of archaic linguistic and literary forms in early modern drama and poetry does not merely illuminate the individual works in which they appear. Instead, it argues, archaism is a crucial barometer of writers' broader engagements with two forms of temporal process: the history of the nation and the development of literary style. When poets or dramatists return to older forms of English, be they in vocabulary, syntax or metre, they make a claim on – and for – the linguistic and poetic resources of the English language; simultaneously, they may explore its place in the construction and manipulation of national history and identity. As Claire McEachern comments in her influential account of the poetics of English nationhood in the late sixteenth and early seventeenth centuries, 'England, English, and Englishness are spoken in many ways in this moment, by many persons and in many places.'[3] Moreover, in creating something new from the fragments of something old, archaist writers both recapitulate and reconfigure their national and literary heritage.

In the preface to his *Fables Ancient and Modern* (1700), John Dryden sets out two parallel literary histories: ancient and modern, Roman and English. 'We must be Children before we grow Men', he declares. 'There was an

Ennius, and in process of Time a *Lucilius*, and a *Lucretius*, before *Virgil* and *Horace;* even after *Chaucer* there was a *Spencer*, a *Harrington*, a *Fairfax*, before *Waller* and *Denham* were in being: And our Numbers were in their Nonage till these last appear'd.'[4] Literary archaism both depends on and resists such teleologies. Archaising writers demonstrate their awareness of historical difference, as evidenced in linguistic and stylistic change, but through their desire to imitate and reinvigorate outmoded styles they also challenge the smooth narrative of progression that Dryden describes. They thus acknowledge the ways in which, to appropriate Annamarie Jagose's description, time might be not linear but 'cyclical, interrupted, multi-layered, reversible, stalled'.[5] Archaists' time is, in the terms adopted by recent scholars, queer time – out of joint, askew, at odds with conventional notions of temporality.[6] In its impersonation of the past, archaism unsettles relationships between past, present and future even as it seemingly attempts to inscribe them.

Archaists reject, implicitly or explicitly, some of the conventions of their own day; however, they do not slavishly imitate outmoded forms. Their relationship with the past is both collusive and competitive; writers who employ archaism express a desire for communion with the dead, but also a longing to outstrip their achievements. Archaism's backward glance is not, therefore, purely nostalgic. Instead, the archaising writer seeks to reshape the past, to mould the present, and proleptically to conjure times yet to come; he or she creates a temporal hybrid that looks forward to its own incorporation into a national and literary future. In these ways, therefore, archaism crystallises the distinctively self-aware stance that early modern writers adopt in relation to their fast-changing language, their literary tradition, and the uncertain contours of English nationhood.

The chapters that follow analyse the various uses of archaism in literary texts written and, in many cases, performed between 1590, the year in which *The Faerie Queene* first appeared, and 1674, when the twelve-book version of Milton's *Paradise Lost* was published. This time frame merits some comment, especially given that it starts a decade after the publication of *The Shepheardes Calender*, a text that is rightly seen as a landmark in the uses of literary archaism. Moreover, the self-conscious use of archaism in English literature did not begin with Spenser.[7] It had a rich tradition among mid-sixteenth-century poets, and its use was intertwined with anxieties about the status of the English language for much of this period, as I will explore in greater detail below. Thomas Wyatt, Henry Howard, Earl of Surrey, Nicholas Grimauld, Alexander Barclay, Barnabe Googe, Thomas Sackville, George Turberville and George Gascoigne all employed

archaic linguistic and literary forms, and in 1553 Thomas Wilson was able
to complain that 'The fine Courtier will talke nothyng but Chaucer'.[8]
Archaism also played a crucial role in literary experimentation; as Veré
Rubel comments, poets such as Wyatt evolved 'a poetic diction that was
new because it was deliberately old'.[9]

Notwithstanding these developments, however, the period between
the Elizabethan *fin de siècle* and the early years of the Restoration was a
distinct phase in the tradition of literary archaism, in which writers
adopted new forms of archaism and evolved distinctive attitudes towards
outmoded style and its uses; it also saw the production of some of the
most intriguing and varied archaist texts ever written. By the 1590s, some
of the century's earlier anxieties about the status of English as a literary
language had eased. But events in the following decades would put new
pressures on notions of Englishness, the relationship of England to other
parts of the British Isles, and the place of English amongst Britain's
languages. As I will explore in the following chapters, these events
included: the accession of James VI of Scotland to the throne of England,
and his project for the union of Britain; the marriage of his son, Charles I,
to the French Catholic princess, Henrietta Maria; the fracturing of Stuart
Britain during the Bishops' Wars and Civil Wars; and the new dominance
of England under the Protectorate. Experiments with medieval literary and
linguistic forms, with genres such as epic and pastoral, and with metrical
archaism, reflected and participated in the debates surrounding these
events.

In terms of archaism itself, 1590 saw the publication of the first three
books of *The Faerie Queene*, a milestone because it saw archaism move out
of pastoral writing – its accustomed home in the 1570s and 80s – and into
epic. The 1590s also saw fast-paced developments in both poetic and
theatrical style, developments that rendered certain metrical forms (notably
the fourteener and poulter's measure) and dramatic genres (in particular the
morality play) archaic, making them available for specific kinds of
stylistic experimentation. However, the changes that made a wider range
of archaisms available also hastened the processes through which archaism
itself eventually slipped out of fashion. By the time that the Stuart
monarchy was restored in 1660, writers were beginning to reject archaism
in favour of a more sustained neo-classicism. Attacks on Spenser's language
intensified, the use of archaism became increasingly restricted to parody
and burlesque, and in 1700 Dryden justified translating Chaucer into
modern English on the grounds that 'as his Language grows obsolete, his
Thoughts must grow obscure'.[10] Furthermore, two of the 1660s' most

prominent engagements with outmoded style, Milton's *Paradise Lost* and Samuel Butler's *Hudibras*, may actually have hastened archaism's decline.

In focusing on this pivotal period, therefore, this book traces both the development of literary archaism and the relationships that writers established between the literary conventions of their own times and those of their medieval and Tudor forebears. Like Peggy A. Knapp in her illuminating study *Time-Bound Words*, I pay close attention to the ways in which an old word 'points to both the horizon it helps define in the Middle Ages, and to a new understanding of society and culture as new conditions arise'.[11] However, in exploring the uses of not only archaic vocabulary but also outmoded grammatical and metrical forms, I attempt in addition to take seriously the cultural work that literary and linguistic style can do. While metre might not be strictly imaginative in itself, it can be used, as Alison Shell points out, 'in a manner similar to allegory and other imaginative devices', carrying both creative and emotional weight.[12] Similarly, Andrew Zurcher's recent case-study of the ways in which the archaic auxiliary 'mote' ('may' or 'must') functions in Spenser's poetry suggests both the author's 'labored care over his language' and the impact that such linguistic forms can have on the overall texture of a literary work.[13]

Arguing for the importance of a range of archaising strategies in the period 1590–1674, this book also makes a case for the range of writers and genres involved. It deliberately balances canonical and non-canonical texts, examining the plays and poems of Jonson, Middleton, Milton, Shakespeare and Spenser alongside those of William Cartwright, Morgan Llwyd, Robert Southwell and Anna Trapnel, among others. In doing so, it insists on both the literary interest of such texts – some periodically dismissed as doggerel or hack-work – and the value of examining works such as *Hamlet* or *The Faerie Queene* alongside texts that do similar aesthetic work or aim for a similar imaginative impact.

Instead of attempting an exhaustive or comprehensive survey, I instead take 'snapshots' of the use of archaic style in different contexts. The structure of the book follows broadly the chronology of the styles being mimicked or resurrected. Chapters 1 and 2 explore two examples of the early modern encounter with medieval literary culture, looking first at the uses in seventeenth-century literature of Old English, the Anglo-Saxon forebear of Early Modern English that was perhaps the ultimate English linguistic archaism, and then at writers' responses to later medieval authors such as Chaucer and Gower. In doing so, these chapters contribute to the burgeoning field of 'medievalism' as an object of study.[14] Chapters 3 and 4 explore the uses of Tudor styles that had become outmoded by the late sixteenth century, focusing on archaism in liturgical texts and religious poetry, and on the reanimation of old-fashioned dramatic genres on the turn-of-the-century stage. Finally, Chapters 5 and 6 focus on the two genres with which archaic style was most often linked in the early modern period: pastoral and epic, traditionally the 'lowest' and 'highest' of literary modes.

Furthermore, each chapter asks different questions of its material and its central texts, exploring in different ways and to different degrees the two central issues on which the book focuses: archaism's relationships with literary history and with national history and identity. In doing so, they focus on the multiple relationships between archaism and issues such as regional identity, obsolescence, religious conservatism and radicalism, prophecy, the interactions between different generations of writers, parody, genre, anachronism and nostalgia. Chapter 1, 'Within our own memory: Old English and the early modern poet', focuses on three literary encounters with Old English: the quotation of Old English phrases in two plays, Thomas Middleton's *Hengist, King of Kent* (1619–20) and William Cartwright's *The Ordinary* (*c.*1635); the self-conscious use of Old English words in William L'Isle's translation of Virgil's *Eclogues* (1628); and the composition of poems in Old English for two university collections in the 1640s and 1650s. In examining these texts, it makes two interrelated arguments, one relating to national identity and the other to literary lineage and inheritance. First, it argues that these texts demonstrate the crucial role that the Anglo-Saxon language could play in the conceptual-isation of national identity in Stuart and Protectorate Britain; second, it contends that in these texts Old English gradually becomes visible – or thinkable – as a vehicle for literary expression, thus helping to facilitate the rediscovery of Old English poetry and the rewriting of literary history that it occasioned. In these ways, therefore, literary archaism enables writers both to come to terms with the political pressures of the present day and to gesture towards unknown futures.

Chapter 2, 'Chaucer, Gower and the anxiety of obsolescence', similarly focuses on medieval literary inheritance. As noted above, two categories of archaism appear in literary texts: the archaism of the text that has grown old, and that of the text that has been deliberately written in an old-fashioned style. In Book 4 of Spenser's *The Faerie Queene* (1596), the Cambridge University play *The Return from Parnassus* (*c.*1598–1600), Shakespeare and George Wilkins' *Pericles* (1607) and Cartwright's *The Ordinary* we find both quotations from the works of Chaucer and Gower and imitations of them. Each of these texts deploys archaism as a means of negotiating their authors' anxieties about linguistic change and the current or future obsolescence of literary works, but they come to two opposing conclusions. *The Faerie Queene* and *The Return from Parnassus* use archaism as a means of expressing their authors' unease about the obsolescence of medieval texts, the corrupting effects of time, and the potential future obsolescence of their own works. In contrast, *Pericles* and *The Ordinary* resist obsolescence, insisting through their very use of archaism that Chaucer and Gower still have an active place in modern literary culture and that their authors will likewise survive the passage of time.

Chapters 3 and 4 move away from medieval literary inheritance to consider styles that had more recently become archaic. Chapter 3, 'Archaic style in religious writing: immutability, controversy, prophecy', explores the most culturally central use of archaism in early modern England: that found in biblical and religious diction. Protestant translations of liturgical texts such as the Bible, the Book of Common Prayer and the Psalms employ archaism in an attempt to mimic the supposed immutability of divine language, and to naturalise their translations as truly 'English'. Outside the Anglican establishment these qualities are put to alternative uses, and, despite their contrasting beliefs, Catholics and Protestant radicals such as the Fifth Monarchists deploy similar archaising techniques. Writing against the tendency for Catholic poets to adopt baroque forms, Robert Southwell and Gertrude More use archaic English metres such as the fourteener and common measure in an attempt to re-naturalise Catholic devotional traditions and to reinscribe their connections with their native land. Writing during the national upheavals of the Civil War, Commonwealth and Protectorate, the Fifth Monarchists Anna Trapnel and Morgan Llwyd exploit the connections of common measure to the English psalter and the prophetic traditions of the Psalms. They use archaic metres to underscore the Fifth Monarchists' claims to national heritage and to link their poetry with the apocalyptic temporality of prophecy, arguing for the central role of their brand of Protestantism in the destiny of the nation. Thus, Catholic and Protestant poets alike exploit archaism's capacity to appeal to the past, and to a disputed national heritage, while simultaneously staking a claim to both the present and future.

While Chapter 3 focuses on the use of archaism in specific non-dramatic contexts, Chapter 4, 'Staging generations: archaism and the theatrical past', analyses the ways in which late Elizabethan and early Jacobean plays exploit Tudor dramatic modes that had become archaic by the turn of the seventeenth century: the morality play; the elite drama and classical translations of the 1560s and 1670s; and the dramatic romance of the 1570s and 1580s. Taking as its starting point allusions to the morality play in Jonson's *The Devil is an Ass* (1616) and *The Staple of News* (1626), it focuses on inset metadramatic sequences in three turn-of-the-century works: *Sir Thomas More* (*c*.1601; revised *c*.1603–4), *Histriomastix* (*c*.1598–1602) and Shakespeare's *Hamlet* (*c*.1600). While medieval styles might be safely consigned to the distant past, Tudor dramatic modes were not sufficiently far away as to be uncomplicatedly archaic. For that reason, the theatrical archaism of the plays discussed here uncovers the processes through which one generation of writers constructs another as archaic, and the range of interactions within and between generations that these processes require. It allows dramatists to recreate and critique earlier modes, to exploit their thematic and aesthetic potential, and to use them in defining their own works' relationship with the literary and theatrical past.

The final pair of chapters considers the uses to which writers put archaism in critiquing or renewing two of the most established literary genres: pastoral and epic. Chapter 5, 'Shepherds' speech: archaism and early Stuart pastoral drama', returns to pastoral, the most important literary vehicle for archaism in the mid-sixteenth century. However, rather than focusing on Spenser and his direct followers and imitators, it explores developments in pastoral drama in the early seventeenth century, and the ways in which new influences from Italy and, later, France complicated pastoral's archaising heritage. While the non-dramatic poetry of Michael Drayton, William Browne, and Giles and Phineas Fletcher largely adheres to Spenserian models, plays such as John Fletcher's *The Faithful Shepherdess* (1607–8), Milton's *A Masque Presented at Ludlow Castle* (1634) and Jonson's *The Sad Shepherd* (*c*.1634–8) use outmoded style in different ways. Juxtaposing the old pastoral technique of archaism with new styles and conventions absorbed from continental theatre, they explore alternative forms such as syntactic archaism and the Skeltonic, and reassess the role of Spenserian archaism. In doing so, they negotiate the paradoxical associations that pastoral had with both low and elevated style, with the rustic and the courtly, with the natural and the artificial, with the comic and the serious, with English and foreign influences, and with the old and the new. Archaism takes on a crucial role in these negotiations, breaking down these binaries in some contexts and reinforcing them in others. It thus assists dramatists in renegotiating the place of pastoral in national, cultural and aesthetic contexts alike.

Moving from the humblest of neoclassical genres to the highest, Chapter 6, 'Archaism and the "English" epic', explores the role of linguistic and metrical archaism in the creation of a local style for epic writing. The association between archaism and epic grandeur was an early modern commonplace, traceable to the ideas of theorists such as Aristotle and Quintilian and to the stylistic innovations of early epic poets such as Homer and Ennius. Owing to archaism's links with medieval writing and the English literary tradition, it became a powerful means for rendering epic stylistically and emotionally 'English', in both original works and translations. However, as the seventeenth century progressed, it also became a way in which writers were able to register the strains within that project. The chapter first compares the use of a single archaic word, 'dight', in *The Faerie Queene* and Edward Fairfax's translation of Tasso's *Gerusalemme liberata* (1600), examining the ways in which archaism assists these writers in adapting Italian epic to English uses. It then turns to metrical archaism, looking at the uses of the fourteener – strongly associated with English epic style in the sixteenth century – in George Chapman's translation of Homer's *Iliad* (1598–1611) and Shakespeare's *Cymbeline* (*c*.1611). The uses to which these writers put the fourteener suggest the potential strengths and weaknesses of English epic form, an issue that is taken up in detail in the next section, which focuses on mock-heroic parodies of the epic in Jonson's 'On the Famous Voyage' (*c*.1610) and Charles Cotton's burlesque adaptation of *The Aeneid*, *Scarronides* (1664–5). Jonson and Cotton suggest through their parody of English epic style that archaism and other aspects of epic diction have become exhausted. The chapter concludes with a reassessment of Milton's *Paradise Lost*, arguing that while Milton – like Jonson and Cotton – deconstructs the traditional role of archaism in the English epic, he also manipulates outmoded linguistic and metrical styles in order to repurpose epic as a Christian and republican form. Finally, a short Coda explores the reasons for literary culture's widespread rejection of archaism in the late seventeenth century.

Four theses

Having set out the scope of this study, in the rest of this introduction I plot its conceptual background. To engage fully with literary archaism, and the issues that it raises, is to delve into a number of areas that have preoccupied scholars in recent years. Notably, because it is entwined with the English language and English literary stylistics, archaism foregrounds writers' attitudes towards linguistic and stylistic change, and its study thus engages with recent detailed exploration of stylistic and rhetorical affect in early modern texts.[15] It also entangles itself with questions of English national identity in the late sixteenth and early seventeenth centuries, the subject of influential studies by Richard Helgerson, Claire McEachern, Mary Floyd-Wilson and John Kerrigan, among others.[16] Further, the imitation of outmoded styles raises questions relating to temporality, historiography and relationships between different periods of literary and national history.[17] In exploring these issues, and seeking to place archaism within its specific cultural, social and political contexts, this book follows a broadly historicist path. Yet it also aims to complicate prevailing models through its attention to the temporal instability of archaic style, and its awareness of the extent to which this instability challenges the stable division between past and present on which many historicist readings depend. If, as Philip Schwyzer notes, literary texts are 'things in the present and witnesses to the past, belonging in different ways to us and the dead',[18] archaist works further complicate our notions of what 'belongs' to the past or present. Literary archaism, which looks backwards and forwards simultaneously, and creates texts that resist belonging fully to any one time-period, is in many respects an 'unhistorical' phenomenon, to adopt Madhavi Menon's term. However, while archaism resists incorporation into a fully historicist model of criticism, its unsettling power becomes evident only when we look in detail at its workings, exploring fully its cultural and aesthetic contexts.[19]

Rather than summarising in detail all of the influences on the approach to literary archaism adopted here, I instead set out four theses about its nature and function:

1. *Archaism is a form of imitation.*
2. *Archaic words and styles undermine linear temporality, reconfiguring relationships between past, present and future.*
3. *Archaism is intertwined with national identity.*
4. *Archaism is self-conscious and artificial, yet capable of arousing strong emotion.*

As I explain in greater detail below, early modern archaism's closest conceptual bedfellows are anachronism and nostalgia; its affinity with anachronism in particular marks its difference from the literary archaisms of some other periods. For instance, some of my theses challenge the model outlined in the fullest study of literary archaism to date, Linell B. Wisner's 'Archaism, or Textual Literalism in the Historical Novel', largely because the nineteenth- and twentieth-century historical novel, Wisner's object of study, pursues different ends and employs rather different techniques from early modern texts. As Wisner notes, his texts do not 'merely sprinkle their narratives with obsolete mannerisms'; instead, they faithfully reproduce an 'antiquated literary idiom', most closely resembling forgeries of older texts.[20] In contrast, early modern archaist writers mingle outmoded linguistic and literary forms with contemporary idioms; they 'sprinkle' their texts with archaism or embed archaising characters or self-contained sequences within their narratives, and the products only rarely resemble forgeries. While archaism may be deployed strategically as an authenticating gesture in early modern texts, its claim to truth is generally complicated or compromised. Moreover, even where a complete work is written in an archaic form – for instance, the seventeenth-century composition of poems in Old English or a cod-Chaucerian style – anachronistic details are included, and archaisms often jostle with neologisms and other forms of temporal dissonance.

While the post-eighteenth-century novel uses archaism extensively, early modern prose fiction employs it only very rarely, even in texts set in the historical past.[21] Furthermore, unlike the historical novel, archaist texts of the sixteenth and seventeenth centuries do not use archaism to represent 'a specific historical experience', as Wisner terms it ('Archaism', 12). Instead, early modern literary archaism has more in common with the techniques used in the temporally hybrid form of steampunk, a recent novelistic and filmic subgenre that often places anachronistic technology in nineteenth-century settings; in steampunk, as Margaret Rose describes, archaisms 'often help the texts to masquerade as Victorian'; they represent 'an engagement with the historicity of the present', playing with what Fredric Jameson has termed 'connotations of pastness'.[22] In a similar fashion, early modern archaism masquerades as Anglo-Saxon, as Chaucerian, as early Tudor, or as the product of a less clearly specified past, but it never expects its masquerade to be fully credited or taken wholly seriously.

1 Archaism is a form of imitation. Archaism requires a writer to mimic older literary and linguistic forms, as a number of the terms used by early modern writers to describe it acknowledge. The term 'archaism' itself appears to have been first used in the mid-seventeenth century, but prior to that writers occasionally used a term closer to the original Greek, 'archaismos'.[23] Writing in the 1530s, Nicholas Udall quotes the fourth-century grammarian Donatus' commentary on Terence's *Eunuch*, defining 'archaismos' as 'an imitation of spekynge of the olde tyme'.[24] This definition stresses both the diachronic and imitative aspects of archaism: a writer is required not merely to refer to past forms, but to seek to recreate them. Archaism might also shade into cacozelia, a rhetorical technique criticised as 'Fond Affection' by George Puttenham in *The Art of English Poesy*

(1589), which often entails imitating the 'wrong' models.[25] Cacozelia is often linked with neologisms taken from other languages, but it can also encompass archaism. In Thomas Elyot's 1538 Latin–English dictionary a 'Cacozelus' is 'an yll folower or imitatour';[26] here, the writer who employs cacozelia chooses the wrong exemplars to imitate, exemplars which might be classical texts, modern works in foreign languages, or older texts from his or her own national tradition. The past is a different country, and archaism as cacozelia is an affected, potentially ill-mannered, form of imitation.

The slightly later term 'Chaucerism', used from at least the 1590s, also foregrounds imitation – here of a specific medieval forebear – while suggesting in addition a certain primitivism of style.[27] Jonson, for instance, complains that Chaucerisms 'were better expunged and banished', while Thomas Fuller comments that Chaucerisms in Spenser's poetry 'are thought by the ignorant to be *blemishes*, known by the learned to be *beauties* to his book; which notwithstanding had been more salable, if more conformed to our modern language'.[28] The term also highlights the intertexual relations that can be created through the imitation of an earlier text or even the use of a single word or metrical form. For instance, when Spenser says in the opening lines of the Proem to *The Faerie Queene* that his 'Muse whilome did maske, / As time her taught, in lowly Shepheards weeds' he not only draws attention to his own archaising style in *The Shepheardes Calender*, but also invokes the literary history of the word 'whilom' itself, and the authors – most notably Chaucer – who used it.

Imitation was central to early modern poetics, but its characteristics and problems are particularly evident when a writer chooses to mimic the style of a predecessor whose work has become outmoded. Terence Cave points out that in literary imitation 'the activities of reading and writing become virtually identified'; readers read with the intention of incorporating a text into their own work, while the imitating writer 'cannot entirely escape the constraints of what he has read'.[29] When the text imitated is an outdated one, and aspects of its form or style have become archaic, the 'writer as imitator' is forced to negotiate carefully the demands of two sets of aesthetic conventions: those of the source text and those of his own day. As Thomas M. Greene notes, imitation 'makes possible an emergent sense of identity, personal and cultural, by demonstrating the viability of diachronic itineraries'.[30] In imitating older texts, the archaising writer constructs his or her own poetic identity through a form of literary time travel, underscoring the network of diachronic interactions on which early modern literary composition depended.

Imitation is crucial to one of the most important early modern critiques of archaism, Jonson's comments in his commonplace book, published posthumously as *Timber, or Discoveries*, in which he sets out some typically stringent advice for the young writer, drawing closely on Quintilian's guidelines for the use of archaism in the *Institutio Oratoria*. '[A]s it is fit to read the best authors to youth first', Jonson writes,

> so let them be of the openest, and clearest. As Livy before Sallust, Sidney before Donne. And beware of letting them taste Gower or Chaucer at first, lest falling too much in love with antiquity, and not apprehending the weight, they grow rough and barren in language only. When their judgements are firm and out of danger, let them read both the old and the new; but no less take heed that their new flowers and sweetness do not as much corrupt as the other's dryness and squalor, if they choose not carefully. Spenser, in affecting the ancients, writ no language; yet I would have him read for his matter; but as Virgil read Ennius.[31]

Typically concerned with avoiding the extremes of poetic style and diction, Jonson suggests that writers such Gower and Chaucer are best left to experienced poets, who will be able to bear the 'weight' and avoid the 'rough[ness]' and 'barren[ness]', the 'dryness and squalor', that imitating older writing might bring. The original work might be good, but in attempting to imitate it a modern writer merely produces a worthless reiteration of its worst stylistic features. Nonetheless, although he condemns writers' love affairs with antiquity, Jonson's comments also hint there is a dangerous allure in the works of Gower or Chaucer. Despite their stylistic limitations, these writers continue to work on the imaginations of their early modern successors.

In fact, Jonson's discussion of archaism becomes more multifaceted the more attention we devote to it. His allusions to the classical writers Ennius (*c*.239–*c*.169 BCE) and Sallust (86–*c*.35 BCE) – the latter taken directly from Quintilian – remind us that archaism has a long history, and one that was intertwined with ideas about imitation. Archaism in Greek texts stretches back at least as far as Homer, and Sander M. Goldberg argues that Roman archaism may be nearly as old as the literature itself, pointing out that it was 'a way to make the legacy of the past legitimize the work of the present'.[32] Archaism in Latin verse is instructively complex. For later writers, much of the archaic quality of Ennius' work derived from its genuine antiquity, but Ennius had also introduced self-conscious archaisms of his own, imitating aspects of Homeric style in his *Annales*.[33] Ennius' works thus embody both forms of archaic text: that which has become old and that which imitates older works. His voluntary archaism was often overlooked; in the *Institutio Oratoria*, for instance, Quintilian writes, 'Ennius we should worship as we do groves whose age has made them sacred, and whose huge and ancient trees have come to have more sanctity about them than beauty.'[34] Sallust, viewed more straightforwardly as a self-conscious archaiser, receives harsher criticism: Quintilian quotes an epigram that describes him as a 'plunderer of old Cato's words', and comments, 'This is sheer pedantry' ('Odioso cura').[35]

Thus, when Jonson juxtaposes Donne with Sallust he criticises what he perceives as the wilful and affected obscurity of Donne's style; when he compares Spenser with Ennius he suggests that on some level Spenser is unable to prevent himself from imitating his medieval forebears.[36] As Anne Barton notes, some of the earliest commentators on *The Shepheardes Calender* claimed that Spenser was 'the Virgil to Chaucer's Ennius'; however, for Jonson in *Discoveries* 'Spenser was Ennius: an important but stylistically primitive writer who should be respected by future poets, but not imitated'.[37] David Scott Wilson-Okamura takes this line of argument further, associating Jonson's statement with Virgil's supposed response to someone who asked why he read Ennius, 'I am combing dung (*stercore*) in search of gold', and commenting, 'the allusion is unmistakable: for Jonson, reading Spenser was like sifting dung'.[38] Jonson here expresses a fierce resistance to archaism. However, as I will describe later in this book, his resistance is accompanied by extensive – though often edgily self-conscious – use of archaism in some of his own works. He thus epitomises early modern culture's simultaneous attraction to and suspicion of the revival of outmoded style.

Considering early modern culture's ambivalent response to archaism also raises the question of another form of imitation: parody. Many early modern writers simply found older words or styles amusing. William Hawkins' school play *Apollo Shroving* (1627), for instance, has a good deal of fun with the use of archaism in erotic poetry, and in particular its stubborn adherence to outmoded forms such as 'eyne' for 'eyes'. In one comic set-piece, the affected Captain Complement attempts to instruct a young boy, Gingle, in wooing technique, only to find that his lesson is derailed when his pupil fails to understand the incongruous poetic archaism in the doggerel lines 'Souse not thy glittering globy eyne / In dreary teary salt sea brine'. Frustrated, Complement asks Gingle, 'Knowst thou not what globy is? I perceiue then thou art no traueller, thou hast not (as I haue done) trauelled about the globe of the earth. Know'st not what eyne be? I see thou art no Poet, thou hast neuer read *Chaucer*. Hast thou neuer heard of eyne twaine?'[39] The comedy of the sequence derives from the assumption that audience members will recognise and understand the phrase 'globy eyne' as a parody of poetic archaism, and from the disparity between their knowledge and the ignorance of the unfortunate Gingle.

In *Apollo Shroving*, Complement attempts to justify his use of archaism by drawing on Chaucer's poetic authority; as this might suggest, diachronic interactions between past and present are important to parodic imitation. Parody encompasses a range of imitative forms, including quotation, allusion, burlesque and pastiche, and all of these forms can draw on older words and styles. Linda Hutcheon usefully defines parody as 'repetition with critical distance, which marks difference rather than similarity', describing it as a process of 'revising, replaying, inverting, and "trans-contextualizing" previous works of art'.[40] Both Hutcheon and Margaret Rose stress parody's capacity to make past and present speak to one another, invoking temporal as well as critical distance. Rose, for instance, argues that it is 'synthetic and analytic and diachronic and synchronic in its analysis of the work it quotes, in that it is able to evoke a past work and its reception and link it with other analyses and audiences'.[41] In recycling older texts and imitating their conventions, a parody establishes interconnections between past and present and between older and newer generations of writers, genres and texts; further, each individual parody becomes part of a multi-temporal network of previous and, potentially, future parodies. Moreover, parody also highlights the fact that archaism's imitation is never a neutral process: writers who introduce older forms into their works do so for specific reasons, and from specific perspectives.

2 Archaic words and styles undermine linear temporality, reconfiguring relationships between past, present and future. Thus far, I have argued that archaism is a form of diachronic imitation; however, the interactions that it creates between past, present and future are more complex than this suggests. Archaism draws on its closest conceptual analogues, anachronism and nostalgia, yet it also complicates some of the assumptions of these two models; in doing so, it has affinities with recent attempts to reconceptualise the temporality of literary texts and other aesthetic objects of the early modern period, and with recent accounts of the cultural workings of memory.

A popular stereotype of Spenserian poetics is invoked by Samuel Daniel in the 1592 version of his sonnet sequence, *Delia*: 'Let others sing of Knights and Palladines,' he writes, 'In aged accents, and vntimely words.'[42] Writing two years after the publication of the first part of *The Faerie Queene*, Daniel vividly evokes its stylistic archaism, but his use of the word 'untimely' also suggests the ways in which archaism violates chronology. The recycling of old linguistic and stylistic conventions invariably pulls the past into the present, even if only by virtue of the fact that the old word is uttered in a new context, or the old convention is juxtaposed with forms that long post-date it. Moreover, archaism depends on the simultaneous presence of what the linguist Manfred Görlach calls 'diachronically different forms of speech'.[43] It does not seek simply to erase temporal difference, but to play with the aesthetic and interpretative possibilities that the combination of old and new forms provides.

As this suggests, archaism carries with it an inherent anachronism. We often think of anachronism as occurring when an author imports something new into an ancient setting – the clocks that strike in Shakespeare's *Julius Caesar*, for example, or Dante's introduction of Virgil into *The Divine Comedy*.[44] However, as Jeremy Tambling points out, the anachronistic is 'what is out of time, the heterogeneous within time', and in an early gloss Thomas Blount defines both 'Anachronicism' and 'Anachronism' as 'an error in Chronology, or an undue connexion of time, a false Chronicling, a repeating of time'.[45] Taking something out of its usual place in time makes it anachronistic. Therefore, when a writer imports something old into a new setting they equally create anachronism; archaism is, in Blount's terms, very precisely a 'repeating of time'. The links between archaism and anachronism are forcibly stated in Greene's discussion of what he terms '*pathetic* or even *tragic* anachronism': 'all of us and all the things we wear and make and build and write . . . are condemned to anachronism insofar as we and they endure into an estranging future'.[46] Greene's examples of pathetic anachronism include old words which have survived into the present and superannuated figures; his comments on the superannuated character might also be applied to old words: such a character 'will typically attract ambivalence, the ambivalence of all historical change, and this divided awareness will affect the posture of the text toward its own historicity'.[47] Greene here engages with the archaism of the text or figure that has become old, but his comments reverberate with the deliberate archaism that concerns me here, in which words or styles that have been allowed to 'die' are brought back to life.[48]

A number of scholars have argued that a sense of anachronism is crucial to the existence of historical consciousness.[49] Margreta de Grazia points out in her elegant recent account of anachronism that the Renaissance is often said to have been 'not only conscious of diachrony but also conscious that it was conscious of it: in recognizing itself as a distinct period, both from remote antiquity (to which it would draw closer) and from the proximate dark ages (from which it would distance itself)'.[50] De Grazia rightly questions the preconceptions about the classical and medieval pasts upon which this model depends; however, her summary suggests some of the connections between archaism and anachronism, and the negotiations that are required – between past and present, between the present day and different versions of the past – when writers choose to write in a self-consciously archaic style. For a word or stylistic element to be archaic, language users must have a sense of the developments within a language over time, and archaism is an intensely and innately self-conscious form of diachrony.

Anachronism, and archaism with it, can also complicate linear models of historical progression. To quote Tambling again, anachronism counters a 'definable historical framework, with "before" and "after", cause and effect';[51] archaism as anachronism aligns the 'before' with the 'after', or even privileges the 'before', confusing and potentially challenging a model of temporality based on cause and effect. Like the Renaissance artworks recently examined by Christopher S. Wood and Alexander Nagel in *Anachronic Renaissance*, literary texts that employ archaism are marked by 'temporal instability', and Wood and Nagel's comments on visual art also hold true for the literary text. Like the artwork, an archaising text points away from the moment of its own making or design backwards towards an earlier point of origin; yet at the same time, 'it points forward to all its future recipients who will activate and reactivate it as a meaningful event'.[52] An artwork thus resists both linear temporality and periodisation; it has the ability 'to "fetch" a past, create a past, perhaps even fetch the future' (18).[53] Literary works share this quality – for instance, in their use of source texts or narratives, and in their frequent appeal to not only contemporary but also future readers. In fact, it could be argued that the literary work is even more temporally unstable than the artwork, as through his or her use of language and literary form – and, in particular, of archaism and neologism – a writer is able to pull together words and styles from different periods.

A further means of conceptualising temporal fluidity, and one that has particular significance here, is set out by Jonathan Gil Harris in his recent book *Untimely Matter in the Age of Shakespeare*, in which he describes the capacity of material objects to 'articulat[e] temporal difference'.[54] Drawing on Bruno Latour and Michel Serres, Harris suggests that early modern objects might be both polychronic and multi-temporal. An object such as a joint-stool might be polychronic because it gathers associations and meanings as it descends through time, while a printing press might be considered to be multi-temporal because it gathers together substances and technologies developed in various historical periods, complicating linear temporality. As Serres argues, 'every historical era is likewise multitemporal, simultaneously drawing from the obsolete, the contemporary, and the futuristic. An object, a circumstance, is thus polychronic, multitemporal, and reveals a time that is gathered together, and with multiple pleats'.[55] For Harris, the early modern 'thing' is not solely or simply early modern: it might be an object that had survived from an earlier time, such as the Roman walls of the city of London, or the items of clothing recycled in the royal courts and the public theatres; its technology might be ancient, as in the case of many industrial tools used during the sixteenth and seventeenth centuries. Such objects are 'of the English Renaissance, yet not of it', and might be characterised as 'untimely matter' (*Untimely Matter*, 3). Harris deals with objects, whereas this book focuses on literary and linguistic style, yet his comments here have a suggestive resonance for the ways in which archaism functions in early modern texts.

To apply a theory of materiality to words and stylistic conventions might seem incongruous, but in an important sense early modern words *were* things, and their function often blurs into the material. Jane Donawerth notes that early modern writers favoured the idea of a 'connection between words and things', and she notes that the popularity of this idea 'may explain some of the reverence in which the ancient words of Latin, Greek, Hebrew and even Anglo-Saxon were held'.[56] Words are here granted the status of prized objects, and we can see how this way of thinking might be applied to archaic terms or concepts: to use a phrase that Elizabeth Fay borrows in turn from Nietzsche, archaisms are 'conceptual mummies', seemingly dead but capable of recovery.[57] Moreover, 'untimely terms' are belated but also, crucially, 'out of joint', to borrow Hamlet's phrase; to adopt another term with bodily connections, they are 'dislocated' – removed from their proper or correct place, disarranged and confused. Words and conventions, like things, might be both polychronic and multi-temporal, and, as I argue in detail below, words – even more than things – have the capacity to carry with them the emotional resonance of their earlier uses.

The temporal fluidity of archaism also associates it with nostalgia, its other conceptual analogue. Like archaism, nostalgia can pull together past, present and future; as Svetlana Boym describes, the nostalgic's 'fantasies of the past, determined by the needs of the present, have a direct impact on the realities of the future', he or she 'feels stifled within the conventional confines of time and space'.[58] The archaist is similarly stifled, but he or she reacts to this confinement in a different fashion from the nostalgic, seeking to recreate and reshape, rather than simply to remember or fantasise. Nostalgia attempts, as Renée R. Trilling has recently argued, 'to reconstruct the lost past in the present moment', and 'its manipulation of material events into aesthetic objects turns the present into history, thereby reifying the separation between present and past'.[59] In contrast, archaism transforms aesthetic objects into new aesthetic objects; in its reinvigoration of old words and conventions, it turns history into the present, undermining the separation enacted by nostalgia. Furthermore, while archaism can invoke nostalgia, and can mimic its conservative tendencies, it is not reducible to nostalgia because it not only looks back to the past but also insists upon the present's ability to match past achievements and even, through the combination of archaism and neologism, to outstrip them. As Harry Berger Jr writes of *The Faerie Queene*, 'Spenser places traditional material in historical perspective by quotation and revision: he depicts it as something old, separates those elements which are still valid from those which are inadequate or outmoded, and transforms it into something new'.[60] Unlike nostalgia, archaism is fundamentally transformative, and it goes to old texts for new answers.

If recent studies underscore the differences between archaism and nostalgia, scholars' accounts of memory offer a more directly productive way of thinking about archaism's configuration of the relationship between past, present and future. In *Matter and Memory*, first published in 1896, Henri Bergson suggests that memory 'imports the past into the present, contracts into a single intuition many moments of duration'.[61] Bergson's description of the way in which memory recovers the past, reshaping it in the process, has marked affinities with the process of the archaising writer, for whom archaic words and conventions function as a form of semi-embodied memory. Further, archaism resonates with the model of 'multi-directional memory' recently described by Michael Rothberg, who argues that

> recollections and representations of personal or political history inevitably mix multiple moments in time and multiple sites of remembrance; making the past present opens the doors of memory to intersecting pasts and undefined futures. Memory is thus structurally multidirectional, but each articulation of the past processes that multidirectionality differently.[62]

Archaism, similarly, is 'structurally multidirectional'. The archaising writer moves backwards and forwards in time, plundering a series of intersecting pasts for material that will suit his or her project; similarly, every archaist work reshapes its material in a different manner, and each will look forward and backwards in a different way.

For example, when Spenser uses the word 'wight' in *The Shepheardes Calender* or *The Faerie Queene*, he looks back to Chaucer, whereas when Shakespeare, Jonson or Milton use the term, it is filtered through Spenser; when 'wretched wight' appears in the opening line of Keats's 'La Belle Dame Sans Merci' (1820) it is an even more self-consciously adopted element of poetic diction,[63] and in later novels such as Charlotte Brontë's *Shirley* (1849) or Charles Dickens's *Bleak House* (1853), it appears in moments of narrative burlesque. Thus Dickens's sardonic description of Sir Leicester Dedlock being treated for his hereditary gout condition concludes with the statement, 'And he is very great, this day. And woe to Boythorn, or other daring wight, who shall presumptuously contest an inch with him!'[64] Dickens's use of the term 'wight' carries the weight of the word's history with it, but, simultaneously, readers of *Bleak House* carry Dickens with them if they turn to Spenser or Chaucer, meaning that the history of the word works both backwards and forwards.

3 Archaism is intertwined with national identity. As described above, the use of archaism raises specifically early modern concerns about the relationship between language and national identity: to quote Paula Blank's useful summary, 'A traditional language, yet one invoked by writers for its novelty, a "pure" English that was foreign to native readers, archaism highlights the complexities of the Renaissance "question of the language" – especially, the question of which version of the vernacular was truly "English".'[65] Archaic forms of English belong to linguistic and, thereby, national tradition, but they also have the capacity to undermine long-standing assumptions about the nature and status of English, England and the English.

Although archaism appears in medieval English texts, it found new prominence in the context of sixteenth-century debates about the status of English as a national and literary language.[66] Many commentators argued that loan-words should be incorporated into English from classical languages such as Latin and Greek, or from modern vernaculars such as French and Italian, yet others insisted that English should instead look to its own past.[67] In the 1530s, when Wyatt was experimenting with Chaucerian forms in his poetry, Thomas Berthelet published an edition of Gower's *Confessio Amantis*, in which he tells Henry VIII, to whom the book is dedicated, that wise readers will not 'throwe asyde' the 'olde englisshe wordes and vulgars' of Gower's text. Instead, Gower's words 'shall as a lanterne gyue him lyghte to wryte cunnyngly and to garnysshe his sentencis in our vulgar tonge'.[68] In Berthelet's powerful metaphor, the older text illuminates not only the past, but the present and, potentially, the future.

In the following years, the idea that the works of earlier authors might provide a fruitful source for linguistic renewal gained traction, partly as a result of the activities of an influential group of mid-sixteenth-century archaisers, including John Cheke and Thomas Smith. In a letter to Edward Hoby appended to the printed text of Hoby's translation of Baldassare Castiglione's *The Courtier* (1561), Cheke argues that

> our own tung shold be written cleane and pure, vnmixt and vnmangeled with borowing of other tunges ... if she want at ani tijm (as being vnperfight she must) yet let her borow with suche bashfulnes, that it mai appeer, that if either the mould of our own tung could serue vs to fascion a woord of our own, or if the old denisoned wordes could content and ease this neede, we wold not boldly venture of vnknowen wordes.[69]

Cheke's emphasis on the purity of an English free from Latinate neologism is underlined in his idiosyncratic orthography, and his vision of a self-sufficient English tongue recurs in the work of both his contemporaries and later commentators such as William Camden, Alexander Gil and John Hare.[70] Although Richard Foster Jones is probably right in his assessment of this project as 'hardly feasible', the idea that English could become self-sufficient through the revival and recasting of old words, and that it might thereby preserve its continuity with its own past, nonetheless exercised a powerful hold on the imagination of writers.[71]

Nearly a generation after Cheke, ideas of national identity, belonging and estrangement were crucial to the period's most influential expression of an archaist stance, E.K.'s letter to Gabriel Harvey, printed as the preface to *The Shepheardes Calender*. The degree to which Spenser's diction is 'genuinely' archaic has been much debated.[72] More intriguing, however, is the strategy that E.K. adopts in defending the poet's use of potentially outmoded words, and the aim of the preface to naturalise archaism as decorous, aesthetically valid and truly 'English'. Among the features of Spenser's verse that E.K. praises are his

> dewe obseruing of Decorum euerye where, in personages, in seasons, in matter, in speach, and generally in al seemely simplycitie in handeling his matter, and framing his words: the which of many thinges which in him be straunge, I know will seeme the straungest, the words them selues being so auncient, the knitting of them so short and intricate, and the whole Periode and compasse of speache so delightsome for the roundnesse, and so graue for the straungenesse.[73]

In using archaic words, E.K. argues, Spenser creates an alluring remoteness and unfamiliarity (see, for instance, the emphatic use of variations on the word 'strange'), which sets off other aspects of his poetry to advantage. This is not a crude way of using language. On the contrary, the words are woven together in a manner that is concise ('short') and intricate, and which produces a pleasing 'roundness', generally glossed as 'fullness' or 'careful finish', of style.[74]

Despite his emphasis on archaism's 'strangeness', E.K. nonetheless sees Spenserian archaism as part of a programme of linguistic renewal; it restores to English writers their national heritage and enables them to reach across time in order to reshape contemporary aesthetics. He writes:

> [I]n my opinion it is one special prayse, of many whych are dew to this Poete, that he hath laboured to restore, as to theyr rightfull heritage such good and naturall English words, as haue ben long time out of vse and almost cleane disinherited. Which is the onely cause, that our Mother tonge, which truly of it self is both ful enough for prose and stately enough for verse, hath long time ben counted most bare and barrein of both. (ll. 77–84)

Echoing the likes of Cheke, he proclaims the self-sufficiency of English, arguing that those who would incorporate 'peces and rags of other languages' merely make 'our English tongue, a gallimaufray or hodgepodge of al other speches' (ll. 86, 90–1). The idea of a 'natural' English is associated here – as elsewhere – with what Blank terms 'the preservation of an original – and threatened – national identity' (*Broken English*, 101). Archaism appears to offer a means of confronting and assuaging anxieties about the status of English as a 'pure' expression of national identity, but the purity that it offers is itself open to question, given that the outmoded words promoted by archaists are no longer part of the living language.

Although Spenser and E.K. brashly announced a 'new' English poetry, Cathy Shrank points out that 'in its consciousness of its own novelty the *Shepheardes Calender* is closer to mid-Tudor writing than that of subsequent decades, when authors generally felt less need to justify their choice of English as a language in which to write'.[75] What brings Spenser closer to late-Tudor concerns is his need not simply to defend writing in English, but to defend the uses of outmoded style. Archaism was becoming somewhat less prominent and credible as a means of linguistic renewal or a literary technique in the 1570s. John Baret spoke for many when he rejected 'olde obsolet words, which no good writer now a dayes will vse' in his 1574 dictionary,[76] and E.K.'s self-defensive stance is suggested in the ways in which he attempts to forestall criticism. Particularly evocative are his comments that some critics on hearing an old word 'crye out streight way, that we speak no English, but gibbrish, or rather such, as in old time

Euanders mother spake' (ll. 93–5). Evander's mother Carmentis, a prophet, was said to have spoken in archaic Greek, and her name became a byword for Roman poets in describing the affected use of obsolete words.[77] The allusion seemingly leads into the statement that the anti-archaists' 'first shame is, that they are not ashamed, in their own mother tonge straungers to be counted and alienes' (ll. 95–7), which recuperates the potentially damning link between archaism and female garrulity. E.K. thus casts them as alienated from their own linguistic, cultural and national heritage. While archaic language is alluring precisely because it is 'strange', to reject it is to leave oneself a stranger or alien, divorced from one's own history and cultural inheritance.

E.K.'s defensive stance and Samuel Daniel's snide comments about 'aged accents, and vntimely words' both suggest that archaism was a controversial technique in the late sixteenth century. Moreover, as I will explore in greater detail in the following chapters, political changes in the seventeenth century were to make its place in literary culture yet more complex. The Elizabethan alignment of linguistic and national identity was itself a convenient fiction given the presence of many non-English speakers within what was still referred to by the regime as the realm of 'England, France and Ireland'. After James Stuart's accession to the English throne in 1603, this picture became yet more complex – what was the status of archaic English in a realm newly re-christened 'Great Britain, France and Ireland', one that incorporated England's powerful neighbour, Scotland, its linguistic traditions, and its own network of European allegiances? The king's assertion that his two kingdoms were 'alreadie ioyned in vnitie of Religion and language' not only elided the existence of Scottish Gaelic, but also belied the important differences between English and Scottish versions of English.[78] Between 1642 and 1660, the national picture became still more fraught; it is perhaps unsurprising that the Restoration saw a turn away from archaism and the linguistic past, as part of a wider retrospective reshaping of a traumatic recent history.

By 1660, neoclassicism was beginning to dominate English literary aesthetics. In earlier years, however, classicism and archaism were held in a more delicate balance. When writers incorporate outmoded linguistic or stylistic forms into their work, they also acknowledge, implicitly or explicitly, the existence of a tradition of writing in English, a tradition that might run counter to – or at least complicate – the ways in which they interact with classical or continental influences. This tension underlies Jonson's comments in *Discoveries* and the hostility of the Caroline poet

George Daniel to the continued influence of Chaucer on literary aesthetics. Daniel sets out his intention

>   to Shew
> A Spring more worthy; whence wee may derive
> With greater Honour, the Prerogative
> Of English Poesie; and Clearlie evince
> Noe Age can be call'd Darke to a Cleare Sence,
> As in the Ancients.[79]

Contrasting antiquity with a 'dark' age, and rejecting Chaucer as 'Mustie
and antiquated', Daniel exhorts his contemporaries to look instead to
Elizabethan greats such as Sidney, Spenser and Jonson, and to classical
poets such as Virgil and Ovid.[80] When a writer deliberately resorts to
archaism they therefore implicitly reject neoclassicism and embrace the
primitive barbarism of Chaucerism. In this respect, the uses of archaism
fall into a pattern observed by Helgerson, in which patterns of thought
taken from either classical antiquity or the middle ages 'provided the
recognized models of civility and barbarity against which English writings
were inevitably measured'.[81] However, Daniel's comments fail to take into
account the extent to which both Elizabethan and classical writings were
themselves open to the uses of archaic style. What looks like a binary
opposition between the archaic and the neoclassical begins to break down.

These debates show us, in addition, the ambiguous place of outmoded
style in relation to the ways in which language creates and maintains
community. As Jonathan Hope argues, 'language existed to communicate
people's ideas to other people – so the best language was that which
communicated to the largest number of people. For most in the Renaissance, language that did not communicate across society – that did not in
fact *create* society – was pointless'.[82] Deliberately to employ obscure,
outmoded terms is potentially to prize the symbolic significance of a word
over its communicative value, to break the circuit of understanding
between speaker and listener, and to refuse to create society. Thus, while
archaist writers may harbour a dream of reviving a 'pure' form of English
and, with it, a renewed English nation, the use of archaism itself splinters
that dream because the revived words, restored from the dead, may no
longer be able to communicate with current speakers or even be recognised
as 'English'. As McEachern argues, the nation itself is 'an ideal of community that is, by definition, either proleptic or passing, ever just beyond
reach'.[83] Archaism, which itself looks both backwards and forwards, has
the capacity both to create that community and shatter it, its vision of
linguistic and national union always just out of reach.

4 Archaism is self-conscious and artificial, yet capable of arousing strong emotion. In his comments about his epic poem *Gondibert* (1650), William Davenant renews the attack on archaism, focusing his attention on Spenser himself. Noting that Spenser's 'obsolete language' is criticised, Davenant explains in detail the reasons for these negative assessments:

> Language (which is the onely Creature of Man's Creation) hath like a Plant, seasons of flourishing, and decay; like Plants, is remov'd from one Soil to another, and by being so transplanted, doth often gather vigour and increase. But as it is false Husbandry to graft old Branches upon young Stocks: so we may wonder that our Language (not long before his time created out of a confusion of others, and then beginning to flourish like a new Plant) should (as helps to its increase) receive from his hand new Grafts of old wither'd Words.[84]

Archaism, in Davenant's view, does not breach merely stylistic decorum, but also temporal decorum; moreover, his comparison of language to a plant suggests the potentially unnatural quality of archaism's desire to reach back in time, and to revive past forms. Attempting to give dead words new life, he argues, is as artificial as trying to graft dead twigs onto living plants.

Archaism is – as Davenant's account suggests – a highly self-aware and self-conscious process. Despite its marked differences from nostalgia, archaism shares its tendency towards the inauthentic or ersatz; Susan Stewart's description of nostalgia as 'the repetition that mourns the inauthenticity of all repetitions and denies the repetition's capacity to form identity' holds equally true for archaism.[85] While E.K. and other proponents of archaism may try to naturalise it, using outmoded literary or linguistic forms can leave an author open to charges of stylistic perversion, affectation or unnaturalness. As a result, the majority of writers who employ outmoded forms are acutely aware of the problematic nature of their claim to authenticity. For instance, Spenser's self-consciousness about using archaic forms is displayed not only in the provision of E.K.'s glosses in *The Shepheardes Calender*, but in the somewhat nervy foregrounding of the word 'whilom' in the first line of the Proem to Book 1 of *The Faerie Queene*.

Nonetheless, archaism's radical inauthenticity is also one reason for its impact on readers and spectators, and the archaist writer's self-conscious imitation of outmoded styles can produce various kinds of aesthetic and emotional effect. Francesco Orlando's resonant discussion of the timeworn object is useful here: 'Time uses up and destroys things, breaks them and reduces them to uselessness, renders them unfashionable and makes people

abandon them; time makes things become cherished by force of habit and
ease of handling, endows them with tenderness as memories and with
authority as models, marks them with the virtue of rarity and the prestige
of age.'[86] Archaism imitates or incorporates timeworn linguistic and literary styles, and, like the timeworn object, it can create a range of responses,
some ambivalent or paradoxically mixed. Encountering an archaic form
might provoke distancing emotions of surprise, derision or awe in readers
or spectators, but it might equally incite more intimate feelings of comfort,
grief or longing. As E.K. notes in his preface to *The Shepheardes Calender*,
quoted above, Spenser's 'pastorall rudenesse' and 'seemely simplycitie of
handeling his matter, and framing his words' result in a work that is both
'delightsome for the roundnesse' and 'graue for the straungeness' (ll. 19,
21–2, 26–7).

   These varied effects permeate the uses of archaism in late sixteenth- and
early seventeenth-century texts. As I explain in detail in Chapter 1, in
Middleton's *Hengist, King of Kent, or The Mayor of Queenborough*, a phrase
in Old English functions as a linguistic alienation effect, distancing the
audience from the treacherous Saxon who speaks it. Elsewhere, archaism is
often calculated to arouse amusement or laughter – as in Dickens's use of
'wight', or Hawkins's 'globy eyne' – and a pervasive anxiety surrounding
the use of archaic words was that they might become not merely obsolete,
but obscene. In Middleton's *No Wit/Help Like a Woman's* (Prince Henry's
Men, 1611), the Widow asks 'How many honest words have suffered
corruption since Chaucer's days? A virgin would speak those words then
that a very midwife would blush to hear now'.[87] As I will explore further
in Chapters 2 and 3, words such as 'jape' and 'occupy' were considered in
the seventeenth century to have been rendered obscene by the passage of
time. Their place in certain contexts, such as literary works and liturgical
translations, was therefore questioned, and the words took on a comic
or satiric quality that was not present in their original use, potentially
rebounding on their innocent users.

   In contrast, Anne Norris Michelin notes that stylistic archaism is
effective because 'older styles make a dual impression, first of novelty,
deviation from the expected, but second of appropriateness and familiarity'.[88] Archaic literary and linguistic styles can be distancing and surprising,
but also – as in pastoral literature or religious diction – homely and
subliminally comforting. In using the word 'whilom' in the opening of
The Faerie Queene, Spenser seeks not only to give his epic the kind of
grandeur that Quintilian and Jonson suggest might be conveyed through
archaism, but also to display his affinity with older literature and to

reinscribe his kinship with Chaucer. In this fashion – to appropriate Carolyn Dinshaw's term – archaism can create 'affective connections'[89] across time through the recycling and reshaping of outmoded styles. When poets compose in Old English, when dramatists weave quotations from Chaucer or morality plays into their texts, when writers inhabit outmoded metrical forms, they express a longing to make contact, to speak for or through the past.

Archaism's affect can also be conjured through the relationship between the outmoded element and the surrounding text. In his account of photography, *Camera Lucida*, Roland Barthes encapsulates the emotional tug of the photograph in terms that resonate strongly with archaism's potential effects:

> A Latin word exists to designate this wound, this prick, this mark made by a pointed instrument: the word suits me all the better in that it also refers to the notion of punctuation, and because the photographs I am speaking of are in effect punctuated, sometimes even speckled with these sensitive points; precisely, these marks, these wounds are so many *points*. This second element which will disturb the *studium* [i.e., the content of the photograph which arouses the intellect] I shall therefore call *punctum*; for *punctum* is also: sting, speck, cut, little hole – and also a cast of the dice. A photograph's *punctum* is that accident which pricks me (but also bruises me, is poignant to me) . . . the *punctum* shows no preference for morality or good taste: the *punctum* can be ill-bred.[90]

In his preface to *The Shepheardes Calender*, E.K. suggests that 'rough and harsh' archaic and dialectal terms 'enlumine and make more clearly to appeare the brightnesse of braue and glorious words. So oftentimes a dischorde in Musick maketh a comely concordaunce: so great delight tooke the worthy Poete Alceus to behold a blemish in the ioynt of a wel shaped body' (Epistle, ll. 68–72). Like Barthes's *punctum*, or the grit in an oyster, an archaic word or style is an aesthetic irritant, rubbing up against its surroundings. Spenser's 'whilom' is a sting, speck or hole, jolting his reader and reminding him or her of the history of both the English language and English poetry. The archaic *punctum* is also indecorous, excessive, 'ill-bred'; Thomas Nashe, in an evocative phrase, refers to archaisms as 'Oouse' – as waste or remnant.[91]

The four theses outlined above link archaism with imitation, temporal dissonance, nationhood and affect; they argue for the multiplicity of the ways in which it functions in texts written between 1590 and 1674, and the various effects that it might have on readers and spectators. Taken together, however, they also suggest archaism's aesthetic and emotional potential, and some of the reasons why it was so consistently appealing to poets and dramatists. Whether archaism is viewed as a debased or elevated form of imitation, a temporal medley or an expression of a particular form of 'pastness', a saviour of national pride or an embarrassment to it, an alienating device or a means of instilling familiarity to a text, it has the capacity throughout this period to disrupt or unsettle aesthetic norms. Literary archaism looks to the past, and to former modes of expression, but it also seeks to reshape the present, and to look forward to new futures.

Coda

In 1642, the Cambridge scholar Henry More published a long philosophi-cal poem, *Psychodia Platonica, or a Platonicall Song of the Soul*. The poem opens with an argument written in common measure, and the main text begins,

> NOr Ladies loves, nor Knights brave Martiall deeds,
>   Yrapt in rolls of hid Antiquity;
> But th'inward Fountain, and the unseen Seeds,
>   From whence are these and what so under eye
>   Doth fall, or is record in memory,
> *Psyche*, I'll sing. *Psyche!* from thee they sprong.
>   O life of time, and all *Alterity!*
> The life of lives instill his nectar strong,
> And Psych' inebriate, while I sing *Psyches* song.[92]

More deliberately echoes Spenser's archaising style. He mimics Spenser's use of the common measure argument, and the first line of the first stanza self-consciously recalls both line 5 of the Proem to *The Faerie Queene*, in which Spenser declares his intention to 'sing of Knights and Ladies gentle deeds', and the opening line of Canto 1. Similarly, More's positioning of 'Yrapt', with its archaic 'y' prefix, at the beginning of the second line, seems to be a calculated echo of Spenser's use of 'Y cladd' in the same place in the first stanza of Book 1. Instead of addressing a Muse, as Spenser does in the first verse of his Proem, More addresses Psyche, and his final line echoes and revises the end of Spenser's Proem, 'Fierce warres and faithfull loues shall moralize my song'. The opening of More's poem is thus a self-aware negotiation with and revision of Spenser's poem, one that turns the semi-hidden '*divine Morality*' of *The Faerie Queene* into its overt theme. As a whole, *Psychodia Platonica* suggests the depth of More's love for Spenser and '*that incomparable Piece of his*', *The Faerie Queene*, which he first encountered when his father read it to him as a boy.[93]

More's use of archaism is in many respects in line with the tendencies that I have described above. He uses outmoded conventions as part of a meditation on memory and temporal difference, underscoring stylistically his untimely subject-matter and narrative. However, *Psychodia Platonica* is doubly archaic: while Spenser's archaic mannerisms were radical in the 1590s, by the 1640s, even his neologisms were gathering dust. It is therefore perhaps not surprising that More's work was met with incredulity from at least one reader, the Oxford philosopher and alchemist Thomas Vaughan. In the course of an increasingly vitriolic dispute with More, Vaughan writes of another poem, 'Hymn in Honour of Charity and Humility',

> Is this an *old Song*, or a *new*? forgive me Sir! now at last I apprehend the *mysterie*; You are neither a *Modern singer*, nor yet an *Ancient one*; You live in *our dayes*, but you imitate *Spencer*, so that *your song* is both *old and new*, and *Truth* perhaps may be had *for it*.[94]

In the context of 1640s and 1650s aesthetics, Spenserian style muddles temporal categories even more comprehensively than it did in the 1590s, with the result that More's poetry, with its use of neologistic terms such as 'alterity', is a temporal hodgepodge, a mixture of ancient and modern, old and new.

More's belated Spenserianism highlights the distance travelled between 1590 and the 1640s; it also presents a complex layering of temporal and literary effects. While his tribute to Spenser is undoubtedly sincere, More's meta-archaic work suggests both the aesthetic power of archaism and its vulnerability to charges of artificiality, obscurity and comic absurdity. In claiming the past through his imitation of a beloved literary forebear, More asserts the worth of the English language and the literature that it has spawned, yet he also implicitly suggests that neither has improved over the last sixty years. In adopting an old-fashioned form, and using it to convey up-to-date philosophical ideas, he fuses past and present, insisting on the capacity of older forms to speak to the present, and to carry his ideas into the future. These characteristics are reiterated and refashioned in the works examined in the following pages. Like More's poems, they are 'both *old and new*', and truth may perhaps be had for them.

CHAPTER I

Within our own memory: Old English and the early modern poet

In the preface to *Ælfredi regis res gestæ* (1574), Archbishop Matthew Parker recounts a remarkable story of linguistic survival at Tavistock Abbey in Devon. According to Parker, after the Norman Conquest 'certain colleges of monks were established by our ancestors'; 'In these colleges', he writes,

> were men who were instructed in knowledge of this language, and who in turn, by communicating it to others, passed it on to posterity. This practice was continued, I believe, up to times within our own memory at the monastery of Tavistock in Devonshire, and in many other monasteries, in order that knowledge of this tongue should not perish entirely, though it was no longer used.[1]

According to Parker, teaching in the forms of English used before the Norman Conquest – known to linguists today as Old English – existed within monastic institutions, a tradition that continued at Tavistock until the Reformation and the monastery's dissolution in 1539. This claim apparently caught the scholarly imagination, and it is repeated by later writers, notably William Camden in his widely cited *Britannia*, first published in Latin in 1586 and translated into English by Philemon Holland in 1610. The English text reads:

> scarcely had this Abbay [*sic*] stood thirty yeeres after it was first founded, when the Danes in their spoiling rage burnt it to the ground: yet it flourished againe, and by a laudable ordinance, lectures therein were kept of our ancient language (I meane the English Saxon tongue) which continued even to our fathers daies; for feare lest the saide language (a thing that now is well neere come to passe) should be forgotten.[2]

Parker's 'within our own memory' ('nostra memoria') becomes Camden's 'even to our fathers daies' ('vsque ad patrum memoriam');[3] although a generation has passed, an affective link still remains. The narrative was repeated by a number of authors, and the refectory at Tavistock, at that point almost intact, became known as the 'Saxon school'.[4] By the late seventeenth century, in Edward Gibson's new edition of *Britannia*, further details had accrued to the legend: 'Farther down the river is *Tavistoke*, where the school in which the Saxon tongue was taught, is still in being; and (as I have heard) there was also in the beginning of the late Civil wars, a Saxon-Grammar printed, in *Tavistoke*.'[5] In this account, Anglo-Saxonist activity at Tavistock is again close at hand, separated not by the Reformation but by another social and cultural cataclysm: the Civil War.

There are hints of truth in these accounts: some medieval scholars could read Old English, and a few could even write it;[6] moreover, Anglo-Saxon manuscripts from the monks' library at Tavistock have survived, and books were printed there in the early sixteenth century.[7] However, the precise claims that Parker, Camden and Gibson make are implausible, and their value therefore lies not so much in the claims themselves, but in the desire that they express for contact with the past, and with a living tradition of Old English that is always tantalisingly positioned just out of reach. They testify to the longing to communicate, to erase historical distance, to touch the past, longings that recur throughout early modern culture's uses of archaism.

This chapter takes the story of the Saxon school at Tavistock as its starting point for an exploration of the interactions between early modern literary culture and Old English, perhaps the ultimate English linguistic archaism. Examining the radically inauthentic appearances of Old English in seventeenth-century drama, classical translation and lyric poetry, it advances two interrelated arguments. First, it contends both that Old English was an important resource for conceptualising national identity in Stuart and Protectorate Britain, and – perhaps counterintuitively – that it actually complicates the presentation of linguistic and national identity presented within these texts. Second, it argues that in seventeenth-century texts Old English gradually becomes visible and viable as a vehicle for literary expression, complicating a widespread scholarly assumption that its use was generally utilitarian in this period. In the years leading up to the publication of the first edition of Anglo-Saxon poetry in 1655, the peculiar, ersatz appearances of Old English in early modern literature begin to make the existence of what John Cleveland was to call a 'West Saxon poet' thinkable.[8] The experiments of seventeenth-century imaginative writers thus helped to facilitate the rediscovery of Old English poetry, and the reconfiguration of literary history that attended it. The texts are part of a process in which Old English is not only figured as 'within' memory, but is incorporated into national and cultural memory. Or, rather, 'memories', since despite polemicists' attempts to sculpt a single, dominant narrative, melding Old English with narratives of English political, linguistic and religious identity, a multitude of narratives and counter-narratives continued to coexist.

In exploring these issues, I first argue for the currency of Old English in early modern literary contexts, summarising the uses of Old English words and phrases in literary texts, the publication history of Anglo-Saxon poetry and scholars' attitudes towards it. In his fine study of twentieth-century poetry's engagements with Old English, Chris Jones identifies a 'contradictory doubleness' in scholarly and poetic attitudes towards Old English, a 'received notion of primitive alterity and coterminous similitude'.[9] For early modern scholars, similarly, Old English is both remote and familiar; moreover, Old English poetry marks the point at which the English language becomes most strange and alienating, despite their increasing familiarity with Anglo-Saxon texts in general.

In this context, I then examine in detail three important examples of early modern literature's engagement with Old English. The first is the quotation of well-known Old English phrases in two contrasting plays: Thomas Middleton's *Hengist, King of Kent, or The Mayor of Queenborough*, a tragedy performed by the King's Men around 1619–20, which depicts the arrival of the first Saxon forces in Britain, and William Cartwright's comedy *The Ordinary*, performed at Oxford University around 1635, which is set in contemporary London. Quotation was a crucial instrument through which readers and, later, playgoers were brought into contact with Old English, and, despite their generic and stylistic differences, both of these plays feature mangled versions of the Old English phrase *nimath eowra seaxes*, 'take your daggers', allegedly used by the Saxon warrior Hengist as a signal for his forces to massacre the British soldiers on Salisbury Plain. For antiquarians, the phrase symbolised the political, social and linguistic conquest of the Saxons over the British, and it was often invoked in the context of discussions of the origins of the English. Like the Saxons themselves, Old English was simultaneously 'English' and 'not-English', and the repetition of *nimath eowra seaxes* in plays such as *Hengist* and *The Ordinary* underlines the extent to which using Anglo-Saxon history also forced writers to engage with linguistic and, thereby, temporal and cultural difference.

My second example is the interaction between Old English and classical literature – specifically the works of Virgil – in the translations of William L'Isle. L'Isle was an important figure in the development of Anglo-Saxon scholarship in the seventeenth century; one of the first scholars to recognise the difference between Old English prose and poetry, he also experimented with composition in Old English. In his translation of Virgil's *Eclogues* (1628), L'Isle follows the example of Edmund Spenser's *The Shepheardes Calender* and self-consciously incorporates Old English words as part of his archaising style. As Hannah Crawforth explains in an important recent essay, Spenser looks 'beyond Chaucer to the Anglo-Saxon roots of English'; his text and E.K.'s glosses draw on the etymology of specific words 'in order to reveal his readers' alienation from the Anglo-Saxon "mother-tongue" and thus from the true English Church'.[10] In his imitation of Spenser, L'Isle not only intensifies the 'Saxon' content of the pastoral, but also establishes a distinctive perspective on Old English. For him, Old English is not solely or simply 'English', but something to which the Scots also have a legitimate claim, and his Virgilian translations establish Old English as part of a complex trans-temporal and trans-national linguistic network.

Such national and temporal interactions are also at play in my final example: three seventeenth-century lyric poems composed in Old English, published in university anthologies in 1641 and 1654.[11] In these works, Abraham Wheelock, William Retchford and Joseph Williamson deploy Old English as a means through which national identity and national destiny might be negotiated. In the context of national and international violence and warfare – the Bishops' War and Irish Rebellion of 1638–41 and the First Anglo-Dutch War of 1652–4 – the use of Old English takes on a potent force. Yet instead of simply signalling English nationalism, composing in Old English enables these writers to reframe the relationships between English, Scots and Irish, and between English and Dutch, and to bring the past to bear on contemporary events.

Very ancient and savage

In his Jacobean translation of Camden's *Britannia*, quoted above, Philemon Holland writes that the passing of Old English into oblivion is 'a thing that now is well neere come to passe'. Holland here translates the 1607 text of *Britannia*, extensively revised by Camden, which reads, 'lectiones in hoc vsque ad patrum memoriam habebantur, *nè quod nunc serè euenit*, huius linguæ cognitio intercideret' (my emphasis).[12] In the 1586 and 1590 editions of *Britannia*, in contrast, Camden writes 'nè quod nunc euênit' ('which has now come to pass').[13] Camden's alteration of his text suggests that advances in the scholarship of Old English had rendered him more optimistic, and it is testament both to the activities of late sixteenth- and early seventeenth-century scholars and to the circulation of at least some of their ideas.

In-depth knowledge of Old English was limited to certain circles and locations – for instance, Robert Talbot, John Leland and Robert Recorde in the 1540s, the scholars associated with Archbishop Parker in the 1560s and 1570s, Cambridge University in the 1630s and 1640s, and Oxford University in the later seventeenth century – and to individuals such as Richard Verstegan, whose influential book *A Restitution of Decayed Intelligence: In Antiquities* was published in Antwerp in 1605.[14] However, fragments of the language circulated more widely – in historical and lexicographical texts, in religious polemic, in legal treatises, and in drama and poetry. The ultimate English linguistic archaism, Old English was also paradoxically current.

The use of Anglo-Saxon texts in early modern religious, legal and political debate has been the focus of sustained attention from scholars.[15] Less well documented, however, is the range of interactions with Old English that can be found in seventeenth-century literary texts – in poems, plays and translations. In addition to the works explored in detail in this chapter, we might look to Ben Jonson's *The New Inn* (King's Men, 1629), which includes a short sequence in which characters quibble over the derivation of the word 'wapentake', defined by Tipto as 'A Saxon word to signify the hundred'.[16] John Selden quotes sources in Old English in his notes or 'illustrations' to the first part of Michael Drayton's chorographical epic *Polyolbion* (1612),[17] and this example is followed in William Slatyer's *The History of Great Brittany* (1621), in which the phrase *waes hail* appears in both the Latin and English texts of the account of the Saxon Rowena's seduction of the British king Vortigern, and other Old English phrases appear in the notes.[18] Words derived from Old English were used self-consciously by poets such as Spenser and John Milton, and the value of the 'Saxon' monosyllable in English poetry was asserted by writers such as Samuel Daniel, George Chapman and Sir John Beaumont.[19]

Perhaps unsurprisingly, early modern poets show little interest in Old English poetry itself, which was barely recognised as such even by specialists. The pioneering scholar Laurence Nowell owned the *Beowulf* manuscript (British Library Cotton Vitelius A.xv) in the 1560s, and his hand can be seen in a handful of other Anglo-Saxon poetic manuscripts. Nowell may have been, as Timothy Graham remarks, the only scholar of his age to show a 'noticeable interest' in Old English poetry,[20] but even he does not appear to have recognised it as poetry. Similarly, while sixteenth-century editions of Anglo-Saxon works occasionally include their inset poems – the earliest is apparently Parker's edition of *Ælfredi regis res gestae*, which includes Alfred's *Metrical Preface* to his translation of Gregory's

Regula pastoralis – no awareness is shown that they are literary texts or that they display literary techniques.[21]

In the seventeenth century, scholars began to be more conscious of the presence of poetry in the Anglo-Saxon manuscripts they handled. Abraham Wheelock's 1643 edition of the Old English versions of Bede's *Historia ecclesiastica gentis Anglorum* and the *Anglo-Saxon Chronicle* includes not only 'Cædmon's Hymn', the text of which appears in the Old English Bede, but also a number of poems embedded in the *Chronicle*.[22] Although he was apparently unaware that these fragments were poems, Wheelock recognised that there was a stylistic difference between prose and verse sections of the text: he comments of the entry for 937, now known as 'The Battle of Brunanburh', '*Idioma, hîc & ad annum 942. & 975. perantiquum, & horridum*' ('the language, here and at the years 942 and 975, is very ancient and savage').[23] Danielle Cunniff Plumer notes that Wheelock's recognition of stylistic difference is significant; yet, like Nowell, 'he evidently did not recognize them as verse'.[24] In the same year the Dutch scholar Johannes De Laet, who used the poetic manuscript now known as Bodleian MS Junius 11 in researching an unpublished dictionary of Old English, told the Danish antiquary Ole Worm '*videturque metra [sic] quondam constare*' ('it appears from time to time to be made up of lines of verse'), quoting the opening lines of Genesis A from that manuscript.[25] Even earlier were the comments of the antiquary, translator and poet William L'Isle – whose work will concern us later in this chapter – who died in 1637. L'Isle heads a manuscript transcription of 'The Battle of Brunanburh' with the comment, 'This is mysticall *and* written in a poeticall vaine obscurely of purpose to avoid the daunger of those tymes *and* needs dechyphring'; he also describes the Chronicle's later poems, 'The Capture of the Five Boroughs', 'The Coronation of Edgar' and 'The Death of Edgar', as 'mysticall'.[26] While he does not appear to have recognised the poems as poetry *per se*, L'Isle's description of them as 'written in a poeticall vaine' suggests that he was aware of their literary or imagistic quality.

L'Isle was unusually alert to the stylistic qualities of Old English, but his comments can be usefully compared with those of John Milton, who read the translations of Wheelock and Henry of Huntingdon in preparing his *History of Britain*. In a section probably composed around 1655–7,[27] Milton describes the Battle of Brunanburh, and relates that the Viking forces

> enterd *England* by *Humber*, and fought with *Athelstan* ... the bloodiest fight, say Authors, that ever this Iland saw, to describe which, the *Saxon* Annalist wont to be sober and succinct, whether the same or another writer, now labouring under the weight of his Argument, and over-charg'd, runs

on a sudden into such extravagant fansies and metaphors, as bare him quite
beside the scope of being understood. *Huntingdon*, though himself peccant
enough in his kind, transcribes him word for word as a pastime to his
Readers. I shall only summe up what of him I can attain, in usuall
language.[28]

Reading Anglo-Saxon poetry in Latin translation, Milton finds it radically
indecorous – extravagant, fanciful and barely comprehensible. Indeed,
even though his use of the phrase 'extravagant fansies and metaphors'
suggests that he is aware of the presence of literary or rhetorical techniques
he seems more inclined to attribute the stylistic shift to the presence of
a second author. His reluctance to engage with linguistic difference is also
suggested in the way in which he refuses 'to wrincle the smoothness
of History with rugged names of places unknown, better harp'd at in
Camden, and other Chorographers' (178). As Barbara K. Lewalski notes,
Milton is preoccupied with narrative style in *The History of Britain*, and
at pains to produce an 'educative humanist narrative' rather than an
antiquarian tract.[29]

Despite Milton's generally low opinion of his Anglo-Saxon sources,
scholars have often sought to find links between *Paradise Lost* and the
first self-consciously planned edition of Old English poetry: Francis
Junius' edition of Bodleian MS Junius 11, *Cædmonis monarchi paraphrasis
poetica Genesios ac præcipuarum sacræ paginæ historiarum*, published in
Amsterdam in 1655.[30] Junius presents the manuscript's metrical paraphrases of the Books of Genesis, Exodus and Daniel, *Christ and Satan*
and a metrical 'Prayer' as the work of the semi-legendary Anglo-Saxon poet
Cædmon, and he adopts, and in some places supplements, the manuscript's metrical pointing. His was, as Plumer notes, the first edition of
Anglo Saxon poetry to identify a 'purely literary element' to its contents;
it was an edition purely composed of poetic texts, and it isolated aspects of
their form.[31] It was not, however, a financial success, and it does not appear
to have reached an audience beyond scholars and antiquarians.[32]

Recovering Old English also involved other quasi-literary practices.
Both Nowell in the sixteenth century and L'Isle in the seventeenth are
thought to have produced additional 'Old English' texts by either translating Latin into Old English (Nowell) or archaising transcripts of early
Middle English texts such as the *Ancrene Wisse* (L'Isle).[33] A more playful
expression of this practice can be seen in the preface to L'Isle's *A Saxon
Treatise* (1623), in which he ventriloquises the voice of Alfred the Great
for a few words in Old English before dropping back into Early Modern
English: 'hereof me thinks I heare already the learned King *Ælfred* thus

expostulating and complaining: **[g]if on þeos gesælig doend gesihþe godes**, &c. or thus rather in our English: If in this happy making sight of God …'[34] Like many of his contemporaries, L'Isle is involved in a process of reanimation and reformulation, making the past speak to the present in both its own and an alien tongue.

These literary and quasi-literary engagements with Old English begin to complicate the perspective provided in the texts examined by Siân Echard, in which 'Old English is the institutional language … the realm of the linguistic, etymological, geographical and the anthropological', and Middle English 'the language of poetry'.[35] This tendency is still more marked in the texts on which the remainder of this chapter focuses, in which Old English becomes not merely a historical relic but an aesthetic tool. 'Ancient and savage' as Old English may have appeared, writers increasingly became alert to its possibilities and the new uses to which it might be put.

'Nemp your sexes!'

The most prominent Old English phrase to appear in early modern texts was *nimath eowra seaxes* ('take your daggers'), which appears in a dizzying number of forms across the sixteenth and seventeenth centuries: 'nenpnith youre sexis' (John Rastell); 'Nemyth, your sexes' (John Hardyng) '*neme your sexes*' (John Foxe), '*Nempt your sexes*' (Raphael Holinshed), '*Nem eour Seaxes*' (Richard Verstegan and John Speed), '*Nemp your Sexes*' (Thomas Middleton), 'Nem esur Saxes' (William Cartwright), '*Nempnith*, your Sepis' (Thomas Heywood), '*Nemet oure saxas*' (Inigo Jones), '*Nemet eour Saxes*' (John Milton), '*NEM ET EOVR SEAXES*' (Edward Stillingfleet) and '*Neme Eour Saxes*' (Robert Brady).[36] In itself, the variety of forms in which the phrase appears suggests the imperfections of early modern knowledge of Old English, and the alien quality that it held for writers, readers and spectators.

Nimath eowra seaxes frequently appears in narrative accounts of Hengist's treachery, but it also features in discussions of etymology, national identity and linguistic origin. For instance, in *The History of Great Britain under the Conquests of the Romans, Saxons, Danes and Normans* (1611), John Speed – like many of his fellow antiquarians – devotes a paragraph to the origins of the Saxons' name. According to Speed, the Saxons

> tooke the appellation from the *Fashion* of the *Weapon* that vsuallie they wore; which was a *Crooked Bowing Sword*, somewhat like vnto a *Sithe*, with the edge on the contrarie side, called by the *Netherlanders*, a *Saisen*, and by themselues *Seaxen*, and the shorter of like fashion for hand-weapons, *Seaxes*;

such as were those that were hid vnder their Garments in the *Massacre* of the *British Nobilitie* vpon *Salisbury Plaine*, when *Hengist* gaue the watchword, *Nem eour Seaxes*, that is, *Take you[r] Swords*.[37]

Speed's politico-linguistic history slips seamlessly – albeit somewhat uneasily – from a narrative about weaponry to one about treachery and conquest, from a physical object to the human that uses it, from a single word to a phrase that embodies a moment of national identity-formation. In this narrative, the violence of the Saxons' conquest is bound up with their name and the very language that they speak – and, thereby, their collective identity.

The role that language plays in conquest and, therefore, the construction of national identity is made still more explicit in other Jacobean antiquarian works.[38] '[T]he *English-Saxon* tongue', Camden writes in *Remains of a Greater Work, Concerning Britain* (1605), 'came in by the *English-Saxons* o[u]t of *Germany*, who valiantly and wisely performed heere all the three things, which implie a full conquest, viz. the alteration of lawes, language, and attire.'[39] Conquest, for Camden, involves not merely territorial expansion, but the erasure or over-writing of a pre-existing culture with that of the invaders; the origin of the English is therefore traced to the Saxon invaders rather than the conquered Britons. Another book published in 1605, Verstegan's *A Restitution of Decayed Intelligence*, makes this case still more strongly, its opening chapter beginning with the words 'Englishmen are descended of German race, & were heertofore generaly called Saxons'.[40] Old English is English, these writers suggest, and the English are Saxons.

This perspective is complicated in *Hengist, King of Kent* and *The Ordinary*. In *Hengist, King of Kent*, the watchword is (unsurprisingly) uttered by Hengist himself, in Middleton's dramatisation of the foundational moment described by Speed. In *The Ordinary*, it is uttered by an antiquary, Robert Moth, whose name might indicate that he is dusty ('Mote') or moth-eaten.[41] Like many antiquaries, Moth has a sustained interest in medieval history, philology and literature.[42] He uses another Old English phrase, *waes heal*, which appears in the chronicles as part of a toast offered to the British king Vortigern by Hengist's daughter Rowena, and he also refers to a famous incident in later Anglo-Saxon history, the treachery of the nobleman Edric against his king, Edmund Ironside. In each play, characters elsewhere speak in standard Early Modern English, with the exception of Moth, whose usual linguistic mode is a highly wrought pastiche of Middle English, much of it adapted from the works of Chaucer. This peculiar diction – which is at odds with the colloquial, often slangy, linguistic milieu of the play in general – creates a strange interplay between Old English, Middle English and Early Modern English, reminding an audience of linguistic change and positioning Moth as a temporal anomaly.

Middleton's account of *nimath eowra seaxes* is drawn largely from the version of events in Raphael Holinshed's *First and Second Volume of Chronicles* (1577).[43] The watchword is first set up between Hengist and his forces:

> *1 Saxon* Give us the word, my lord, and we are perfect.
> *Hengist* That's true, the word; I lose myself. *Nemp your sexes.*
> It shall be that.
> *1 Saxon* Enough sir; then we strike.[44]

It then appears for a second time as the two armies meet on Salisbury Plain. Hengist tells his men, 'Calm looks but stormy souls possess you all' (4.3.27), and the British king – here called Vortiger – and his unsuspecting lords approach:

> *Vortiger* We see you keep your words in all points firm.
> *Hengist* No longer may we boast of so much breath
> As goes to a word's making than of care
> In the preserving of it when 'tis made.
> *Vortiger* You're in a virtuous way, my lord of Kent,
> And since both sides are met like sons of peace,
> All other arms laid by in signs of favour
> If our conditions be embrac'd –
> *Hengist*   They are.
> *Vortiger* – we'll use no other but these only here.[45]
> *Hengist Nemp your sexes!*
> [*The* SAXONS *draw their daggers and slay the* BRITISH LORDS]
> *British Lords* Treason, treason!
> *Hengist* Follow it to the heart, my trusty Saxons!
> It is your liberty, your wealth and honour.   (4.3.28–39)[46]

Having been primed with the first use of '*nemp your sexes*', spectators will be aware that the Saxons will attack as soon as they hear the watchword, even if they do not know the phrase or recognise it as Old English. The prominence of the phrase in historical accounts of this event might also mean that they could be alert to the ironies in the use of 'word', 'point' and 'arms' in the preceding dialogue; the Saxons will keep to their watchword, which precisely entails not keeping their 'word'. No translation is provided, although a visual gloss might be provided when the Saxons draw their daggers. Nonetheless, even if the Old English phrase is unintelligible to an audience member, and functions purely as sound, the alien language becomes a signal for conspiracy and betrayal, and for national and linguistic difference.[47] Although elsewhere in the play they speak standard Early Modern English, even to each other, the Saxons have the capacity to use a tongue incomprehensible to the British.

Old English is not, however, purely 'foreign'; rather, as an archaic ancestor of Early Modern English it both is and is not alien. Furthermore, at the moments when the phrase '*nemp your sexes*' is spoken the play moves away from realism and towards a kind of linguistic alienation effect, in which Hengist effectively quotes from early modern accounts of the events on Salisbury Plain even as he inhabits those events within the dramatic representation. English spectators are alienated from their own past, and from their putative national and linguistic origins, through their inability to understand Hengist's words, spoken in what commentators such as Camden and Verstegan called the 'English-Saxon' tongue.[48] Thus, even as Middleton draws on historians' and antiquarians' accounts of the origin of the English, he resists this identification, aligning his spectators' sympathies not with the alien, invading Saxons but with the conquered British.

The reasons for such a manoeuvre become clearer when we look to the Jacobean context of the play, and a widespread cultural investment in the idea of 'Britain' following the accession of James VI of Scotland to the throne of England.[49] James notoriously styled himself 'King of Great Britain, France and Ireland', and argued that his accession reunited 'these two mightie, famous, and ancient Kingdomes of England and Scotland, under one Imperiall Crowne'.[50] In an important sense, the English were now 'British'; in a play written at the height of the debate about the Union of England and Scotland, Edward Sharpham's *The Fleer* (1606), the somewhat dissolute gallant Ruffle admits 'I did pray oftener when I was an Englishman but I have not prayed often, I must confess, since I was a Briton'.[51] If the English had become 'Britons', the English language was one of their few remaining links to the Saxon invaders. Moreover, English-speaking Scots might equally be 'Saxons', an issue to which I will return later in this chapter.

Perhaps surprisingly, a similar negotiation with the Saxonist narrative of English national origin can be found in Cartwright's comedy *The Ordinary*, performed around 1635.[52] *Hengist, King of Kent* appears to have been revived by the King's Men around this time, and it is possible that the theatrically aware Cartwright was directly inspired by Middleton's play.[53] *The Ordinary* features a comic replay of Hengist's betrayal, as the antiquary Moth faces an attack from the aggressively drunken Have-at-All. The use

of Old English is set up in the initial lines of the encounter, as Moth greets
Have-at-All with the words, 'Waes heal thou gentle Knight', drawing (with
comic disregard for context) on the account of Rowena's first encounter
with Vortigern.[54] As Speed relates,

> in the midst of [Vortigern's] cups, *Rowena* (so was the damosell called) with
> a low reuerence and pleasing grace, saluted the *King* with a cup of gold
> full of sweet wine, incharming it with these words in her language; **Waes
> heal hlaford Cyning**, which is in our English, *Be of health Lord King*: he
> demanding the meaning, would be taught to answer to her owne vnder-
> standing, and said, **Drinc heal**, that is, *Drinke health*[.] (*History*, 389)[55]

Although Moth adapts the phrase to address a 'gentle Knight' rather than a
'Lord King', it is perhaps unsurprising that Have-at-All responds to his
approach not with the phrase *drinc heal* but with violent rejection: 'Waes
heal thou gentle Knight? speak what art thou? / Speak quickly doe: Villain
know'st thou not me?' (ll. 1698–9). Unlike the willing Vortigern, Have-at-
All resists being drawn into an alien linguistic and social interaction, which
in Cartwright's version is comically translated from a heterosexual to a
homosocial context.

   In the exchange that follows, Have-at-All becomes progressively more
irate and Moth progressively more desperate to avoid injury. Characteristically, the antiquary appeals to history and romance, presenting Have-at-All
with negative exemplars of treacherous violence and positive exemplars of
heroic chivalry. Intriguingly, his examples of treachery all derive from
Anglo-Saxon history. As Have-at-All continues to beat him, he cries, 'flet
Englond, flet *Englond*: / Dead is *Edmond* ... I nis not *Edmond Ironside*
God wot' (ll. 1724–5, 1727). Moth refers to the story of the struggle
between Edmund Ironside and Cnut for the English throne, during which
the mendacious Saxon nobleman Edric is said to have tried to convince the
English forces that Edmund was dead in order to aid the invader. The
narrative appears in Holinshed's *Chronicles*, but Moth's version appears to
derive ultimately from Henry of Huntingdon's Latin *Chronicle*: 'videns dux
Edricus ruinam Dacorum imminere, clamauit Anglorum genti, **Flet Engle,
flet Engle: ded is** *Edmund*' ('seeing the ruin of the leader of the Danes
was imminent, Edric called out to the English people, "Flee Englishmen, flee
Englishmen: Edmund is dead"').[56] The result of Edric's treachery is the death
of 'omnis flos nobilitatia Brittaniae' ('all the flower of the British nobility') –
an intriguing conflation of 'English' and 'British' on Huntingdon's part.
Moth recalls this historical act of treacherous violence, but he apparently
confuses Edric's fiction of Edmund's death with the real thing.

Moth's final allusion to Anglo-Saxon history is a response to Have-at-All's threat, 'I'l seal thy lips', to which he replies,

> A twenty Devil way![57] So did the Saxon
> Upon thylke plain of *Sarum*, done to death
> By treachery, the Lords of merry *Englond*
> Nem esur Saxes.   (ll. 1729–32)

The confusion between 'England' and 'Britain' recalls that of Huntingdon, and it is perhaps the result of Moth's conflation of Hengist's betrayal with that of Edric. The beleaguered antiquary casts himself as the betrayed Briton/Englishman and Have-at-All as the treacherous Saxon/Dane. Have-at-All's initial response is to demand, 'Villain dost abuse me / In unbaptized language?' (ll. 1732–3), interpreting Old English as both alien and unholy. Attempting to mollify him, Moth stops speaking altogether and instead *entreats by signs* (ll. 1743–4SD), apparently reaching the final point of a linguistic descent from Early Modern English, through Middle English and Old English, eventually relying on gesture alone. Have-at-All is predictably unimpressed, declaring, 'this is more / Unsufferable than your old patch'd gibberish; / This silence is abuse' (ll. 1736–8). He then threatens the frantically gesticulating Moth:

> I'l send thee to
> The Place of it, where thou shalt meet with *Oswald,*
> *Vortigern, Harold, Hengist, Horsey, Knute,*
> *Alured, Edgar,* and *Cunobeline.*   (ll. 1738–41)

Have-at-All earlier rejected Moth's appeals to historical exemplars – his response to the reference to Edmund Ironside is a physical attack and the emphatic exclamation 'Take that for history' (l. 1725). Yet he clearly recognises Moth's allusion to the treacherous attack upon the British forces, as his references to '*Vortigern*', '*Hengist*' and '*Horsey*' (a comic misremembering of 'Horsa', the name of Hengist's brother) suggest. He ironically rejects the identification made between himself and Hengist even as his violent behaviour foregrounds the comic similarity between the two aggressors.

If we take the use of the phrase *nimath eowra seaxes* in isolation, *The Ordinary* appears to create a dynamic similar to that of *Hengist, King of Kent*: Moth casts himself as the beleaguered Briton, with Have-at-All as the treacherously violent Hengist. However, Moth's reference to 'the Lords of merry *Englond*' complicates this picture through its conflation of English and British, and his other allusions to Anglo-Saxon history confuse things even further. In his reference to Edmund Ironside, Moth himself utters the words of the traitor who had aligned himself with the invading Danes, while in his use of the phrase *waes hail* he implicitly casts himself as Rowena to Have-at-All's Vortigern. Furthermore, it is not Have-at-All who utters the treacherous phrase *nimath eowra seaxes*, but the antiquary himself. Old English scholarship cannot save Moth; indeed, his over-immersion in his area of study apparently creates and intensifies his predicament.

The use of Old English therefore complicates notions of national and personal identity, alienating English spectators from their putative national origins and alienating Moth from himself, his native language and, eventually, any form of speech. Moreover, it does so through its archaism. In *Hengist*, the phrase *nimath eowra seaxes* functions either because it is incomprehensible owing to its antiquity or – if a spectator knows their Speed, Holinshed or Verstegan – because it is recognisable as a historical touchstone. In *The Ordinary*, it symbolises both Moth's status as an antiquary and the extent to which he is out of touch with his own time and its linguistic and behavioural conventions. Like the sexual, behavioural and economic practices associated with 'queer time' by Judith Halberstam,[58] archaic Old English phrases are at odds with conventional notions of what is appropriate to a particular time and place; the extent to which Moth is 'queered' by his linguistic proclivities is underlined in his comically misplaced quotation of Rowena's words of seduction. Middleton and Cartwright both exploit the aural qualities of outmoded language, creating a polytemporal aesthetic in which Old English functions either as alienating device, as in *Hengist*, or as part of the temporally confused speech of the clownish Moth. The plays also suggest, however, that Old English was becoming part of cultural memory, and a key element in the formation of national history and identity.

The freedom of a translator

Gather vp the fragments that remaine, that nothing be lost.[59]

In *Hengist, King of Kent* and *The Ordinary*, Old English moves out of chronicle, antiquarian treatise and polemic, and onto the stage. In doing so, it is incorporated into a form of writing that would have been viewed in its own day as sub-literary at best, despite the cultural pretensions of many of its proponents. In the work of William L'Isle, in contrast, we see Old English in contexts that are simultaneously more 'literary' and more scholarly. As noted above, L'Isle was an important figure in early seventeenth-century Anglo-Saxon scholarship. His edition of Ælfric's letter to Sigeweard on the Old and New Testaments was published in 1623 as *A Saxon Treatise Concerning the Old and New Testament*, and further projected editions of Anglo-Saxon texts survive in manuscript.[60] He also wrote extensively about his experiences of learning Old English in the preface to *A Saxon Treatise*.

L'Isle was also active as a translator, and his version of Virgil's *Eclogues*, published in 1628, is a resonant attempt to mediate classical literature through a temporally and nationally hybrid form of English.[61] Taking Spenser's *Shepheardes Calender* as his immediate model, L'Isle weaves archaic words into his text, and he also supplies explanatory glosses alongside a running interpretative commentary that draws on, quotes and translates earlier editors such as Juan Luis Vives.[62] In doing so, he develops his forebear's interest in both the temporality and trans-national capacities of the English language. Hannah Crawforth has demonstrated the ways in which Spenser self-consciously combines words with Middle English and Old English derivations; moreover, Willy Maley has argued that his archaising style is shaped not only by his reading in Chaucer but also by his exposure to the variety of English used by Catholics of Norman English descent in the English Pale in Ireland – who were known, confusingly in this context, as the 'Old English'.[63] The English of the 'Old English' was thought to represent an outmoded form of the language: Richard Stanihurst, for instance, describes it as 'the dregs of the old ancient Chaucer English'.[64] Its use in *The Shepheardes Calender* thus adds another layer to Spenser's multi-temporal and multi-national linguistic hybrid. These qualities are incorporated and intensified in L'Isle's *Eclogues*.

In his commentary notes, L'Isle flags up four words as 'Saxon': 'sicker', 'sib', 'herry' and 'queme'.[65] The words were not new discoveries; each had appeared in *The Shepheardes Calender*, albeit without being described as 'Saxon', and L'Isle acknowledges his source in his note to 'queme': 'please: a Saxon word: *Spencer*' (F6r). Yet the translator's desire to flag up the origins of these words, and to brand them as 'Saxon', where other words are credited to Chaucer and Spenser, draws attention to the long history of English, and of changes within the language. The fact that L'Isle is translating Virgil adds to the polychronic effect of his text. While Spenser's original work draws on Virgilian generic and stylistic models, and Chaucerian and Saxonist vocabulary, L'Isle's translated Virgil moves forward in time from the classical past, and the Latin language, to inhabit simultaneously three different phases in the development of the English language: Old English, Middle English and Early Modern English. Old English is thus incorporated into both linguistic and, potentially, literary history.

Counterintuitive as the association might seem, for L'Isle there was nothing incongruous about mediating Virgil through Old English; indeed, he had already brought them together in print. *A Saxon Treatise* is prefaced by an archaising imitation of Virgil's fourth Eclogue, in which Prince Charles is hailed as the nation's redeemer. The poem opens with an appeal to '[Y]EE Nine that leaue twi-pointed *Pernas* hill, / To dwell on double-trenched *Gogmagog*', depicts King James as 'mightie *Pan*', and praises Prince Charles, whose lineage draws together formerly contending nations: 'The *Norman*, th'*English*, and *Dardaniane* [i.e. Trojan] / (O royall Impe) are ioyned by thy Sire; / And thou fro [*sic*] mothers side draw'st bloud of *Dane*.'[66] In a short poem printed beneath the Prince of Wales' emblem, which faces the first page of the eclogue, L'Isle writes of the Germanic motto 'Ich dien', *'That Word still Saxon, shewes he doth protect / From throat of time our ancient Dialect'* (*A Saxon Treatise*, title-page verso). To praise Charles in this simultaneously Virgilian and Saxonist context is to hail him as the protector not only of the nation but of its language and linguistic heritage.

The connection that L'Isle drew between Virgil and Old English is best explained by a passage in the preface 'To the Reader' in *A Saxon Treatise*, in which he describes the 'vneasie way' through which he learned Old English. According to his own account, L'Isle began by first reading German and Dutch, and worked his way back through the oldest forms of English that he could find. However, this strategy caused him problems:

> diuers good bookes in this kinde I got, that were neuer yet published in print; which euer the more ancient they were, I perceiued came nearer the Saxon: But the Saxon, (as a bird, flying in the aire farther and farther, seemes lesse and lesse;) the older it was, became harder to bee vnderstood[.] (*A Saxon Treatise*, c4v)

A pivotal moment came when he encountered a perhaps unlikely source:

> At length I lighted on *Virgil* Scotished by the Reuerend *Gawin Dowglas* Bishop of *Dunkell*, and vncle to the Earle of *Angus*; the best translation of that Poet that euer I read: And though I found that dialect more hard than any of the former (as neerer the Saxon, because farther from the Norman) yet with helpe of the Latine I made shift to vnderstand it, and read the booke more than once from the beginning to the end. Wherby I must confesse I got more knowledge of that I sought than by any of the other. For as at the Saxon Inuasion many of the Britains, so at the Norman many of the Saxons fled into Scotland, preseruing in that Realme vnconquered, as the line Royall, so also the language, better than the Inhabitants here, vnder conquerors law and custome, were able. (c4r–d1r)

L'Isle argues that just as Scotland preserved the Saxon royal line through the marriage of Margaret, granddaughter of Edmond Ironside and great-niece of Edward the Confessor, to Malcolm III, so Middle Scots has preserved Old English. Old English is 'this outworne dialect of our forebeers; which *England* hath kept best in writing, *Scotland* in speech' (e4v); it is a linguistic heritage shared by English and Scots alike. Like the twentieth-century Scottish poets discussed by Chris Jones, he is aware of an 'intertwined dual evolution of Anglo-Saxon in both England and Scotland' (*Strange Likeness*, 164). In this context, it becomes perhaps less surprising that L'Isle describes James I in his poem to Prince Charles in *A Saxon Treatise* as '*Norman* ... *English*, and *Dardaniane*' rather than as Scottish; from his perspective, the Scots are in some respects more English than the English. And although recent scholars have been sceptical about the utility of Douglas's Middle Scots translation of *The Aeneid* as an Old English primer,[67] there is an important sense in which, for L'Isle, Old English is both Scottish and Virgilian, and Virgil, correspondingly, is Anglo-Saxon.

In the preface to *Virgil's Eclogues Translated into English*, L'Isle discusses the role of the translator, saying,

> my homely Muse drest the whole feast, according as shee knew it would best please my own tast and dyet, (*Coquus enim Domini debet habere gulam*:)[68] & I used the freedome of a Translator, not tying my selfe to the tyranny of a Grammaticall Construction, but breaking the shell into many peeces, was onely carefull to preserve the kernell safe and whole, from the violence of a wrong, or wrested Interpretation[.] (¶¶5v–6r)

The belief that preserving the spirit of the original text is more important than to follow it word for word appears to liberate L'Isle; as Andrew Wallace argues, he 'counterintuitively casts the freedom with which he has translated the *Eclogues* as evidence of his fidelity to Virgil'.[69] The precise nature of this freedom is suggested by L'Isle's punning use of the word 'homely', which in addition to meaning 'plain' or 'unadorned' can also describe something domestic, familiar or intimate.[70] His translation self-consciously adopts a rustic style often associated with Virgil's work by commentators, and it also simultaneously domesticates the Roman writer, embedding him in English linguistic and literary tradition.[71]

Two stanzas from L'Isle's version of the first Eclogue demonstrate his technique. The Latin text reads:

> Urbem, quam dicunt Romam, Meliboee, putavi
> stultus ego huic nostrae similem, quo saepe solemus
> pastores ovium teneros depellere fetus.
> sic canibus catulos similes, sic matribus haedos

noram, sic parvis componere magna solebam.
verum haec tantum alias inter caput extulit urbes,
quantum lenta solent inter viburna cupressi. (ll. 19–25)

[The city which they call Rome, Meliboeus, I, foolish one! thought was like
this of ours, whither we shepherds are wont to drive the tender younglings of
our flocks. Thus I knew puppies were like dogs, and kids like their dams; thus
I used to compare great things with small. But this one has reared her head as
high among all other cities as cypresses oft do among the bending osiers.]

L'Isle's translation runs as follows:

> Sicker, yee mee to thing doo'n timely tempt,
> Which erst, I bet, than yee did never ken:
> Ah fon, (friend *Melibe*) I whilome dempt,
> That famous Citty, which I now and then
> In common chat, amongst our Countrimen,
> Haue heard ycleeped, by the name of *Rome*,
> Certes for all the world, sibb, to our homely home.
>
> Where we poore shepheards, woont attend our Lamms,
> And tender younglings weane. So did I dare
> Kids, liken, to their Goates, Whelpes to their Damms,
> And Mowle-hills, woont, to Mountaines, to compare.
> 'But sooth, to it all other Citties are
> 'As to huge Firre-trees, the young tender plants,
> '(So high her haughty head she 'boue them doth enhance.)
>
> (*Virgils Eclogues*, A2r–v)

Sicker, glossed by L'Isle as 'an old Saxon word; as much as verily, or surely'
(A8v), echoes *The Shepheardes Calender*, where it appears twelve times. The
word 'bett' ('a word contracted from better') is credited to Chaucer and
Spenser (A8v), 'ycleeped' ('named or called') to Chaucer (B1r), and 'fon'
('a contraction from fondling') and 'dempt' ('for deemed, or imagined') to
Spenser (B1r). 'Sibb' receives a longer, etymological note:

> *Sibb*: an old Saxon word, as much as of kinred or alliance: from hence coms
> our word Gossip; corruptly so written and spoken; if being indeede, God-sib:
> that is, a kinred in God: all such as are Godfathers and Godmothers together
> at the christning of a child, by the Popes Canons, become Sib to each other,
> and of a spirituall kindred, so neere allyed, that such Godsibs may not marry
> together, without speciall dispensation from his Holinesse. (B1r)

In his preface to *A Saxon Treatise*, L'Isle argues for the importance of Old
English in studies of the etymology of contemporary words and names
(f1v–f2v). Here he puts theory into practice, but tracing the origins of the

word 'sibb' leads him into an odd engagement with Roman Catholic practice, odd because elsewhere he claims that one of the primary uses of Old English is in support of Protestant doctrine and practice (*A Saxon Treatise*, dıv, c3v). Using Old English in literary contexts seems to render it simultaneously less insular and less appropriate for straightforwardly polemical uses.

Something of this tendency can also be seen elsewhere in the translation. L'Isle naturalises Virgil as an indigenous poet, transforming his predecessor's plants and flowers into their English equivalents: in the second Eclogue, for instance, Virgil's 'alba ligustra' ('white privets') and 'vaccinia nigra' ('dark hyancinths') (l. 18) become L'Isle's '*Hurtles . . .* blacke' and '*Dazies* [. . .] white' (A5v).[72] Further, L'Isle's English Virgil is also a British poet, one whose diction encompasses not only Anglo-Scottish Old English but also Irish Gaelic. In the first Eclogue he translates 'pressi copia lactis' ('a wealth of pressed cheeses') (l. 81) as 'curds galore' (A4r), the latter word glossed as 'An Irish word, and signifies plenty, and abundance' (B5v). This is the earliest use of 'galore' that has been traced in an English text,[73] and although the word is clearly chosen to rhyme with 'store' it adds to the verbal texture of the translation and to its trans-nationalism. L'Isle is also markedly less anxious than Spenser about his combination of English and Irish linguistic resources.[74] If we recall L'Isle's description of Douglas's translation of *The Aeneid* as 'the best translation of that Poet [Virgil] that euer I read', we realise that his archaised British Virgil is a tribute to the powerful hold that the Scots poet's work had on him.

Although he may have been only dimly aware of the presence of poetic techniques within the Anglo-Saxon texts he studied, L'Isle's translation of Virgil's *Eclogues* shows no sign of embarrassment about bringing together classical literature and Old English vocabulary. Instead, the translation makes an implicit claim for the status of not only Early Modern English but all versions of English as vehicles for literary expression. Simultaneously, it suggests that Old English is not simply or purely 'English' but a shared linguistic heritage between English and Scots. Such a view complicates the perspective established in texts such as *Hengist, King of Kent*, in which Old English is associated purely with the Saxons, and it foreshadowed the new uses to which the language was to be put in the following decades, notably in a new innovation: the composition of poetry in Old English.

West-Saxon poets

William L'Isle may well have possessed the ability to compose verse in Old English; if he did, none of his attempts has survived. However, some of his contemporaries not only composed in Old English but also saw their compositions into print: Abraham Wheelock and William Retchford contributed poems in Old English to a 1641 Cambridge University collection, *Irenodia Cantabrigiensis*, and Joseph Williamson followed their example in *Musarum Oxoniensium*, printed in Oxford in 1654. Like L'Isle's experiments with Old English, these poems are a by-product of seventeenth-century scholarship in Anglo-Saxon texts and Old English. Wheelock was University Librarian at Cambridge, Professor of Arabic, and, from the late 1630s, the holder of a (somewhat ad hoc) lectureship funded by Sir Henry Spelman with the aim of encouraging the study of Old English.[75] William Retchford was one of his pupils.[76] Joseph Williamson, later Clerk of the Privy Council and Secretary of State, took his BA at Queen's College, Oxford, in 1654, the year in which his Old English poem was written, and in 1679 he established a lectureship in Anglo-Saxon there.[77]

The books in which these poems were published, *Irenodia Cantabrigiensis* and *Musarum Oxoniensium*, were products of the early modern culture of panegyric, poetic miscellanies compiled and published within the universities in praise of the ruler at particular, politically momentous moments.[78] *Irenodia Cantabrigiensis* consists of verses praising Charles I on his return from Scotland in November 1641, following the peace settlement that concluded the so-called 'Bishops' Wars', while *Musarum Oxoniensium* praises Oliver Cromwell on the successful conclusion of the first Anglo-Dutch War in 1654. Each volume includes a wide variety of classical languages and vernaculars: Latin, Greek, Hebrew, French, Welsh, English and Old English. The three Old English poems exemplify this multilingual approach: Wheelock's Old English poem (see Figure 2) is a translation of his other contribution, written in Hebrew; Retchford's poem begins with four lines in Latin, followed by fourteen in Old English (see Figure 3); and Williamson's consists of fourteen lines in Old English followed by another sixteen in French.

The inclusion of English and other vernaculars in official university collections was a Caroline innovation, adopted by Oxford poets in 1633 and by Cambridge poets as late as 1640.[79] As James Loxley argues of the Oxford volumes, these works seek to bind together the English language and the 'British Stuart dynasty' that Charles and Henrietta Maria were busily establishing during the 1630s; 'vernacular poetry takes its place in the formal relations between the university and the monarch'.[80] Thus, *Irenodia Cantabrigiensis* uses the English language as part of an attempt to bolster the authority of the British Stuart monarchy at a moment of national crisis. In the 1654 volume, in contrast, multiple languages are

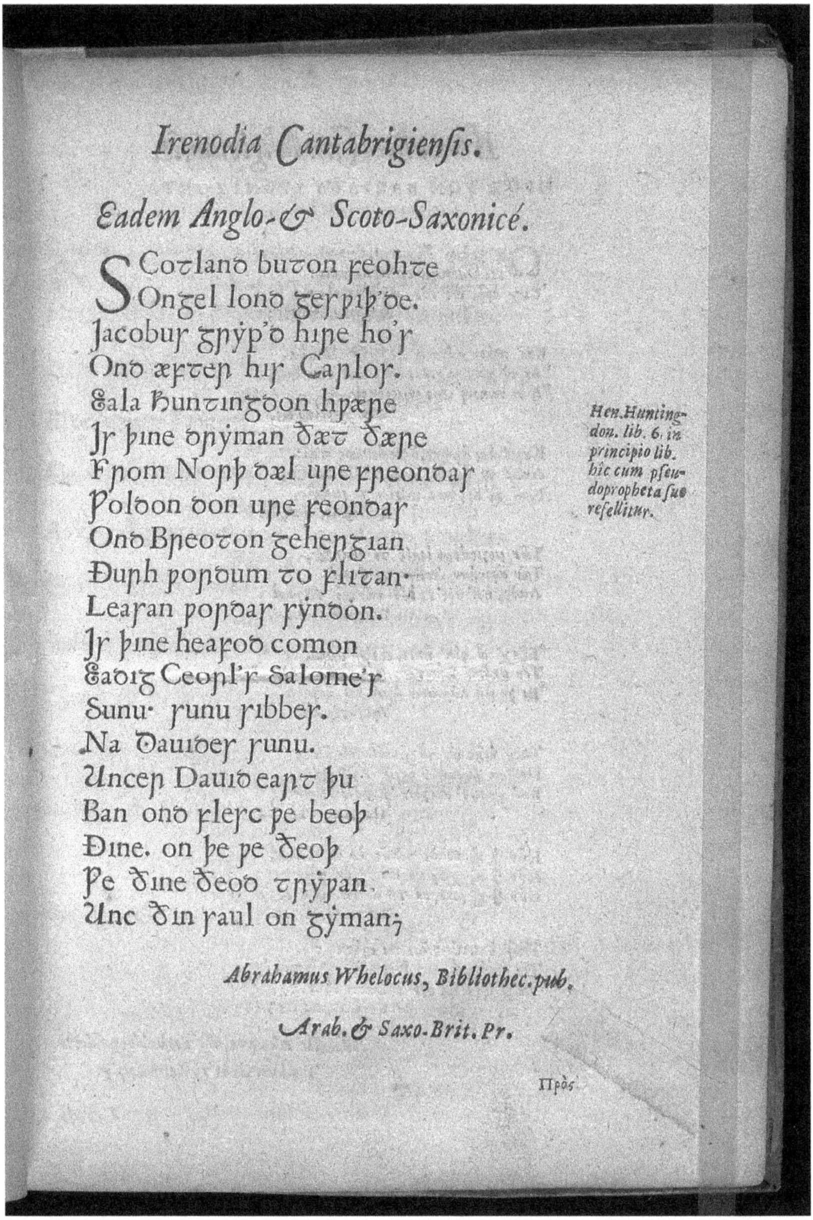

Irenodia Cantabrigiensis.

Eadem Anglo-& Scoto-Saxonicé.

SCotland buton feohte
Ongel lond gerpiþ de.
Jacobus gnyp'd hine ho'f
Ond æfter hif Caplof.
Sala huntingdon hpæpe
If þine dryman ðæt ðæpe
From Norþ dæl une freondar
Poldon don une feondar
Ond Breoton gehergian
Duph pordum to flitan·
Leafan pordaf fyndon.
If þine heafod comon
Sadig Ceopl'f Salome'f
Sunu· funu fibbef.
Na Dauidef funu.
Uncer Dauid eart þu
Ban ond flefc þe beoþ
Dine. on þe pe ðeoþ
Þe ðine ðeod tpypan.
Unc ðin faul on gyman;

Hen. Hunting-
don. lib. 6. in
principio lib.
hic cum pseu-
dopropheta suo
refellitur.

Abrahamus Whelocus, Bibliothec.pub.

Arab. & Saxo-Brit. Pr.

Πρὸς

Figure 2 Abraham Wheelock, 'Eadem Anglo- & Scoto-Saxonicé', in *Irenodia Cantabrigiensis* (Cambridge, 1641), A4r.

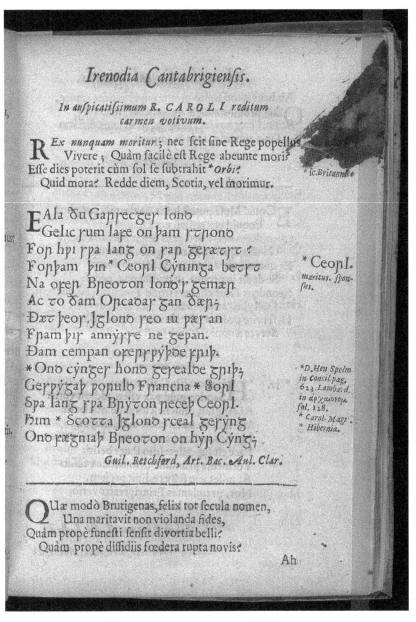

Figure 3 William Retchford, 'In auspicatissimum R. CAROLI reditum carmen votivum', in *Irenodia Cantabrigiensis*, G4r.

instead gathered in an attempt to reconceptualise the relationship between ruler and nation in the wake of Cromwell's installation as Lord Protector in December 1653. The place of Old English within each volume is ambiguous, however. *Irenodia Cantabrigiensis* places its Old English poems among the ancient languages, while *Musarum Oxoniensium* positions Williamson's poem in a section written mainly in modern vernaculars. This may be due to Wheelock's use of Hebrew and Retchford's of Latin in the Cambridge volume, and Williamson's of French in the Oxford volume, but the difference highlights the fact that Old English was anomalous in terms of both classical and modern languages: too ancient and obsolete to be a true vernacular, but too obscure, indecorous and barbaric to be fully incorporated among the classical languages.

Wheelock and Retchford's poems are also striking visually, marking the first appearance in print of the elegant Anglo-Saxon types apparently designed for use in Wheelock's edition of Bede.[81] This visual authenticity is misleading. None of these poets attempts to write in authentic Old English forms; indeed, it is unlikely that they had any idea of the conventions of Old English poetry.[82] Instead, they effectively write seventeenth-century lyric poems in Old English, employing modern rhyme schemes and metres, and weaving in a series of biblical and classical references, in the style of contemporary panegyric. These poems are not the product of a historicist imagination, but of a somewhat irreverent desire to employ a new linguistic facility in very modern contexts; thus, they display archaism's characteristic tendency to look both backwards and forwards. Nonetheless, the choice of Old English is striking, especially in the context described by Loxley – if the English language was aligned with the Stuart dynasty in the 1630s and early 1640s, where did that leave Old English? And what did the use of Old English signify in the mid-1650s?

The poems' linguistic failings have been discussed in detail by scholars;[83] what has been less widely recognised – and what interests me here – is the way in which the resurrected language is made to speak to mid-seventeenth-century concerns and, in particular, the way that it is invoked as part of a poetic dialogue about the nature and status of the 'British' nation. In Wheelock and Retchford's poems, Old English is employed in the context of tensions between the British nations – not only the Scottish invasion of England and the ineffectual attempt of the monarch to impose his authority on his rebellious northern kingdom, but also the Irish rebellion, which broke out in October 1641. In Williamson's poem, Old English appears in the wake of Cromwell's subjugation of Ireland and

Scotland and his assumption of the title of Lord Protector, and of the peace treaty signed in May 1654 between the United Provinces of the Nether-lands and the Protectorate of England, Scotland and Ireland. It thus speaks to a recent reconfiguration of the relationship between the British nations, and a reassessment of the relationship between the British and the Dutch. All of these poems are thus embedded in contemporary debates, and – as I will explore in detail – the use of Old English mediates and inflects the political stance that each takes.

The complex ways in which Wheelock and Retchford use Old English become clear if we examine in more detail the political context in which their poems appeared. Published in Cambridge late in 1641, *Irenodia Cantabrigiensis* celebrates an apparently peaceful conclusion to three years of turmoil in Scotland and northern England. The imposition of a Laudian prayer-book in Scotland led to a rebellion in 1638, followed by the 'Bishops' Wars', during which the Scots defeated an English army at Newburn on 28 August 1640 and occupied Newcastle, Durham and a large swathe of north-east England. Charles travelled to Scotland in person in August 1641, and a peace treaty was finally agreed in early September; various forms of panegyric were written to celebrate the king's return to England in November. However, optimism was strongly qualified by fears about the Irish uprising, which began in late October, and by the passing of the Grand Remonstrance by the House of Commons on 23 November, two days before Charles's official entry into London.[84]

Irenodia Cantabrigiensis and a companion volume published in Oxford, *Eucharistica Oxoniensia*, reflect this divided mood, attempting to negotiate the conflicting demands of panegyric and political realism. Even as they celebrate what they term a 'bloodless' victory, contributors are painfully aware of the difficulties caused by Charles's absence from England and the Irish rebellion. Tensions in London are summarised by Robert Cresswell, a friend and room-mate of Abraham Cowley:

> The Town beset with watches and with fears
> More terrible then th' Halberts, now not cares
> For train-bands virtue, or Artilleries power,
> Nor puts much confidence in London Towre.[85]

Other poets refer directly to political events. In a Latin poem, Charles Rich writes, 'Ah propera! Cernis quam fulget Hibernia in armis? / Te vocat Imperii cura secunda Tui' (I2v) ('Ah, make haste! You see how Ireland shines forth in war? / The next responsibility of your empire calls you'),[86] while Thomas Yardley alludes more delicately to the situation, concluding his contribution with the lines 'For whom so mild a Prince cannot appease, / That people's rougher then the Irish Seas' (K4v).

These themes are developed in Retchford's poem:

In auspicatissimum R. CAROLI reditum carmen votivum.

Rex nunquam moritur, nec scit sine Rege popellus
Vivere; Quàm facilè est Rege abeunte mori?
Esse dies poterit cùm sol se subtrahit [87] *Orbi?*
Quid mora? Redde diem, Scotia, vel morimur.

Eala ðu Garsecges lond
Gelic sum lafe on þam strond
For hwi swa lang on sar gesaetst?
Forþam þin [88] Ceorl Cyninga betst
Na ofer Breoton lond's gemaer
Ac to ðam Orcades gan ðaer;
Ðaet þeos Iglond seo iu waes an
Fram þis annysse ne gewan.
Ðam cempan oferswyþðe friþ.
[89] Ond cynges hond gesealde griþ;
Geswygaþ woruld Francna [90] Eorl
Swa lang swa Bryton receþ Ceorl.
Him [91] Scotta Iglond sceal gesyng
Ond faegniaþ Breoton on hyr Cyng;   (G4r)

[*A votive poem for the most auspicious return of King Charles.*

The king never dies; nor do the masses know how to live without a king; how easy is it to die in the king's absence? Can there be day when the sun withdraws itself from the world? Why delay? Restore the day, Scotland, or we die.

Alas, you land of ocean, why have you sat so long in grief, like some widow on the shore? Because your husband, the best of kings, goes not beyond Britain's border, but to the Isles of Orkney, so that this island which was once one has not struggled [away] from this unity. 'And a king's hand gave peace.' The lord of the Franks quiets[92] the world as long as Britain cares for Charles. The Irish isle shall celebrate him, and Britain rejoice in its king.]

The Latin section of the poem opens with a proverb often cited in accounts of English common law and the succession: because the office of king is not coterminous with the body of an individual king, the king can never be said to die.[93] Retchford then casts Charles as the sun, without whose light his people cannot survive, in an image that recurs throughout the collection.[94] The Old English section approaches the same issue from a different angle, and the 'Garsecges lond' ('land of ocean') – apparently here England rather than Britain – is figured as a wife mourning the absence of her husband. The poet reassures her, saying that Charles has gone 'Na ofer Breoton lond's gemaer / Ac to ðam Orcades' ('not beyond Britain's border, but to the Isles of Orkney'); the king has not left his kingdom, even though he has travelled to its farthest extent. Orkney, which was not part of Charles's itinerary in 1641, here appears as a metonymic stand-in for Scotland itself. In addition, the allusion evokes the distance that the king may travel without leaving his realm; not only was Orkney towards the northern edge of Charles's Scottish kingdom, but it was also sometimes associated with the 'ultima Thule' mentioned in Virgil's *Georgics*, 1: 30.[95] The next lines, 'Ðaet þeos Iglond seo iu waes an / Fram þis annysse ne gewan' ('so that this island which was once one has not struggled [away] from unity'), suggest that Britain's unity is strengthened, not threatened, by the king's journey. Like other poets in *Irenodia Cantabrigiensis*, such as Yardley, William Fairbrother or John Cleveland, who argue for Charles's ubiquity or omnipresence throughout his kingdoms, Retchford evokes a paradoxical absence/presence that England should celebrate rather than mourn.[96]

After eight lines focusing on the king's absence, the poem turns – in a sonnet-like volta – to proverb and prophecy. Quoting an Anglo-Saxon law published in the collections of William Lambarde and Henry Spelman,[97] Retchford writes, 'Ond cynges hond gesealde griþ' ('And a king's hand gave peace'), the proverbial phrase apparently lending Charles its authority, and reinforcing the idea that Charles's 'victory' was achieved through his kingly influence rather than through force or bloodshed. However, to quote this material in 1641 was to allude to an ongoing debate about the nature of monarchical power. Anglo-Saxon laws had long been a subject of study in early modern England, and for some Caroline writers they came to symbolise ancient rights under the common law, and the liberty of parliament, both of which were thought to be threatened by Charles's personal rule. For example, as Jessica Dyson notes, common lawyers who were opposed to what they saw as the illegal use of royal prerogative identified 'a continuity in English common law from the Saxons (whose laws were made by consent of the people) through to the present'; for this reason, they argued that 'the king was not above the law, nor was he its origin'.[98] Thus, while Retchford's quotation appears to support royal authority, it also perhaps alludes implicitly to challenges to that authority.

The next couplet, 'Geswygaþ woruld Francna Eorl / Swa lang swa Bryton receþ Ceorl' ('The lord of the Franks quiets the world as long as

Britain cares for Charles'), also draws on an exterior source. According to Retchford's note, the 'Francna Eorl' is Charlemagne ('*Carol Magna.*'), and he apparently alludes to a prophecy supposedly discovered at Magdeburg, translated by the Scottish antiquary James Maxwell in *Admirable and Notable Prophesies* (1615) as follows:

> Of the blood of the Emperour *Charles* the Great, and of the kings of *France*, shall arise an Emperour named *Charles*, who shall rule Imperially in *Europe*, by whome the decaied estate of the Church shall be reformed, and the ancient glorie of the Empire againe restored. For there shall come a people, which shall bee called a people without a head, and then woe shall be vnto Priests. The ship of S. *Peter* shall suffer great violence, but the flouds and waues shall in end waxe calme. Horrible mutations of all kingdomes are at hand, and the estimation of Monkes shall perish. The Beast of the West, and the Lyon of the East shall beare rule ouer all the world. Christians for fifteene yeres shall trauaile ouer *Asia* in great security, and safety, but afterwards terrible things shall bee heard of Antichrist.[99]

In an earlier book, *A Monument of Remembrance* (1613), Maxwell had associated the prophecy with Charles, who had recently become heir to the throne following the death of his older brother, Prince Henry. Here he refuses to make a 'personall application', commenting, 'I loue not to be censured, neither for a false prophet, if mine application should faile, nor for a flatterer' (35–6). Encouraged by the events of 1641, the attacks on episcopy, and, perhaps, the fact that Charles was allied by blood to the French crown, Retchford is able to be less cautious. Charles I – often referred to as 'Carolus Magna', 'Great Charles' or even 'Charlemagne' in Caroline panegyric – will gain dominance in Europe and, it is implied, preserve the true faith, as long as Britain retains its loyalty to him.[100] The prophecy's reference to '[h]orrible mutations of all kingdomes' and the downfall of monks may also underlie Retchford's reference to 'Scotta Iglond', which, as his note makes clear, means Ireland. Ireland will celebrate Charles – that is, the Irish rebels will be made to celebrate him with their speedy submission to his authority? – and the whole of Britain will rejoice. The anachronistic use of rhyme – 'gesyng' / 'Cyng' – fore-grounds the political closure that the poet envisages.

Retchford's poem thus combines three antiquarian resources – the Old English language, Anglo-Saxon laws and a medieval prophecy – to underline Charles's perceived position as a king of England who holds together a British realm, and who may, in time, turn his attention to international affairs. Old English is not, however, an uncomplicated vessel for these sentiments, as the potentially double-edged associations of the

Anglo-Saxon law suggest. Moreover, Caroline writers' uneasy command of the language meant that a text's range of meanings might slip out of their control. A good example of this is the word 'Ceorl', which Retchford uses twice; the first time he glosses it as 'husband' ('*Maritus. sponsus.*'), while the second time it stands in for Charles's Christian name. He apparently interprets the word in the same way as L'Isle, who writes in *A Saxon Treatise*, '*Charles*, our chiefe Saxon name … signifies *one of masculine strength or virtue*, as the dutch tongue yet hath it, and in this old English, *a married man*' (f2r–v). However, Retchford cannot have been unaware of the word's other associations and its widely cited relationship with the Early Modern English 'churl'; John Selden, for example, writes that 'the *Ceorle*, [or] *Churle*, was ignoble, or the yeoman'.[101] Referring to Charles as 'Ceorl', therefore, draws on good antiquarian precedent but also, perhaps inadvertently, associates the king with low-status churlishness. In addition, the primary association of 'Ceorl' with 'husband' is itself not unproblematic, given widespread anxiety about the influence of Queen Henrietta Maria in the 1630s and 1640s.

Similar problems are evident in the collection's other Old English poem. Wheelock was all too aware of the disturbances in the country at large during 1640 and 1641; in an undated letter written after the Battle of Newburn he told Sir Simonds D'Ewes:

> Scots care not much for Antiquitie … I would hast beyond seas if I could, if troubles increase. Newcastle is much abused by them, & we here alreadie quake for want of coles: I humblie crave of you that if you heare that they come this way, to direct us wheare to hide under ground these Reverend Saxon sermons &c. for their good & o^rs & o^r posteritye.[102]

In this context, the Old English version of Wheelock's poem is a defiant statement about the important of 'Antiquitie' and the renewed protection it gains from the returning king:

Eadem Anglo- & Scoto-Saxonicé.

> Scotland buton feohte
> Ongel lond geswiþ'de.
> Jacobus gryp'd hire ho's
> Ond æfter his Carlos.
> Eala Huntingdon hwære
> Is þine dryman ðæt ðære[103]
> From Norþ dæl ure freondas
> Woldon don ure feondas
> Ond Breoton gehergian
> Ðurh wordum to flitan·

> Leasan wordas syndon.
> Is þine heafod comon
> Eadig Ceorl's Salome's
> Sunu· sunu sibbes.
> Na Dauides sunu.
> Uncer Dauid eard þu
> Ban ond flesc we beoþ
> Ðine. on þe we ðeoþ
> Þe ðine ðeod trywan
> Unc ðin saul on gyman;   (A4r)

[The same English and Scottish Saxons.

Scotland conquered England without battle; James gripped its heel, and after [that] his Charles. O Huntingdon, where is thy sorcerer who would make our friends in the North our enemies and harry Britain, to quarrel with words? They are lying words. Thy chief is here: blessed Charles, Solomon's son, son of peace. Not David's son. Thou art our David; bone and flesh we are thine. In thee we thrive, we thy true people; by us be thy soul protected.]

After its resonant title, the poem opens with an allusion to the peaceful conquest of England by Scotland in 1603. James is figured as a Jacob, gripping the heels of England (or perhaps, by extension, Elizabeth I),[104] which then descends to Charles as his son. Like L'Isle, Wheelock appears to see Old English as the shared national inheritance of English and Scots, who are 'Eadem ... Saxonicé'. Writing in Old English is therefore less a statement of English superiority and more an expression of nostalgia for a lost amity and unity, and relief at its apparent re-establishment.

These associations continue in the following lines. Like Retchford, Wheelock draws on medieval sources, citing Henry of Huntingdon's chronicle for the prophecy of the 'dryman'. In Huntingdon's account a man of God ('quidam vir Dei') in the time of Æthelred predicts that the drunkenness of the English and their negligent treatment of churches will leave them open not only to the attacks of the Normans – a prophecy fulfilled by the Norman Conquest – but later those of their most hated enemies, the Scots ('Praedixit etiam, quòd non ea gens solùm, verùm & Scottorum, quos vilissimos habebant, eis ad emeritam confusionem dominaretur').[105] For John Weever in *Ancient Funeral Monuments* (1631), this prophecy had been fulfilled, contrary to expectations, in King James's accession; he writes,

> Thus for a king to ouercome, was but to come, and to be welcome, to bee receiued of his Subiects in all places, with shouts and acclamations of ioy, demonstrations of truest loyaltie, loue, and obedience, and to be conducted and guarded with an admirable confluence of his Nobilitie, Gentrie, and Commons, vnto the Throne of his lawfull inheritance.[106]

In Wheelock's poem, similarly, the accession of James fulfils the prophecy and reunites the English and Scottish Saxons; the Scots who rebel against his son are therefore merely liars, with no prophetic force behind them and no genuine religious grievance.

Wheelock concludes with another series of biblical allusions: Charles is the son of Solomon – a favoured comparison of James I – and thereby the son of peace;[107] simultaneously, he is not David's son (that is, Solomon), but David himself. Wheelock is able to draw on typological traditions in which temporality is fluid – allowing Charles to be both Solomon's son and his father. The allusion to David recurs elsewhere in *Irenodia Cantabrigiensis*: in the opening poem the Cambridge vice-chancellor, Richard Holdsworth, writes, 'Sic in Te David est, in Te redivivus & Orpheus; / Nam Tu saxa moves, & Tu quoq; robora flectis' (¶2r) ('So David is in you reborn, and Orpheus; / You move the rocks, and you bend the oak'). Wheelock thus weaves conventional references into his linguistically unconventional poem.

Wheelock is far more circumspect here than in a Greek poem written on the ostensibly similar subject of Charles's return from his Scottish coronation in 1633, in which the light-bearing king dispels a 'Scottish' darkness from England.[108] However, his Old English poem may nonetheless slip beyond its intended meanings. The Huntingdon prophecy is more politically ambivalent than the poet suggests: with its allusions to religious neglect and Scottish aggression, the text had an obvious appeal to those unsympathetic towards Charles during the Bishops' Wars, and it was extracted and cited in early 1640s pamphlets such as Thomas Asladowne's *The Copy of a Letter sent from one of the Queene's Servants at the Hague to a Gentleman in Westminster ... With the Predictions of Henry of Huntington* (1642) and *Mercurius Propheticus. Or, A Collection of Some Old Predictions* (1643). It is possibly for this reason that Wheelock so strenuously calls the prophet a 'dryman' who speaks 'Leasan wordas'.

The allusion to Charles as 'Eadig Ceorl's Salome's / Sunu' ('blessed Charles, Solomon's son'), with its oddly anachronistic punctuation, is also double-edged. Wheelock's use of the word 'Ceorl' (here with an extra 's' to bring it closer to 'Charles'), is just as ambiguous as that of his student. Moreover, Solomon's son and successor was Rehoboam, best known for his susceptibility to flattering courtiers and for the rebellion of his people over taxation, which led the ten northern tribes of Israel to break away and form a separate kingdom.[109] The parallel was not lost on Wheelock's contemporaries. In *A Discourse Concerning Puritans* (1641), Henry Parker writes that 'Vnfortunate *Rehoboam* stands as a Seamarke to warne all

Princes how to shun this rocke of violent counsell against a people violently inraged and aggrieved'.[110] Furthermore, in January 1642 Henry Walker published a 'perrillous Petition' (as the hostile John Taylor termed it) called *To Your Tents O Israel*, its title alluding to the account of Rehoboam in 1 Kings 12:16, which he distributed in the streets and even threw into Charles's coach as he passed.[111] Wheelock may have intended the publication of his poem in Hebrew and Old English to protect him against the criticism later faced by the likes of Walker; on the other hand, the description of Charles as 'Salome's / Sunu' may simply have been a compliment that had the potential to rebound on him.

Irenodia Cantabrigiensis's 1650s successor, *Musarum Oxoniensium*, is likewise the product of a very specific political and cultural moment, and Old English again forms part of a meditation on national and linguistic identity. Summer 1653 saw the last major battle of the first Anglo-Dutch war, the Battle of Schevening (also known as the Battle of Texel), following which Cromwell and his allies again put forward a plan, first broached in 1651, for political union between Britain and the United Provinces.[112] The States-General rejected the proposal but a peace treaty, the Treaty of Westminster, was eventually signed between the two nations on 8 May 1654. In the meantime, Cromwell had been sworn in as Lord Protector on 15 December 1653. On 12 April 1654 an ordinance was published for the union of England and Scotland, underlining England's domination of what was now the 'Protectorate of England, Scotland and Ireland' in the wake of Cromwell's campaigns in Ireland and Scotland.

The Protectorate may have seen what David Norbrook calls a 'drift towards monarchism';[113] yet the situation in 1653–4 was more fluid and contested than is often recognised. In their focus on Cromwell's role as leader, *Musarum Oxoniensium* and a Cambridge volume, *Oliva pacis*, revived the discontinued tradition of volumes celebrating the ruler, a gesture than can be viewed alongside other adoptions of quasi-monarchical style: Cromwell was to be referred to as 'His Highness'; he made a ceremonial entry into London in February 1654; and new coins replaced the image of Parliament with one of the Protector on horseback, mimicking the image on Charles I's seal.[114] Nonetheless, the poems of *Musarum Oxoniensium* also react to distinctively Protectorate concerns, not least of them the need to find persuasive forms for praising a leader's successful conclusion of a foreign campaign, and to deal with the recent proposals for Anglo-Dutch union. In addition, as Edward Holberton has pointed out, *Musarum Oxoniensium*'s response to the Protectorate was shaped by Oxford University's recent experience with the Barebones Parliament, which had planned to do away with it. Holberton sees the volume more as a negotiation with the new regime than an uncomplicated celebration of it, suggesting that it 'probes the auspiciousness of the peace'.[115] Despite its professed loyalty, *Musarum Oxoniensium* is remarkably hard-headed in its portrayal of Cromwellian authority.

Joseph Williamson's poem appears in the second part of the volume, which otherwise consists of poems in the modern vernaculars of English, French and Welsh, and its use of Old English fuels its engagement with Protectorate politics:

On thære sibbe betweox Breotone & Holland

To tham Hollandiscum.

ANNE theod aetforan wæron we,
Anes modores sunu, oth thæt sæ
(Swa men secgeath) us todælod.
Æfter that anne heorte and heafold
We begen hæfdon othæt æft
Totwæmth thruh us sæs-cræft.
Ac thonne ure Mars Neptun acwealde,
Waes ylc Apollo, ond sibbe sealed.
Ac thyles us æft ge gehergiath,
Beoth ge gemindig nu we habbath
Davides Hearpan for ure freondas,
Georges Blod-Rode for ure feondas.
Soth sy eower frith, welswa flite todæloth,
Ge Neptunes Sunu, We his Hlaford boeth.

Yvrongne d' Espée! va t'en coucher
   Dans la gaine;
N'ose pas nous cy-apres toucher.
   Pour la haine
Qu'avoins, voy-cy l'Amitiè.
   Nostre Terre
De ce Nouveau-Monde fait une moitiè,
   L'autre leur Mer.
Quand soif auras, Va (c'est l'Arrest)
   À l'estang
Du Croissant, qui, pâle qu'il est,
   A trop de sang.
Leur Lyon domptè, & nostre Croix
   Se joindront,
Faisans le Sainct Agneau, à mesmes loix
   Combattront.[116]

[On the peace between Britain and Holland.

To the Dutch.

We were formerly one people, one mother's son, until the sea (so men say) divided us. After that we shared one heart and head, until trade later divided us in anger. But then our Mars subdued Neptune, Apollo too, and bestowed peace. But lest you later harry us, remember that we now have David's harp for our friends, George's bloody cross for our enemies. May peace be truly yours as long as you avoid strife; be you Neptune's son, we his lord.

Drunkard sword! Go and sleep in the scabbard; do not dare to touch us hereafter. For the hate which you had, here is friendship. Our land makes one half of this new world, their sea the other. When you will thirst, go (that is the decree) to the pool of the crescent which, pale as it is, has too much blood. Their tamed lion and our cross will join together, acting as the holy lamb, they will fight to the same laws.][117]

Like the work of Retchford and Wheelock, Williamson's bilingual poem recycles a common stock of imagery: the image of the subdued Neptune, for example, appears elsewhere in *Musarum Oxoniensium*, in Henry Harby's statement: '*Cromwello* concede tuum, Neptune, Tridentem, / Ac metuant alium Pontus, & Unda Deum' ('Grant Cromwell, Neptune, your trident; / And let the sea and wave fear another god') (D3v). Williamson generally eschews the hyperbolic praise of Cromwell that is a dominant strategy elsewhere in the volume; nonetheless, his poem appears at first glance to display a nationalism that is reflected in some other contributions, and which was in line with the new Protector's own motto: *pax overitur bello* ('peace through war'). For instance, John Ford writes, 'This little Molehill now can Mountaines shake: / At ENGLAND'S look what Nation doth not quake?' and gloatingly sets out England's superior position within the British Isles: 'The *Scot* his Bonnet vailes, the *Irish* crew / Are sunk into their Boggs, no more in view' (L2v). Similarly, Henry Beeston recalls 'the series of the *War* / From *Marston-Moore* to *Dublin* and *Dunbar*' (L3r), aligning the destiny of the nation with the conquests of its leader in all parts of his new realm.

Given his use of Old English, we might expect Williamson's poem to be written, like those of Ford and Beeston, from an explicitly English perspective. However, this is not the case, as Williamson speaks of 'Britain' rather than England and alludes to the two national symbols – the English cross of St George and the Irish harp of Erin – found on the Commonwealth's flag and coat of arms: 'Davides Hearpan for ure freondas, / Georges Blod-Rode for ure feondas' ('David's harp for our friends, George's bloody cross for our enemies'), the fusion between them reinforced by the compound rhyme on 'freondas' / 'feondas'. Rather than asserting England's power within the British Isles, Williamson seems to imagine a powerful union of the nations within the Commonwealth.

Moreover, rather than emphasising English or even British superiority over the United Provinces, 'On thære sibbe betweox Breotone & Holland' looks forward to a renewal of old amity. The French section of the poem concludes with an image of British and Dutch joining together '*à mesmes loix / Combattront*', the rhyme on *joindront* and *Combattront* underlining its presentation of the two Protestant republics fused in religious war. In its emphasis on restored unity, the poem is similar to many others within the collection. Robert Gorges, for example, sees a union between British and Dutch rivers: 'The noble *Thames*, doth now the *Texell* wed, / As old *Alphëus Arethusa* did' (I1r), while William Godolphin concludes his poem with the lines,

> *Hermophroditus* so and *Salmacis*
> (Whose Bodyes Joyn'd in a perpetuall Kisse)
> With our two States receiv'd like Union;
> VVent *Two* into the *Streame*, Return'd but *One*. (L2r)

These tendencies are intensified in Williamson's poem by his use of Old English. The opening lines, 'ANNE theod ætforan wæron we, / Anes modores sunu' ('We were formerly one people, one mother's son'), suggest that he has in mind the close relationship between Old English and Old Dutch, a connection underlined in the early seventeenth century by the scholarship of Verstegan, and in the 1640s and 1650s by that of De Laet and Junius.[118] Language here is a point of connection between formerly divided peoples.

The effect can be compared with that of Marvell's 'The Character of Holland', probably written around February–March 1653, which opens with a mocking revision of the union image, describing 'Holland, that scarce deserves the name of land, / As but th'off-scouring of the British sand'.[119] Like Williamson, Marvell uses details of language to analyse the relationship between British and Dutch, dropping in Dutch words that were widely understood in English, such as '*Hans-in-Kelder*' (l. 66). He twice incorporates such words in evoking the notorious drunkenness of the Dutch – a characteristic that Williamson also refers to at the start of his second stanza – declaring that 'as they over the new level ranged / For pickled herring, pickled *Heeren* changed' (ll. 33–4) and describing the 'spectacle' of their 'skipper gross ... Tunned up with all their sev'ral towns of beer; / When stagg'ring upon some land, snick and sneer' (ll. 93–6). In his use of such loan-words, as John Kerrigan argues, Marvell 'deftly traces threads of interconnectedness that make Dutch attempts to fight their neighbours absurd as well as vain' and he figures the Dutch as 'comic dialect speakers' rather than aliens.[120]

Like Marvell's use of Dutch words in 'The Character of Holland', Williamson's use of Old English is performative: the poem enacts the unity that the poem also evokes on a narrative level. Nonetheless, the poem also occupies a different place in Anglo-Dutch relations because it was written after the peace between Britain and Holland had been agreed. For all its abuse of the Dutch, therefore, 'On thære sibbe betweox Breotone & Holland' uses the language of its title and first stanza to underline the interconnection of the two nations. Moreover, as John Considine points out, the word 'sæs-cræft' is not authentic Old English, but instead appears to be adapted from the Dutch 'zeekracht' (sea-power).[121] Old English in this poem is not merely insular, but the symbol of a shared history, and of possible future alliance or even unity. Williamson uses the archaic language as part of a movement beyond the mere praise of Cromwell, responding to what Laura Lunger Knoppers has called 'the complex and shifting political culture of 1654'.[122] Indeed, the Protector himself is a marginal figure within this poem. Williamson invokes the national symbols of the Commonwealth, rather than the rapidly emerging insignia of the Protectorate, and Cromwell is not mentioned by name; instead, in a gesture reminiscent of Marvell's 'Horatian Ode', he is 'ure Mars' ('our Mars'), the instrument of the British people. Given the associations between Old English and the common law, described above, Williamson's use of this language thus perhaps underlines his implicit scepticism about Cromwell's place in the new regime. By 1655 he was tutoring Royalist pupils in France.[123]

The poems of Retchford, Wheelock and Williamson represent not merely the desire of scholars to display a new skill, but a fascinating attempt to put Old English to use as part of an ongoing debate about national identity and the role of the ruler. Like L'Isle's translations, they suggest that the close alignment between Old English and English national identity, pursued by scholars such as Verstegan and reflected in *Hengist, King of Kent*, was only one interpretation. These poems thus present a far more complex vision of national and international unity and division than has previously been recognised, reconfiguring Old English as a shared linguistic heritage that had a renewed relevance to contemporary events. In addition, they demonstrate their authors' awareness that the outmoded language might be used in the pursuit of poetic and aesthetic effect, and despite their linguistic failings they represent a genuine attempt to fuse the archaic and the contemporary. Old English vocabulary, quotations from genuine Anglo-Saxon texts, and allusions to medieval prophecies are merged with seventeenth-century poetic structures to create works that not only look back but also suggest the ways in which the past might be brought to bear on the present.

Conclusion

The literary texts explored above engage in different ways with the two issues that are at the heart of this chapter: the role of Old English in conceptions of national identity, and the possibility of its use for aesthetic expression. In *Hengist* and *The Ordinary*, the use of the Old English phrase *nimath eowra seaxes* signals Middleton and Cartwright's engagement with scholarly narratives concerning English identity and linguistic and national descent, and their apparent desire to complicate or question such narratives. Moreover, the playwrights expose their audiences to the sound of Old English, using its alien quality to underline both the foreignness of the Saxons and the temporal dislocation of the antiquary. In L'Isle's translations and the original poems, Old English becomes not a sign of English racial origin and purity, but a shared linguist inheritance between English, Scots and, potentially, Dutch, and a tool to probe the authority of the ruler.

Simultaneously, the aesthetic possibilities of Old English are explored. In *Hengist* and *The Ordinary*, the quotation of phrases in Old English draws attention to the linguistic texture of the surrounding text. Moreover, in the work of Cartwright and L'Isle, Old English is part of a self-consciously multi-temporal collage of different phases in the development of the English language. Yet where Cartwright's Old English is juxtaposed with Early Modern English and pastiche Middle English, L'Isle's is incorporated into a temporally and nationally hybrid linguistic tapestry. By the mid-century, and the anthology poems of Wheelock, Retchford and Williamson, Old English has become the primary vehicle for poetic expression, its potential underlined by its juxtaposition in the university collections with established literary languages such as Latin, Greek and French. Despite the linguistic shortcomings of these poems, they begin to make the idea of an Old English poetic canon thinkable.

Not long after the publication of *Irenodia Cantabrigiensis*, one of its contributors, John Cleveland, weighed into the then-current pamphlet war involving 'Smectymnuus', the pseudonymous author of the anti-Episcopal tract *An Anti-Remonstrance, to the Late Humble Remonstrance to the High Court of Parliament* (1641).[124] Cleveland's poem, 'Smectymnuus, or the Club-Divines', opens with the lines,

> *Smectymnuus?* The Goblin makes me start:
> I'th' Name of Rabbi *Abraham,* what art?
> *Syriac?* or *Arabick?* or *Welsh?* what skilt?
> Ap all the Bricklayers that *Babell* built.
> Some Conjurer translate, and let me know it:
> Till then 'tis fit for a West-Saxon Poet.[125]

The name Smectymnuus – a combination of the initials of the five writers involved with *An Anti-Remonstrance* – becomes, for Cleveland, the epitome of linguistic disorder, as his reference to Babel suggests. Yet the allusion in the last line quoted here indicates that he still had an eye on *Irenodia Cantabrigiensis* and, in particular, Wheelock, the man who was not only lecturer in Anglo-Saxon but the Cambridge chair in Arabic.[126] In Cleveland's view, a 'West-Saxon Poet' is a temporal anomaly, just the sort of literary barbarian who might approve of a coinage such as 'Smectymnuus'.

Despite Cleveland's obvious scorn for the scholarly pursuit of Old English, his poem nonetheless hints that as a result of the work of Wheelock and Retchford it was possible by this time to conceive such a thing as a 'West-Saxon Poet'. And if there could be a seventeenth-century Saxon poet, there might also have been a tenth-century Saxon poet. Frequently positioned by commentators as being on the outer edge of memory – 'within our own memory'; 'continu[ing] even to our fathers daies'; 'in the beginning of the late Civil wars' – within these seventeenth-century texts Old English becomes increasingly close at hand, increasingly fully embodied through the efforts of its modern proponents. Old English poetry was beginning its slow entry into cultural memory.

CHAPTER 2

Chaucer, Gower and the anxiety of obsolescence

Ye knowe ek that in forme of speche is chaunge
Withinne a thousand yeer, and wordes tho
That hadden pris, now wonder nyce and straunge
Us thinketh hem, and yet thei spake hem so,
And spedde as wel in love as men now do;
Ek for to wynnen love in sondry ages,
In sondry londes, sondry ben usages.

Geoffrey Chaucer[1]

Obsolete. Olde, stale, growne out of vse.

John Bullokar[2]

Language is subject to time, and old words may not survive. Chaucer was aware of this tendency, describing in *Troilus and Criseyde* the process through which words that were previously held dear become 'nyce' – that is, absurd or foolish – and 'straunge' – unfamiliar or foreign.[3] His early modern successors were no less aware of linguistic development and decay, and, for them, Chaucer's own language was becoming increasingly suspect. As early as the first decades of the sixteenth century, John Skelton expressed ambivalence about the capacity of Middle English to speak to modern readers. In 'The Garland of Laurel' (1523), he describes Gower 'y^t first garnished our *e*nglishe rude' and Chaucer 'that nobly entreprised / How y^t our englishe myght freshely be ennewed'.[4] However, in an earlier poem, 'Philip Sparrow' (*c*.1508), the young female speaker, Jane Scrope, argues that although she considers Chaucer's 'englishe wel alowed' for at least some of her contemporaries it was becoming difficult: 'And now men wolde haue ame*n*ded / His englyshe where at they barke / And marre all they warke' (T2v). Skelton's own perspective appears to be clear in his narrator's critique of Chaucer's 'barking' critics:

>Chaucer that famous Clarke,
>His tearmes were not darcke
>But pleasaunt easy, and playne;
>No worde he wrote in vayne[.] (T2v)

In the face of those who have become hostile towards Chaucer's style, Skelton asserts both the value of the older writer's work and the ease with which it can (still) be read, the second assertion implicitly reinforced by the fluency of the phrase 'pleasaunt, easy, and playne'. Jane's assessment of Chaucer appears, however, to be an exception to her general opinion of Middle English. Of Chaucer's great contemporary, Gower, she remarks that although Gower's 'matter is worth gold / And worthy to be enrold' his style is more problematic: 'Gowers englyshe is olde / And of no value is tolde' (T2r). A distinction is drawn between the content, which still has value, and the form, which is now obsolete.

This chapter focuses on the relationship between archaism and the process implicit within Chaucer's description of changes within the English language, and both acknowledged and resisted within Skelton's poem: that linguistic change could leave a poet's work obscure, unintelligible or even, as time went on, obscene. The first section examines the general issues raised by the increasing linguistic obscurity of older literary works – such as difficulties in communication, hostility towards older styles of writing, and anxieties about English's status as a literary language in comparison with Italian or classical Greek and Latin – and explores some of the solutions proposed by early modern writers. Those who argued that older works should be allowed to 'die' and those who thought that they merely demanded greater effort from readers represent two extremes. More moderate, and practical, solutions were offered by those who sought to connect old texts with new readers through tactics such as glossing, updating and various forms of translation.

This discussion sets up the second and third sections, in which I examine four literary texts that do not merely argue for the ongoing relevance of medieval texts but actively engage in archaism, employing such techniques as citation, quotation and imitation. However, these texts adopt different stances in relation to the works on which they draw. First, I examine two works written late in the reign of Elizabeth I which display what I will term the 'anxiety of obsolescence': Book 4 of Spenser's *The Faerie Queene*, published in 1596, and a Cambridge University play, the first part of *The Return from Parnassus*, performed at St John's College around 1598–1600. In Book 4, Spenser turns directly to Chaucer for the first time in *The Faerie Queene*, singling him out by name and then providing a continuation to the older poet's *Squire's Tale*, a text that is, notoriously, incomplete. In *The Return from Parnassus*, a poet composes an imitation of Chaucer for his patron; his poem quotes from *Troilus and Criseyde* and concludes with a well-known example of Chaucerian archaism. While *The Faerie Queene* betrays a fear that time will erode even the greatest literary works, *The Return from Parnassus* engages with the flip-side of that problem: that words will not die but will instead be corrupted by time and even rendered obscene, leading the works in which they feature to become degraded and devalued.

I then turn to two later texts, both of which strive against obsolescence and its pernicious effects: George Wilkins and William Shakespeare's *Pericles*, first performed at the Globe playhouse by the King's Men in 1607–8, and a second university play, William Cartwright's *The Ordinary*, performed at Oxford University around 1635. *Pericles* is narrated by a resurrected John Gower, whose *Confessio Amantis* (*c*.1386–93) is one of the sources on which the play draws, while *The Ordinary* features (as we saw in Chapter 1) an antiquary, Robert Moth, whose dialogue is based on quotations from Chaucer's works. In contrast with *The Faerie Queene* and *The Return from Parnassus*, each of which attempts to speak for Chaucer but clearly fears that his works may not endure, *Pericles* and *The Ordinary* feature a variation on what Angus Vine has called 'imaginative antiquarianism'.[5] The works of Gower and Chaucer are made to speak directly to playhouse audiences, and each play suggests, in its own way, that they might have an ongoing cultural life.

Obsolescence and the medieval poet

In spite of Chaucer's high status as cultural and literary exemplar, many late sixteenth- and early seventeenth-century commentators agreed that the increasing age of medieval poetry posed a challenge. '*Chaucer* is harde euen to our vnderstandings: who knowes not the reason?' writes John Marston in the introduction to his 1598 collection of satires.[6] Many comments on Chaucer's works betray a pervasive fear that they are hurtling towards obsolescence. In Samuel Daniel's 'Musophilus', published a year after Marston's satires, Musophilus (lover of the muse) discusses the value of learning with Philocosmus (lover of the world). In the course of a jeremiad on the passing of time and the cultural barrenness of his own day, Musophilus laments that Chaucer is nearing the end of his literary afterlife:

> For what hy races hath there come to fall,
> With low disgrace, quite vanished and past,
> Since *Chaucer* liu'd who yet liues, and yet shall,
> Though (which I grieue to say) but in his last[.]

The rhetorical patterning of the penultimate line here, with its movement from the past tense to the present and future, and its repetitions of 'live' and 'yet', underlines the current vibrancy of Chaucer's work. However, this confidence is undercut in the final line, with its edgy parenthesis and its final emphasis on the rhyme-word 'last'.

Musophilus doubts, moreover, that any of his contemporaries will have even Chaucer's cultural longevity:

> Yet what a time hath he wrested from time,
>   And won vpon the mighty waste of daies,
>   Vnto th'immortall honor of our clime,
>   That by his meanes came first adorn'd with Baies,
>   Vnto the sacred Relickes of whose rime
>   We yet are bound in zeale to offer praise?
> And could our lines begotten in this age
>   Obtaine but such a blessed hand of yeeres,
>   And scape the fury of that threatning rage,
>   Which in confused clowdes gastly appeares,
>   Who would not straine his trauailes to ingage,
>   When such true glory should succeed his cares?
> But whereas he came planted in the spring,
>   And had the Sun, before him, of respect;
>   We set in th'Autumne, in the withering,
>   And sullen season of a cold defect,
>   Must taste those soure distastes the times do bring,
>   Vpon the fulnesse of a cloid neglect[.][7]

Poetic heritage is figured in national terms, and Chaucer's writing is implicitly positioned as the first challenge mounted by English verse to the domination of the classics. However, the passage of time potentially leads not to greater glory but to confusion, as the jaded palates of a degenerate later age are unable to appreciate either Chaucer or his poetic inheritors. The life-span allowed to poetic works appears to be contracting. While Chaucer says that linguistic change will render words ridiculous 'Withinne a thousand yeer', Daniel worries that Chaucer's work is breathing its last after only 200 years, and that his own work and that of his contemporaries will not last even this long.

The obsolescence of medieval writers was crucial in part because early modern literary theory frequently sought to position Chaucer as the 'father' of English literature, and Chaucer and Gower as pivotal figures in the development of English as a literary language. Philip Sidney, for instance, writes, 'in the Italian language the first that made it aspire to be a treasure-house of science [i.e. knowledge] were the poets Dante, Boccaccio, and Petrarch. So in our English were Gower and Chaucer'.[8] The comparison with Italian poets discloses, however, the vulnerability of older English poets. While early modern English writers were all too aware of linguistic change as it affected their poetic forebears, they were often convinced that Italian was immune to such fluctuation. Writing more than a generation after Sidney, Kenelm Digby compares Italian with the classical languages, arguing that the influence of great writers

> is the cause that after the great lights of learning among the GRECIANS their language receiued no further alterations. and that the LATINE hath euer since remained in the same state whereovnto it was reduced by CICERO, VIRGILL, and the other great men of that time: and the TUSCANE tongue is at this day the same as it was left about 300 yeares agoe by DANTE PETRACHE and BOCCACE.[9]

Even when English writers contend that Chaucer and Gower sought, like the Italian poets, to perfect their language, changes within English mean that they must either argue that this language has since degenerated, or that Chaucer and Gower were merely the first stage of a more lengthy process of correction and purification. In comparison with what they knew or assumed about Greek, Latin and Italian, English appeared to these writers to be dangerously mutable and unstable.

Anxieties about communication, aesthetics and the ongoing mutability of English colour the ways in which early modern writers attempted to come to terms with or counter the archaism of Chaucer and Gower's works. At one extreme, some writers proposed that medieval English writers should simply be ignored, and written out of literary tradition. As we saw in the introduction to this book, the Caroline poet George Daniel expresses this opinion in its most aggressive form, arguing that English poetry has been misled by its reverence for its medieval forebears and that it should instead look to the classics. In 'An Essay: Endeavouring to Ennoble our English Poesie by Evidence of Latter Qvills; and Reiecting the Former', he contends that it is ridiculous that modern writers should imitate Chaucer, drawing an unfavourable comparison with classical writers. 'Shall wee derive', he asks, scornfully, 'Our English fflame, our Glories Primitive / From antique Chaucer? ... He doth not rise / Like ancient Poets, in huge Extasies / Of vncontrolléd ffancie, to Survay / Inestimable Nature.'[10] The pun on 'antique' underlines his scorn: not only is Chaucer worn with age, but his work has also become antic: grotesque, bizarre or uncouth.[11] Later in the poem Daniel renews his attack on 'in-authenticke' Chaucer (l. 80), apparently casting the older poet as untrustworthy and lacking in authority, and rejecting him as a poetic prototype.[12] The rejection of Chaucer's assumed authority is sealed in the bald statement that he 'Adds nothing to our Poesie, in his Store; / Nor let vs call him Father anie more' (ll. 81–2).

Other writers, in contrast, argued that the incomprehensibility of Chaucer lay not in the writer, but in the reader. Aston Cokain, for instance, writes,

> Our good old *Chaucer* some despise: and why?
> Because say they he writeth barbaro[u]sly.
> Blame him not (Ignorants) but your selves, that do
> Not at these years your native language know.[13]

The word 'barbarous' here carries with it the force of neoclassical distaste; as George Puttenham writes in *The Art of English Poesy*, 'when any strange word not of the natural Greek or Latin was spoken, in the old time they called it *barbarism*, or when any of their own natural words were sounded and pronounced with strange and ill-shaped accents, or written by wrong orthography . . . they said it was barbarously spoken'.[14] However, Cokain defiantly asserts that the fault lies not with Chaucer but with seventeenth-century readers. Mirroring the language of E.K.'s preface to *The Shepheardes Calender*, discussed in the introduction to this book, he positions these ignorant critics of Chaucer's English as paradoxical native foreigners, unable to comprehend their own tongue: not to understand old words is to leave oneself a stranger in one's own language and, by extension, land.

In the face of such opposed and entrenched views, many writers offered more practical solutions, such as annotation, modernisation and trans-lation. In doing so, they frequently sought to connect Chaucer to modern readers and to bolster his cultural authority. Particularly important are Thomas Speght's 1598 and 1602 editions of *The Works of our Ancient and Learned English Poet, Geoffrey Chaucer*. These volumes have received illuminating attention from a number of scholars in recent years; my aim is, therefore, to focus specifically on the strategies through which Speght seeks to counter accusations of obsolescence against Chaucer's works.[15] In a dedicatory letter included in both editions, Francis Beaumont (probably the father of the dramatist) recounts a series of objections against Chaucer that he says that Speght has mentioned in their private conversations:

'as first that many of his wordes (as it were with ouerlong lying) are growne too hard and vnpleasant, and next that hee is somewhat too broad in some of his speeches, and that the worke should therefore be the less gratious'.[16] I will come back to the issue of indecency later in this chapter; here, my concern is with the measures that Beaumont credits to Speght in his edition: 'by your interpretation of the most vnusuall words, that hardnesse and difficultie is made most cleare and easie: and in the paines and diligence you haue vsed in collecting his life, mee thinkes you haue bestowed vpon him more fauorable graces then *Medea* did vpon *Pelias*: for you haue restored vs *Chaucer* both aliue again and yong again' ([a]4v–[a]5r). Whereas Medea's claim to be able to rejuvenate the aged Pelias was a cruel trick, the Chaucerian editor is able to bring his subject back to life and comprehensibility. For Beaumont, Speght has reconnected Chaucer with his modern readers, allowing them access both to the man himself, by fleshing out his biography, and to the works, by glossing difficult and obscure words. Speght's 1598 edition comes with a glossary of 'The old and obscure words of Chaucer, explaned', corrected and updated in the 1602 edition,[17] and this example was followed by other writers as a means of connecting old texts with new readers. For instance, in *Ancient Funeral Monuments* John Weever adds marginal glosses to his quotations from Chaucer and from earlier medieval writers such as Robert of Gloucester.[18]

The presence of the glossary in Speght's editions should not, however, blind us to the other means that were used to make Chaucer's writing more palatable to modern readers. Like those of other sixteenth-century editors, Speght's text is selectively modernised, especially in terms of its orthography and punctuation,[19] and, as we have seen, Skelton suggests that there was a demand in his day for Chaucer's English to be 'amended'. Similar tactics were adopted in the publication of other medieval texts, such as Robert Crowley's 1550 edition of Langland's *Piers Plowman*, here entitled *A Godly Dyalogue & Dysputacyon Betwene Pyers Plowman, and a Popysh Preest Concernyng the Supper of the Lorde*, or the tale of Fortunatus from Thomas Hoccleve's version of the *Gesta Romanorum* in William Browne's *The Shepherd's Pipe* (1614), where it is retold by Roget, representing George Wither.[20] A 1634 edition of Malory's *Morte D'Arthur*, published by Jacob Bloom and printed by William Stansby, claims on its title-page to present the text 'Newly refined'. The preface asserts, accordingly, that the text is corrected 'not in language but in phrase', on the grounds that 'King *Arthur* or some of his Knights were declared in their communications to sweare prophane, and vse superstitious speeches'. Now that these have been 'amended or quite left out', he claims, 'it may passe for a famous piece of Antiquity, reuiued almost from the gulph of obliuion, and renued for the pleasure and profite of present and future times'.[21] Even where archaic 'language' is allowed to pass, specific phrases that contravene modern social decorum must be amended. Or, at least, the claim must be made: recent scholars have identified very few alterations to the Bloom/Stansby text beyond the modernisation of spelling.[22]

These processes of mediation can be found in a more extreme form in the wholesale translations of Chaucer's works that replaced new editions after 1602.[23] Translation takes different forms but displays related concerns. Richard Brathwaite's *A Comment upon the Two Tales of our Ancient, Renowned, and Ever Living Poet Sr. Jeffray Chaucer, Knight*, which was apparently completed by 1617 but not published until 1665, consists of detailed glosses of *The Miller's Tale* and *The Wife of Bath's Tale*.[24] These glosses explain and expand on Chaucer's text, and they also negotiate with its bawdy. For instance, in his comments on the comic climax of *The Miller's Tale*, Brathwaite does not gloss the moment at which Absolon kisses Alison's 'naked ers' (l. 3734), but he toys with his reader in his glosses on the surrounding lines. For instance, lines 3718–19, here given as '**Wilt thou than go thy way therwith qd she? / Yecertes lemman, qd this Absolon**', are followed by the comment,

> Small favours would not be neglected, because they may be Introductions to higher Curtsies when occasion is offered. Mean time *Absolon* prepares his Cynamon mouth for a tast of an unsavoury Curtsie. He takes his corporal Oath of his constant fidelity, and makes *Alyson's* **Posteriora's** the Book he swears by. Whence observe, with what intollerable petulancy she jeers the poor Cloysterer![25]

At such moments, Brathwaite's text must be read with Chaucer's if a reader is to understand the narrative; his glosses supplement the tale and direct the reader, but without fully echoing or endorsing its frankness.

Brathwaite is concerned not only to connect Chaucer with modern readers, but also to rehabilitate two notoriously bawdy *Tales*, and similar concerns can be seen in the handling of Chaucer elsewhere. In 1630, Jonathan Sidnam translated *Troilus and Criseyde* into 'our Moderne English. For the satisfaction of those. Who either cannot, or will not, take ye paines to vnderstand. The Excellent Authors. Farr more Exquisite, and significant Expressions Though now growen obsolete, and out of vse'.[26] However, he only includes the first three books, commenting in a sequence appended to Book 3,

> But yet let him that list, goe on to tell
> The wanton slipps of this deceitful Dame.
> And what misfortunes afterwardes befell
> Poore Troilus, who vnderwent the shame.
> Of her misdeedes, though he deseru'd noe blame.
>   For I am loath to doe true loue that wrong.
>   To make her fall, the subject of my song.[27]

Like Brathwaite's versions of *The Canterbury Tales*, Sidnam's *Troilus* both is and is not Chaucer's text. By the end of Book 3 it has become 'my song', as the translator seeks to rehabilitate the older poet's work through his own intervention.

Reflecting George Daniel's assumption that the classics are less prone to decay than vernacular works, Chaucer's work even appeared in Latin translation. Francis Kynaston's translation of the first two books of *Troilus and Criseyde*, here titled *Amorum Troili et Creseidæ*, appeared in 1635, accompanied by a swathe of commendatory verses in both Latin and English, mirroring the book's presentation of Latin and English text on facing pages.[28] In his dedication to Patrick Young, the Royal Librarian, Kynaston justifies his project, writing, 'conservatio huius poematum gemmæ ab interitu & oblivione, quæ ferè amissa erat, & a nostratibus vix intellecta, (saltem nemini in deliciis) ob verborum in eâ obsoletorum ignorantiam, quæ in desuetudinem abiêre' ('I desired the preservation from ruin and oblivion of this gem of poems, which was nearly lost and scarcely understood by us [at least as the favorite of none] because of ignorance of the obsolete words in it which have fallen into disuse').[29] As Tim William Machan notes, Kynaston 'stresses – if not exaggerates – the obscurity of Chaucer's language'.[30] The reasons for this tactic are plain, as the obsolescence of Chaucer's text is the pretext for Kynaston's own work.

The dedicatory poems follow Kynaston in their approach to Chaucer. For instance, William Cartwright – to whose work I will return later in this chapter – tells Kynaston "Tis to your Happy cares wee owe, that wee / Read *Chaucer* now without a Dictionary', endorsing the idea that Latin is less mutable than English.[31] Somewhat paradoxically, Francis James is moved to write his dedicatory poem in a self-consciously archaic, cod-Chaucerian style, praising Kynaston in these terms:

> For that thy boke beareth alder prize,
> That I nat how unneth thou couth devise,
> To maken *Chaucer* so right wise and sage
> Who couth all craft in werkes, take pilgrimage

> To *Rome*, and sothly there lerne Latine verse
> In little throwe, so seemelyche to reherse.[32]

Adopting 'Chaucerian' archaisms such as 'unneth', 'couth' and 'seemelyche', James also mimics the supposed metrical roughness of medieval verse, and his poem is presented in black letter, a font increasingly being used to signal the archaism of older English writing and, in particular, that of Chaucer himself.[33] The pastiche and its 'typographic nostalgia', to use Zachary Lesser's term,[34] serves to prove its own point: Chaucer is indeed archaic and in need of linguistic reformation. It is perhaps, therefore, unsurprising that a reader of Kynaston's translation would also encounter the English text of *Troilus and Criseyde* in black letter, the Latin text in Roman. Chaucer's poems thus make a 'pilgrimage / To *Rome*' in more ways than one.

James's poem suggests one of the rhetorical uses to which Chaucerian archaism might be put in the context of debates about literary longevity and obsolescence. In contrast, the works that I discuss in the second part of this chapter seek not to distance their readers or spectators from Chaucer's works, but to forge connections between them. They differ, however, in their degrees of optimism about the potential success of this project, and even where James's cynicism is rejected a high level of anxiety can adhere to the use of archaic style.

The anxiety of obsolescence

The work of Spenser, the period's most notorious proponent of literary archaism, expresses in striking terms the unease about obsolescence created by the self-conscious use of old-fashioned styles. Although they admired Spenser's achievements, seventeenth-century critics were clearly nervous about the capacity of his work to survive the passage of time. Sidney had criticised Spenser's archaism in *The Shepheardes Calender* on the grounds of generic decorum,[35] but his successors – who had been able to read not only Spenser's pastorals but also *The Faerie Queene* – took a more wide-ranging approach. In *Hypercritica* (*c*.1618), a style-manual for aspiring historians, Edmund Bolton is willing to admit Spenser's *Hymns* as a model; however, he writes,

> I cannot advise the allowance of other his Poems, as for Practick *English*, no more than I can do *Jeff. Chaucer, Lydgate, Peirce Ploughman*, or *Laureat Skelton*. It was laid as a fault to the charge of *Salust*, that he used some old outworn Words, stoln out of *Cato* his Books *de Originibus*. And for an Historian in our Tongue to affect the like out of those our Poets would be accounted a foul Oversight.

If a historian uses old words they risk becoming like Sallust who – as we saw in the introduction to this book – was notorious for his deliberate archaism. Archaism, Bolton argues, should not be used by the historian 'unless perhaps we cite the Words of some old Monument … or what else soever of the ancients'.[36] He is, however, keen to point out that 'My judgement is nothing at all in Poems or Poesie', and elsewhere he confirms this verdict, including Spenser in a list of those commended for their use of English and acknowledging him as 'the most learned Poet of our Nation', even though he describes him as 'very little for the vse of history'.[37] However, Bolton's doubts about the utility of Spenser as a model were also shared by poets such as William Davenant and Ben Jonson, who in *Discoveries* follows his strictures relating to Chaucer and Gower with the notorious assertion that 'Spenser, in affecting the ancients, writ no language'.[38]

The impact of such criticism is clear in the comments of Kenelm Digby, who is described by R. M. Cummings as 'the most exact and probably the best of Spenser's early critics'.[39] Digby claims that in Spenser's works 'weight of matter was neuer better ioyned *with* propriety of language and *with* maiestey and sweetnes of verse'.[40] He devotes considerable energy, however, to defending the poet's use of language. '[I]f any', he writes,

> should except against his reuiuing some obsolete words, and vsing some ancient formes of speech, in my opinion he blameth that w*hich* deserueth much prayse; for SPENCER doth not that out of any affectation (although his assiduity in CHAUCER might make his language familiar to him) but onely then when they serue to expresse more liuely and more concisely what he would say: and whensoeuer he vseth them, he doth so polish their natiue rudenes, as retaining the maiesty of antiquity the[y], want nothing of the elegancy of our freeshest speech. (148–9)

For Digby, the 'maiesty of antiquity' – the grandeur that archaic words and forms of speech can lend to a literary text – outweighs their potential 'rudenes' or rusticity, a quality that Spenser has in any case polished out of them. Through the poet's mediation, old words become 'fresh'.

Intriguingly, this firm statement leads Digby into an extended consideration of the effects of language change and the ability of writers in different linguistic traditions to transcend them or to 'fix' language in perpetuity. These comments are worth quoting at length:

> I hope that what he hath written will be a meanes that the english tongue will now receiue no more alteration and changes, but will remaine & continue settled in that forme it now hath; for excellent authours doe draw vnto them the study of posterity, and whosoever is delighted w*ith* what he

readeth in an other, feeleth in himselfe a desire to expresse like thinges in a like manner: and the more resemblance his elocutions haue to his authours, *the* neerer he perswadeth himselfe he arriueth to perfection: and thus, much converstation [*sic*] and study in what he would imitate, begetteth a habite of doing the like . . . If it is true that the vicissitudes of things (change being a necessary and inseperable condicion of all sublunary creatures) and the inundations of barbarous nations may overgrow and ouerrune the vulgar practise of the perfectest languages, as we see of the forementioned GREEKE and LATINE; yet the vse of those tongues will flourish among learned men as long as those excellent authours remaine in the world. Which maketh me confident that noe fate nor length of time will bury SPENCERS workes and memory, nor ideed [*sic*] alter that language that out of his schoole we now vse vntill some generall innouation happen that may shake as well the foundations of *our* nation as of our speech[.] (149)

Spenser's works are themselves evidence of linguistic change within English, but Digby speculates – or, perhaps, fantasises – on the possibility that this change might be halted, and Elizabethan literary language be preserved, as in aspic. Writerly reading and poetic influence here lead not to change but to stylistic and linguistic stability. Whereas Jonson alienates Spenser from linguistic tradition, Digby assimilates him into 'our speech', a linguistic tradition of which Jonson himself is said to be the next great exemplar (149–50). Far from writing 'no language', Spenser becomes both a model and final point of development for English, one to be followed until such a time as the nation itself is destroyed. Linguistic stability, it seems, mirrors national stability.

In his desire to position Spenser as the great shaper of English within a continuing literary tradition, Digby follows the implicit argument laid out within works such as *The Shepheardes Calendar* and *The Faerie Queene*. With the help of E.K., Spenser positions himself as heir to all that is best in literary English. We recall, for instance, E.K.'s preface to *The Shepheardes Calender*, with its opening tribute to 'the olde famous Poete Chaucer . . . the Loadestarre of our Language', itself a quotation from John Lydgate, and the statement that 'hauing the sound of those auncient Poetes still ringing in his eares, [Spenser] mought needes in singing hit out some of theyr tunes' (ll. 1–4, 34–6). Within the works, however, Spenser's position as heir to Chaucer becomes a source of greater anxiety, and his use of the older poet as a literary model is not only a strength but also a potential liability, a hostage to an uncertain future. As Craig Berry points out, Chaucer can function as both an 'authoritative hedge against misreading and ill reception' and a source of ambivalence, raising doubts about the capacity of writing to survive, the value of the English poetic canon, and the very viability of a writing career.[41]

While the printed text of *The Shepheardes Calender* foregrounds at a notably early stage the work's links with Chaucer and the English literary tradition, *The Faerie Queene* is initially rather more circumspect. It is only in Book 4, printed as part of the second instalment of the poem in 1596, that Spenser turns explicitly to Chaucer. Having introduced the knights Cambell and Triamond, and their lovers Cambina and Canacee, Spenser writes,

> Whylome as antique stories tellen vs,
>   Those two were foes the fellonest on ground,
>   And battell made the dreddest daungerous,
>   That euer shrilling trumpet did resound;
>   Though now their acts be no where to be found,
>   As that renowmed Poet them compyled,
>   With warlike numbers and Heroicke sound,
>   Dan *Chaucer*, well of English vndefyled,
> On Fames eternall beadroll worthie to be fyled.
>
> But wicked Time that all good thoughts doth waste,
>   And workes of noblest wits to nought out weare,
>   That famous moniment hath quite defaste,
>   And robd the world of threasure endlesse deare,
>   The which mote haue enriched all vs heare.
>   O cursed Eld the cankerworme of writs,
>   How may these rimes, so rude as doth appeare,
>   Hope to endure, sith workes of heauenly wits
> Are quite deuourd, and brought to nought by little bits?
>
> Then pardon, O most sacred happie spirit,
>   That I thy labours lost may thus reuiue,
>   And steal from thee the meede of thy due merit,
>   That none durst euer whilest thou wast aliue,
>   And being dead in vaine yet many striue:
>   Ne dare I like, but through infusion sweete
>   Of thine owne spirit, which doth in me suruiue,
>   I follow here the footing of thy feet,
> That with thy meaning so I may the rather meete. (4.2.32–4)

The word 'whilom' is a characteristic Spenserian archaism, used throughout *The Faerie Queene*. But a reader who knows his or her Chaucer will quickly realise that the first line goes beyond the incorporation of a single word, and is a direct quotation of the first line of *The Knight's Tale*, the first of *The Canterbury Tales*. Even before Chaucer's name is mentioned, such a reader is alerted to the negotiations in the following sequence. Similarly, the last four lines of stanza 33 are an imitation of part of the preamble to Chaucer's *Anelida and Arcite* (another incomplete text), in which the poet laments the effects that time can have on literary works:

> This olde storie, in Latyn which I fynde ...
> That elde, which that al can frete and bite,
> As hit hath freten mony a noble storie,
> Hath nygh devoured out of oure memorie[.] (ll. 10, 12–14)

In Spenser's version, the image of 'cursed Eld the cankerworme of writs' vividly encapsulates the malignant process through which time attacks literary works, the cankerworm being a caterpillar that attacks buds and leaves, consuming new and fresh growth.[42] A similar image appears in William Covell's 'A Letter from *England* to her Three Daughters, Cambridge, Oxford, Innes of Court' (1595), in which the works of Chaucer and Lydgate are said to be under threat from 'the fretting cancker worme of mouldie time'.[43] The word also highlights in itself the passage of time, and linguistic change, as it has not been traced in English before 1530; its broader use to signify a 'highly malignant and corrupting influence that spreads and consumes' became prominent in the following decades.[44] Time's attack is, paradoxically, newfangled, the product of a degenerate later age which is unable to appreciate the work of its forebears, and Spenser's line of argument is strikingly similar to that of Samuel Daniel in 'Musophilus', discussed above, with which *The Faerie Queene* is almost contemporary.

   Despite the quotations from *The Knight's Tale* and *Anelida and Arcite*, the 'ancient story' here is Chaucer's *Squire's Tale*, the unfinished state of which was the subject of much early modern debate.[45] Spenser suggests that the complete *Squire's Tale* has been lost, and his story of Cambell, Canacee and the three brothers is presented as a recuperation of Chaucer's now incomplete narrative. He will, he declares, be infused with Chaucer's spirit, and will 'follow here the footing of thy feete' (4.2.34.8). Things are not, however, as straightforward as they appear. As the later poet John Lane points out, with some asperity, Spenser 'dealth with [*The Squire's Tale*] promiscuously, and not in couplet*es* (suiting to the Authors institute!)'.[46] Spenser does not precisely 'follow ... the footing of [Chaucer's] feete' even though *The Faerie Queene* as a whole mimics aspects of Chaucerian diction and syntax. Indeed, even Chaucer's metre does not go untouched; in his quotation from *The Knight's Tale* Spenser compensates for the loss of a second syllable in 'olde' by substituting 'antique'.[47]

Spenser's adjustments also affect narrative. The statement 'Whylome as antique stories tellen vs, / Those two were foes the fellonest on ground' presents the struggle between Cambell and Triamond as part of Chaucer's lost story. But this is not what the 'antique stories tellen vs'. Triamond appears nowhere in *The Squire's Tale*, and the storyline that Spenser picks up from Chaucer is only one of a number of narrative possibilities presented there. Having devoted his second section to the tale of Canacee's encounter with the falcon, Chaucer's narrator says that he will break off from this story and instead 'my proces holde / To speken of aventures and of batailles / That nevere yet was herd so grete mervailles' (ll. 658–60). He then outlines his plans:

> First wol I telle yow of Cambyuskan,
> That in his tyme many a citee wan;
> And after wol I speke of Algarslif,
> How that he wan Theodora to his wif,
> For whom ful ofte in greet peril he was,
> Ne hadde he ben holpen by the steede of bras;
> And after wol I speke of Cambalo,
> That faught in lystes with the bretheren two
> For Canacee er that he myghte hire wynne.
> And ther I lefte I wol ayeyn bigynne. (ll. 661–70)

In responding to Chaucer's incomplete tale, Spenser thus makes a conscious choice about what to include or exclude; his first act of adaptation is to select not Cambyuskan's conquests or Algarslif's wooing of Theodora, but the puzzling suggestion that Cambalo will fight with two (not three) brothers in order to 'win' Canacee, with its hints of an incest narrative that is rejected elsewhere in *The Canterbury Tales*.[48]

This appropriative stance is noticeable in other respects. Spenser has comparatively little interest in Canacee, who is by far the most fully developed character in Chaucer's version, and instead his narrative focuses on Cambell and the brothers Priamond, Diamond and Triamond. Similarly, the actual continuation of Chaucer's narrative is confined to an inset narrative recounting past events; it is embedded into the broader narratives of friendship that constitute Book 4, and its characters become part of that book's proliferation of knights and ladies through their participation in the tournament sequence of Canto 4.[49] In some respects this control may be a response to the remarkably edgy treatment of narration in *The Squire's Tale*, in which the narrator repeatedly claims to find it difficult to tell his story, or to control its style adequately.[50]

Spenser's version, therefore, both is and is not a continuation of *The Squire's Tale*. Furthermore, the links with Chaucer's narrative mean that the story of Cambell, Canacee and the three brothers always has the potential to transgress the boundaries that are set around it. In particular, the anxieties about longevity and immortality that underline the discussion of time's effects on literary works in 4.2.33 are embodied in *The Faerie Queene*'s version of *The Squire's Tale*. Priamond, Diamond and Triamond are not just brothers but triplets, brought 'forth at one clap' (4.2.43.9), and their close relationship and identification with one another is underlined in Spenser's description:

> Stout *Priamond*, but not so strong to strike,
>   Strong *Diamond*, but not so stout a knight,
>   But *Triamond* was stout and strong alike:
>   On horsebacke vsed *Triamond* to fight,
>   And *Priamond* on foote had more delight,
>   But horse and foote knew *Diamond* to wield:
>   With curtaxe vsed *Diamond* to smite,
>   And *Triamond* to handle speare and shield,
> But speare and curtaxe both vsed *Priamond* in field. (4.2.42)

The stanza divides into three triplets, each of which begins and ends with a different brother, and each of which initially picks up the brother named in the final line of the preceding triplet. In each of the summarising lines the attributes or implements listed as the strengths of the first two brothers are combined in the third. The stanza eventually circles back on itself, mimicking the bond shared by the siblings.

The brothers already love each other 'As if but one soule in them all did dwell' (4.2.43.3), but they become even more tightly bound together when their fairy mother, Agape, makes a bargain with the Fates to preserve and prolong their lives, asking that when the eldest brother dies

> Eftsoones his life may passe into the next;
>   And when the next shall likewise ended bee,
>   That both their liues may likewise be annext
> Vnto the third, that his may so be trebly wext. (4.2.52.6–9)

Like the final line of Spenser's stanza, the life of Triamond will be extended, as his brothers' souls enter his body. In the battle with Cambell that fills the next canto, the deaths of Priamond and Diamond, and the entry of their souls into their younger brother, allow Triamond to match Cambell, who is himself protected by Canacee's magic ring. At the moment at which he would have died, only one soul leaves Triamond's body, and his revival is presented as a resurrection:

But nathelesse whilst all the lookers on
    Him dead behight, as he to all appeard,
    All vnawares he started vp anon,
    As one that had out of a dreame bene reard,
    And fresh assayld his foe, who halfe affeard
    Of th'vncouth sight, as he some ghost had seene,
    Stood still amaz'd, holding his idle sweard;
    Till hauing often by him stricken beene,
He forced was to strike, and saue him selfe from teene. (4.3.31)

The hero returns from the dead, just as Spenser's text reanimates the literary work that time has 'defaste'. However, Triamond is not immortal; his life has merely been prolonged through the artificial means of his mother's bargain with the Fates. Furthermore, as William Kamowski points out, Spenser's recuperation of the fragment of *The Squire's Tale* – a narrative fragment within a textual fragment within a work that is incomplete – takes place in a text (*The Faerie Queene*) that is itself incomplete. Spenser's impetus, he claims, 'is as medieval as his sensibilities'.[51] But there is nonetheless an anxiety in Spenser's interaction with Chaucer's narrative and a certain nervousness about his engagement with medieval literary culture.

This anxiety is, I suggest, heightened by Book 4's other explicit allusion to a literary figure. Spenser pauses during his account of the arrival of Cambina, who finally ends the battle between Cambell and Triamond, to draw a comparison between her magical drink, Nepenthe, and a literary predecessor:

        Much more of price and of more gratious powre
            Is this, then that same water of Ardenne,
            The which *Rinaldo* drunck in happie howre,
            Described by that famous Tuscane penne:
            For that had might to change the hearts of men
            Fro loue to hate, a change of euill choise:
            But this doth hatred make in loue to brenne,
            Any heauy heart with comfort doth reioyce.
        Who would not to this virtue rather yeeld his voice? (4.3.45)

Spenser probably alludes to Lodovico Ariosto's *Orlando Furioso* (1532), although he may be thinking of Matteo Boiardo's *Orlando Inamorato* (1495), itself a source for Ariosto's poem.[52] In either case, the allusion is part of a general turn away from Italian romance – a formative influence on Book 2 and, especially, Book 3 of *The Faerie Queene* – in the 1596 additions to Spenser's poem. The reference to 'that famous Tuscane penne' is crucial. As Berry argues, Spenser pointedly refers to his Italian predecessor and the language in which he wrote: unlike Chaucer, described as the 'well of English vndefyled' (4.2.32.8) and the 'pure well head of Poesie' (7.7.9.4), 'the river of Italian romantic epic is an impure source'.[53] However, the set of relationships is perhaps more complex than this suggests. In view of Digby's comments on the immutability of literary Italian, a move away from Ariosto and/or Boiardo and towards Chaucer is also a move away from linguistic stability and towards instability and flux. The works of older English authors are also, in linguistic terms, an 'impure source'.

A different – albeit perhaps implicitly related – kind of impurity is also at stake. Berry argues that Spenser turns to the 'serious' Chaucer in order to dispel his previous borrowing from the 'reputedly frivolous' Ariosto.[54] This may well be true, but it downplays another species of impurity – that is, the fact that Chaucer himself was increasingly viewed as 'frivolous', and even obscene, during the course of the sixteenth century.[55] In his translation of *Orlando Furioso*, published in 1591, John Harington attempts to defend Ariosto on the grounds that 'our *Chawcer* ... in both words & sence, incurreth far more the reprehension of flat scurrilitie, as I could recite many places, not onely in his millers tale, but in the good wife of Bathes tale, & many more, in which onely the decorum he keepes, is that that excuseth it, and maketh it more tolerable'.[56] Such attitudes appear to have hardened as time went on. Writing in the 1630s, George Daniel attacks those who defend Chaucer 'cause you have bene told / Your Grandsires Laugh'd once at his Baud'rie / Laid out in Rime' ('An Essay', ll. 84–6), castigating a taste for Chaucer as both old-fashioned and improper. For these reasons, to turn to Chaucer was not to find a 'pure' source in terms of either linguistic or sexual decorum, and these problems are heightened when the Chaucerian source is *The Squire's Tale*, with its hints of incest.

The issue of sexual impurity, implicit in Spenser's uneasy negotiations with Chaucerian narrative, is prominent in my second example of the 'anxiety of obsolescence', the first part of *The Return from Parnassus*, performed not long after the publication of the second instalment of *The Faerie Queene*. Deeply concerned with literary reputation and the workings of the literary marketplace, *The Return from Parnassus* examines in its own way the question of Chaucer's scurrility and, with it, the possibility that linguistic change might render previously innocuous language indecorously bawdy. The play focuses on the careers of four former students, Studioso, Philomusus, Ingenioso and Luxurio, and their attempts to secure a profitable vocation. While Studioso is engaged as a tutor and Philomusus as a sexton, Ingenioso and Luxurio enter into the late-1590s trade in literature, Ingenioso working for a printer and attempting to gain a wealthy patron, and Luxurio writing and selling ballads. During the third act, Ingenioso is patronised by a rich idiot, Gullio, a pretender to the status of poet who models himself on a notable literary forebear:

> I had in my dayes not vnfitly bene likned to Sr Phillip Sidney, only with this diference, that I had the better legg, and more amiable face. His *Arcadia* was prettie, soe are my sonnetes; he had bene at Paris, I at Padua; he fought, and so dare I; he dyed in the lowe cuntries, and soe I thinke shall I; he loued a scholler, I maintaine them, witness thy selfe, nowe[.]^{57}

Gullio is a debased imitation of Sidney, as the innuendo of 'he dyed in the lowe cuntries, and soe I thinke shall I' suggests – and the ironies that his genealogy provokes multiply as the play progresses.

The tipping point in the relationship between poet and patron comes when Gullio instructs Ingenioso to write love lyrics for him to submit to his would-be mistress, 'in two or three diuers vayns, in Chaucers, Gowers and Spencers, and Mr Shakspeares' (ll. 1027–8). The poems are accordingly presented in Act 4, in a sequence that merits quoting at length. Gullio declares 'Lett mee heare Chaucers vaine firste, I loue antiquitie, if it be not harshe' (ll. 1144–5) – echoing the terms used by Beaumont in his preface to Speght's Chaucer – and Ingenioso reads the poem:

> Euen as the flowers in the coulde of night
> Yclosed slepen in there stalkes lowe,
> Redressen them [against]^{58} the sunne brighte
> And spreaden in theire kinde course by rowe,
> Right soe mine eyne when I vp to thee throwe,
> They bene y cleard; therfore, o Venus deare,
> Thy might, thy grace y heried be it here.
>
> Nor scriuenly^{59} nor craftilie I write;
> Blott I a litell the paper with my teares,
> Nought might mee gladden while I [did]^{60} endite
> But this poore scroule, that thy name y bears.
> Go blessed scroule, a blisfull destinie
> Is shapen thee, my lady shalt thou see.
>
> Nought fitteth mee in this sad thinge I feare
> To vsen iolly tearmes of meriment;
> Solemne tearmes better fitten this mattere
> Then to vsen tearmes of good content:
> For if a painter a pike woulde painte
> With asses feet, and headed like an ape,
> It cordeth not soe were it but a iape. (ll. 1146–65)

On the word 'jape' Gullio interrupts, saying:

> Noe more, nowe in my discreet iudgment, this I iudge of them, that they
> are dull, harshe and spiritless; my M^{ris} will soone finde them not to sauoure
> of my sweet vayne. Besides, thers a worde in the laste canto, which my chaste
> Ladye will neuer endure the readinge of: thou shouldest haue insinuated soe
> much, and not toulde it plainlye. What is becomne of arte? (ll. 1166–72)

Ingenioso defends his language, saying 'S^r, the worde as Chaucer vseth it,
hath noe vnhonest meaninge in it, for it signifieth a ieste', but Gullio
retorts, 'Tush, Chaucer is a foole, and you are another for defendinge of
him' (ll. 1176–9). For the ignorant patron, Chaucer is not only antique – a
fault that might just have been overlooked – but also obscene. However,
the ironies of the play's interaction with Chaucer intensify if we look
further into the specific ways in which it handles its source.

The poem itself is constructed around a series of quotations from Book
2 of *Troilus and Criseyde*. The first stanza adapts, with minor amendments,
a description of Troilus in lines 967–73. The final three lines of the third
stanza and the first two lines of the second stanza are taken from Pandarus'
advice on the composition of love-letters (ll. 1041–3, 1026–7), the former
retaining their allusion to the opening lines of Horace's *Ars poetica*.[61] The
final lines of the second stanza quote Troilus' declaration, 'Lettre, a blisful
destine / The shapyn is: my lady shal the see!' (ll. 1091–2). The remaining
lines mimic Chaucer's style, including archaisms such as the 'y-' prefix in
'y bears' (l. 1156), and the '-en' inflection in the plural verb 'vsen' and the
infinitive 'fitten' (ll. 1160–1); they also imitate the supposedly rough
Chaucerian metre. The quotations mean, of course, that the joke is on
Gullio, who is unable to recognise real Chaucer and who condemns the
whole poem as 'dull, harshe and spiritless', the opposite of his own 'sweet'
style (implicitly one comparable with that of Shakespeare and other early
modern sonneteers).

This misrecognition does not, however, alter the fact that Gullio dislikes
Chaucer's style, whether it is real or pastiche. Moreover, his scepticism
about Chaucer is one of the only genuinely Sidneian things about Gullio;
despite Sidney's professed admiration for Chaucer as a crucial figure in the
development of literary English, he is ambivalent about his works, writing
in *An Apology for Poetry*,

> Chaucer, undoubtedly, did excellently in his *Troilus and Criseyde*; of
> whom, truly, I know not whether to marvel more, either that he in that
> misty time could see so clearly, or that we in this clear age walk so
> stumblingly after him. Yet had he great wants, fit to be forgiven, in so
> reverent antiquity. (110)

While *Troilus and Criseyde* is 'excellent', Chaucer's 'antiquity' makes him stylistically suspect; Sidney, a perceptive critic, finds this excusable, but Gullio focuses more on Chaucer's 'wants' than his visionary excellence. Moreover, although Ingenioso impeccably follows Sidney's guidance in adapting lines from *Troilus and Criseyde* rather than *The Canterbury Tales*, even this care cannot preserve him – or Chaucer – from the charge of obscenity.

Crucially, Chaucer's lack of propriety was increasingly perceived as one of his worst defects, a fact emphasised in Beaumont's comment that Chaucer was thought to be 'somewhat too broad in some of his speeches'. As Harington's criticism of *The Miller's Tale* and *The Wife of Bath's Tale* indicates, much of the opprobrium centred on *The Canterbury Tales*; however, the word 'jape', found not only in *The Canterbury Tales* but also in *Troilus and Criseyde*, was also the focus of popular disapproval and innuendo. For Chaucer and his contemporaries 'jape' had two primary meanings: a trick, or a joke or jest.[62] By the early sixteenth century, and perhaps earlier, the word appears to have collected an additional meaning: the act of sexual intercourse; this meaning was uppermost in the minds of late sixteenth-century commentators, for whom it had become an obsolete curiosity.[63] George Puttenham in *The Art of English Poesy* warns his would-be poet against 'such words as may be drawn to a foul and unshamefast sense, as one that would say to a young woman, "I pray you let me jape with you"' (340), and the word appears in a similar context within literary works, often attached specifically to Chaucer. For instance, in *The Passionate Morris* (1593) a man deserting his pregnant lover tells her, 'I am assured thou art not so foolish as to build of any thing I haue saide, or of that I haue done, but as of a iest', at which the allegorical figure of Honesty comments, 'Doe you tearme such dooing iesting? . . . if *Chaucers* iapes were such iestes, it was but bad sporte.'[64] 'Chaucer's jest' was also used as a synonym for sexual intercourse.[65]

'Jape' is not glossed in the 1598 edition of Speght's Chaucer, but it appears in the extended glossary in 1602:

Iape, (prolog.) Iest, a word by abuse growen odious, and therfore by a certain curious gentlewoman scraped out in her Chaucer: whereupon her seruing man writeth thus:

> My mistres cannot be content,
> To take a iest as Chaucer ment,
> But vsing still a womans fashion
> Allows it in the last translation:
> She cannot with a word dispence,

> Although I know she loues the sence.
> For such an vse the world hath got,
> That words are sinnes, but deeds are not. (3T6r)

The origins of the poem are unclear, but a version of the first six lines is set as a round for three voices in Thomas Ravenscroft's *Melismata* (1611), and it also appears in early modern manuscript miscellanies.[66] The force of the gentlewoman's reaction to the word 'jape' – which leads her physically to obliterate it from her copy of Chaucer's works – is meant within the anecdote to reinforce her hypocrisy; it also argues, however, for the increasing force of sixteenth-century literary culture's rejection of this word.

The fact that *Troilus and Criseyde* was not thought to be an exception to Chaucer's regrettable tendency to bawdry is suggested in Nicholas Breton's comment in 'In the Praise of his Mistress' (1591), 'For *Venus* was a toy, and onely feigned fable / And *Cressed* but a *Chawcers* ieast, and *Helen* but a bable.'[67] Here, Criseyde is reduced to her presumed sexual function, used as a synecdoche for the text's sexual impropriety. Such a perspective is reflected in *The Return from Parnassus*, in which the disputed use of the word 'jape' appears in a quotation from *Troilus and Criseyde*, albeit in a passage in which Pandarus warns Troilus about what not to include in a love-letter. As Paula Glatzer points out, Gullio 'doesn't get Ingenioso's joke because he didn't get Chaucer's in the first place'.[68] His attention is instead caught by the word 'jape' itself. Like the 'seruing man' in the poem printed by Speght, Gullio thinks that his mistress will be too squeamish to read the word 'jape' and – as in the poem – it is assumed that she will be more receptive to innuendo. Archaic language is comically positioned as 'rude' (in both senses of the word) and indecorous, a kind of textual id that expresses all too clearly the intentions that the speaker would rather veil.

The sequence's focus on innuendo is also clear in the presentation of Ingenioso's Spenserian poem, which opens 'A gentle pen rides prickinge on the plaine, / This paper plaine, to resalute my loue' (ll. 1181–2). Gullio again interrupts – this time after only two lines – saying 'Stay man, why thou haste a very lecherous witt, what wordes are these? Though thou comes somwhat neare my meaninge, yet it doth not become my gentle witt to sett it downe soe plainlye' (ll. 1183–6). Again, the issue is not what is said, but the way in which it is expressed, and the ironies in Gullio's dirty-minded response to 'Chaucer' and 'Spenser' are intensified when he takes at face value Ingenioso's smutty parody of Shakespeare's *Venus and Adonis*, declaring, 'let this duncified worlde esteeme of Spencer and Chaucer, Ile worshipp sweet Mr Shakspeare' (ll. 1200–1) and assuming that Shakespeare's style is the one likely to attract women.[69]

In *The Return from Parnassus*, the anxiety that archaism arouses is not only that old words can become 'dull' or 'harsh', but that they can become semantically slippery, rebounding posthumously on their users. Works that are both stylistically and chronologically 'new' are placed in opposition to the old and the faux-antique, but the object of satire is not the older works themselves, but the contemporary literary marketplace and its (perceived) perversion of literary value. Chaucer and Spenser are grouped together as the bawdy antithesis of 'sweet Mr Shakspeare', and Gower appears to drop out altogether. Foolish readers such as Gullio are assumed to be incapable of accepting archaism as a necessary stylistic and aesthetic element in both old and new works; instead, they are easily distracted by the newfangled associations of individual words, and only too willing to project their own sexual proclivities onto old texts. Ingenioso himself is presented as a reader who is able to look beyond time's corruption of language – his gloss on the word 'jape' is historically correct, after all – but he is nonetheless implicated in the debasement of literary culture through his willingness to pander to Gullio's desire.

The incorporation and imitation of the archaic Chaucerian text in *The Faerie Queene* and *The Return from Parnassus* thus display the anxiety of obsolescence in two interrelated forms, with both works betraying a pervasive unease about the stability of English, and about time's effects on old words. Time's erosion of language and its corruption of individual words are two sides of the same coin: processes through which literary status becomes uncertain, and through which an early modern writer's poetic forebears might become lost. It is also significant that *The Return from Parnassus* groups Chaucer and Spenser together as obscene and therefore unsupportable; if the antiquity of literary works is a problem, so too is the imitation of those works.

Against obsolescence

In *The Return from Parnassus*, Gullio's negative reaction to Ingenioso's Chaucerian poem apparently means that his imitation of Gower – promised in Act 3 – is not delivered. To a certain extent, this suppression mirrors the downward trajectory of Gower's reputation in the late sixteenth and early seventeenth centuries: allusions to Gower generally accompany references to Chaucer – unlike Chaucer, he is seldom referred to independently – and his stylistic star fades along with that of his more famous contemporary.[70] However, Gower, not Chaucer, was to be fully embodied on the early modern stage, in Shakespeare and Wilkins' *Pericles*, and was thereby the subject of one of the period's most sustained attempts to assert the value of archaic style.

The depiction of Gower in *Pericles* has been the subject of a good deal of interest from critics, and many have pointed out the ways in which this 'exceedingly bookish play' (as Barbara Mowat terms it) constructs its self-consciously 'ancient' presenter.[71] Especially powerful is the connection that Jennifer Summit draws between the representation of Gower in *Pericles* and the treatment of the poet as a 'memorial writer' in Weever's *Ancient Funeral Monuments*: 'Where Shakespeare's Gower comes from ashes,' she writes, 'Weever's comes from manuscripts . . . whose very age underscores both their authority and their distance from the present.'[72] Building on this work, I argue that *Pericles* is in itself antiquarian, in that it imaginatively recreates archaic narratives, linguistic and poetic conventions, and social rituals. To view the play in this way is to take seriously F. David Hoeniger's suggestion that Gower 'was meant to appeal to an audience that had developed a liking for things old-fashioned and antiquarian'.[73] Through their imaginative antiquarianism, Shakespeare and Wilkins challenge the assumptions about archaism's obsolescence that are anxiously negotiated in *The Faerie Queene* and *The Return from Parnassus*.

As Graham Parry and others have described, the activities of early modern antiquarians were often textual rather than archaeological, and antiquarian works are full of allusions to and quotations from classical and vernacular literary works, including those of Chaucer and Gower.[74] This emphasis is reflected in the satiric character of 'An Antiquary' presented in John Earle's *Micro-cosmographie* (1628). Earle describes the antiquary as someone 'that hath that vnnaturall disease to bee enamour'd of old age, and wrinckles', who 'loues all things (as Dutchmen doe Cheese) the better for being mouldy and worme-eaten'.[75] In addition to his interest in broken statues and old monuments, coins and pictures of Caesar, saints' wells and ruined abbeys, crosses and stone foot-stools, the antiquary 'reades onely those Charactars, where time hath eaten out the letters' (C2r), and he

> loues no Library, but where there are more Spiders volums then Authors, and lookes with great admiration on the Antique worke of Cob-webs. Printed bookes he contemnes, as a nouelty [*sic*] of this latter age; but a Manu-script [h]e pores on euerlastingly, especially if the couer be all Moth-eaten, and the dust make a Parenthesis betweene euerie Sillable. (C2v–C3r)

Although Earle's portrait is exaggerated, there is an element of truth to it. Antiquarians were proud of their work with manuscript sources, and many took great pains to track them down. However, as Angus Vine argues in his fine recent study of early modern antiquarian writing, stereotypical representations such as Earle's do not capture fully the 'dynamic, recuperative, resurrective response to the past' that is presented in the work of writers such as Leland, Camden, Stow and Selden. Theirs is, he argues, 'an essentially imaginative response to the past ... the antiquary conceived of himself as bridging the gap between past and present, affording "olden time" presence so that it might speak to or inform the current time'.[76] John Aubrey, writing in the late seventeenth century, compares antiquarianism to 'the Art of a Conjuror who makes those walke and appeare that have layen in their graves many hundreds of yeares: and represents as it were to the eie, the places, customs and Fashions, that were of old Time'.[77] Aubrey is especially sensitive to what Richard Bauman and Charles L. Briggs term 'temporal disjuncture' or 'temporal dislocation',[78] but antiquarians throughout the century felt similar impulses.

Pericles responds to the imaginative element within antiquarianism, as Gower returns from the grave in order to resurrect, in turn, a story that he famously told in *Confessio Amantis*. The prologue sets up these interactions:

> To sing a song that old was sung
> From ashes ancient Gower is come,
> Assuming man's infirmities
> To glad your ear and please your eyes.
> It hath been sung at festivals,
> On ember eves and holidays,
> And lords and ladies in their lives
> Have read it for restoratives.
> The purchase is to make men glorious,
> *Et bonum quo antiquius eo melius.*
> If you, born in these latter times
> When wit's more ripe, accept my rhymes,
> And that to hear an old man sing
> May to your wishes pleasure bring,
> I life would wish, and that I might
> Waste it for you like taper light.[79]

These lines associate Gower closely with the interests of early seventeenth-century antiquaries such as Camden, Selden or Weever. Like them, Gower invests value in the sheer antiquity of what he presents. In the first line, the modulation of tenses in 'To *sing* a song that old was *sung*' emphasises the temporal gap between the material and its new audience. Similarly, Gower presents himself as having returned from the dead, not merely having come from the grave, but having been reconstituted from 'ashes'. He is interested in ancient cultural practices, here the 'festivals', 'ember eves' and 'holidays' at which the story has received oral presentation, and the 'lords and ladies' who have read it in earlier versions. The Latin tag, 'Et bonum quo antiquius eo melius' ('and the older a good thing is, the better it gets') encapsulates Gower's stance, but the quotation of a pre-existing phrase also allies him with the proverb-hunting antiquarians.[80] Similarly, the later line 'I tell you what mine authors say' associates him not only with medieval writerly habits and phraseology, but also with the antiquarians' dependence on textual authority. This impression is reinforced in the close paraphrase of Gower's own *Confessio Amantis* in lines 29–30, in which Gower's 'And suche delit he tok therinne / Him thoghte that it was no sinne' (8: 345–6) is conflated with the proverbial dictum 'custom makes sin no sin' to become 'But custom what they did begin / Was with long use accounted no sin'.[81]

As scholars have often noted, Gower's style in the choruses is also modelled on medieval literary conventions. The tetrameter couplets either mimic those used by the historical Gower in his English poetry, or are written in a generalised approximation of the style of medieval verse – in Robert Greene's prose fiction *Greene's Vision* (1592), both Chaucer and Gower are introduced with short verses written in this form.[82] Even more extreme than the archaism of Gower's verse form is that of his diction. The Act 2 Chorus, for example, includes such fragments of a recreated Gowerian English as the declaration that Pericles 'Is still at Tarsus, where each man / Thinks all is writ he speken can' (2.0.11–12) and the statement that 'All perishen of man, of pelf, / Ne aught escapend but himself' (2.0.35–6). Shakespeare and Wilkins' Gower thus both promotes and embodies older forms of the language.

Earle concludes his character of the antiquary with a sketch of his physical appearance: 'His verie atyre is that which is the eldest out of fashion, and you may picke a Criticism out of his Breeches. He neuer lookes vpon him self til he is gray-hair'd, and then he is pleased with his owne Antiquity' (C3r–v). A similarly antiquarian impulse appears to have been at work in the King's Men's performance of *Pericles*. Wilkins' prose reworking of the play, *The Painful Adventures of Pericles, Prince of Tyre* (1608), advises its readers to 'receiue this Historie in the same maner as it was vnder the habite of ancient Gower the famous English Poet, by the Kings Maiesties Players excellently presented', and the title-page presents a picture of Gower in medieval costume.[83] The Gower that stalked the Globe's stage, apparently clad in medieval costume, embodies the antiquarian impulse, and the linguistic archaisms of the choruses both reinforce and vocally embody the negotiations with the historical, literary, cultural and material pasts with which he is engaged. We might even compare the choruses with the black-letter quotations from medieval writers in the works of Camden or Selden – the choruses, like the quotations, lend an aura of authenticity to the 'text' (to use Gower's suggestive term) that surrounds them.

Other aspects of the play's dramaturgy contribute to this antiquarian effect, such as the extensive use of dumb shows. As I will explain at greater length in Chapter 4, the dumb show was not in itself particularly archaic in the early seventeenth century, despite critics' assertions to the contrary.[84] However, its appearance in three of the choruses that punctuate the action of *Pericles* (2.0.16.1–6, 3.0.14.1–7 and 4.4.22.1–5) nonetheless contributes to the play's performative antiquarianism because the staged action and Gower's narration foreground the act of the recuperation of the past. Like many similar devices, the dumb shows in *Pericles* prescribe in detail the physical action and gestural conventions required. The Act 2 dumb show requires '*talking*', the display of a letter, and the reward and knighting of a messenger (2.0.16.1–5), while a similar sequence in Act 3 requires kneeling, the display of another letter, '*rejoic[ing]*' from Thaisa and '*tak[ing] leave*' (3.0.14.2–3, 5). The dumb show in Act 4, Scene 4 makes particular demands on the actor playing Pericles, who is required to convey his reaction to the news of his daughter Marina's apparent death through physical gestures that are keyed to Gower's words:

> *Enter* PERICLES *at one door with all his train;* CLEON *and* DIONIZA *at the other. Cleon shows Pericles the tomb, whereat Pericles makes lamentation, puts on sackcloth, and in a mighty passion departs. [Exeunt Cleon and Dionyza at the other door.]*

> GOWER See how belief may suffer by foul show.
> This borrowed passion stands for true-owed woe,
> And Pericles in sorrow all devoured,
> With sighs shot through and biggest tears o'ershadowed,
> Leaves Tarsus and again embarks. He swears
> Never to wash his face nor cut his hairs,
> He puts on sackcloth and to sea he bears
> A tempest which his mortal vessel tears,
> And yet he rides it out.　　　　(4.4.22SD–31)

Introducing this dumb show, Gower emphasises the role of visual story-telling in bringing the dead to life, and the importance of the audience's active imagination as a supplement to the dramatic action: 'Like motes and shadows see them move awhile; / Your ears unto your eyes I'll reconcile' (4.4.21–2). The dramatist, like Aubrey's antiquarian, mimics 'the Art of a Conjuror'; but where the antiquarian works on the reader's imagination, representing 'as it were to the eie, the places, customs and Fashions, that were of old Time', the stage is able to grant its representations a physical presence.

Rather than undermining the antiquarian impulse of *Pericles*, the play's temporal mixture reflects the eclectic concerns of contemporary scholars. While Gower's choruses display linguistic and stylistic medievalism, the dramatic action of the play takes place in the ancient world. It is, however, an ancient world that includes the spectacle of the tournament (2.3), itself a remarkable example of Elizabethan and Jacobean medievalism.[85] This mixture even echoes the antiquarians' presentation of their sources on the printed page, where quotations from medieval English writers jostle with lines taken from Homer, Virgil and other classical writers. In Selden's notes on the eleventh song in Drayton's *Polyolbion*, for instance, a quotation from Robert of Gloucester (in black letter) is followed by quotations from Tacitus' *Annals* and Bede's *Historia* (in italic) (see Figure 4).

In contrast with *The Faerie Queene* and *The Return from Parnassus*, *Pericles* assumes that its audience are not only willing but able to connect intellectually and emotionally with its antiquarian 'author' and his archaic style. Indeed, the play is confident enough in its material to play with spectators' expectations and, at times, to subvert them. As has often been noted, the hero of Gower's narrative is Apollonius of Tyre, and Shakespeare and Wilkins were the first to call him 'Pericles'. What is less often noted is the way in which Pericles' name is introduced. Although it appears in the title of the play, and presumably appeared on the play-bills that advertised its performance at the Globe, the name is not heard until twenty-six lines into the first scene, at the point at which Antiochus cautions 'Prince Pericles' on the dangers of courting his daughter. In contrast, Antiochus' name is introduced during Gower's prologue, and is used by Pericles in his first line of dialogue (Prologue 17; 1.1.3). Having alerted spectators to the fact that the Apollonius of Tyre narrative is being adapted, Shakespeare and Wilkins almost flaunt their independence from their source in their willingness to change the hero's name, to subvert both Gower and his own 'authors'. Similarly, the major prose scenes featuring the fishermen (2.1) and the brothel (4.2, 4.5) deliberately transgress both the classical setting of the narrative and the medieval ambience of Gower's choruses, featuring a series of anachronistic references to religious and

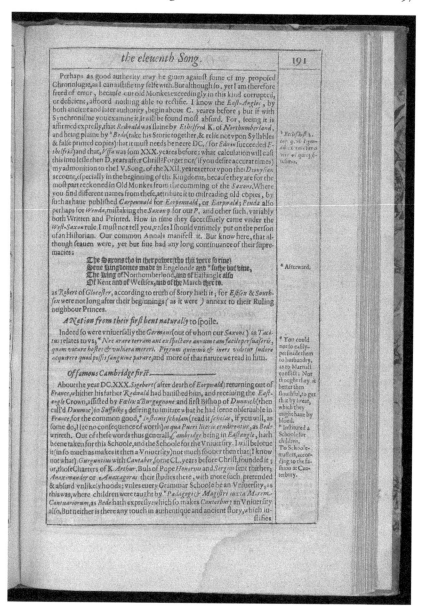

Figure 4 John Selden's notes on the eleventh book of Michael Drayton's *Poly-Olbion* (London, 1612), R6r, with quotations from Robert of Gloucester (in black-letter) and Tacitus and Bede (in italic).

social customs, clothing and even the newfangled disease of syphilis. These elements are combined, for example, in Bawd and Bolt's gleeful account of the French knight, 'Monsieur Verolles' – his name derived from the French word for the pox – who 'offered to cut a caper' on hearing Marina described and will, according to Bawd, 'come in our shadow to scatter his crowns in the sun' (4.2.98, 99, 104).

In the 'Ode to Himself', Ben Jonson famously criticises *Pericles* as a 'mouldy tale . . . stale / As the shrieve's crusts, and nasty as his fish-/ Scraps, out every dish / Thrown forth and raked into the common tub'.[86] I have argued here that *Pericles* may indeed be 'mouldy', but its mouldiness is not that of decaying food, but that of the antiquary. *Pericles* loves its 'mouldy and worme-eaten' sources in the same way as Earle's antiquary loves his ancient documents, and its presiding deity – Gower – is as pleased with his grey hairs as is Earle's character. As we have seen, Spenser's archaism caused anxiety amongst his contemporaries and immediate successors, who worried about his poetry's ability to withstand time. In contrast, the archaism and imaginative antiquarianism of *Pericles* appear to have fuelled its lasting appeal to Jacobean and Caroline audiences, and it was still current on the stage in the 1630s.[87]

The antiquarianism of *Pericles* finds a fascinating echo in William Cartwright's *The Ordinary*, performed at Oxford University in 1635, in which the antiquary Robert Moth also engages in performative antiquarianism. Like Shakespeare and Wilkins' Gower, he speaks in a reanimated form of Middle English, here based on a patchwork of quotations from Chaucer; however, his dialogue is much less precise in its recreation of Middle English than Gower's, suggesting either that Cartwright did not have the necessary knowledge or inclination to polish it, or that Moth's linguistic incompetence is itself part of the joke. Although antiquarians appear in other plays of the period – notably Shakerley Marmion's *The Antiquary* (Queen Henrietta Maria's Men, c.1634–6) – Moth is unique in the way in which he embodies his preoccupations linguistically. However, the kind of linguistic impersonation in which he engages is also evoked by Earle, and by Samuel Butler in a sketch written before 1680 but not published until 1759. Earle begins his description by saying that the antiquary is 'a man strangely thrifty of Time past, & an enemy indeed to his Maw, whence hee fetches out many things when they are now all rotten and stinking' (C1v).[88] Butler's antiquary, similarly, 'has a great Veneration for Words that are stricken in Years, and are grown so aged, that they have out-lived their Employments – These he uses with a Respect agreeable to their Antiquity, and the good services they have done'.[89]

Butler may be recalling Cartwright's play, and his depiction of Moth, but – as we have seen – a focus on language and textuality was by no means uncommon in discussions of antiquarianism, and in the work of the antiquarians themselves.

In contrast with *Pericles*, in which archaic style is limited to Gower's choruses, in *The Ordinary* Cartwright does not confine Moth to a metatheatrical device, but instead integrates him into the body of his comedy. Moth, a figure who behaves as if he is a man out of time, nonetheless has to function within the hetero-erotic structures of Caroline London, and he paradoxically does so with the aid of Chaucer. Apart from his fight with Have-at-All, which I discussed in Chapter 1, Moth's main involvement in the plot of *The Ordinary* is in his wooing of a vintner's widow, Joan Potluck, who is introduced in the play's second scene as the exploited landlady of a group of ne'er-do-well gallants. Each of the young men refuses to marry her, either finding a pretext – including a (fictional) castration – or rudely insulting her, but later in the act Hearsay and Meanwell agree to set up their 'good toothlesse Countesse' with Moth, Meanwell commenting 'Hee'l surely love her, 'cause she looks like some / Old ruin'd peece, that was five Ages backward'.[90] As elsewhere, the antiquary is assumed to have a natural affinity with anything that is old, or that appears to be old.

On his first appearance in the play, in Act 2, Scene 2, Moth is immediately marked out by his language and his antiquarian interests. The scene opens *in medias res*, with Meanwell trying to convince Moth to enter into his romantic plot:

> *Mean[well]*. If what I speak prove false, then stigmatize me.
> *Mo[th]*. I nas not what you mean; Depardieux you
> Snyb mine old years, Sans fail I wene you bin
> A Jangler, and a Golierdis.
> *Mean[well]*.   I swear
> By these two *Janus* heads you had of us,
> And your own too, as reverend as these,
> There is one loves you that you think not on.   (ll. 683–9)

Moth's first speech sets the tone, as he uses the Chaucerian archaisms 'nas' and 'Depardieux' (in God's name), and quotes from the description of the Miller in the General Prologue to *The Canterbury Tales*.[91] Similarly, Meanwell draws attention to the stereotypical preoccupations of the antiquary in his reference to the goods that he and his friends have dealt Moth; he suggests, moreover, that the romantic 'goods' he offers are as genuine as his antiquarian ones, and as legitimate a subject for Moth's interest.

The scene derives much of its humour from the incongruous integration of the antiquary, with his querulous tone and archaic speech-patterns, into a romantic plot. This is especially true of the preening little soliloquy with which Moth ends the scene:

> Cembeth thy self, and pyketh now thy self;
> Sleeketh thy self; make cheere much Digne good Robert:
> I do arret thou shalt acquainted bin
> With Nymphs and Fawny, and Hamadryades;
> And y'eke the sisterne nine Pierides
> That were transmued into Birds, nemp'd Pyes,
> Metamorphoseos wat well what I mean.
> I is as Jollie now as fish in Seine.   (ll. 724–31)

Here, Moth draws successively on *The Merchant's Tale* (l. 2011), *The Knight's Tale* (l. 2928) and the Introduction to *The Man of Law's Tale* (ll. 92–3), creating a collage of Chaucerian fragments that begins with a fairly sensible borrowing from the description in *The Merchant's Tale* of Damian's preparations after May has left a letter for him, but becomes progressively sillier as his flight of fantasy continues. Moth attempts to bring his learning to bear on his current situation, putting Chaucer to practical, if incongruous, uses.

The uses to which Moth puts his learning are further demonstrated in Act 3, when he and Potluck appear together on stage for the first time, and the antiquary is given the chance to try out his somewhat idiosyncratic courtship techniques. The sequence is worth quoting at some length. Having serenaded Potluck with a mish-mash of lines from *The Miller's Tale*, Moth compliments her as 'fresh' and 'lycand' (pleasing or attractive) (l. 1018).[92] The object of his affections demurs, commenting, 'I could plant red, where you now yellow see; / But painting shews an harlot' (ll. 1022–3). Potluck's use of the word 'harlot' sets Moth off into etymology: 'Harlot, so / Called from one *Harlotha* Concubine / To deignous *Wilhelme*, hight the Conqueror' (ll. 1024–6). Picking up the word 'harlot', she then apparently cuts him off in full flow, saying,

> Were he ten *Williams*, and ten Conquerors
> I'd have him know't, I scorn to be his Harlot.
> I never yet did take presse-money to
> Serve under any one   (ll. 1027–30)

Even Moth manages to pick up the marked sexual innuendo of her references to 'press-money' and to 'serv[ing]' under; he replies: 'Then take it now', kisses her, and exclaims,

Werme kisse! Thine lips ytaste like marrow milk;
Me thinketh that fresh butter runneth on them.
I grant well now, I do enduren woe,
As sharp as doth the *Titius* in Hell,
Whose stomack fowles do tyren ever more,
That highten Vultures, as do tellen Clerkes. (ll. 1030–5)

Potluck approves of the emotion behind this speech, even if she does not
follow his precise meaning, and they reach an agreement:

> *Pot.* Can you be constant unto me as I
> Can be to you?
> *Moth.* By *Woden* God of Saxons,
> From whence comes Wensday, that is Wodensday,
> Truth is a thing that ever I will keep,
> Unto thylke [day] in which I creep into
> My Sepulchre; I'l be as faithfull to thee,
> As Chaunticleere to Madam Partelot.
> *Pot.* Here then I give away my heart to you,
> As true a heart as ever widow gave.   (ll. 1048–57)

Cartwright's knowledge of Middle English may have been imperfect, but
he plays knowledgeably with the original contexts of the lines he quotes.
Moth's exclamation when he first kisses Potluck is a close paraphrase of
Troilus and Criseyde, 1.785–8:

> I graunte wel that thow endurest wo
> As sharp as doth he Ticius in helle,
> Whos stomak foughles tiren evere moo
> That hightyn volturis, as bokes telle[.]

In Chaucer these words are part of Pandarus' sympathetic description of
Troilus' sexual frustration, uttered shortly before he discovers that the
object of the young man's attraction is his niece, Criseyde. Here, the lines
likewise suggest erotic tension, as Potluck's kiss inflames Moth; they are
both appropriate and comically misplaced, given the unhappy conclusion
of the love affair between Troilus and Criseyde. Similarly, Moth's assertions about 'truth' (ll. 1052–4) are taken from *The Canon's Yeoman's Tale*
(ll. 1044–6), in which the Canon – described some twenty lines later as the
'roote of al trecherie' (l. 1069) – discusses not love but financial propriety.
When Moth refers to another Chaucerian couple, Chanticleer and Pertelot,
the chicken hero and heroine of *The Nun's Priest's Tale*, the comparisons
are perhaps happier, albeit equally incongruous, especially given the
fact that Chanticleer had seven wives, 'Whiche were his sustres and his

paramours' (l. 2867). It is noticeable, however, that the allusion comes in an exchange of vows that is reminiscent of those undertaken by Troilus and Cressida in Shakespeare's version of the story (*Troilus and Cressida*, 3.2.168–203).

In contrast with *The Return of Parnassus*, where Chaucer's bawdry makes him unfit for use as an erotic tool, in *The Ordinary* Moth is apparently able to deploy Chaucerian quotation in a way that makes him available – even attractive – to the object of his desires. Moreover, while Moth's Anglo-Saxon scholarship renders him vulnerable to Have-at-All's attack, and dangerously at odds with heterosocial norms, his reading in Chaucer actually aids him in his pursuit of Joan Potluck. The dual rehabilitation of antiquary and ancient writer reaches its climax in Act 5, when Moth and Potluck enter as man and wife, and he announces,

> *Denuncio vobis gaudium magnum,*
> *Robertus de Tinea electus est in sedem Hospitalem,*
> *Et assumit sibi nomen Galfridi.*
> Joy comes to our house. I *Robert Moth* am
> Chesen into thylk Hospitall seat,
> Thylk Bason of *Jone Potluck*, Vintners Widow,
> And do transmue my name to Giffery.
> New foysons byn ygraced with new Titles. (ll. 2257–64)

Like his archaic English, Moth's use of Latin in everyday conversation, and his adoption of the new name 'Geoffrey', a tribute to Chaucer, is part of his performative antiquarianism. However, his willingness to translate his own Latin declaration perhaps suggests his greater integration into society, and this tendency is underlined through the stage action, in which he again kisses Potluck (ll. 2265–6).

Where *The Return from Parnassus* presents Chaucer's reputation for bawdy as a romantic handicap, Moth's tribute to Chaucer in his new name is a testament to the erotic uses to which he has put the poet's lines. Cartwright may also have had in mind the lines from *Troilus and Criseyde* quoted at the beginning of this chapter, in which Chaucer writes that men a thousand years ago 'spedde as wel in love as men now do' (2.26). The entire plot concerning Moth is thus a kind of 'Chaucer's jape', with the sexual success of the poet's archaic devotee standing in as the joke's punchline. While *The Ordinary* satirises both the antiquarian and Chaucer's contemporary reputation, it nonetheless contends, in its comic fashion, that medieval poets still have their uses.

Conclusion

In the preface to a compilation of Latin and English adages, published in 1621, Bartholomew Robertson writes: 'All ages are not alike, many words fall and dye, and daily other reuiue; all is one, if we speak as the now and then time affords. If *Chaucer* could arise, he should learne a new phrase, and scarsly could vnderstand, vnlesse he went to schoole againe.'[93] Robertson imagines a reborn Chaucer who is unable to communicate with his successors, and is therefore forced to adapt himself to linguistic change. Intriguingly, however, he also suggests that while words 'fall and die' they also have the capacity to be brought back to life. The works examined in this chapter – *The Faerie Queene*, *The Return from Parnassus*, *Pericles* and *The Ordinary* – all exhibit, in their varying ways, a refusal to speak only as 'the now and then time affords'. Instead, they mingle old and new, inserting not only archaic words and linguistic structures, but also extended quotations from medieval literary works. They thus create a multitemporal collage in which the selection of particular texts, and quotations from those texts, create a complex network of meanings and associations.

As we have seen, the works examined in detail here vary in the attitudes that they take towards the medieval authors that they quote, appropriate and embody. *The Faerie Queene* and *The Return to Parnassus* both express an anxiety that medieval literary works are subject to corruption at the hands of time. Here, Chaucer's works are seen as vulnerable not just to incomprehension but also to damaging forms of linguistic corruption or misreading, processes that could leave a formerly prized author an obscene laughing-stock. Implicitly, both texts betray a fear that the only viable approaches to literary obsolescence are either heavy-handed explication of the kind emerging in print editions of Chaucer, or translation, updating and rewriting. Medieval authors may survive, but only in radically altered or mediated forms.

In contrast, and despite Cartwright's own professed unease about Chaucer's longevity, both *Pericles* and *The Ordinary* assume that audiences in London and Oxford are capable of making an effort to engage with Middle English, both genuine and pastiche. The antiquarian impulse of *Pericles* is crucial to its dramatic and commercial success, and its impact depends on its audience's willingness to engage with Gower and to 'accept [his] rhymes'. In *The Ordinary*, Cartwright apparently assumes that not all audience members will understand every word that the antiquary says, and he uses the comments of other characters, such as Meanwell, Have-at-All and the bemused Potluck to support and mediate Moth's utterances. However, the play requires its audience to follow and engage with Moth's story, and to be amused by his efforts to function within a cut-throat contemporary London. Moreover, the narrative itself – with Moth's sexual triumph and his explicit tribute to Chaucer – suggests in its sardonic fashion that older literature has an ongoing function. In these works, medieval authors are not to be put to school, but to use.

CHAPTER 3

Archaic style in religious writing: immutability, controversy, prophecy

In the course of his dispute with Gabriel Harvey in 1592, Thomas Nashe paused to lecture his adversary on the correct use of archaisms. If Harvey were not his enemy, Nashe writes, 'I would teach thy olde *Trewantship* the true vse of words, as also how more inclinable verse is than prose to dance after the horrizonant pipe of inueterate antiquitie'.[1] The assumption that archaism is more suitable to verse than other forms of writing pervades early modern culture, but there was one important area in which outmoded style appears in both poetry and prose: religious writing. Linguistic and stylistic archaisms play a central role in liturgical translations, and religious verse similarly danced to what Nashe terms the 'horrizonant' – roaring, or terrible-sounding – 'pipe of inueterate anti-quitie'.[2] Religious writing would thus have been the main venue in which the majority of early modern English readers encountered archaism, and its uses here have important implications for the workings of outmoded style in literary culture more generally.

This chapter compares the use of archaism at the heart of the Anglican establishment – in translations of the Bible, the Book of Common Prayer and the Psalms – with that in the work of translators and poets associated with two groups stigmatised by that establishment: Catholics and the radical Protestant Fifth Monarchists. It argues that in the works of each of these groups archaism identifies the texts with earlier, 'purer' or plainer forms of the language, thus playing a central role in the religio-political project of naturalising a particular version of Christianity as domestic and familiar. Yet this process was often fraught with complications. While linguistic and stylistic archaisms in liturgical texts were a key tool in the conservative presentation of religious doctrine, they were also a potential source of anxiety, impeding understanding or even permitting a dangerous ambiguity of meaning. Archaism is not merely a form of generic decorum – one rudely broken by iconoclasts such as John Donne – but an aesthetic tool in itself, and part of a more complex negotiation of the tensions between biblical and poetic style. In religious verse, the unchangeable and timeless meet and clash with the mutable and topical, and archaism is at the heart of this tension.

The first part of the chapter, 'Archaism and religious diction: traditions and transitions', explores in detail the aesthetic and political uses to which archaic language and style were put in religious translation, analysing the ways in which Protestant and Catholic translators of liturgical materials negotiated the demands of representing biblical language in English, and the pressures that the passage of time put upon their techniques. Part two, 'Catholic poets and the plain style', looks at the work of two Catholic poets from different generations: the Elizabethan Jesuit Robert Southwell and the Caroline nun Gertrude (née Helen) More. In the face of a sustained movement towards a Latinate and Baroque aesthetic for English Catholicism, both of these poets instead turn to archaic metres and the 'Saxon' monosyllable, occupying aesthetic spaces generally associated with Protestantism and attempting thereby to re-naturalise Catholicism as a truly 'English' faith. Part three, 'Radical Protestantism and prophecy', looks briefly at the verses of the early Caroline prophet Jane Hawkins before focusing on two Fifth Monarchist poets: Anna Trapnel and Morgan Llwyd. While Trapnel and Llwyd employ the same metrical resources as Southwell and More, they do not draw uncomplicatedly on the associations between archaism and Englishness, a tactic that would have been made difficult by Llwyd's forcefully articulated sense of his national identity as a Welshman. Instead, they exploit the strong association between archaic metre and Protestant translations of the Psalms – one of the few forms of set worship that the Fifth Monarchists did not reject – and the Psalms' own connection with inspired speech, and they weave archaic forms into a complex vision of apocalyptic revelation. The comforting timelessness of certain archaic metres, which by the 1650s were almost beyond literary fashion, thus combines with the radical a-temporality of prophecy – the 'eternal prophetic present', as James Holstun terms it – to form a potent aesthetic whole.[3] When poets imitate the conventional form of the Psalms they invoke a kind of cultural nostalgia, but when they do so within prophecy they also stake a claim to the future.

Archaism and religious diction: traditions and transitions

Assumptions about the nature of divine utterance are crucial to the use of archaism in religious writing. Many early modern writers held that only divine language was immutable; all earthly languages were subject to change and decay. A 1640 translation of a tract by Sebastian Franck (1499–1542) summarises this perspective:

> In the word of God alone, which proceedeth out of the mouth of god, is seated the rule of all things ... All other arts they be variable whatsoever they be to time, fortune, vanitie, death, and oblivion; and not onely these arts, but also the Letters, bookes, formes, masters, tongues, which we use, doe perish, and others after them, which succeed in their places, so that nothing is constant & of long continuance in the earth, but all things according to their visible nature, are frayle, mutable, and momentary.[4]

Writers and translators of devotional materials therefore faced a stylistic quandary: should they use up-to-date forms, implicitly acknowledging the transience of earthly language, or should they resist linguistic change, attempting to forge a timeless diction that would more closely resemble an immutable divine language? English Protestant translators turned to archaism in an attempt to 'fix' language, and to resist temporal change, aligning it with the immutable power of religious doctrine. Yet religious writing also brought archaism into direct contact with contemporary controversy, as writers and translators sought to connect themselves with earlier traditions of their native language and, thereby, to root the Church of England as authentically 'English'.

The role of archaism in the Anglican Bible is clear in the 'Authorised' or King James Bible.[5] Two examples demonstrate some of the varied ways in which the translators employ outmoded words or linguistic forms:

> Blessed *shall be* the fruit of thy body, and the fruit of thy ground, and the fruit of thy cattell, the increase of thy kine, and the flocks of thy sheepe. (Deuteronomy 28:4)

> John did baptize in the wildernesse, and preach the baptisme of repentance, for the remission of sinnes. (Mark 1:4)

Archaism appears here in the two forms outlined in the introduction to this book: older words and forms are retained from earlier translations, and, more surprisingly, newly imported. The first quotation, from Deuteronomy, retains the weak plural 'kine', which was rapidly becoming archaic in the early seventeenth century.[6] It prefers the increasingly old-fashioned pronoun 'thou' over 'you',[7] and it repeatedly uses 'and' to translate the Hebrew *waw*, a stylistic marker of Protestant Bible translation from Tyndale onward.[8] It also displays the stubborn refusal to introduce colloquial contraction that gives liturgical English something of its archaic tonality. The second, from Mark, adds the heavy auxiliary 'do' that was slipping out of fashion in 1611;[9] it does not appear in earlier translations.[10]

In its retention and amplification of outmoded vocabulary and syntax, the King James Bible thus used archaism as a stylistic tool, and this translation was itself a crucial channel through which archaic style was circulated and perpetuated in seventeenth-century England.

Archaism also appeared or persisted in other liturgical texts. As I will explore in detail below, the Book of Common Prayer was criticised by Presbyterian ministers in the early 1660s for its inclusion of 'obsolete words'.[11] The Psalms were yet more marked by their use of archaic diction. A disgruntled William Barton claimed in 1656 that the century-old translation by Thomas Sternhold and John Hopkins, published in the late 1540s, featured 'Many obsolete words; as, *glory goodly dight; the woful hearted wight; thousands of Neat and Kine; the springing wels and bourn, ay, eke, agast, revere*, and many more'.[12] Some of these words had been archaic even in the sixteenth century, when they were first adopted, and by the seventeenth century they were increasingly showing their age.

Furthermore, the Psalms also opened up an alternative form of archaism in the distinctive metre used in early translations: alternate lines of eight and six syllables, often with cross-rhymes linking them into four-line stanzas, termed common measure, ballad measure or Sternhold's measure. Scholars have debated whether Sternhold adapted a style already being used in popular ballads, or ballads adopted the style from his metrical Psalms. Beth Quitslund argues in her recent study of the psalter that, although common measure came over the course of the sixteenth century to be associated with ballads, 'very few examples of ballad or Common Meter songs before Sternhold's are even plausibly "popular" in the sense of being "not courtly"'.[13] Instead, Quitslund follows Edward Doughtie in arguing that Sternhold adopted his metre from that of the Earl of Surrey and other courtly poets and thus '*made* the meter popular', leading to its adoption in ballads and other demotic forms.[14]

No matter what common measure's origins were, it gradually gathered a weight of tradition and associative memory behind it, and became connected with Englishness through its links with both the national church and popular forms of literature. By the 1580s, however, common measure was rarely used outside ballads and the Psalms, and the archaic aesthetic of the Psalm translations, which were now perceived as barren and primitive, came under attack.[15] Joseph Hall argued in 1607, 'since our whol Tra[ns]lation is now vniuersally reuised; what inconuenience or showe of innouation can it beare, that the verse should accompanie the prose', criticising the 'rude & homely' quality of English poetry 'in those times, compared with the present'.[16] Similarly, George Wither observed in 1619 'what poore esteem those incomparable Hymns haue amongst the common sort of man, in respect of that which the elegancie of prophane *Poems* hath obtained, beeing trimmed vp in those their naturall ornaments of *Poesy*, which the *Psalmes* haue bin in some sort depriued of'.[17] While secular poetry had developed and become progressively more refined, the Psalms had been fossilised. Hall blames the conservative taste of English congregations, writing, 'This fault (if any) will light vpon the negligence of our people; which endure not to take paines for any fit variety',[18] but the persistence of common measure also suggests that it met an emotional and aesthetic need, its comforting familiarity a bedrock in the face of religious turmoil.

The linguistic conservatism of much sixteenth- and seventeenth-century liturgical translation is underlined in the rules set for the translators of the King James Bible.[19] The first rule stipulated, 'The ordinary Bible read in the Church, commonly called the Bishops' Bible, to be followed, and as little altered as the truth of the original will permit'. The second required 'The names of the prophets, and the holy writers, with the other names of the text, to be retained, as near as may be, accordingly as they are vulgarly used'. The third demanded 'The old ecclesiastical words to be kept, *viz.*: the word "Church" not to be translated as "Congregation" etc.', referring to a controversy about the translation of specific biblical terms that had been rumbling since William Tyndale preferred 'congregation' over 'church' in his translation of the New Testament, first published in 1525.[20] Religious 'truth' here appears to reside in form as much as content. The overall aim of the King James Bible is set out clearly in a report to the Synod of Dort: 'In the first place caution was given that an entirely new version was not to be furnished, but an old version, long received by the Church, to be purged from all blemishes and faults.'[21] As we have seen, the goal of producing not a 'new' translation but a newly improved 'old' one was achieved partly though conserving the vocabulary and syntax of earlier translations and partly through introducing new archaisms modelled on those of the earlier translations. The archaism of the Anglican Bible was a conscious strategy, and one that ran counter to prevailing aesthetics.[22]

This strategy of archaising simplicity was itself long established. Archbishop Matthew Parker instructed the contributors to the Bishops' Bible (1568) 'to followe the Commune Englishe Translacion vsed in the Churches and not to reede from yt but wher yt varieth maifestlye from

the Hebrue or Greke orginall'.[23] His 1567 edition of the Psalms includes
a poem, 'Of the Vertue of Psalms', in which he defends the use of
old-fashioned vocabulary in the following translations:

> Conceyue in hart: no griefe to sore,
>   wordes olde so ofte to vewe:
> Thy gayne therby: is wrought the more,
>   though wordes be neuer newe.
>
> How can we féele: sacietie,
>   in fourmes of godly speache:
> The soule which féelth: aduersitie,
>   loues playnes health to seache.[24]

Parker self-consciously juxtaposes polysyllabic, Latinate words such as
'satiety' and 'adversity' with the monosyllables that he prefers in his own
writing, and he specifically defends his use of 'old' words, suggesting that
they have an inherent worth and emotional authenticity lacking in more
gaudy linguistic display. His use of common measure in the poem also
associates it with Psalm translation itself, casting both as part of a longer
tradition, and a particular, Anglican, aesthetic.

Thus, a powerful tendency within sixteenth- and seventeenth-century
culture associated religious language with linguistic stasis – itself associated
with the timelessness of religious truth – and with aesthetic and cultural
conservatism. This was not, however, the only approach to the temporality
of religious language. Gregory Martin, translator of the Catholic New
Testament published in Rheims in 1582, rejected the plain style and the
now-familiar diction of the Protestant translations in favour of new,
Latinate coinages. He outlines his intentions:

> we wish it to be most sincere, as becommeth a Catholike translation, and
> haue endeuoured so to make it: we are very precise & religious in
> folowing our copie, the old vulgar approued Latin: not onely in sense,
> which we hope we always doe, but sometime in the very wordes also and
> phrases, which may seeme to the vulgar Reader & to common English
> eares not yet acquainted therewith, rudeness or ignorance: but to the
> discrete Reader that deeply weigheth and considereth the importance of
> sacred wordes and speaches, and how easily the voluntarie Translatour
> may misse the true sense of the Holy Ghost, we doubt not but our
> consideration and doing therein, shal seeme reasonable and necessarie:
> yea and that al sortes of Catholike Readers wil in short time thinke that
> familiar, which at the first may seeme strange, & wil esteeme it more,
> when they shal otherwise be taught to vnderstand it, then if it were the
> common knowen English.[25]

Martin's linguistic approach differs crucially from that of his Protestant counterparts. Rejecting 'the common knowen English', he seeks the origins of religious 'truth' in the long-established Latin Vulgate, and he thus employs Latinate diction rather than the archaic 'English' forms of the Anglican liturgy. While Latinate language is – like Parker's archaism – a marker of authenticity, authenticity here lies in the translator's stylistic imitation of his source text, the 'old vulgar approued Latin' or 'authentical Latin', as the title-page calls it, which he prefers to the Greek and Hebrew texts favoured by Tyndale and the other Protestant translators.

Despite his confidence that the Latinate terms will become familiar to English Catholics, Martin nonetheless acknowledges the risk that they may alienate readers, including an appendix in the back of the volume, 'The Explication of Certaine VVordes in this Translation' (5E2r–v). The appendix demonstrates Martin's vulnerability to the inevitable attack from Protestant propagandists: that his English was not truly 'English', but a Romish counterfeit. William Fulke includes a mocking reprint of it in his 1583 confutation of the Rheims translation, and he comments on the passage quoted above, 'Not the desire of sinceritie, but rather of obscuritie, hath made you to thrust in a great number of words … you affect noueltie of wordes, to obscure the Gospel, as much as you can'.[26] Obscurity and neologism, according to Fulke, are deliberate tactics: there may now be a Catholic translation of the Bible, but it is one that the majority of Catholics cannot readily understand. As late as 1625 James Hyatt criticised the Rheims translation for speaking 'to the common people in an vnknowne tongue, and vsing such an affected sublimitie of phrase, and such a Romish English (as one fitly calls it) that plaine Englishmen can no more vnderstand what is spoken, then if he that preacheth, were a Barbarian to them, and they to him', singling out the use of 'absolete and barbarous wordes'.[27] For Hyatt, Latinate neologisms are obsolete because they are not capable of being understood by their intended audience; they are, he implies, the diametric opposite of 'plain' English, meaning that 'Romish English' is merely a debased dialect, with no true claim to represent the English nation.

Protestant translators were, nonetheless, similarly open to charges of neologism. As we have seen, Tyndale was attacked for translating the Greek *ekklesia* as 'congregation', and he was also criticised for rendering the Greek *presbuter* as 'senior' or (in the 1534 version) 'elder' rather than 'priest', and *agape* as 'love' rather than 'charity'.[28] In 1583, the year after the publication of the Rheims New Testament, William Rainolds defended

its Latinate approach by attacking Protestant translations as 'newfangled',
and it is clear that he still has Tyndale in mind:

> For looke what old words you haue vpon newfanglednes (as it might seeme)
> altered and taken out of the Bible by the working of Satan, those verie
> thinges you haue remoued from the hartes of men, and cast out of the
> churches which you haue inuaded. With the name *priest*, went away the
> office of *priest*, with the *altar*, that which was the proper seruice of God, &
> done at the *altar*. with taking away the word *penance*, you haue withdrawen
> the people from al *doyng of penance*, and in altering the word *church*, you
> haue cut them cleane from the *church*, & more estraunged them from the
> communion of it, then some barbarous and faithles nations that neuer
> heard of Christ.[29]

In Rainolds' view, when the translators alter words they signal their
intention to do away with the things themselves. For Catholic and
Protestant translators alike, there is a fine line between authenticity and
corruption; neologistic or iconoclastic approaches to the Bible might be
presented as a return to source, but they might also expose translators to
the accusation that they were merely perverting the biblical text and
turning it to polemic ends, using words to alter practices.

   Doing away with old words provoked anxiety, but archaism in religious
diction might itself cause unease because it could draw attention to the
existence of linguistic change and instability. In a treatise first published in
Latin in 1597, the Scottish preacher Robert Rollock attempts to counter
such anxieties, commenting that 'the whole translation needes no renuing,
but some words which happily are become obsolete and out of vse'.[30]
Rollock seems to be at ease with the idea of updating translations when
necessary; at any rate, he does not seem to think that the potential future
obsolescence of individual words is a reason not to translate at all. By the
mid-seventeenth century, the need to 'renew' obsolete words in religious
texts was more pressing. William Barton, quoted above, attacks the
'unseemly phrases' of the Sternhold/Hopkins translation of the Psalms
and its 'Many obsolete words', referring caustically to the 'ruines of an old
Psalm-book'.[31] Similarly, in an account of debates surrounding the 'review
and alteration' of the Book of Common Prayer in the early 1660s, Richard
Baxter summarises Presbyterian requirements 'That all obsolete words in
the Common-Prayer, and such whose use is changed from their first
significancy ... may bee altered unto other words generally received, and
better understood'.[32]

   As Baxter's comments suggest, the obscurity of old words was not the
only problem: they could, in addition, take on meanings unintended by

the original authors or translators. This anxiety often focused on words in the translations that had taken on sexual connotations. Baxter urged that 'obsolete Phrases [*With my Body I thee Worship*, &c.] should be changed'; here, the phrase is apparently 'obsolete' because it recalls the supposed crudity of an earlier age, rather than because the individual words themselves have become obscure.[33] Henry Jessey, a Nonconformist minister who was heavily involved with plans for a revision of the King James Bible in the early 1650s, similarly advocated reform on the grounds that 'Obscure words should be made more plain for mean people to understand, of which many instances might be made, but we shall onely (for brevity sake) mention this one old word [*Occupy*] which hath various significations'. Jessey mentions that 'occupy' could mean '*trade, or traffic*', 'occupied' '*used or wrought with*', 'occupyeth' '*supplyeth or fills*' and '*that have been occupied therein*' '*that have walked about therein*'.[34] Implicit, however, is the fact that 'occupy' – like 'shame' – had sexual connotations, a usage that became more common during the seventeenth century. As David Norton suggests, the King James Bible 'was not only somewhat archaic (Jessey's ostensible point) but insensitive in retaining "occupy", which sounded lewd to dirty ears'.[35]

It was not only the vocabulary of liturgical texts that was vulnerable to archaism. As noted above, the dominant metre used in the Sternhold/Hopkins psalter, and its effect on other aspects of language, was also criticised. The Psalms tread water between liturgical text and poetry, and they were thus put under pressure on both religious and aesthetic grounds. In the early seventeenth century, Hall singled out the metre of the Psalms for criticism, writing, 'to say truth, I neuer could see good verse written in the wonted measures. I euer thought them most easie, and least Poeticall'; Wither similarly attacked those 'who allow of *Metre* but will give way to no new *versions*'.[36] A generation later, the pressures had increased. In 1651, Henry King complained that he tied himself '*to the old Meter and old Tunes*' in an attempt not to alienate '*the Congregation, perfect in their antient Tunes*'; his aim was to render the Psalms

> rather with perspicuity and plainesse for the vulgar use, then Elegance. For this the disadvantage of the Measure (of All others least gracefull) wherein most of the Psalmes run, allowes not: especially when by designe I deny my selfe the liberty of those words and Phrases, which either suit not the Gravity of the Subject, or capacity of the Meanest[.][37]

King chafes against the restrictions and the perceived aesthetic limitations of common measure. However, writers nonetheless continued to use common measure, many, like King, being swayed by the familiarity of such forms among congregations; as I. M. Green argues, people 'may well have come to regard metrical Psalms as a kind of folk music'.[38] To use common measure between the 1590s and the 1650s was thus to draw on a collective history, a shared heritage, and a powerful affective connection between present and past.

The use of archaism in liturgical texts, in its varied forms, thus suggests a complex network of associations. Archaism gives a translation authority and roots it in English linguistic history, something that was particularly important for the Protestant translators; it also lends it simplicity and familiarity, creating an affective bond between text and reader and binding together past and present in an immutable and timeless space. Yet, at the same time, the retention of archaic forms within liturgical texts could leave them open to charges of aesthetic barrenness – as in the case of the Psalms – or even obscenity. Nonetheless, liturgical archaism paved the way for the use of outmoded style in the work of both Catholic and Protestant poets, and it became a crucial means through which writers could express religious identity and emotion, make claims to both authority and national identity, and negotiate the place of the individual believer in the face of apocalyptic revelation.

Catholic poets and the plain style

As we have seen, Catholic translators of the Bible in the 1580s rejected the archaising plain style of their Protestant counterparts. Some Catholic poets nonetheless used archaism and plainness as a means of negotiating the tensions between national identity and confessional allegiance. As Christopher Highley points out, early modern Catholicism is often viewed as 'antithetical to the very idea of English nationhood', and is instead associated predominantly with continental counter-Reformation culture.[39] However, Highley convincingly argues that both Catholic exiles and those who remained in England actively asserted their English nationhood and identity. Something of this project can be seen in the publication and translation of Anglo-Saxon texts such as Bede's *Historia ecclesiastica gentis Anglorum*, as both Catholics and Protestants attempted to lay claim to the early English church.[40] But an implicit negotiation of Englishness and the national past through archaic style can be seen elsewhere, in the use of outmoded poetic conventions in the English poetry of the Catholic poets Robert Southwell and Gertrude More. Both of these writers spent the bulk of their lives outside England. Southwell, a Jesuit priest, passed most of his adult life on the continent before embarking on a mission to England that ended with his execution in 1595.[41] More left England in 1623, at the age of seventeen, to enter the English Benedictine Abbey of Our Lady of Consolation at Cambrai, which her father, Cresacre More, had financially endowed; she died there from smallpox in 1633.[42] Although a generation apart, Southwell and More thus shared a religious vocation and a life conditioned by official hostility towards Catholicism, and they both use stylistic archaism as a means of negotiating the potentially competing demands of faith and nation.

In both his poetry and prose, Southwell stresses his loyalty to England despite the state's hostility towards his religion and towards him specifically as a Jesuit priest. *An Humble Supplication*, his response to Elizabeth's 1591 proclamation against Jesuits and seminary priests, stresses the Englishness of his fellow priests and casts their attempts to convert England to Catholicism as the utmost expression of patriotism:

> if wee seeke with out deepest perrills to plant it in our Realme, and to winne soules from misbeleefe vnto it, we thinke that we owe a most sincere, and naturall love vnto our Countrie: for euen by Christs own testimonie, no mans Charitie reacheth to any higher point, then to yeeld his life for the benefit of his friend.[43]

The repeated use of 'our' – 'our Realme', 'our Countrie' – underlines Southwell's allusion to John 15:13: 'Greater loue then this no man hath, that a man yeld his life for his frendes.'[44] England is presented as an erring friend for whom the Jesuit mission is prepared to sacrifice all.

The very decision to write poetry in English was loaded. Anne Sweeney points out that for Southwell's generation of priests, 'Latin was the language of the angels, while the vernacular was a weapon of war'.[45] To express religious devotion in English was therefore in some respects to enter enemy territory, and to fight his opponents with their own weapons. Although – or perhaps because – English was a 'weapon of war', Southwell was alert to its stylistic effects, and the specifics of the forms that he adopts are crucial. His poems are in many ways out of kilter with the literary fashions of their day, despite their posthumous popularity and the professed admiration of poets such as Ben Jonson for his most famous poem, 'The Burning Babe', and his style is resolutely 'English' rather than Latinate or baroque.[46] As Sweeney notes, Southwell did not employ a baroque style in most of his English poems; on the contrary, he developed a 'poetically narrated, scriptural passion-play that he suited to the English cultural climate'.[47] It is telling, in this context, that Edmund Bolton – who, as we saw in Chapter 2, was sceptical about Spenser's style – praised

Southwell's poems, 'the *English* whereof as it is most proper, so the sharpness, and Light of Wit is very rare in them'.[48] Bolton found Southwell's English not alien but familiar and correct.

Stylistic archaism is a crucial means through which Southwell achieves this effect of familiarity. He uses common measure extensively, as in 'Seek Flowers of Heaven':

> Soare upp my soule unto thy reste
>   Cast of this loathsome loade
> Long is the date of thy exile
>   Too long thy strait aboade
> Graze not on worldly withered weede
>   It fitteth not thy taste
> The flowres of everlasting spring
>   Do growe for thy repaste.[49]

As we have seen, common measure was strongly associated with English Protestantism and with the ballad. When Southwell adopts it he makes a certain kind of claim to national identity, one mirrored by Catholic ballads, which also adopted common measure. As Alison Shell comments, 'Catholics had an underdog's interest in exploiting oral methods of communication', including ballads, 'methods which were versatile, labile and difficult to censor';[50] appropriating the ballad allowed writers to mediate between Protestant and Catholic, spiritual and secular, elite and popular cultures.

Southwell also, however, employs other archaising techniques alongside common measure. I will pause here over one poem, 'A Child my Choice', which first appeared in print in the hugely popular collection *Saint Peter's Complaint* (1595) and is also to be found in manuscripts associated with Catholic households, such as the Waldegrave manuscript, now held at Stonyhurst College.[51] The poem reads:

> Let folly praise that phancy loves I praise and love that childe
> Whose hart no thought, whose tong no word, whose hand no deed defilde
> I praise him most I love him best all prayse and love is his
> While him I love in him I live and cannot lyve amisse
> Loves sweetest mark, lawdes highest theme, mans most desired light
> To love him life to leave him death to live in him delighte.
> He myne by gift I his by debt thus ech to other Dewe
> First frende he was best frende he is all tymes will try him trewe.
> Though yonge yet wise though small yet strong though man yet god he is
> As wise he knowes, as stronge he can as god he loves to blisse
> His knowledge rules his strength defendes his love doth cherish all

His birth our joye, his life our light, his death our end of thrall
Alas he weepes he sighes he pantes yet do his Angells singe
Out of his teares his sighes and throbbs doth bud a joyfull springe
Almightie babe whose tender armes can force all foes to flye
Correct my faultes, protect my life direct me when I die.[52]

Strikingly, Southwell employs fourteener couplets, a form that had been popular in poetry and drama of the 1560s and 1570s, but was falling out of fashion in the 1580s and had become almost obsolete by the 1590s. Since Southwell uses other metrical forms elsewhere, it is not simply a question of the exile being unaware of developments in English poetry. Instead, Southwell chooses the metre specifically because of its associations with English poetry, just as George Chapman would choose it for his translation of the *Iliad* later in the 1590s.

Southwell handles the fourteener with deceptive ease. He does not always break the line into the conventional eight and six pattern, with a caesura after the eighth syllable; instead, it often falls into triplets in a four, four, six pattern (see ll. 5, 9), and it thereby resists the 'swing' to which the long line is prone. The fourteener also enables Southwell to make extensive use of repetition within the long line. Words are repeated, as in 'I praise him most I love him best all prayse and love is his' (l. 3), and he also reproduces the same syntactic structure with different nouns and verbs; this occurs both within the line, as in 'Whose hart no thought, whose tong no word, whose hand no deed defilde' (l. 2), and across lines, as in 'Alas he weepes he sighes he pantes yet do his Angells singe / Out of his teares his sighes and throbbs doth bud a joyfull springe' (ll. 13–14). Southwell's extensive use of alliteration may also have registered as outmoded in the 1590s. In line 6, for instance, we find a studied patterning of 'l' and 'd', the latter introduced in the second half of the line: 'To love him life to leave him death to live in him delighte'. Similarly, the use of monosyllables and very few polysyllabic words is at odds with the fashionable norms of 1590s poetry. The cumulative effect is to create an apparently 'plain' style that is in fact very tightly controlled and patterned, and to produce new poems that are also, simultaneously, 'old'.

There is a specific context for Southwell's stylistic and metrical archaism, one that alerts us to the affective and polemic uses to which aspects of English style might be put. As I will explore in greater detail in Chapter 6, the fourteener had an established reputation within English literary culture and as a poetic signifier of national identity, and was widely referred to as 'English' metre; common measure had taken on similar associations as a result of its use in Psalms and ballads. A connection with 'Englishness' was also thought to adhere to the use of monosyllables. To quote George Puttenham, discussing stress patterns in English: 'in words monosyllable, which be for the more part our natural Saxon English, the accent is indifferent, and may be used for sharp or flat and heavy at our pleasure. I say Saxon English, for our Norman English alloweth us very many bissyllables, and also trissyllables, as: *reverence, diligence, amorous, desirous,* and such like'.[53] Drawing a line between 'Saxon English' monosyllables and 'Normane English' polysyllables, Puttenham suggests that the former might be associated with an ancient or authentic 'English' aesthetic or acoustic. The truth of Puttenham's argument can be seen in the ways in which the monosyllable was used in seventeenth-century poetry.[54] The Jacobean poet John Beaumont argued that 'Our Saxon shortnesse hath peculiar grace / In choise of words, fit for the ending place', advice that Southwell follows in 'Seek Flowers of Heaven' and 'A Child my Choice'.[55] In 1620 William Loe, pastor of the English Church in Hamburg, published a volume of biblical paraphrases written entirely in monosyllables and common measure; he comments in his preface that he sought '*to knovve vvhether vve might express our harts to god in our holy soliloquies by monasillables in our ovvne mother tongue, or no*', arguing that monosyllables were the '*true idiome*' of English '*vntill it came to be blended, and mingled vvith the commixture of Exotique languages*'.[56] Sincere religious expression, he argues, demands the use of 'true' English. Southwell's poetry, like Parker's poem on the Psalms, thus foregrounds what Puttenham calls 'natural Saxon English' rather than the affected Latinate or 'blended' diction favoured by more courtly or pretentious poets.

One of the functions of poems such as 'A Childe my Choyce' and 'Seeke Flowers of Heaven', therefore, is to create an aesthetic for Catholic poetry that is both accessible and plain, and also, subliminally, comfortingly 'English'. In a recent essay, Sadia Abbas critiques the assumption that Southwell's style indicates an estrangement from his native tongue; on the contrary, she argues,

> Southwell's tendency to use heavy alliteration, fourteeners, and versions of poulter's measure could, and I believe should, be as easily interpreted as evidence of his cultivation of a native, English, medieval style ... Southwell appears to have chosen a vernacular, alliterative style not only as a repudiation of contemporary poetic practice but also because such a style makes a statement about continuity and patriotism.[57]

Although I would dispute Abbas's characterisation of Southwell's style as 'medieval', given that the fourteener, poulter's measure and common measure are all strongly associated with Tudor aesthetics, she rightly highlights the extent to which the poet simultaneously rejects late Elizabethan poetic norms and lays a claim to the historical, religious and cultural past. The contrast with the Rheims Bible, with its attempt to bypass contemporary English by returning to the Vulgate's Latin, is marked, but Southwell's archaising poems have a similar polemic purpose: he reclaims Catholicism as English, and England and the English as Catholic.

Southwell's verse may have established a pattern among Catholic poets, for similar procedures can be seen in the work of Gertrude More a generation later. Caroline Bowden points out that English nuns on the continent asserted both the English national identity of the convents and 'their sense of a mission to preserve English Catholicism' through their use of vernacular texts, which had the function of 'emphasising both Englishness and a sense of continuity with the distant past in England'.[58] It is therefore unsurprising that More should write poetry in English, and that she should follow Southwell's example by challenging the claim of Protestant poets to archaic forms such as common measure.

More's poems were produced within a culture of meditation and of submission to God's authority, precepts in which Father Augustine Baker, the controversial spiritual adviser to the Abbey at Cambrai, had instructed her.[59] Baker also collected and edited More's works, which circulated in manuscript and were printed two decades after her death.[60] Many of the poems were gathered as 'Confessiones Amantis. The Confessions of a Louing & Pious Soule to Allmighty God', a title seemingly given to them by Baker, and they are appended to More's lengthy defence of her spiritual adviser, 'This Devout Souls Advertisement to the Reader'.[61] The 'Confessiones Amantis', which More apparently referred to as 'Amor ordinem nescit and Ideots deuotions', are modelled on St Augustine of Hippo's *Confessions*, and in them More interweaves prose meditations and poems written in common measure. The first confession is typical of this technique, the poem summarising and crystallising the prose section:

> O that all *loues* might be wholy conuerred to *thee*! At least lett those who haue dedicated themselues to *thee*, cease to desire any thing out of *thee*; Send them meanes to know how sweet it is to haue no friend but *thee*, and to be neglected by all but *thy* sweet mercy.

> > *O can that soule that* loues *her* God
> > *For very shame complaine*
> > *To any other then* himselfe
> > *Of what she doth sustaine!*

No way to her was euer sound,
       Nor euer shall there be,
But taking vp thy Crosse my Lord,
       Thereby to follow thee.
This is the Way, the Truth, the Life,
       Which leadeth vnto heauen,
None is secure, but only this,
       Though seeming nere so euen.[62]

Like Southwell's, More's language is simple and direct, employing plain, non-Latinate diction, and depending upon the balance of monosyllables and disyllables.

Arthur Marotti argues that this 'deliberate artlessness' is 'part of a strategy of self-effacing religious plain-speaking consistent with Baker's and More's ideals of contemplative prayer, which included an avoidance of distracting sensuous particularity'.[63] However, this interpretation of the aesthetic impact of More's poetry is perhaps challenged, or at least complicated, by some of the poems, such as that addressed to St Augustine himself. More writes,

> I haue no friend to speake, or treat with but *thee*, and some of thy Saints, to whom *thou* hast giuen charge of me, and to whom I fly when my sinnes affright me; amongst whom next after thy Deare Mother, the Queene of mercy, is my beloued *S. Augustine.*

O Glorious Saint *whose hart did burne,*
       And flame with Loue *Diuine,*
Remember me most sinnefull wretch,
       Who hunger staru'd doth pine.
For want of that which thou enioyest
       In such aboundant measure;
It is my God *that I doe meane,*
       My ioy, *and all my* treasure.
Thy words O *Saint are truly sweet,*
       Because thou dost addresse
Them vnto him *who's only meet*
       Our mis'ries to redresse.   (2: 13)

Like many religious poets, More fuses erotic and divine imagery; the difference here is that Augustine rather than the speaker is portrayed as 'flaming' with the love of God, a love that gives him the power to act as an intermediary for the 'starved' wretch. Further, in her use of common measure, More creates a powerful synthesis of the Catholic meditative tradition and the Protestant Psalm tradition; there is a marked irony in the use of this form for a poem on the intercession of saints, as More self-consciously fuses Catholic practices and Protestant aesthetics.

In doing so, moreover, More encroaches on Protestant territory. Her poetry has significant affinities with that of Protestant contemporaries such as Ann Collins, Ann Montagu, Elizabeth Richardson and Frances Cooke. All of these poets use common measure, and Elizabeth Clarke and Jonathan Gibson suggest that the metre's connection with the Psalms may have reinforced the idea that this was 'legitimate rhetorical endeavour', suitable for both religious subject matter and for the female poet.[64] The contexts in which their work appeared encourage such an interpretation. Richardson's 'My owne Prayer in Meeter' appears in a book of prayers and meditations, entitled *A Ladies Legacy to her Daughters* (1645);[65] Cooke's 'A Psalm Gathered out of the Psalms of David' is appended to *Mistress Cooke's Meditations*, a volume celebrating her close escape on the Irish Seas in 1650;[66] and Collins' appear in *Divine Songs and Meditations* (1653).

The Catholic More perhaps has a different, more oppositional relation to Psalm tradition. Like Southwell's, her work stakes a claim to English identity, rather than assuming it as a right. Common measure becomes a space for contestation, similar to the physical spaces – such as churches, the court, the scaffold, the bed, the household and the prison – described by Frances E. Dolan and Anthony Milton in their accounts of Stuart Catholicism.[67] Like physical spaces, literary forms are 'saturated with meaning' and Catholics' 'politically charged attitude towards space' also extends to textual expression.[68] While English Protestants occupied the ecclesiastical spaces formally used for Catholic ritual, English Catholics occupied the metrical spaces established by Protestant translations. More's work thus appears to appropriate the decorous religious voice of Protestant women, turning it to alternative devotional ends, rather than fully inhabiting it.

Radical Protestantism and prophecy

It is too simple, however, merely to sketch a contrast between decorous and unthreatening Protestant poetry and appropriative Catholic poetry in relation to the use of common measure. In addition to using common measure in devotional meditation, Protestant women also used it in the more politically and socially disruptive context of prophecy. The combination of prophecy and archaism is a potent one. As Angus Fletcher writes, certain kinds of prophecy balance 'anticipation of the future with a concern for the past and, even more important, for the present', their method is 'to hold the eternal and the ephemeral in simultaneous copresence'.[69] Furthermore, as Sue Wiseman argues of Anna Trapnel's works, the prophet is permitted by the form's conventions 'to encode in Biblical language a criticism of the present which is offered as underwritten by God'.[70] The topical and the eternal are held in productive suspension, aided by the trans-temporal associations of biblical language and style. Thus, it is appropriate that prophetic poetry should employ archaism, drawing on its associations with biblical language and with the past, and on its potential – through the active *recreation* of older modes – to gesture towards the future. Casting a prophecy in common measure allows poets to link their work with culturally resonant forms such as the ballad and, especially, the Psalm; given that the Psalms themselves were often viewed as prophetic works, the combination is particularly appropriate. As Erica Longfellow points out, the Psalm is 'variously a song of praise, instruction, a polemical statement of doctrine and prophecy of forthcoming events'.[71] This powerfully mixed message is crucial to poets' use of common measure in prophecy, in which the archaic metrical form underlines their desire to speak to and on behalf of a popular audience.

An early example of the use of common measure in prophecy is that of Jane Hawkins of St Ives, Cambridgeshire, a fragment of whose verse prophecies survive in the state papers dealing with her case.[72] On 28 April 1629 John Williams, Bishop of Lincoln, wrote to Dudley Carleton, Viscount Dorchester, Secretary of State, with an account of Hawkins' prophecies. According to Williams,

> in a rapture or extasie, into the wch she fell the .24. of March last past, [Hawkins] hath uttered straunge thinges in verse (wch she will not confesse she could ever make before or can doe nowe) in matters of divinitie, and state ... Fayninge herself in a trau*n*ce, she began (like the Eleventh Sibill) to preach in verse. But not any thinge (as the report went) concerning the state or the Governme*n*t of the Church. But onely by waye of Aunswer to private Temptations of hir owne, and magnifienge the Ministrye of M^r. Tokey (the viccar) and his power (togeither with Christs) in gettinge hir the victorye over Sathan[.][73]

The bishop claims that Hawkins uttered her poetry for three days and three nights, to an audience of nearly 200 people, most of them women. He describes the process through which the prophecies were taken down, and the apparent plans of the vicar, Job Tookey, to disseminate them:

> The viccar, and one M^r. Wise, his wise Curat, and another scholler, sitting composedlye at the beds feete, and coppienge out the verses, wch the poore weoman (for she is but a pedlar) did dictate, w^ch (amountinge to so*m*me

thousands) they had transcribed and written over fayre, wth intent to print and divulge them, when comminge thither suddenlye I seazed upon the Coppye and the Originalls.

Williams is at pains to discredit Hawkins, describing her as 'a wittye and a craftie Baggage. And the chief in this Imposture'. He declines to enclose any of the verses, on the grounds that 'there is nothinge in them relatinge to the state', saying that 'Sometimes they are in Rime, but seldom in any reason'.

Yet Williams' attitude towards the verse prophecies and their author is inconsistent. Within the letter he claims that they are both the product of private grievances and ambition, and 'straunge thinges in verse ... in matters of divinitie, and state'. Similarly, Hawkins herself is both 'the chief in this Imposture' and the tool of more powerful and ambitious men. Williams thus appears to be caught in a double bind, keen both to downplay the importance of Hawkins' utterances and to emphasise the need for his swift action in suppressing them. The bishop's late-seventeenth-century biographer, John Hacket, in contrast, claims that Hawkins' verses were 'full of Detraction and Injury to the Authority of the Bishops, to the Church-way of *England* in the Liturgy, and not sparing some Occurrences of the Civil Government', arguing that Hawkins had indeed sought to criticise the established church.[74]

Williams eventually persuaded Tookey publicly to reject Hawkins and her prophecies, and he reported to Dorchester on 5 May, '(as I am enformed) it hath fully satisfied those people, and that they crye out against the weoman, for this Imposture'.[75] This time, he enclosed a section of the verses, commenting, 'All that, may haue any reflection upon the states, I haue transcribed & enclosed in this peece of paper'. The enclosed verses read:

> O lett it bee for euer told
> to ages that suceed
> That they may lay it vp in store
> for then will bee most need.
> When that you see these fearfull times
> W^ch now in *parte* you feare,
> For they are sure to come to vs
> o they draw wondrous neare.
> And then (good truth) you may beleiue,
> I take it still for grant,
> that punishment will follow sinn
> & euer will it haunte.

And therefore now in shortest speech
o labour to beleiue
least afterwards it bee too late,
when you so sore shall greiue.[76]

If this extract is representative, Hawkins' verses positioned the prophet as the mediator between past, present and future, appealing to 'ages that suceed' and addressing the sinful and fearful 'you' of the present day, a collective which by implication includes powerful clerics such as Williams himself. The use of common measure, with its links to both ballads and Psalms, underlines the appeal to a broad, popular audience, which is also signalled in the repeated use of the vocative or intensifying 'O'.

Hawkins' appeal to a popular audience is also suggested by Hacket, who writes that Hawkins

> utter'd such Brainless Verses, as might justifie the common Ballads of the City; and was as bad at an *English* Verse, as the old Monks were at a *Latin*, stufft with such frigid Jests, as were able to cool the Bath ... Yet the more vile and plain, they lik'd the better with the rural Hobs: and would have spread into Fairs, and Markets, and been sung by Fidlers Boys, if it had not been prevented.[77]

The comparison that Hacket draws between Hawkins' verses and 'the common Ballads of the City' suggests that he was alert to their form and its implications. His allusion to the Latin verses of pre-Reformation monks suggests both his desire to dismiss Hawkins and his uneasy awareness of the political uses to which her verses might be put. Simultaneously, he insinuates that it is the prophecies' very plainness that might enable their circulation. Although he strenuously asserts the aesthetic worthlessness of Hawkins' verses, Hacket nonetheless fears that they could have had a broad appeal, given the chance to circulate within the local and, perhaps, national community. In exploiting common measure's association with ballad forms, Hawkins thus gives her prophecies a dangerously populist appeal.

In 1629 it was relatively easy for Williams to suppress Hawkins' prophetic verses and to force her supporters to recant, and apocalyptic and millenarian prophecies were also suppressed elsewhere in Caroline England.[78] In the fervid atmosphere of the 1640s and 1650s suppression was no longer so easy, and – as scholars have described in detail – a number of prominent female prophets emerged, including Mary Cary, Elinor Channel, Katherine Chidley, Lady Eleanor Davies, Anna Trapnel and Sarah Wight.[79] While many of these prophecies are in prose, a number also use verse. Common measure appears sporadically in the work of Davies,[80] and more extensively in that of Trapnel, whose published texts fuse the prophetic tradition exemplified by Jane Hawkins and the meditative traditions with which Gertrude More, Elizabeth Richardson, Frances Cooke and Ann Collins are associated. It is perhaps no coincidence that Collins uses common measure in a poem entitled 'A Song Composed in the Time of the Cruel War, When the Wicked did Much Insult over the Godly', which opens with the lines, 'VVith *Sibells* I cannot Devine / Of future things to treat', an ironic glance at the activities of her contemporaries.[81]

Trapnel's use of common measure also, however, intersects with the work of religious radicals such as the Ranters, Diggers, Quakers and, in particular, Fifth Monarchists. Fifth Monarchists believed that the fifth empire, the reign of King Jesus, as prophesied in the Book of Daniel, was imminent; Protectorate England was the last days before the coming of '*the Lord to his Temple*'.[82] They featured prominently in the Barebones Parliament of 1653, and were among the most disappointed by its dissolution and Cromwell's assumption of the title of Lord Protector. Crucially, as Holstun argues, Fifth Monarchists 'differed from so many of their contemporaries not by the mere fact of their millenarianism, but by its specifically *popular* quality'.[83] Although they had some support from gentry allies, the majority of Fifth Monarchists were engaged in trades, especially the clothing trade, and they were widely assumed to be hostile to rank and social hierarchy. In one of his *Aenigmatical Characters*, published in 1654, Richard Flecknoe suggests that a '*Fifth Monarchy Man*' 'is more familiar with the *Lord*, than to stand on *Ceremonies* with him any more; and he so hates a *Gentleman*, as he can't endure *God* should be served like one'.[84]

Archaic forms were central to the Fifth Monarchists' project of religious and social plainness. Flecknoe may allude to the Fifth Monarchists and Quakers' insistence on addressing their social superiors with the familiar 'thou' rather than the respectful 'you'. In 1651 the Quaker George Fox was brought before a magistrate and 'because I did not put off my hat and said Thou to him, he asked the man that rode thither before me whether I was not mazed or fond; but the man told him, no, it was my principle'.[85] Similarly, when Thomas Venner and his fellow Fifth Monarchists were brought before Cromwell in 1657, it was said that they would 'not put off their hats to the Protector, and *thou* him at every word that they speak to him'.[86] They thus revived an increasingly obsolete form of address and imbued it with new meaning and social power.[87] However, as linguists have noted, the sectarians' use of 'thou' appears to have hastened its decline among other English speakers; it became an ever-more-obvious signal of their refusal to move with linguistic fashion.[88]

Common measure was similarly linked to religious radicalism. While it appears sporadically in the work of Anglicans and royalists such as George Herbert and Henry Vaughan, it is found more often in the work of Nonconformists and republicans.[89] In *The Ranters Ranting*, published in 1650, John Reading associates common measure with the Ranters, claiming that they sang 'blasphemous songs in the tunes of *Davids* Psalms' and 'vile and filthy songs to the tune of Psalms, and uttered many oaths (or asseverations of oaths) and execrations'. He prints two songs, one of which is in common measure.[90] The description of the Ranters alternately singing profane songs to the tune of the Psalms and uttering blasphemous oaths functions in Reading's text as a grotesque parody, but the use of common measure also appears in more authentic works by radical writers. Gerrard Winstanley, leader of the Diggers, wrote verse in a variety of old-fashioned metres, including common measure, fourteeners and poulter's measure.[91] These poems are interspersed within Winstanley's prose texts and on their margins – for instance, on title-pages and as tailpieces – and they draw explicitly on key biblical prophecies such as those of Revelation, Daniel and Ezekiel. For instance, 'Commander in Chief is God Himself', which appears at the end of *The Breaking of the Day of God* (1650), includes six marginal glosses to Revelation and four to Daniel, and concludes with the lines, 'For now the Image of the Beast: / appears to act his part; / But he's a falling, and Saints shall sing / *Haleluja* with joy of heart.'[92]

Winstanley's work may have influenced the forms adopted by leading Fifth Monarchist writers later in the 1650s. Like Winstanley's, Fifth Monarchist works draw extensively on biblical prophecy, notably, but not exclusively, the Books of Daniel and Revelation. The title of Trapnel's first and best-known publication, *The Cry of a Stone* (1654), is taken from the apocryphal second book of Esidras (or Ezra), and she aligns herself with Elisha, who was given 'a double portion of thy spirit' by his father Elijah (2 Kings 2:9).[93] Vavasor Powell wrote a metrical paraphrase of Jeremiah, and Morgan Llwyd's poems include 'The Third Trumpet, or Last Alarm', its title drawing on Revelation 8:10.[94] Similarly, the common-measure Psalm was one of the few set forms not rejected by Fifth Monarchists, and they composed and extemporised their own Psalms and hymns. Trapnel and Llwyd use the form most extensively, but it also appears in the work of Powell and Christopher Feake, both of whom composed hymns in common measure.[95] Common measure is a crucial element in Fifth Monarchist style, one that underlines their commitment to plain speaking, to the commons and to republican ideals.

I focus here on the work of Trapnel and Llwyd, exploring in detail the formal qualities of their verse and the effects of archaic metres on its political and imaginative impact. My emphasis on form might seem counter-intuitive, given that Trapnel and Llwyd's poetry – like Gertrude More's – has traditionally been dismissed as doggerel. However, studies of Trapnel by scholars such as Pamela S. Hammons and Erica Longfellow, and reappraisals of Llwyd's English verse by Nigel Smith and John Kerrigan, support the view that there is more to their work in formal and aesthetic terms than has often been recognised.[96] Building on these studies, I analyse the archaising strategies of their poems – the use of common measure and the fourteener, and the 'Saxon' monosyllable – examining their role in four key areas of the Fifth Monarchist project and aesthetic: populism; the Psalm; plainness; and prophecy. In the writings of Trapnel and Llwyd stylistic archaism is part of a powerfully apocalyptic aesthetic, in which popular politics, involuntary and voluntary utterance, and lyricism and plain-speaking, are fused.

As described above, Fifth Monarchists challenged political elites and sought to reach a broad public. Trapnel's verse was composed in an atmosphere of fevered sensation, and it appears to have been part of a conscious strategy. In December 1653 she accompanied Powell to Whitehall, where he was examined for treason; following his release in January 1654, she was 'seized upon by the Lord' and produced a set of prophecies during the period of eleven days and twelve nights that she spent in a trance, alternately praying and rhapsodising in verse (*Cry of a Stone*, 1). Her words were taken down by one of her associates, who describes himself as 'the relator' and his work as '*a true and faithful Relation of so much as for some 7 or 8 dayes could be taken from her by a very slow and unready hand*' (a2v). Just as the Bishop of Lincoln and his biographer worried about the potential of Hawkins' verses to circulate in print, so Marchamont Nedham wrote to Cromwell on 7 February 1654 declaring that Trapnel's Fifth Monarchist supporters were planning 'to print her discourses & hymnes' and to send her around England. The 'prophesies and hymnes' are, he claims, 'unsufferably desperate against your highnes person, family, religion, friends, and the Government'; they may be 'frivolous in themselues, yet the vulgar is a superstitious Animal, naturally doting upon such vanities'.[97]

Nedham's concern was justified. The Whitehall prophecies were printed in *The Cry of a Stone, or a Relation of Something Spoken in Whitehall* (1654), the title-page of which describes them as 'Visions of GOD. RELATING To the *Governors, Army, Churches, Ministry, Vniversities*: And the whole NATION'. Reworked versions appeared in *Anna Trapnel's Report and Plea*,

printed later in 1654. A second book of prophecies was printed around 1658 in
a large folio, a far more prestigious format than the quartos of *The Cry of a
Stone* and *Anna Trapnel's Report and Plea*. Only one copy has survived,
without its title-page and, possibly, three other preliminary leaves.[98] The
volume includes comparatively little prose, and it collects prophetic
songs delivered in 1657–8.[99] The songs on the first fifty pages also appear
in *A Voice for the King of Saints and Nations*, published in quarto in 1657,
which was possibly intended for wider circulation than the folio book.[100]
These forms of production left their mark on Trapnel's work. As Matthew
Prineas has argued, she becomes 'increasingly concerned with the authority
and dissemination of her songs as *written* works', referring to them as 'books',
'scrolls' or 'records'.[101] She is also at times aware of the relator, telling him
at one point, 'O brother dear, then learn now / To be more nimble in your
Pen / To take this matter, and how, / In what manner it doth come down'
(Folio, 76). Trapnel's work is the product of both divine inspiration and a
specific set of human interactions. Like that of Hawkins, her verse is 'mediated writing' – to adopt Ramona Wray's term – produced through a set of
interactions between poet, amanuensis, supporters and printer, and it similarly aims to communicate with both the converted and a mass audience.[102]

In contrast, few of Llwyd's poems were printed, although others apparently circulated in manuscript.[103] Although they did not reach as broad a
public as Trapnel's, they nonetheless seek to forge connections across
a local and national community. Llwyd's community is based on common
knowledge and shared assumptions and beliefs, but it is also one that must
be carefully maintained. In 'An Appendix of the Letter Sent to the
Differing Brethren', he writes,

> Two woes are past, the third begins, the judge is now at hand
> the tides do turne, the nation reeles. stand now (yee faithfull) stand.
>
> Fine webs are spun, backslidings great, strange tryalls new are neare
> A mascked Pope dispute in some, be warnd my brethren deare.
>
> Lett us hold fast with hand & heart and foord the flowing streams
> Abide in love, and Christ will guide and keepe us from extreams.
>
> (*Gweithiau*, 16)

The successive appeals to 'yee faithfull' and 'my brethren deare' bind his
intended readers together, until they merge with the speaker in the 'us' of
the final stanza quoted here. While Llwyd seeks to bind his community
together through his verse, he also uses it to rebuke them. 'An Appendix'
opens with the line 'I am comanded to exhort, rebuke, convince, informe';

in 'The Third Trumpet, or Last Alarm', he addresses 'All yee that have an eare to heare'; and in 'Awake, O Lord, Awake Thy Saints' the penultimate stanza asks the churches 'why should yee kicke your brethren sweet / & bedstraw still embrace' (*Gweithiau*, 15, 52, 80). Trapnel speaks to some extent from within a community, as its representative looking out towards the nation, whereas Llwyd seeks to heal divisions within the community, or to attract others to it. Both poets, however, use common measure as a means of reaching a broad audience, and of forging affective connections with it.

Llwyd's poetry also raises questions about the nature of the community to which it appeals. While Trapnel's poetry – like that of Southwell and More – uses archaism in order to authenticate a particular branch of Christianity as 'English', the position of Llywd's work is more complex, given his Welsh nationality. In 'The Excuse', the opening section of his long meditation on the climactic year 1648, he self-consciously addresses England, Scotland and Wales in turn: 'All English swans that are alive and Scottish cuckowes sing / and some Welsh swallowes chirpe and chime to welcome pleasant spring' ('1648', *Gweithiau*, 18). Llwyd wrote the bulk of his literary prose works in Welsh, and his poems are occasionally bilingual, such as 'Come Wisdom Sweet', written in fourteener couplets:

> Come wisdome sweet, my spirit meet, for at thy feet I fall
> Oh chiefest thing, my wealth, my wing, my rest, my ring, my all.
>
> My love, my light, my song, my sight, my bread, my bright eternall one
> Hee doth not cease, to give increase, with Peace and ease in one
>
> Sinne Death and Satan (crabbed foes) are kings of woes and wrath
> (as wind, fire, brimstone joyne in one) our Christ all conquered hath
>
> O Drymmed cri, a wnaethem ni, pe basit ti o Dduw
> Heb ladd y tri, ath laddlodd di, in llwyddo ni i fyw.[104]   (*Gweithiau*, 37)

Llwyd uses the fourteener, strongly associated with English verse, to bring together his two languages, establishing stylistic patterns that extend from English into Welsh. In the first two stanzas, he sets up a pattern of internal rhymes within the fourteener line. These rhymes intensify in line 4 ('cease ... increase ... Peace ... ease') until they almost take over the entire line; they disappear or move to a different beat at the crisis point of the poem – Christ's conquest of Sin, Death and Satan – before returning to their former pattern in the final, Welsh stanza. The poem thus epitom-ises the ways in which the Fifth Monarchist project extended across England and Wales, and through his use of the archaic fourteener line Llwyd speaks for English and Welsh alike.

The Psalm and common measure are another means through which Fifth Monarchist poets seek to bind their public together and to speak for and to the nation. Llwyd composed paraphrases of the Psalms in both English and Welsh, and they are a pervasive influence on his work. Nonetheless, Trapnel is more self-conscious about her role as Psalmist and, as Longfellow notes in her fine account of Trapnel's work, she establishes her own authority through the connection that she draws between her 'singing' and the Psalms.[105] Trapnel repeatedly calls her songs '*Davids Psalm*' in the Folio songs,[106] and meditates self-consciously on their status:

> O the Psalm it is very choice,
> It is composed well:
> Souls, if you do consider it,
> It will your sins expel.
> It is a Psalm with a Doctrine,
> And with such reasons too,
> As the Application doth bring home,
> And sweetly apply to you.
> O it is a most royal Psalm,
> It doth come from the King;
> And tidings of its love it doth
> Unto your spirits bring.
> It is a very publick Psalm,
> It speaks to each and all
> O do not let one tittle of it
> Unto the ground then fall. (Folio, 118)

Trapnel insists that the entire Psalm genre is prophetic, stating that 'the Psalmist declares his works and word / By a Spirit of Prophecie' (Folio, 866). In using the common measure, therefore, Trapnel lays an implicit claim to divine authority, a claim that she reinforces with her explicit references to the Psalms' own status as prophecy. While her 'Psalm' is 'composed', it is not entirely clear who the composer is, and by the end of the section quoted here the 'publick' Psalm appears to have taken on its own agency.

The popular appeal of Fifth Monarchist poetry is underlined by the use of common measure and other archaising techniques, which become part of a performance of plainness. Further, in drawing on common measure's associations with the Psalms, both Trapnel and Llwyd exploit its relationship with song. The relator in *The Cry of a Stone* describes Trapnel as singing her prophetic songs or 'Hymnes', and she often casts herself as a singer within them. For instance, when she calls on Cromwell to repent and accept God's will, comparing him with the Hebrew general and judge Gideon, she tells him, '*Oh Gideon would that I could sing / a triumph here for thee*'

(*Cry of a Stone*, 53). Her prophecies also deploy the repetitions, exclamations and vocatives often found in religious song, and in one extended section in the Folio she constantly returns to a refrain of 'hallelujah', weaving other words – here, in particular, 'children' and 'Covenant' – in and out:

> O Lord, thou dost revive thy own,
> Thy revivings are great:
> O hallelujah that thou
> Thus carries to thy seat.
> O hallelujah to thee,
> Unto thy children:
> O hallelujah to thee
> For thy Covenant so new.
> For all things through the Covenant
> Thy children can do:
> Blessed be thou for the Covenant,
> Hallelujah we will sing;
> And for thy Covenant, O Lord,
> Thanksgiving we will bring.
> O hallelujah, O Lord,
> For thy most powerful grace,
> With hallelujah, O Lord,
> Thy Saints do thee embrace. (Folio, 749)[107]

Although Trapnel's metre is often irregular, the structure of these lines suggests that she pronounced 'hallelujah' with five syllables ('hal-e-lu-i-ah'), the word becoming a drawn-out expression of praise and joy; polysyllabic loan-words stand out against the plain 'Saxon' monosyllables that comprise much of the rest of the text.

A number of Llwyd's poems were intended to be sung by his congregation, and he uses similar techniques to Trapnel's, albeit within a tighter poetic structure; we might look, for instance, to the first and last stanzas of 'Great is our God':

> Great is our God and very kind.
>   Jehovah is his name
> Great is his word, his arme, his mind.
>   Great is his love and fame.
>
> . . .
>
> fill us with faith & make us strong
>   Teach us to know thy name.
> And since the worlds to thee belong
>   lord fill them with thy fame. (*Gweithiau*, 69, 70)

In the first stanza, the repetition of 'great' creates a circling effect, and this circle is completed in the final stanza, as Llwyd repeats the rhyme on 'name' and 'fame' with which he began. Again, the polysyllabic loan-word 'Jehovah' stands out in a sea of monosyllables and, like Trapnel, Llwyd uses common measure and the 'Saxon' monosyllable to create a paradoxical impression of ecstatic plain speaking.

The performance of plainness also inflects Fifth Monarchist verse in other ways. Trapnel's attacks on the university-educated clergy, and their hostility to inspired prophecy, take on a harsh, quasi-satiric voice, and she contrasts her song's lack of ornament with the inflated speech of the clergymen:

> You have so much of your fine Gold,
> And of your brave cloaths about,
> That the Lamb looks too mean for you
> That are of a high proud mouth.
> Prophesie speaks too plain for them,
> That makes them it disdain,
> Because it tells them of their faults,
> And deals with them so plain. (Folio, 58)[108]

The 'high proud mouth[s]' of the clergy are incapable of speaking with common measure's plain 'voice', which here aligns the speaker/poet with the 'mean' Lamb of God; Trapnel's claim that they are resistant to the asceticism of prophecy is part of her political and aesthetic point.

For Llwyd, common measure is similarly a crucial means through which he can create the impression of plain speech, but it is nonetheless part of a carefully crafted structure. He is comfortable enough with his 'hopping rime', as he terms it in '1648' (*Gweithiau*, 18), to experiment with it, using cross-rhyme as well as couplets and employing feminine endings in poems such as 'Some Dutch are Deep Suspicious Birds'. Llwyd often combines common measure with monosyllables, creating an aura of almost limpid calm; one poem reads, in its entirety,

> There's peace enough within,
> and worke enough to do,
> and strength enough to do the worke,
> and wages for it too.   (*Gweithiau*, 41)

The anaphora on 'and' has the same effect as it does in Protestant translations of the Bible, generating an impression of simplicity and plainness. Moreover, Llwyd frequently uses homely images to conjure instability, chaos or change: 'the nations are on potters wheeles'; 'Nations look like a stubblefield'; 'The kingdoms all as potters clay' (*Gweithiau*, 22, 27, 71). Thus, the aesthetics of Llwyd and Trapnel's songs are in tune with the character of Fifth Monarchist radicalism, and their poetic and linguistic choices – common measure and monosyllabic plainness – restate implicitly their claim to popular appeal and authority.

In drawing on the timeless qualities of common measure, Trapnel and Llwyd's poetry also illustrates what M. H. Abrams calls the 'recursive' procedures of apocalyptic literature, and the capacity for prophetic biblical texts to represent 'the present and the future by replicating or alluding to passages in earlier biblical texts'.[109] This tendency is exacerbated, in turn, within texts that quote from these biblical prophecies, as these texts look backwards to their biblical origin and forward to the Apocalypse that they predict. In Trapnel's work, past, present and future are pulled together in the timeless space of common measure, just as the self and other are confused and conflated within her prophetic voice. Similarly, '1648' and Llwyd's other prophetic poems, such as 'The English Triumph' and 'The Third Trumpet', combine multiple temporalities, bringing current events to bear on biblical prophecy, and vice versa.

In some respects the authority of the prophet is ambiguous, since it derives from the prophetic speaker's willingness to become a mouthpiece for the spirit. As H. W. Robinson argues, religious prophecy 'submits the human will wholly to the divine . . . the word will be more or less detached from its human speaker, and become an independent event'.[110] For female prophets, this tendency is intensified, and the ability to compose poetry is often presented as an involuntary impulse. In 1629, Bishop Williams claimed that Hawkins 'hath uttered straunge thinges in verse (wch she will not confess she could ever make before or can doe nowe)'; while 'B.T.', a witness to Trapnel's trance in 1654, noted that '(she saith) she cannot make a verse when she is hir self'.[111] A prophetic poet's inability to compose while not divinely inspired paradoxically authenticates their verse, assigning away at least part of its authorship. This effect is particularly marked at the points in Trapnel's Folio verses at which her voice becomes fragmented, both 'I' and not 'I', self and other:

> The voice it doth come down and cast
> All that is of self away:
> But what's of Christ, it doth shew forth;
> For it is that must bear sway.
> That voice which is mine, pass sentence on;
> But what is of the Lord,
> Do thou most sweetly utter forth,

And O spread it abroad.
That voice which is mine, is very dross,
It is filthy dregs also:
But what is of the lord Christ, is that
For which the Spirit doth blow. (Folio, 257)

Trapnel denies the agency of her own voice elsewhere – notably in *The Cry of a Stone* – but these lines are especially vehement in their rejection of a mixed and impure human voice in favour of one that is unified, eternal and immortal. Metre and rhyme hold together a set of words and images that might otherwise become utterly fragmented.

In Llwyd's poems, prophecy shapes a set of personal encounters between the speaker and his audience and between the speaker and the divine. In the 'Summer' section of '1648', for example, Llwyd fuses the Song of Songs and prophecies of the conversion of the Jews:

19. Harke what a sound the dead bones make
The Jewes with Jesus rise
O Tartar, East and Caspian hills
Deliver up your prise.

20. Make way, Remoove the blocks, stand by
O wellcome Jewes by mee
A shulamite in Jesus coach
I long thy face to see.

21. Thy face shall brighten all these lands
Thy moone looks like the sun
The sun like seven. The bridegroom now
that famous race will run. (*Gweithiau*, 26)

The 'shulamite' of the second stanza quoted here is the Bride of the Song of Solomon (6:13), and the third stanza reworks the biblical text more directly: 'Who is she that looketh forth as the morning, faire as the moone, cleare as the sunne, and terrible as an armie with banners?' (6:10). Specific biblical allusions thus help to depict the conversion of the Jews as an intimate, quasi-erotic, conjunction.

In Llwyd's *An Honest Discourse ... Between Goodman Past, Goodman Present, and Goodman Future*, Goodman Past explains the uncanny temporality of prophecy to Present and Future, telling them, 'there shall be no rest, till the End of all things hath found the Beginning; till *Alpha* be (apparently to man) united to *Omega*; till the end of the world overflow the beginning thereof; till the onely blessed Being swallow up all beings; and judge them himself, to his own deserved honour'.[112] Prophecy looks to a time when past and present will fused, and it enacts that conjunction within its own narrative and formal structures. Thus, in the central 'Summer' section of '1648', Llwyd describes the temporality of the last days:

> 23. How long will this faire summer last?
>   Above a thousand years
>   Our weeping lasted. lord wipe off
>   at once our teares and feares.
>
> 24. The Judgment day is not a day
>   of twenty foure houres long
>   for Christ (as Judge) beings with Pope
>   and ends with Magog strong.
>
> 25. Its (plurally) oft called Times
>   Times of refreshing sweet
>   and Times of restitution great
>   and Times when all shall meet.
>
> 26. A sixe day session but one court
>   A seaven years Parliament
>   A thousand years but as one day
>   A day most strangely spent.
>
> 27. Call me a chiliast if you please
>   or giddy headed foole
>   when those dayes come whereof I speake
>   your wisdoms will bee coole. (*Gweithiau*, 26–7)

Llwyd draws on the narrative of Revelation, in which God encourages the saints during the reign of the Beast by scourging his enemies through the opening of the seven seals, the sounding of the seven trumpets and the emptying of the seven vials of wrath. After 1,260 days, Satan is bound and Christ and the saints rule for 1,000 years (Revelation 20:3–6). When this time has elapsed, Satan is released and the battle of Armageddon begins (20:7–8); Satan is cast into 'the lake of fire and brimstone, where the beast and the false prophet are' (20:10) and the Last Judgement begins.

As Bernard Capp points out, the Fifth Monarchists were unusual in their willingness to speculate on what would happen during Christ's thousand-year rule.[113] However, Llwyd's concern here is apparently less with the specifics of Christ's kingdom and more with the fluid quality of post-Apocalyptic time. The repetition of 'Times' in stanza 25 reinforces the point made in stanza 24: the Day of Judgement is not a conventional twenty-four-hour day, but a point at which time becomes plural and different time-schemes are collapsed. Similarly, stanza 26 pulls together the six days of the Creation, the seven years since the beginning of the Long Parliament, and the thousand years of Revelation 20:10; the quotation in the third line from 2 Peter 3:8, 'one day is with the Lord as a thousand yeeres, and a thousand yeeres as one day', underlines Llwyd's message about the effects of the Apocalypse on time. The plain, almost colloquial language in stanza 27 draws attention to Llwyd's scornful use of the polysyllabic word 'chiliast' (millenarian), and his desire to present biblical prophecy as a matter of fact rather than of doubt or speculation.

For many commentators in the 1640s and 1650s, the sectarian prophets were a disruptive and disconcerting novelty. However, as we have seen, in their use of familiar metrical forms and monosyllables Trapnel and Llwyd seek to forge connections with readers and listeners, arguing both explicitly and implicitly for their right to speak to and for the post-Revolutionary nation and its people. Adopting and adapting the voice of the Psalmist enables these writers to create a mode that is both topical and radically a-temporal, and a poetry that is both simple and ecstatic. Stylistic archaism here enacts a form of communication that is tied to content but which also, at times, transcends it, speaking to readers even when the radical content of the verse might otherwise alienate them.

Conclusion

As we saw in the first part of this chapter, biblical translators attempted to resist or bypass linguistic change, and to present the divine word as immutable and unchanging. At the heart of the Anglican establishment was a commitment to archaism as a mechanism for creating and maintaining an impression of timelessness, and for rooting biblical translation within the English language and its traditions, undertakings that contrast sharply with Catholic translators' recourse to Latinate neologism. However, while Anglican writers such as Joseph Hall, George Wither and Henry King came to chafe at the restrictions that stylistic archaism placed on the Psalms, Catholic and Fifth Monarchist poets exploited archaism as a means of connecting with prior traditions and using them to their own ends.

Robert Southwell, Gertrude More, Anna Trapnel and Morgan Llwyd have in common their commitment to simplicity and plainness, and archaic forms such as common measure and the fourteener, and the use of monosyllables, play a crucial role in their poetry and its articulation of national, confessional and political identity. In the work of Southwell and More, archaic form is an occupied space: in using the fourteener and common measure these Catholic poets emphasise their Englishness and simultaneously demonstrate their willingness to appropriate forms associated with English Protestantism. Like the poetry of Southwell and More, the Fifth Monarchist verse composed by Trapnel and Llwyd inhabits the metrical spaces established by the Anglican church and draws on other literary devices strongly associated with Englishness. However, their social radicalism and apocalyptic edge – the latter appropriately conveyed in common measure because of its association with the Psalms – means that they simultaneously challenge the conservative assumptions of the Anglican establishment, the position of which was itself threatened by the events of the 1640s and 1650s. 'I was the child of a Christian woman and not the whelp of a tiger,' wrote Southwell from prison to his kinsman Robert Cecil.[114] Familiar, comforting, archaic language enabled Catholic and radical Protestant poets alike to forge connections with their fellow countrymen. Timeless but intensely topical, domestic but alien, reassuring but estranging, their poetry demonstrates another facet of archaism's hold on the literary imagination.

CHAPTER 4

Staging generations: archaism and the theatrical past

Some blame deep *Spencer* for his grandam words[.]

Edward Guilpin[1]

But you must know your father lost a father,
That father lost lost his[.]

William Shakespeare[2]

Why does Edward Guilpin refer to Edmund Spenser's archaising style as 'grandam words'? On one level, the phrase simply conveys the old-fashioned fustiness that some critics would associate with literary archaism and the recycling of outmoded styles. Yet it also raises concerns crucial to the ways in which archaism was conceptualised in early modern England and to the ways in which it functions within texts: namely, the role that generations, and the perceived differences between generations, play in the construction of archaism and the categorisation of any individual word or style as archaic. These issues have particular resonance for this chapter, which focuses on the ways in which dramatic modes of the early and mid-Tudor period functioned as archaisms in the theatre of the late 1590s and early 1600s.[3] Whereas Old English or Chaucerian modes could be securely associated with the distant past, Tudor styles of drama were less stably 'archaic'. Their use in later plays thus lays bare the range of interactions within and between generations that leads to a style being positioned as archaic.

Archaism depends implicitly on the capacity of words and styles first to be perceived as 'old' and, second, to be renewed through their revival and reanimation. It is precisely the perceived gaps between generations, and the interactions between them, that create archaism: changes in taste between generations cause selected styles to become outmoded, but the connections and continuities between generations allow them to be revived. In a process that is both antagonistic and collusive, the linguistic and stylistic forms of their parents and grandparents simultaneously repel and attract younger writers. When playwrights such as Thomas Middleton, Thomas Heywood and John Fletcher compare shifts in dramatic taste with changes in sartorial fashion,[4] when Guilpin suggests that Spenser is castigated for his 'grandam words', or when E.K. claims that opponents of archaism charge that 'we speak ... as in old time Euanders mother spake',[5] they all argue for the central role of generations in creating and maintaining archaism as a potent literary mode.

The classic work on intergenerational relationships in a literary context remains Harold Bloom's *The Anxiety of Influence*, first published in 1973, in which he argues that 'strong' writers reach their potential through reading and misreading their predecessors. In a 1997 preface to a reissue of the book, Bloom describes the 'strong' poems produced by this act of misreading as 'omens of resurrection', commenting, 'The dead may or may not return, but their voice comes alive, paradoxically never by mere imitation, but in the agonistic misprision performed upon powerful forerunners by only the most gifted of their successors.'[6] I am, of course, concerned here with the idea that the voices of the dead might be resurrected, but, in contrast with Bloom, my attention is caught by what he terms the 'mere imitation' of earlier voices; although individual writers figure prominently in my discussion, I am more interested in the interplay between stylistic 'generations' than in the interaction between great authors.

More helpful in many respects for this project is work by theorists of generations in the social sciences. In her recent book, *Generations: The Time Machine in Theory and Practice*, the sociologist Judith Burnett defines generation as 'a two-legged race consisting of both a kinship network which structures us in time on a diachronic axis and an age set network which structures us in time on a synchronic axis'.[7] This description resonates with the structures of early modern literary generations. Here, the diachronic axis is structured around earlier and later groups of authors and texts, while the synchronic axis is represented by a group of writers working at the same time, often – but not necessarily – of a similar age, and working in similar cultural contexts. Archaism is produced by the interaction between these diachronic and synchronic networks; it is the product not only of a writer's ability to see a particular word, figure or mode as 'old', but also, crucially, their ability to judge it in relation to what is 'new', and their desire to revive it and place it alongside those new forms. As such, it is produced by diachronic and synchronic relationships between and within generations, and is a literary expression of these interactions and tensions.

Generation theory also suggests a vocabulary for describing these inter-actions. In *Generations*, Burnett argues that both diachronic and syn-chronic networks involve 'complex systems of structure and agency; obligation and exchange; reciprocity and the exercise of power', providing for 'intimacy and conflict; the markers of boundaries; and the constant re-creation of the We, the I, the Them and the Us'; diachronic networks allow in addition 'the reproduction of inheritance and systems of stratification' (2). Similarly, for Sigrid Weigel, generations are 'die Schwelle zwischen Entstehung und Fortgang, zwischen Abstammung und Erbschaft, zwischen Prokreation und Tradition, zwischen Herkunft und Gedächtnis' [the threshold between beginning and end, between ancestry and heritage, between procreation and tradition, between origin and memory].[8] Power, obligation, reciprocity, identity, conflict, memory, ancestry, tradition, procreation: these terms are as relevant for considering stylistic and aesthetic generations as they are for considering those based on family or age-cohort.

These ways of thinking about generations belong to a tradition stretch-ing back as far as Karl Mannheim's 'The Problem of Generations', origin-ally published in 1928, and Mannheim's own ideas have important implications for the study of cultural generations.[9] At any one time, Mannheim argues, a series of processes are ongoing:

(a)   new participants in the cultural process are emerging, whilst
(b)   former participants in that process are continually disappearing;
(c)   members of any one generation can participate only in a temporally limited section of the historical process, and
(d)   it is therefore necessary continually to transmit the accumulated cultural heritage;
(e)   the transition from generation to generation is a continuous process.[10]

The use of archaism represents, I suggest, a specific aspect of this process in its literary or cultural context, during which writers look beyond their own 'temporally limited section of the historical process', producing new works that, paradoxically, re-embody older forms. In these ways, 'accumulated cultural heritage' is transmitted into the future, but it is also reshaped and reworked in the process.

In part because of fast-moving stylistic changes in the late sixteenth century, theatre offers an especially intriguing example of the ways in which intergenerational exchanges produce and maintain archaism. More-over, the narratives of plays themselves connect the aesthetic and thematic workings of generations, as the two epigraphs at the head of this chapter suggest. I look first at parodies of the Tudor morality play in two Jacobean works by Ben Jonson: *The Staple of News* (King's Men, 1626) and *The Devil is an Ass* (King's Men, 1616). For Jonson, the morality play becomes the ultimate example of theatrical archaism; the form and its conventions attract him and exercise a shaping influence on his work, but he also fiercely resists them. His characteristically ambivalent response to archaism here leads him to attempt to control the responses of his audiences towards archaic forms – aligning spectators with their own generation and in opposition to the works of the past – yet he also admits the theatrical pleasure that these forms produce. These interactions with the theatrical past are yet more complex in the three plays dating from around the turn of the seventeenth century that are examined in the remainder of the chapter: *Sir Thomas More* (auspices uncertain, *c.*1601; revised *c.*1603–4), written by Anthony Munday, Henry Chettle, Thomas Dekker, Thomas Heywood and, probably, Shakespeare;[11] *Histriomastix, or The Player Whipped* (auspices uncertain, *c.*1598–1602), to which John Marston may have contributed; and Shakespeare's *Hamlet* (Chamberlain's Men, *c.*1600). All of these plays feature metadramatic sequences in which professional theatre companies mount performances in outmoded theatrical forms. Yet archaic style has different functions in *Sir Thomas More*, *Histriomastix* and *Hamlet*, and each play adopts a different stance in relation to the theatrical past and its relationship with the present.

In *Sir Thomas More*, Munday and his collaborators productively exploit the long history of the Tudor morality play, thrusting passages from works that long post-date More's death back into the Henrician past, into a play in which More himself is forced to take a part. In doing so, they complicate *Sir Thomas More*'s presentation of its martyred protagonist, re-inscribing the trauma of the Reformation and the resulting tensions between Catholic and Protestant that the play would prefer to forget. *Histriomastix* uses a broader range of archaic theatrical forms, parodying the morality play and its successors and incorporating references to late sixteenth-century theatrical fashions. In doing so, it tells an alternative history of the popular stage, using theatrical archaism as a tool in a wholesale deconstruction and rejection of its practices and aesthetics.

The play with which the chapter concludes, *Hamlet*, combines something of the techniques of *Sir Thomas More* and *Histriomastix*: like *Sir Thomas More*, it uses archaic theatre to structure its engagements with tragic form, and like *Histriomastix* it uses theatrical archaism to consider the status of the late-Elizabethan commercial stage. However, it also knits together stylistic and thematic treatments of generation to a much greater extent than either of these plays. Shakespeare incorporates into *Hamlet* skilfully handled pastiches of two generations of Elizabethan Senecan aesthetics; in doing so, he brings together familial and aesthetic generations, reflecting on the nature and purpose of the turn-of-the-century revenge tragedy, and the place of the Hamlet narrative within that tradition.

The extent to which the plays examined in this chapter are implicated in inter- and intra-generational tensions is clear: even as they look back to their various theatrical pasts they are simultaneously engrossed by the theatrical present, incorporating explicit allusions to plays that were recent or current at the time of their first performance, or referring to aspects of the late-Elizabethan theatre industry or its personnel. Archaism is thus propelled by a preoccupation not only with the old but also with the new, and by a younger generation's sense of its own innovation. Dramatists use it as a tool in both establishing their own stylistic generation and forging connections across the generations, and it leads them to devote sustained attention to the interactions between the theatrical past and present.

Staging parody: *The Staple of News* and *The Devil is an Ass*

Jonson's critique of the theatrical past often engages explicitly with the idea of generations. In the Induction to *Bartholomew Fair* (Lady Elizabeth's Men, 1614), the fictional contract between playing company and audience that is recited by the Scrivener includes the provision that 'He that will swear *Jeronimo* or *Andronicus* are the best plays yet shall pass unexcepted at here, as a man whose judgement shows it is constant and hath stood still these five and twenty or thirty years'.[12] Shakespeare's *Titus Andronicus*, probably first performed a couple of years after *The Spanish Tragedy*, has here joined Thomas Kyd's play as an exemplar of all that is old-fashioned in the theatrical repertory. Jonson jokingly promises to tolerate playgoers with old-fashioned tastes, but he appears to view them as temporally aberrant.

Jonson's specific animus here is against old plays that were still current in the theatrical repertory, but he also devotes attention to more securely archaic forms, such as the Tudor morality play. The strongly defined conventions of the morality play were a source of its dramatic and commercial success, but they also left it open to parody. In its classic form, it traces the progress of a vulnerable protagonist – Everyman, Mankind, Juventus, Wit, Moros – through an environment in which he is assaulted by allegorical vices and virtues of varying kinds. The earliest examples that have been located, such as *The Castle of Perseverance* (1405–25), *Wisdom* (1450–1500) and *Mankind* (1465–70), date from the fifteenth century, but the tradition persisted for over a century, flourishing in the 1560s and 1570s in such disparate plays as Thomas Preston's *Cambises* (*c.*1561, printed *c.*1569), Ulpian Fulwell's *Like Will to Like* (1562–8), Thomas Garter's *The Most Virtuous and Godly Susanna* (1563–9), and the anonymous *The Conflict of Conscience* (*c.*1571–80).[13] It finally dropped out of fashion on the stage in the 1580s, but morality characters and narrative structures persist in mutated and submerged forms in later drama, as Alan C. Dessen and others have explored in detail.[14]

Jonson treats the morality play as the ultimate example of theatrical archaism; he amuses himself by parodying and critiquing it, but he also cannot help but admit its theatrical power. *The Staple of News*, performed in 1626, includes a sustained allusion to the morality play and its conventions within a series of framing inter-act sequences featuring a group of women, Gossip Mirth, Gossip Tattle, Gossip Expectation and Gossip Censure. Described as *'four gentlewomen, ladylike attired'*, the gossips interrupt the Prologue and mount the stage, Mirth claiming, 'we are persons of quality, I assure you, and women of fashion, and come to see and to be seen'.[15] Like the high-status spectators who sat on stools on the Blackfriars stage, they assert their right not only to 'see and be seen', but to pass judgement on what they see and hear. The age of the women is suggested in Mirth's response to the Prologue's complaint that the 'wits' who normally sit on the stage might object: 'Why, what should they think? But that they had mothers, as we had, and those mothers had gossips (if their children were christened), as we are, and such as had a longing to see plays and sit upon them, as we do, and arraign both them and their poets' (Induction, ll. 15–18). Jonson thus establishes a generational opposition – and, implicitly, a gender opposition – between the young men who would usually occupy this theatrical space and position as arbiters of taste and the older women who have usurped them.

This set-up is crucial to the women's dialogue in the inter-act sequences, in which they criticise *The Staple of News* harshly for its failure to meet their expectations. In the first of these sequences Tattle comments, 'My husband, Timothy Tattle (God rest his poor soul), was wont to say there was no play without a fool and a devil in't' (First Intermean, 25–6). The expectation that a play should include a fool and a devil was a cliché by the late sixteenth century; Thomas Lodge comments to his reader in *Wit's Misery* (1596), *'my Commedie is pleasure, the world is my scœne and stage, and mine actors so well trained, that without a foole and a Deuill I passe*

nothing.[16] By the seventeenth century it was often associated with unin-
formed or non-metropolitan spectators; writing in 1624, John Gee
comments,

> It was wont, when an Interlude was to bee acted in a Countrey Towne, the
> first question that an Hob-naile Spectator made, before hee would pay his
> penny to goe in, was, *Whether there bee a Diuell and a Foole in the play?* And
> if the Foole get vpon the Diuels backe, and beate him with his Cox-combe
> till hee roare, the play is compleat.[17]

As I will explore in further detail in Chapter 5, archaism was often
associated with the regional or provincial; in *The Staple of News* the
London-based gossips are presented as sharing their rural counterparts'
tastes. However, the fact that they also refer in the First Intermean to
Jonson's own play *The Devil is an Ass* and another Jacobean play, *The
Merry Devil of Edmonton* – albeit in the context of their fondness for
theatrical devils – means that they are not entirely ignorant of seventeenth-
century drama. The anxiety raised, therefore, is that the gossips are not
merely ignorant, but that their preference for older forms is an informed
choice. Jonson's quarrel is not with theatrically ill-informed spectators but
those who actively prefer outmoded styles.

The gossips focus more squarely on the Tudor morality play in the
Second Intermean. Censure repeats the complaint that the play lacks a
devil or fool, but they then move to discuss the figure of the Vice in detail:

MIRTH ... How like you the Vice i'the play?
EXPECTATION Which is he?
MIRTH Three or four: old Covetousness, the sordid Pennyboy; the money-bawd
     who is a flesh-bawd too, they say.
TATTLE But here is never a fiend to carry him away. Besides, he has never a
     wooden dagger! I'd not give a rush for a Vice that has not a wooden dagger
     to snap at everybody he meets.
MIRTH That was the old way, gossip, when Iniquity came in like Hocus-Pocus,
     in a juggler's jerkin, with false skirts like the Knave of Clubs. But now they
     are attired like men and women o'the time, the Vices, male and female!
(Second Intermean, 5–14)

As Janette Dillon comments, the gossips 'look for a Vice and dismiss
those characters who come closest to that archaic mode because they don't
fulfil all the old expectations'.[18] Yet the gossips are more eclectic in their
tastes that this comment suggests, and the interplay between different
periods of theatrical history in *The Staple of News* is more complex than
is generally acknowledged. The question 'Which is he?' is crucial: in the
sartorial and theatrical confusion of Caroline London, the Vice has lost his

distinctiveness and, thereby, his power. The gossips describe in detail the Vice's costume and some of his stage business, and they apparently draw on their own memories, underlining the generational distinctions that Jonson is at pains to draw. However, their diagnosis is not inaccurate: in the Caroline theatre it *is* less easy to tell vice from virtue, and the Vices have indeed taken on new costumes and identities.

In the form of allusion, it is relatively easy for Jonson to contain and control an audience's response to the theatrical past. We sense the pleasure that their memories provide for the gossips, but we cannot access those memories at first hand, and they cannot compete with the material that is dramatised within the play proper. Even though the gossips' references to more recent plays might suggest that their preferences are not based merely on ignorance or prejudice, Jonson nonetheless attempts to regulate the theatrical past, and stigmatises it by associating it with both women and the older generation. In contrast, in *The Devil is an Ass*, he provides his audience with a greater level of access to outmoded dramatic forms, displaying a greater degree of creative archaism than is found in *The Staple of News*. Accordingly, the theatrical past is more capable of providing direct pleasure for its audience, and its effects become richer and less predictable.

The opening scene of *The Devil is an Ass* takes place in Hell, where a junior devil, Pug, persuades a reluctant Satan to allow him to go on a mission to Jacobean London. Pug's lack of fashionable polish, and his failure to keep up with the times, are underlined by his desire to take with him a Vice as his aide. He eventually settles on 'old Iniquity',[19] a Vice with a strong dramatic pedigree: in addition to being mentioned by Gossip Mirth in *The Staple of News* he features in two extant Tudor morality plays, *The Nice Wanton* (1547–53) and *King Darius* (c.1558–65), appears in an inset play in *Histriomastix* and is referred to by Shakespeare on two occasions.[20] Iniquity appears here with a flourish, brandishing his wooden dagger, and speaking in a style that combines an old-fashioned poulter's measure, alternating lines of twelve and fourteen syllables, with more regular fourteeners: 'What is he calls upon me, and would seem to lack a Vice? / Ere his words be half spoken, I am with him in a trice' (1.1.44–5). Jonson thus reanimates the figure described by the gossips in *The Staple of News*, giving him a renewed theatrical life and physical presence on the stage, and retaining his distinctive appearance.

Given Iniquity's antiquated appearance and his archaic speech-patterns, it is perhaps unsurprising that his knowledge of theatrical, linguistic and material fashions is comprehensively out of date. The Vice tells Pug,

> I will teach thee to cheat, child, to cog, lie, and swagger,
> And ever and anon, to be drawing forth thy dagger;
> To swear by Gog's nowns, like a Lusty Juventus,
> In a cloak to thy heel, and a hat like a penthouse,
> Thy breeches of three fingers, and thy doublet all belly,
> With a wench that shall feed thee with cock-stones and jelly. (1.1.48–53)

In addition to the archaism of his metre, Iniquity's speech is larded with proverbial saws and features a rather old-fashioned oath, 'Gog's nowns'. His speech incorporates references to the eponymous anti-hero of a morality play, *Lusty Juventus*, to the stage-business associated with the Vice, and to dated styles of clothing (a long cloak, a sloping hat, and padded breeches and doublet), which he apparently believes are still current. Outmoded theatrical and sartorial fashions are identified with each other, the comparison underlining the perceived incongruity of stylistic archaism. Continuing this theme, in his next speech the Vice appears to be ignorant of how the fabric of London has changed since the mid-sixteenth century. For instance, he tells Pug, 'I will fetch thee a leap / From the top of Paul's steeple to the Standard in Cheap' (1.1.55–6), despite the fact that the steeple on St Paul's had been struck by lightning in 1561 and had never been replaced.

Iniquity may be antiquated but he is nonetheless thoroughly engaging; Pug exclaims 'Is it not excellent, chief? How nimble he is!' (1.1.54), and his delight may be shared by an audience, whether or not they are familiar with the conventions that he embodies. The theatrical representation threatens to exceed the boundaries that Jonson imposes, and he apparently shuts down the insurgent potential of the theatrical past with Satan's heavy commentary on theatrical fashion and Iniquity's failings, which directs laughter at, rather than with, Pug and Iniquity:

> Art thou the spirit thou seem'st? So poor? To choose
> This for a Vice t'advance the cause of hell
> Now, as vice stands this present year? Remember
> What number it is: six hundred and sixteen.
> Had it but been five hundred, though some sixty
> Above – that's fifty years agone, and six,
> When every great man had his Vice stand by him,
> In his long coat, shaking his wooden dagger –
> I could consent that then this your grave choice
> Might have done that, with his lord chief, the which
> Most of his chamber can do now. But Pug,
> As the times are, who is it will receive you? (1.1.77–89)

In 1616, Satan declares, Londoners will accept only the most up-to-date vices – 'Unless it be a Vice of quality / Or fashion now, they take none from us' (1.1.111–12) – and Iniquity is barely fit to be taken out in public or to inhabit the Jacobean stage. Even Hell, it seems, is subject to the passing of time and the vagaries of fashion. Pug – and, by extension, any audience member who has taken pleasure from Iniquity's appearance – is stigmatised as a culturally backward 'Hob-naile Spectator' of the kind described by Gee.

In the opening scene of *The Devil is an Ass*, the archaic theatrical past is firmly controlled and, seemingly, suppressed. If Jacobean London has invented new forms of vice, Jonson suggests, it has also invented a new form of drama – the satiric city comedy – in order to represent and regulate them. Both of these things are portrayed as being beyond the capabilities of the morality play. However, Jonson admits fissures in this unyielding treatment of the theatrical past, and he is conscious of the pleasure that archaic theatre can still evoke. In the first place, he cannot fully control the effects of Iniquity's presence on the stage, and the ways in which spectators react towards him, and it is not clear that he entirely wishes to. Moreover, the firm treatment of the morality play cannot hide the debt that the city comedy itself owes to the older form of drama. Iniquity's name – taken directly from the morality play tradition – has the side-effect of reminding us of the origin of the naming convention used for characters such as Merecraft, Engine, Fitzdottrel, Wittipol and Manly. Jonson also suggests his awareness of this lineage in *The Staple of News*, where Mirth comments that contemporary theatrical Vices 'are attired like men and women o'the time'.

Crucially, in addition, the morality play comes back in the final act of *The Devil is an Ass*, as Pug is returned to Hell on the Vice's back, amid much fire and smoke. This reverses the conventional stage business of the morality play, in which the Vice was carried by the Devil, suggesting again Jonson's parodic stance in relation to the theatrical past.[21] However, as Jan Frans van Dijkhuizen points out, Fitzdottrel, the would-be machiavel of the play's main plot, for whom Pug has worked as a servant, 'confesses his fraud when he hears that Pug was a real devil'; if the traditions of the morality play are satirised, 'they are also called upon to resolve the plot'.[22] Older drama may be satirised as the product of an earlier, more ignorant, generation, but its influence and its theatrical power cannot be entirely elided.

Staging history: *Sir Thomas More*

While *The Devil is an Ass* pulls the morality play into the Jacobean era, only to stigmatise it as archaic, *Sir Thomas More* situates it in the historical past. This does not, however, make the play's use of theatrical

archaism more straightforward. Instead, *Sir Thomas More*'s representation of a particular historical milieu sharpens its interactions with
the morality play, bringing three generations into dialogue with each
other: the Henrician period in which the narrative is set; the post-
Reformation period in which the inset play's sources were written
and performed; and the turn of the seventeenth century, when the play
itself was composed. *Sir Thomas More* thus brings three distinct periods
of religious and political history to bear on each other through the
medium of the morality play, and each influences not only the form and
presentation of theatrical archaism, but also its narrative and thematic
implications.

Sir Thomas More recounts events of the late 1520s and 1530s, culminat-
ing with More's refusal to subscribe to the Act of Supremacy and his
execution in July 1535. While it deals with the Reformation and Henry
VIII's break with Rome, it does so in a remarkably evasive fashion: the
king never appears on stage, although he is a heavy off-stage presence, and
religious politics are rarely invoked explicitly. This elision of religious
dispute is perhaps unsurprising; although More retained his status as a
humanist thinker and wit, representing a Catholic martyr on the 1590s
stage was a difficult task, as the play's history of censorship suggests.[23] *Sir
Thomas More* therefore registers the shock of the Reformation primarily
through the effect of Henry VIII's policies on one man and his family. But
the religious tensions of the Reformation are not entirely dismissed; they
instead appear in the gaps and margins of representation, notably in a
play-within-a-play that is mounted within More's own household, the
self-conscious archaism of which sets off a series of negotiations between
generations. Religious division is central to the particular kinds
of anachronism that archaism creates in *Sir Thomas More*, and these
anachronistic forces are crystallised at the moment at which More himself
steps into the inset play.

The preparations for the performance of a morality play called *The
Marriage of Wit and Wisdom*, and its interrupted performance, appear at
the centre of *Sir Thomas More*, in Scene 9.[24] As scholars have noted, the
dramatists draw on Nicholas Harpsfield's account of More's life, in which
More is said to have acted impromptu parts during Christmas festivities
when he was a boy in Cardinal Morton's household; however, they
relocate his theatrical endeavours to his maturity.[25] Donna B. Hamilton
notes the 'strategic placing of the play-within-a-play between the anti-alien
riots and More's refusal to subscribe to the oath of supremacy'; it thus
represents the high point in More's worldly fortunes.[26]

The Marriage of Wit and Wisdom may look like a nod to the period setting, even though the rest of the play is – like the majority of early modern history plays – spoken in contemporary, late sixteenth-century English. The morality play existed in the late 1520s and early 1530s, and the inset play is surrounded by historicising details. The players are described as 'My lord Cardinal's players' (9.50) (a reference to Cardinal Wolsey or, possibly, More's patron Cardinal Morton, neither of whom appears in the play), and the structure of their company and its playing strategies – which are in line with early and mid-sixteenth-century norms – are described in some detail.[27] A player also lists the company's repertoire, which includes works dating from between the 1520s and the 1570s that are either extant or are known to have existed: '*The Cradle of Security*, / *Hit Nail o'th' Head*, *Impatient Poverty*, / *The Play of Four P's*, *Dives and Lazarus*, / *Lusty Juventus*, and *The Marriage of Wit and Wisdom*' (9.60–3).[28]

However, *The Marriage of Wit and Wisdom* is less authentic than it might appear. Its title apparently alludes to Francis Merbury's play *The Marriage Between Wit and Wisdom*, which survives in a manuscript dated 1579. Munday may have had access to this manuscript early in his career; if so, he apparently recalled the title, and its emblematic potential, when he and his collaborators were working on *Sir Thomas More*.[29] Merbury's actual play appears by this time to have been unavailable. However, rather than writing an entirely new piece the dramatists instead created a collage of new and old material, drawing on at least three morality plays available in print: Thomas Ingelend's *The Disobedient Child* (c.1558–69, printed c.1569),[30] from which the prologue derives; R. Wever's *Lusty Juventus* (c.1547–53; printed in at least three editions after 1558),[31] from which the bulk of the play is taken, and which is listed as part of the repertory of the Lord Cardinal's Men earlier in the scene; and *The Trial of Treasure* (?1560s; printed 1567), on which some of the Vice's lines are based and from which his name is taken.[32] All of the source texts date from the decades after More's death; furthermore, they are all in their own ways enmeshed in the politics of the Edwardian and Elizabethan Reformation. *The Disobedient Child* and *The Trial of Treasure* are imbued with Protestant ideology in their presentation of sin and the family, while *Lusty Juventus* is an explicitly anti-Catholic work, written to fulfil the needs of both drama and polemic. Even to include the figure of the Vice in *Sir Thomas More* was to gesture to religious politics; as scholars such as Bernard Spivack and John D. Cox have argued, the Vice did not become fully established until the 1530s, and he was closely associated with the Reformation drama of John Bale and others.[33]

The use of *Lusty Juventus* is particularly striking. An exchange between Juventus, Hypocrisy (a subordinate Vice in *Lusty Juventus*, who represents the Roman Catholic church, and is disguised as Friendship) and the seductive Abominable Living (disguised as Unknown Honesty) is adapted for Wit, the Vice Inclination, and Lady Vanity, who is disguised as Wisdom.[34] An extract demonstrates the way in which the dramatists combine old and new material (sections adapted from *Lusty Juventus* are in bold type):

> WIT. *And is her name Wisdom?*
> INCLINATION.   *Ay, sir, a wife most fit*
> *For you, my good master, my dainty sweet Wit.*
> WIT. **To be in her company my heart** *it* **is set.**
> **Therefore I prithee to let us be gone,**
> *For unto Wisdom Wit hath inclination.*
> INCLINATION. *O sir,* **she will come herself** *even* **anon,**
> **For I told her before where we would stand,**
> **And then she said she would beck us with her hand.**
> *(flourishing his dagger)*
> *Back with those boys and saucy great knaves.*
> *What, stand ye here so big in your braves?*
> *My dagger about your coxcombs shall walk*
> *If I may but so much as hear ye chat or talk.*
> WIT. **But will she take pains to come for us hither?**
> INCLINATION. **I warrant ye, therefore you must be familiar with her.**
> **When she cometh in place,**
> **You must her embrace**
> **Somewhat handsomely,**
> **Least she think it danger,**
> **Because you are a stranger,**
> **To come in your company.**
> WIT. *I warrant thee, Inclination,* **I will be busy.**
> *O, how Wit longs to be in Wisdom's company!*   (9.202–23)[35]

The *Thomas More* dramatists omit the Catholic oaths ('by gods foote' and 'By the masse') uttered by the Vice in *Lusty Juventus* and *The Trial of Treasure*, but they add some archaic touches in the syntax, such as the pleonastic 'it' in line 204.[36] Although their additions are generally in pentameter or hexameter couplets, they retain some of the mixed and ragged metre of the original, as in the short lines given to the Vice in lines 216–21. Otherwise, however, they are generally unconcerned with preserving the rhyme royal (and variations thereon) that is characteristic of the morality play of the 1550s and 1560s. The material taken from the morality play is adapted to late-Elizabethan tastes, but a distinctive flavour of the earlier style is retained. Furthermore, like Iniquity in *The Devil is an Ass*, Inclination retains his attractive and flamboyant theatricality, cheerfully insulting his on-stage audience in lines that echo those of the Vice in *The Trial of Treasure* and shaking his wooden dagger at them.

The crisis point in the performance arrives when Luggins, who is supposed to play Good Counsel, fails to return from his errand to the wig-maker and cannot, therefore, 'enter to admonish Wit that this is Lady Vanity and not Lady Wisdom' (9.258–9). His place is taken by More himself, who improvises his lines in a series of newly composed speeches:

> WIT. *Art thou Good Counsel, and wilt tell me so?*
> *Wouldst thou have Wit from Lady Wisdom to go?*
> *Thou art some deceiver, I tell thee verily,*
> *In saying that this is Lady Vanity.*
>   MORE [*as Good Counsel*]. *Wit, judge not things by the outward show.*
> *The eye oft mistakes, right well you do know.*
> *Good Counsel assures thee on his honesty*
> *That this is not Wisdom, but Lady Vanity.*   (9.275–82)

More mimics the style of *The Marriage of Wit and Wisdom*, and is complimented by the actor who plays Inclination, who tells him 'In troth, my lord, it is as right to Luggins' part as can be' (9.271–2). The shift of register is noticeable in More's use of couplets (elsewhere in *Sir Thomas More* he speaks in either prose or blank verse), proverbial language ('*judge not things by the outward show*'), the third person ('*Good Counsel assures thee*'), and somewhat awkward or old-fashioned syntax ('*right well you do know*'). Momentarily, More is incorporated into the morality play, becoming an emblematic figure rather than a historical individual or dramatic hero. Moreover, his progressive absorption into the morality mode is signalled even earlier in the sequence when he comments 'This is Lady Vanity, I'll hold my life. / Beware good Wit, you take not her to wife' (9.226–7), adopting the inset play's style even though at this point he remains a spectator.

Despite its historicising touches the temporality of the play is complex: it belongs to three different generations, and the inset drama is both of its supposed historical moment and far removed from it. Most of the repertory of the 'Lord Cardinal's Men' dates from the 1560s and 1570s, as does the material quoted and appropriated, and Luggins departs to fetch his beard from 'Ogle's', seemingly a reference to John Ogle, a maker of wigs and theatrical props who is known to have been active from the early 1570s until as late as 1600.[37] The play thus refuses to treat *The Marriage of Wit and Wisdom* as something that is fully of the past, and its version of the morality play is far more post- than pre-Reformation. Indeed, the dramatists' decision to adapt anti-Catholic moralities such as *Lusty Juventus* and *The Trial of Treasure* carries with it a good deal of irony, especially in a play that is in general far more comfortable in presenting More as humanist wit than as Catholic martyr. The sequence featuring the inset play thus pulls together three temporally dissociated elements: a narrative and plot deriving from the 1530s; quoted texts from the mid-sixteenth century; and generic structures and newly composed dialogue from around 1600.

In fusing these disparate generations, *The Marriage of Wit and Wisdom* underlines and embodies the adjustments that the dramatists make in their representation of More. It offers a hagiographical portrait of More as the meta-dramatic embodiment of 'Good Counsel'. As James Simpson comments, just as the 'old, but not so old' morality genre 'is capable of bearing significant truths ... so too does the play itself remind its audience of the contemporary significance of More's courageous and adroit counsel, theatrically delivered'.[38] However, paying attention to specifics of the inset play's archaism and the interplay of generations within the metadramatic sequence complicates this picture. The material incorporated into *Sir Thomas More* is indeed 'old, but not so old', post-dating More's death and embedded in the religious disputes in which the historical More played an important early part. Furthermore, although *The Marriage of Wit and Wisdom* omits the oaths that signal the Vice's religious allegiance in *Lusty Juventus*, it cannot entirely contain the unease that this material invokes. Thus, the dramatic irony created by More's performance as 'Good Counsel', in view of later events and the king's rejection of his 'counsel', is marked. While More ably presents the role of Good Counsel in the metadramatic sequence, the play itself cannot elide fully the reasons why he failed in the real-life equivalent of this role, or the wider context and effects of the political events with which he became embroiled.

The use of anti-Catholic moralities in *The Marriage of Wit and Wisdom* thus underlines in a somewhat grotesque fashion the continued religious turmoil of the mid- and late sixteenth century, and the continued schism between Protestant and Catholic. The inset play proleptically invokes the Reformed, anti-Catholic morality play of the mid-century; as Robert Weimann argues, the morality play 'readily adjusted to economic, social, and political shifts', unlike More himself.[39] Although it is presented at the high point of More's political career, *The Marriage of Wit and Wisdom* thus emblematises the political and historical tensions, the elisions and evasions, that came with representing such a figure at the turn of the seventeenth century. Remarkably, while the play in general presents a hagiographic portrayal of More's career, its metadramatic sequence appropriates the voice of Elizabethan anti-Catholic polemic; the inset play, and its blurring of temporal lines, thus registers – in a way that the rest of the work cannot – the grim history of religious turmoil that followed More's death.

Staging players: *Histriomastix*

In contrast with the other plays considered in this chapter, which draw on widely recognisable generic patterns – history, tragedy, city comedy – *Histriomastix* is idiosyncratic in both structure and genre, and its treatment of theatrical archaism is similarly distinctive. Its *six* acts present an allegorical and cyclical narrative of human progress and decline, as the world is successively ruled by Peace, Plenty, Pride, Envy, War and Poverty; at the end of the play, Peace returns and Astraea – representing Queen Elizabeth – '*mounts vnto the Throne*', attended by Fame, Fortitude, Religion, Virginity and the Arts.[40] A group of players start the play as tradesmen and take on a new profession as actors in Act 1, calling themselves Sir Oliver Owlet's Men; they are one of three social groupings who reappear in each act, the others comprising a group of noblemen and women and a group of lawyers and merchants and their wives. *Histriomastix* thus stages in parodic form the origins of the 'trade' of acting and the professional stage in Elizabethan England. The players' fortunes fluctuate with those of society as a whole, until in Act 6, the age of Poverty, they are expelled from the commonwealth when they refuse to contribute properly to the relief of the poor. The play's title, which, as its subtitle indicates, means 'the player whipped', both draws attention to its central interest in the theatre industry and suggests something of its attitude towards commercial theatre.

Despite its interest in the theatrical profession, *Histriomastix* does not appear have been performed by a professional or semi-professional troupe. It is more likely to have been performed by students at the Inns of Court than by a group such as the Children of Paul's, to which it has often been assigned.[41] Evidence suggests that it was produced, if not originally composed, in the late 1590s or early 1600s – there is a reference to 'play[ing] the *Tamburlaine*' (G1r), which suggests performance after the first performance of Marlowe's play, and it features a number of words that were probably coined in the 1590s.[42] In addition, it seems to contain references to *Hamlet*, as Charles Cathcart has argued, and to *A Midsummer Night's Dream*.[43] It is also possible, though not certain, that John Marston – a quintessential late-1590s writer – had a hand in its composition.[44] *Histriomastix* thus represents a peculiar mixture of the materials associated with different cultural generations. Its language is studded with 1590s neologisms, while its construction harks back to older forms that had taken on new life in the Elizabethan *fin de siècle*.

Within this nexus, the material performed by Sir Oliver Owlet's Men presents a self-conscious imitation and incorporation of older theatrical forms, as *Histriomastix* uses various forms of theatrical archaism to mount a pointed critique of the development of the sixteenth-century theatre industry. In contrast with the more measured treatment of the playing company in *Sir Thomas More*, the travelling players of *Histriomastix* are the subject of considerable mockery – Roslyn Lander Knutson describes them, not unfairly, as 'a dystopian caricature of a bad company'.[45] The players appear at regular intervals, and their repertory is carefully delineated. In Act 2, during the time of Plenty, Posthaste the poet works on a 'new plot of the prodigall childe', and he reads a section for the players, breaking off when he becomes overcome by his own writing and 'cannot read for teares' (C1r–v). The lines quoted from the new play include '*Huffa, huffa, who callis for mee? / I play the Prodigall child in iollytie*' (C1r), a paraphrase of the Henrician morality *The Interlude of Youth* (*c.*1513–14; printed 1532–3), in which Riot cries 'Huffa, huffa! who calleth after me? / I am Riot, full of jollity'.[46] Posthaste thus appears to believe that a morality play in the style of the early sixteenth century is a suitable offering for his company.

However, when the players reappear later in the act, their repertory has moved on a generation or two. Posthaste lists their plays for Lord Mavortius' Gentleman Usher, including '*Mother Gurtons needle*', a reference to *Gammer Gurton's Needle*, performed around 1562–3 and printed in 1575, and '*The Diuell and Diues*', probably the Elizabethan play about Dives and Lazarus that is also mentioned in *Sir Thomas More*.[47] When the actors later perform for Lord Mavortius their play combines morality and romance elements. Although this may appear incongruous, it mimics a form of drama that was emerging in the 1570s. As David Bevington describes, extant plays such as *Clyomon and Clamydes* (*c.*1570–83) and *Common Conditions* (*c.*1570–6) are 'hybrids of romantic and allegorical figures' in which Vices (Subtle Shift in *Clyomon and Clamydes* and the title character in *Common Conditions*) feature in comic scenes that intercut the romance narratives.[48]

The inset play opens with a song advertising the troupe, '*Some vp and some downe, ther's Players in the towne*'; this is followed by a prologue written mainly in fourteeners, which suggests that the play will be a dramatic romance about Troilus and Cressida:

Phillida was a faire maid; I know one fairer then she,
Troylus was a true louer; I know one truer then he:
And *Cressida* that dainty dame, whose beauty faire & sweet,
Was cleare as is yᵉ Christall streame, that runs along yᵉ street.
How *Troyll* he that noble knight, was drunk in loue and bad goodnight,
So bending leg likewise; do you not vs despise.   (C3v)

After these lines, which are not unfairly castigated by the nobleman
Landulpho as 'Most vgly lines and base-browne-paper-stuffe' and 'prophane absurds' (C3v), the opening of the play – an exchange between
Troilus and Cressida – is conducted in tetrameter couplets: 'Come *Cressida*
my Cresset light / Thy face doth shine both day and night' (C4r). The
romantic mood is shattered, however, by a sudden interruption:

> *Enter a roaring Diuell with the Vice on his back, Iniquity in one hand;*
> *and Iuventus in the other.*
>
>   *Vice.* Passion of me sir, puffe puffe how I sweat sir,
> The dust out of your coate sir, I intend for to beat sir.
>   *Iuv[entus].* I am the prodigall child, I that I am,
> Who saye; I am not, I say he is too blame.
>   *Iniq[uity].* And I likewise am *Iniquitie*
> Beloued of many alasse for pitty.
>   *Diuell.* Ho ho ho, these babes mine are all,
> The *Vice*, *Iniquitie* and child Prodigall.   (C4r)

Iniquity, who features as the Vice in *The Devil is an Ass*, is here presented as
a junior vice, accompanied by the equally traditional figure of the prodigal
Juventus. The inset play replicates conventional stage business associated
with the Vice, who – as noted above – was often carried on or off the
stage on the Devil's back, amid a good deal of roaring and puffs of smoke.
The play-within-the-play thus mimics with some precision the details of the
romance–morality hybrid of the 1570s, and the parody is sharpened by the
fact that the dialogue itself is almost meaningless, composed predominantly
of nonsense, non sequiturs and ridiculously forced rhymes.

    In Act 4, the age of Envy, the players are seen debating the roles that
they might take in a new play, and their discussion suggests that they have
again shifted a generation, from the drama of the 1570s to that of the late
1580s and 1590s. Gulch comments, 'here be huffing parts in this new
booke' (F1r); 'huffing', meaning 'swaggering' or 'blustering' is used in a
number of 1590s texts to refer to the dramatic or rhetorical high style:
Gabriel Harvey, for instance, criticises the 'flaunting and huffing braueries'
of Thomas Nashe's 'railing tropes, and craking figures'.[49] Gutt then asks,

'Haue I er'e a good humour in my part?', to which Gulch replies, 'Thou hast neere a good one out of thy part', apparently referring to Jonson's hit comedies, *Every Man in his Humour* and *Every Man out of his Humour*, performed by the Chamberlain's Men in 1598–9. Belch declares, 'Ile play the conquering King that likes me best' – probably with a Marlovian role such as Tamburlaine in mind – and Gutt counters with 'Thou play the cowardly knaue; thou dost but ieast' (F1r). Sir Oliver Owlet's Men are seemingly keeping up to date with two of the most influential theatrical fashions of the late 1580s and 1590s: the huffing Marlovian tragedy and the comedy of humours. This impression is reinforced in Act 5, the age of War, in which the players are pressed into service as soldiers. Clutching the players' apparel, a soldier tells them,

> Come on Players, now we are the Sharers
> And you the hired men: Nay you must take patience,
> Slid how do you march?
> Sirha is this you would rend and teare the Cat
> Vpon a Stage, and now march like a drown'd rat?
> Looke vp and play the *Tamburlaine*: you rogue you. (G1r)

The soldier refers to practices within the professional theatre industry of the late sixteenth century, in which sharers in the company had institutional and financial power over the hired men whose wages they paid. He also describes the stereotypical performance style of the late Elizabethan tragedian, invoking specifically the bravura role of Tamburlaine, originally played by Edward Alleyn.

Archaism and novelty in *Histriomastix* thus serve as markers of temporal change, as the theatre mirrors the development of the play's society through its six ages. However, the incorporation of stylistic features associated with different generations, and the representation of the movement from one generation to another, also serves to complicate notions of temporality and of progress and decay within the play. The narrative structure of *Histriomastix* charts a cyclical movement in which the initial rise and subsequent decline of society through the ages of Peace, Plenty, Pride, Envy, War and Poverty is halted only by the intervention of Peace, who banishes Poverty and hails Astrea – representing Queen Elizabeth – as the guarantor of peace and national glory. She tells her,

>   liue as long
> As Time hath life, and *Fame* a worthy tongue.
> Still breath our glory, the worlds *Empresse*,
> *Religions* Gardian, *Peaces* patronesse;

Now flourish Arts, the Queene of *Peace* doth raigne,
Vertue triumph, now shee doth sway the stemme,
Who giues to *Vertue*, honours Diadem.   (H2v)

As long as she lives, Elizabeth will sustain the conditions in which peace, true religion, the arts and virtue can flourish. In the last action of the play, Plenty, Pride, Envy, War and Poverty 'enter and resigne their seuerall Scepters to *Peace*, sitting in Maiestie' (H3r). However, the play's final message is mixed. Peace has returned to her place of glory, suggesting that the narrative has come full circle; similarly, the reign of Elizabeth is represented as having put a halt to the cyclical movement shown in the preceding six acts. Yet the return of Peace also suggests that the cycle might begin again. Moreover, at the point at which the play was performed, in the late 1590s or early 1600s, spectators must have been aware that Elizabeth's reign was nearing its end. The queen could not 'liue as long / As Time hath life', and time could not come to a halt with the Elizabethan period, tantalising as the fantasy may have been to some.

The representation of the players, and the invocation of novel and archaic theatrical forms, contributes to this temporal uncertainty. While the play depicts a cycle, the theatrical modes associated with Sir Oliver Owlet's Men trace a linear movement through the generations, from Henrician morality play, through the mid-Elizabethan morality–romance hybrid, to Marlovian tragedy and Jonsonian comedy. Theatre ends, with the play, in the Elizabethan *fin de siècle*, but because the players are banished there is no hint of cyclical renewal. *Histriomastix* looks forward to a new era in which the arts will flourish, but this is apparently to come not from the theatre but from other art-forms. In terms of the dramatic forms presented, there is linear movement, but does it represent progress? The play encourages its audience to giggle at archaic theatrical forms through its presentation of *The Prodigal Child* and the Troilus and Cressida play, and equally to snigger at references to the over-the-top histrionics of late-Elizabethan tragedians. In this alternative history, all theatrical fashions are equally risible, whether they are old or new. The play thus uses theatrical archaism to deconstruct the very mode in which it is written, and its stylistic aberrations – its six acts, its recourse to emblematic traditions – begin to look like part of a deliberate rejection of the traditions of the commercial stage that applies to all generations equally.

Staging tragedy: *Hamlet*

Archaism similarly comes into contact with the traditions of the commercial stage in *Hamlet*, but rather than satirising the theatrical past, Shakespeare here uses parodies of outmoded forms to position in generational terms his own versions of an old narrative and a long-established genre. As Margreta de Grazia has recently suggested, despite the frequent identification of *Hamlet* with 'the beginning of the modern age' early allusions to it suggest that it was initially 'considered behind the times rather than ahead of them'; she describes it, resonantly, as 'timeworn on arrival'.[50] *Hamlet* is simultaneously old and new, nostalgic and future-orientated, novel and archaic, and these qualities inflect its handling of its own narrative – which is echoed and re-doubled throughout the play – and its treatment of generations and intergenerational relations.

Like the author(s) of *Histriomastix*, Shakespeare juxtaposes different phases of the theatrical past, drawing on the two distinct generations of English Senecanism recently delineated by Jessica Winston: first, the 1560s – a decade that saw the publication of the Seneca translations of Jasper Heywood, Alexander Neville, John Studley and Thomas Nuce, and the production of Senecan plays such as *Gismond of Salerne* and Thomas Norton and Thomas Sackville's *Gorboduc* – and second, the period between the late 1580s and the early 1600s, a time of Senecan imitation by dramatists such as Kyd, Marlowe, Shakespeare and Marston.[51] The first generation is represented in *Hamlet* by the play-within-the play, *The Murder of Gonzago*, in Act 3, Scene 2; the second by Aeneas' speech to Dido, delivered by the First Player in Act 2, Scene 2. As Madeleine Doran points out, these are places in which Shakespeare 'affects to quote something'; in fact, of course, he composes his own 'quotations', 'but he sets them off in styles utterly different from the body of the play'.[52] As Doran's phrasing suggests, the 'styles' of the two sequences are not identical: they mimic the attempts of two different generations of English writers to represent Senecan tragic style.

Although Aeneas' speech is often described as archaic, it is not especially old-fashioned in its language or style. Instead, its Latinate diction and vivid imagery mimic the Senecan pastiche of Shakespeare's contemporaries, writers such as Kyd and, later, Marston, whose *Antonio's Revenge* is so close in date to *Hamlet* that scholars have been unable to prove conclusively which play came first.[53] In the first section of Aeneas' speech, the Player describes how

> roasted in wrath and fire,
> And thus o'ersized with coagulate gore,
> With eyes like carbuncles, the hellish Pyrrhus
> Old grandsire Priam seeks.[54]

There are clear affinities in tone and diction between the style adopted in this speech and the exaggeratedly Senecan manner of Marston's villainous Piero, who declares in the opening scene of *Antonio's Revenge*,

> I am great of blood,
> Unequal'd in revenge. You horrid scouts
> That sentinel swart night, give loud applause
> From your large palms.[55]

Both Shakespeare and Marston employ words that were long-established in English but were nonetheless comparatively unusual: 'coagulate', 'carbuncles' and 'swart'; both make heavy use of alliteration, and both use inflated language to cast the revenger as an excessive, blood-soaked figure.

In contrast, *The Murder of Gonzago* echoes the stiffer and more stylistically restrained mode adopted by Senecan translators and imitators in the 1560s. It features a dumb show followed by a sequence that differs from the dominant blank verse of *Hamlet* in its use of tetrameter (in the prologue) and pentameter couplets. Lines are generally end-stopped, and an often-strained word order enables the couplets to be maintained; some individual words, such as 'operant', may also be deliberate archaisms.[56] In addition, we might note, with G. R. Hibbard, 'the long-drawn-out sententious commonplaces, the repetition of ideas, the laboured periphrases [and] the references to classical mythology'.[57] The limpid and circular quality of the initial exchange between the Player King and Queen is typical:

> PLAYER KING *Full thirty times hath Phoebus' cart gone round*
> *Neptune's salt wash and Tellus' orbed ground*
> *And thirty dozen moons with borrowed sheen*
> *About the world have times twelve thirties been*
> *Since love our hearts and Hymen did our hands*
> *Unite commutual in most sacred bands.*
> PLAYER QUEEN *So many journeys may the sun and moon*
> *Make us again count o'er ere love be done.*
> *But woe is me, you are so sick of late,*
> *So far from cheer and from our former state,*
> *That I distrust you. Yet, though I distrust,*
> *Discomfort you, my lord, it nothing must.*
> *For women fear too much, even as they love,*
> *And women's fear and love hold quantity –*
> *Either none, in neither aught, or in extremity.*   (3.2.148–62)[58]

The repetitions of 'thirty', 'distrust' and 'women('s) fear' contribute to the circularity of the exchange, and also, perhaps, create an impression of naivety. Like Aeneas' speech, *The Murder of Gonzago* contains Latinate coinages (such as 'commutual' in line 152), but its style is infinitely stiffer. It is also insistently euphemistic: the sun is *'Phoebus' cart'*; the sea *'Neptune's salt wash'*, the earth *'Tellus' orbed ground'*. As Philip Edwards points out, variations between the second quarto and Folio texts suggest that Shakespeare had trouble in finishing the Player Queen's speeches, 'perhaps not finding it easy to get exactly the right kind of prosy sententiousness without becoming positively tedious'.[59]

Various attempts have been made to identify the style that is parodied here. O. B. Hardison Jr suggests that the 'stiff decasyllabic couplets' of the play-within-the-play were 'probably as close Shakespeare dared come to the fourteeners of the older drama except in overtly comic episodes like the performance of Pyramus and Thisby in *A Midsummer Night's Dream*'.[60] He seems to have in mind plays such as Preston's *Cambises* and the anonymous *Clyomon and Clamydes*, which are written predominantly in fourteeners, but their style is not much like that of *The Murder of Gonzago*. As Ralph de Someri Childs has argued, a closer equivalent is the style of sixteenth-century elite tragedies such as Norton and Sackville's *Gorboduc* (1562), George Gascoigne and Francis Kinwelmerche's *Jocasta* (1566), Thomas Hughes and his collaborators' *The Misfortunes of Arthur* (1588) and Robert Wilmot's *Tancred and Gismond* (1591: itself a revision of *Gismond of Salerne*, written in 1566/8), all of which feature dumb shows between the acts.[61]

Yet these observations overlook the ambiguous position of the pentameter couplet in sixteenth-century drama. Tragedies such as *Gorboduc*, *Jocasta* and *The Misfortunes of Arthur* are written primarily in blank verse; *Tancred and Gismond* features some couplets, but the bulk of the play is a combination of blank verse and cross-rhymes. Pentameter couplets are often found as part of a medley style in both the plays performed by Queen Elizabeth's Men in the 1580s and their predecessors, such as William Wager's *Mary Magdalene* (c.1547–66, printed c.1566), R.B.'s *Apius and Virginia* (c.1559–67, printed 1575), Fulwell's *Like Will to Like*, Preston's *Cambises*, Richard Edwards' *Damon and Pithias* (1565, printed 1571), John Pickering's *Horestes* (printed 1567), and George Whetstone's *Promos and Cassandra* (printed 1578).[62] However, in most of these plays pentameter couplets are mainly used by comic and low-status figures, while tragedy and high emotion is conveyed in fourteeners.

Only a handful of surviving sixteenth-century plays are written predominantly in pentameter couplets; these include *King Darius* (c.1558–65, printed 1565) and Thomas Nuce's translation of the pseudo-Senecan tragedy *Octavia* (printed 1566), in which the pentameter is combined with tetrameter. While *King Darius*'s couplets are much plainer and more vigorous than those of *The Murder of Gonzago*, Nuce's *Octavia* provides a reasonably close equivalent, and it seems likely that this Elizabethan Seneca is what Shakespeare has in mind:

> *Oct[avia]*. Nay, sooner shall the roaring frothy seas,
> And mounting, flashing flawes ymatch the skie,
> And smoking, stiffling parching fyer drye,
> With danckish pooles agree, and watrie fenne.
> And griesly *Plutos* filthie feltred denne,
> With starbright heauen shall sooner coupled bee,
> And shining light, with glomie shades agree,
> And with the cleare drye daye, the dewy night,
> Than vnto seruile lore of husband wyght,
> That brutish wise in bloud takes his delight,
> My heauy woefull mynd can I addresse,
> Whyle brothers death my heart doth still possesse.[63]

Words such as 'wight', and the use of the 'y' prefix, were not especially archaic in literary writing in the mid-1560s, when Nuce composed his translation, but they would have seemed dated by the turn of the century, as would the end-stopped couplets and the heavy use of rhetorical devices such as anaphora and alliteration.

As Dieter Mehl stresses in his classic study of the early modern dumb show, the dumb show was not in itself archaic in the 1590s; indeed, it was 'enjoying an ever increasing popularity'.[64] What is archaic about *The Murder of Gonzago* is its diction, its syntax and, in particular, its use of rhyme, a strategy that came under increased pressure in the 1590s and early 1600s. We might draw a comparison with George Chapman's *The Gentleman Usher*, first performed by the Chapel Children around 1601, in which a parodic inset play written by the idiotic schoolmaster Sarpego features both pentameter couplets and poetic archaisms such as 'maugre', 'eke', 'wights', 'cleped' and 'welkin'.[65] Intriguingly, one character, the 'rush-man' declares that it is his duty 'To make rush ruffle in a verse of ten' (2.1.250), suggesting a certain self-consciousness about the pentameter couplets in which he is speaking. The style of *Hamlet*'s inset play therefore *makes* the dumb show archaic, rather than vice versa.

I dwell on *The Murder of Gonzago* because defining precisely the nature of its archaism has important ramifications for how we view the thematic and stylistic interactions between generations in *Hamlet*. The incorporation of the two Senecan modes, with their invocation of two different generations of writers, is part of *Hamlet*'s remarkable temporal ambiguity, the difficulty that this play has in fully separating past, present and future. Further, in contrast with the metatheatrical elements in *Histriomastix*, which move forward in time, the imported elements in *Hamlet* work backwards, in a movement that runs counter to the progression of the main narrative but which is in line with the temporal ambiguity presented elsewhere. For Terence Hawkes, *The Murder of Gonzago* 'marks Hamlet's most recursive moment: the point at which time runs most obviously backwards, and where the play does not just glance over its shoulder, so much as turn fully round to look squarely at the most prominent action replay of them all'. Simultaneously, however, since the inset play aims to 'generate events that will forward the action', it also points towards the future.[66] In its dramatisation of a narrative similar to that of *Hamlet* itself, and in its stylistic archaism, *The Murder of Gonzago* is both an 'action replay' of past events and a catalyst for projected future events. Furthermore, its temporal dissonance seeps out into the drama that surrounds it; the inset play crystallises Shakespeare's presentation of multiple versions of Hamlet and the *Hamlet* narrative, and also links them inevitably to the institution of theatre itself.

Furthermore, *The Murder of Gonzago* is part of a network of interrelations between diachronic and synchronic generations, which are evident on a narrative and thematic level and on a stylistic and generic level. *Hamlet* is an intensely generational work, invoking the 'systems of structure and agency; obligation and exchange; reciprocity and the exercise of power' described by Burnett and the thresholds 'between beginning and end, between ancestry and heritage, between procreation and tradition, between origin and memory' invoked by Weigel. On a thematic level, intergenerational interactions include the demands that the older generation make on the younger, be they Old Hamlet's desire for his son to avenge him, Polonius' willingness to use his daughter as a pawn in diagnosing Hamlet's condition, or Claudius' manipulation of Laertes. The play also sets up implicit comparisons between Hamlet and alternative revengers such as Laertes, Fortinbras and Pyrrhus, and mirroring figures such as Old Hamlet, Ophelia and, potentially, Claudius. On an aesthetic level, *Hamlet* not only draws on but incorporates earlier texts, creating an intrageneric system in which the debt to earlier generations of tragedies creates its own set of tensions.

Thematic and aesthetic generations are combined in *The Murder of Gonzago*, an 'action replay' (to use Hawkes's term) of the primal moment of the Hamlet narrative itself: the murder of Old Hamlet at the hands of his brother. It does not, however, merely reiterate the play's back-story.

The Murder of Gonzago presents a version of this narrative that is revision-ary in both content and style: husband and wife declare their love for one another at length, the wife vows never to marry after her husband's death, and the murderer's intervention (*'Thoughts black, hands apt, drugs fit, and time agreeing, / Considerate season else no creature seeing'* [3.2.248–9]) breaks through the comforting antique patina of the preceding exchange. In its presentation of king, queen and murderer, *The Murder of Gonzago* seems calculated to present the narrative from Hamlet's perspective. Further-more, the archaism of the dialogue between the Player King and Queen, and its recollection of the tragic theatre of its spectators' parents and, even, grandparents, is not burlesqued. As Richard Dyer notes, recent produc-tions have had problems in conveying the 'affective power' of these sequences in addition to their qualities as pastiche, 'Yet without that emotional truth, the point of these pastiches is lost'.[67]

In some respects, therefore, the use of archaic style in *The Murder of Gonzago* is affective, intended to appeal to the deep-seated emotions and theatrical memories of its earliest audiences. It gives the dysfunctional interactions of the Danish royal family the status of archetype, casting a comforting nostalgia around the relationship between the mother and father of the absent child and suggesting the trauma of the nephew/uncle's intervention. The insistent repetition surrounding *The Murder of Gonzago* begs again Gertrude's question to Hamlet, 'Why seems it so particular with thee?' (1.2.75). What is 'particular' about Hamlet's father? About his story? The inset play also presents in its theatrical archaism one of a number of implied pasts that haunt the narrative of *Hamlet*, others including the play's insistent references to suppressed religious rites, and its interest in classical narratives such as those surrounding Hercules, Pyrrhus and Hecuba.[68]

The specific question of the theatrical past also, however, begs further consideration. The replay and revision of the *Hamlet* narrative in *The Murder of Gonzago* does not emphasise only the commonplace aspects of Shakespeare's narrative, or the play's investment in the interplay between generations. In the context of *Hamlet*'s interest in two different forms of English Senecanism, it also underlines the play's close affinity with the English revenge tragedy tradition and, thereby, a new set of intergenera-tional relationships. *Hamlet* draws heavily on the conventions established in Kyd's *Spanish Tragedy*, and it appears to be linked with an earlier play about Hamlet, known as the Ur-*Hamlet*, of which Philip Henslowe records a performance on 9 June 1594, during the short season that the Admiral's Men and the Chamberlain's Men mounted together at the

Newington Butts playhouse.[69] The Ur-*Hamlet* was already old in 1594, since Thomas Nashe mocked it in 1589, and it has been strongly argued both that it preceded *The Spanish Tragedy*, and that Kyd himself may have written it.[70]

Nothing survives of the Ur-*Hamlet* beyond allusions and quotations. Two of the most evocative descriptions occur in the prose works of men who also wrote plays. In *Wit's Misery* Thomas Lodge describes how 'Hate-Virtue' 'walks for the most part in black vnder colour of grauity, & looks as pale as the Uisard of ye ghost which cried so miserally [i.e. miserably] at ye Theator like an oisterwife, *Hamlet, reuenge*' (H4v). Similarly, in criticising dramatists from lowly social backgrounds who presume to write tragedy, Nashe comments, condescendingly, 'English *Seneca* read by candle light yeeldes manie good sentences, as *Bloud is a begger*, and so foorth: and if you intreate him faire in a frostie morning, he will affoord you whole *Hamlets*, I should say handfulls of tragical speaches'.[71] This Hamlet play included a ghost, and it presented an 'English *Seneca*'. Moreover, the phrases '*Hamlet, reuenge*' and '*Bloud is a begger*' align the Ur-*Hamlet* with the second phase of English Senecanism, and suggest that Senecan excess was an essential part of the English *Hamlet* tradition from its earliest phases.

James J. Marino has recently argued that scholars have been too keen to separate the Ur-*Hamlet* from Shakespeare's *Hamlet*; early modern audiences, in contrast, may have seen not two distinct plays but a gradually evolving set of variations on the *Hamlet* narrative. 'Rather than displaying a clear lineage of authority and derivation,' he suggests, 'the *Hamlet* texts are surprisingly interdependent.'[72] David Scott Kastan evokes a more antagonistic relationship between old and new plays: for Shakespeare to call his play *Hamlet* 'is not a gesture of respect toward a worthy model but a revisionary proclamation ostentatiously announcing its own originality'.[73] These viewpoints may be less irreconcilable than they appear, and I suggest that *The Murder of Gonzago* and Aeneas' speech, with their recycling of old and new forms of English Senecanism, argue not so much for a clear division between *Hamlet* and Ur-*Hamlet*, or a complete lack of any such division, but for an intertextual interplay between older and newer versions of the narrative, and with closely related texts such as *The Spanish Tragedy* and *Antonio's Revenge*. Shakespeare attempts to distinguish between his version and the older one, as Kastan suggests, but he nonetheless appears to acknowledge the impossibility of fully separating his play from the established tradition.

Thus, in the sequence centring on *The Murder of Gonzago* Shakespeare compulsively rewrites the theatrical past and present in order to assert his play's own paradoxical modernity as a turn-of-the-century revenge tragedy. In the first quarto and Folio versions of *Hamlet* the troupe are said to have left the city because of the commercial (and, possibly, political) threat posed by a troupe of boy players.[74] These passages seem to refer directly to the renewed activity of the Children of Paul's (from 1599) and the Children of the Chapel (from 1600), and their deliberate appeal to a (would-be) cultural elite.[75] Elsewhere, we find allusions to late-Elizabethan plays. The First Player's speech revisits material dramatised by Marlowe and Nashe in *Dido, Queen of Carthage*, performed by an earlier incarnation of the Children of the Chapel in the mid-late 1580s and printed in 1594. Similarly, the by-play between Polonius and Hamlet – 'I did enact Julius Caesar. I was killed i'th' Capitol. Brutus killed me.' 'It was a brute part of him to kill so capital a calf there.' (3.2.99–102) – seems deliberately to remind an audience of the parts taken by the two actors, John Heminges and Richard Burbage, in Shakespeare's recent play *Julius Caesar*. In the middle of *The Murder of Gonzago* itself, Hamlet tells the actor playing the murderer, Lucianus, 'leave thy damnable faces and begin. Come, "the croaking raven doth bellow for revenge"' (3.2.246–7), adapting two lines from *The True Tragedy of Richard III*, a play first performed by Queen Elizabeth's Men around 1591.[76] *The Murder of Gonzago* is therefore surrounded by references to a set of late-Elizabethan tragedies, some of them drawing on the revenge tragedy tradition in which *Hamlet* itself is so heavily invested. While they insist upon the currency of Shakespeare's play, these allusions also underline through contrast and juxtaposition both the archaism of *The Murder of Gonzago*, and the antiquity of the Senecan tradition that it embodies.

It is worth returning at this point to Aeneas' speech, with its appropriation of the late sixteenth-century Senecanism of Kyd and Marston. Hamlet's immediate reaction to this speech in the soliloquy beginning 'O, what a rogue and peasant slave am I!' (2.2.485) has been fiercely debated, but most relevant here is the extent to which it later shapes Hamlet's own verbal style, and his very conception of himself as a revenger. In the aftermath of the performance of *The Murder of Gonzago*, and immediately before he goes to Gertrude's chamber, Hamlet declares,

> 'Tis now the very witching time of night
> When churchyards yawn and hell itself breaks out
> Contagion to the world. Now could I drink hot blood
> And do such business as the bitter day
> Would quake to look on.   (3.2.378–82)[77]

Hamlet momentarily casts himself as a blood-soaked revenger in the mould of Pyrrhus or Marston's Piero. He encounters the apparently praying Claudius immediately after this speech, leading to the moment at which he comes closest to embodying the traditional revenger: 'And now I'll do it' (3.3.74).[78] Ultimately, however, the Senecan model is rejected, and Hamlet declines to become Pyrrhus.

The metadramatic sequences in *Hamlet* track English Senecanism back to a point at which it can be deconstructed, allowing Hamlet to experiment with, and finally reject, the persona of the Senecan revenger. Hamlet's reaction to the Aeneas speech encapsulates in miniature the reaction to Senecan convention in *Hamlet*, and the ways in which the theatrical past and present are both represented as inadequate behavioural and aesthetic models. Shakespeare appears to be irresistibly drawn to revenge tragedy's conventions – clichés, even – but he is unable to indulge in them fully, and instead compulsively reworks and reinvigorates them. *The Murder of Gonzago* encapsulates this appropriative process. Hamlet does not only ask the First Player 'can you play *The Murder of Gonzago?*', he also asks to be allowed to amend it, and to twist it to his own purposes: 'You could for need study a speech of some dozen lines, or sixteen lines, which I would set down and insert in't, could you not?' (2.2.474, 476–8). Even though Hamlet's revision of the inherited work is far less thorough than Shakespeare's may have been, he adopts, adapts, and re-presents the older play in a specific cultural and political context, one in which its antiquity is both a strategic advantage and (potentially) an aesthetic liability. The play-within-the-play acts as a locus for the archaism that might otherwise be associated with the revenge tragedy, allowing Shakespeare to posit his tragedy as the modern culmination and revision of this tradition.

Hamlet thus presents a series of interwoven negotiations between different kinds of generations. In thematic terms, Hamlet is subject to the demands of the older generation, which hopelessly compromise his dealings with members of his own generation such as Ophelia and Laertes. He also, however, attempts to control the older generation through his interactions with Gertrude and, as strikingly, through his presentation of his family's story in *The Murder of Gonzago*. Simultaneously, the play-within-the-play acts as a locus for anxieties about aesthetic generations, and about the Hamlet narrative, its generic associations, and its classical and modern influences. Like Jonson, Shakespeare attempts to control the impact of his archaic theatrical 'quotations'. Yet he is also – again, like Jonson – prepared to exploit their aesthetic and affective power and their powerful associations with established genres, to take advantage of archaism's potential to make something new from the bones of something old.

Conclusion

In tracking the generational production of theatrical archaism in *The Devil is an Ass*, *Sir Thomas More*, *Histriomastix* and *Hamlet*, I have also traced a series of stories that the early modern theatre told itself about its own development and place in history, about the relationship between different parts of the theatrical landscape, and about the place of particular outmoded forms. These stories centre on, and are embodied by, quotations from and parodies of earlier works, as archaic characters and sequences provide focal points around which diachronic and synchronic generational networks are invoked and negotiated. Dramatists' uses of archaism demonstrate not only the aesthetic and narrative utility of the theatrical past, and the debt that they owe their forebears, but also the need for one generation to distinguish itself from another, and to forge synchronic as well as diachronic networks.

In a preface to the printed text of *The Roaring Girl* (1611), Middleton uses a sartorial metaphor to draw a line between the theatrical past and the theatrical present:

> in the time of the great-crop doublet, your huge bombasted plays, quilted with mighty words to lean purposes, was only then in fashion; and as the doublet fell, neater inventions began to set up. Now in the time of spruceness, our plays follow the niceness of our garments: single plots, quaint conceits, lecherous jests dressed up in hanging sleeves[.][79]

As we have seen, dramatists use archaism to reverse this process and make theatrical time run backwards, or to confuse the boundaries between past and present, between one theatrical generation and another. Yet to recreate the theatrical past too fully would be to risk entering a recursive loop, in which both dramatist and audience might lose their temporal bearings. Accordingly, each of the plays discussed here delicately balances past and present, and each establishes a clear perspective or narrative 'line' on theatrical archaism. Archaism serves different functions: directing spectators' reactions; complicating historical narrative; eliciting affect. Nonetheless, these disparate plays share a common desire to make the theatrical past communicate with contemporary audiences, and to make theatrical generations touch across the stylistic divide.

CHAPTER 5

Shepherds' speech: archaism and Stuart pastoral drama

In the second act of *The Knave in Grain*, performed at the Fortune playhouse in the mid to late 1630s, a young man named Antonio survives a murderous attack from his friend Francisco, who is – wrongly – convinced that he has had an affair with his wife.[1] Despite the play's generally urban setting, the confrontation takes place in a grove, and the wounded Antonio is rescued by a shepherd. In Act 3, Antonio encounters Francisco's wife, Cornelia, and her sister, Phemone, who have fled the city in disguise. Antonio is now dressed as a shepherd himself and in order to keep his identity secret he decides to mould his speech to suit his clothes. He therefore addresses Phemone thus:

> *Bonny wight, what e're you be,*
> *Lucke be in your company.*
> *Are you* Sylvanus, *say to me?*
>   *Phem[one].* None such, good Shepheard.
>   *Ant[onio]. Deft and trim ones mickle glee,*
> *Be you what you please to be,*
> *Some disaster tend by yee.*
>   *Corn[elia].* Never, never more.
>   *Phe[mone].* A me unfortunate.
>   *Ant[onio]. Welladay, now by my Creed,*
> *And my merry Oaten Reed,*
> *Sike another rousing sigh*
> *Would well split me gay and blith:*
> *Let a loutish Clowne partake,*
> *Why this sobbing dole you make?*[2]

Antonio's speech here is a litany of archaic terms, all of them deployed in the pastorals of Spenser and his followers, and many of them glossed by E.K. in *The Shepheardes Calender*.[3] The genuine shepherd does not talk in this manner, so it seems that the dramatist is having fun with the high-status Antonio's ignorance of the lives of real shepherds, evidenced in his conviction that to talk like a shepherd is to employ as many pastoral archaisms as possible and, moreover, to frame one's speech in the trimeter couplets sometimes used by pastoral poets. For a reader of the play, the artificiality of these linguistic and poetic conventions is under-lined by the printer's use of italics for Antonio's speeches. The sequence thus suggests not only the strength of pastoral archaism as a literary convention by the 1630s, when *The Knave in Grain* was performed, but also its vulnerability to satire and mockery.

This chapter takes Antonio's comic appropriation of pastoral style as its starting point, examining the crucial role that archaism played in pastoral drama of the early seventeenth century. This was a period during which experiments in pastoral by Italian and French playwrights brought new pressures to bear on both the aesthetic form and political associations of English dramatic pastoral. In the work of Samuel Daniel, John Fletcher, John Milton, Walter Montagu, Ben Jonson and others, pastoral stylistics negotiate a series of apparently binary oppositions, many of them high-lighted in *The Knave in Grain*. On the one hand, pastoral style was often characterised as low, rustic, natural, resolutely 'English', comic and deter-minedly old-fashioned; on the other, alternative versions of the genre positioned it as elevated, courtly, artificial, classical or continental in its derivation, serious and novel. Pastoral is a marriage of apparent contradic-tions, a factor that actually appears to have fuelled its productive appeal for sixteenth- and seventeenth-century writers. As a crucial marker of pastoral style in sixteenth-century poetry, archaism had the capacity both to reinforce and, perhaps counter-intuitively, break down such binaries, suggesting to seventeenth-century playwrights ways in which pastoral drama might reformulate and reinvigorate itself.

After a brief examination of the debate about archaism's role in pastoral stylistics, I focus on three especially provocative interventions in dramatic pastoral: Fletcher's *The Faithful Shepherdess* (*c.*1608; revived 1634); Milton's *A Masque Presented at Ludlow Castle*, also known as *Comus* (1634); and Jonson's *The Sad Shepherd* (*c.*1634–8). Although notoriously archaic in its style, *The Faithful Shepherdess* self-consciously rejects many of the stylistic markers of Spenserian pastoral, instead using syntactic archaism as part of a strategy in which various pastoral traditions – English, Italian and classical – are brought into ironic and slyly allusive dialogue with one other. In so doing, Fletcher appears to reject rural festivity and to reposition pastoral as elevated and newly courtly in its priorities. Yet *The Faithful Shepherdess* is courtly only insofar as it relates to the cultural priorities of Anna of Denmark, the patron of the company that first performed it, and it rejects

the masculine priorities of Italian pastoral in favour of a renewed engagement with Anna's quasi-oppositional stance in relation to her husband's
policies.

When *The Faithful Shepherdess* was revived in 1634, it moved from the
orbit of Anna of Denmark to that of her successor as queen consort,
Henrietta Maria. In the process, it was brought into dialogue with new
French-influenced works such as Montagu's *The Shepherds' Paradise* (1633),
an aristocratic revision of pastoral, performed by the queen and her court,
that almost entirely eschews archaic style. However, Milton's *A Masque*
and Jonson's *The Sad Shepherd*, both written not long after *The Shepherds'
Paradise*, reclaim archaism as a stylistic tool while nonetheless drawing on
new, continentally inflected theatrical conventions. In these dramas, 'old'
Spenserianism is juxtaposed with novel staging techniques, and both works
engage with newly revived debates about the political status of rural mirth.
Like *The Faithful Shepherdess*, *A Masque* engages with an alternative
cultural centre – in this case the Ludlow seat of John Egerton, Earl of
Bridgewater – and it represents a calculated synthesis of pastoral archaism's
'low' and 'high' associations. *The Sad Shepherd* similarly draws on the
mixed associations of pastoral style, reinforcing archaism's connections
with 'real' regional dialect but also introducing additional literary
artificiality in the form of an archaic verse form, the Skeltonic. Jonson
pointedly rejects some continental influences, but his localising strategy
also exposes – like that of Milton – the fault-lines between pastoral and the
countryside that it purports to represent. Thus all three dramas explore the
nature and the limits of pastoral diction, using archaism to probe and
reconfigure the genre's often troubled aesthetic, national and political
position.

Familiar stuff

Antonio's attempt to mimic the speech of a shepherd is a relatively late
intervention in a long-running debate: what kind of language was appropriate to literary and dramatic pastoral? As long ago as the 1560s, George
Turberville had argued for the generic and social decorum of adopting a
lowly style in pastoral poetry, commenting, 'as ye conference betwixt
Shephierds is familiar stuffe & homely: so haue I shapt my stile and
tempred it with suche common and ordinarie phrase of speach as Coun-
treymen do vse in their affaires'.[4] Turberville's example was followed by
Spenser in *The Shepheardes Calender*, and it was adopted by Spenserian
poets such as William Browne, Giles and Phineas Fletcher, George Wither

and Michael Drayton, the last of whom declared in 1619 that the subject and language of pastoral '*ought to be poor, silly, & of the coursest Woofe in appearance*'.[5] This stance reflected early modern preconceptions about the style of classical pastoral. One theory held, for example, that the word 'eclogue' itself meant 'goat-speech' (from Greek *aix* [goat] and *logos* [word]), while late-classical writers such as Servius and Donatus referred to pastoral's characteristic style as *humilis* (humble or low) and *tenuis* (low, meagre or 'eked-out').[6] As David Scott Wilson-Okamura points out, classical pastoral generally eschews rhetorical figures such as epic simile, apostrophe and personification, thought to characterise the high style, instead aiming for a consistent plainness of diction.[7]

But did this humble style necessarily require the writer of pastoral to revive old words? Theocritus and Virgil use outmoded terms and grammatical constructions only sparingly, leading some early modern commentators to argue that archaism had no classical warrant. Although Philip Sidney concedes that *The Shepheardes Calender* 'hath much poetry in his eclogues, indeed worthy the reading, if I be not deceived', he comments that his 'framing of his style, to an old rustic language I dare not allow, since neither Theocritus in Greek, Virgil in Latin, nor Sannazzaro in Italian did affect it'.[8] Yet archaism seeps into Sidney's own pastoral fiction, in an eclogue delivered towards the end of Book 3 of *The Old Arcadia*, which includes lines such as 'The welkin had full niggardly enclosed / In coffer of dim clouds his silver groats, / Ycleped stars', 'for my sheep I dreaded mickle more' and 'He said the music best thilke powers pleased / Was jump concord between our wit and will'.[9] The eclogue is placed in the mouth of Philisides – Sidney's surrogate in the romance – but its archaism and its use of the beast fable also mean that the poet here inhabits the style of Spenser and, in particular, that of the February Eclogue in *The Shepheardes Calender*.[10] Moreover, Sidney draws attention to its aberrant aesthetic in the divided reception that the eclogue finds within his narrative:

> According to the nature of diverse ears, diverse judgements straight followed: some praising his voice; others the words, fit to frame a pastoral style; others the strangeness of the tale, and scanning what he should mean by it. But old Geron ... took hold of this occasion to make his revenge and said he never saw thing worse proportioned than to bring in a tale of he knew not what beasts at such a banquet when rather some song of love, or matter for joyful melody, was to be brought forth. 'But', said he, 'this is the right conceit of young men who think then they speak wiseliest when they cannot understand themselves.' (225–6)

Ultimately, the comments on Philisides' eclogue draw attention to questions of decorum: while some find his voice, the song's diction and its use of allegory appropriate to pastoral, Geron is clearly discomforted by both its style and its content. Scholars have likewise been divided on the purpose of archaism in this poem. It has been described variously as 'a joke both at Spenser's expense and the "archaic" mentality of the young, unfallen Philisides', a sign that archaic diction is 'an idealized speech, a literary idiom that has nothing to do with the "rustical" language of sixteenth-century northerners', a signal that Sidney is 'thinking more of the threat to English than to continental liberty', and a sign of his adoption of 'the traditional rugged persona of the plain-speaking, anti-courtly shepherd'.[11] Like Geron's judgement, these comments return us to the binary models of pastoral that I outlined at the start of this chapter, and the crucial role that archaism plays in constructing pastoral as 'English' or 'rustic' or 'literary'. What appears to unsettle critics – within the poem and outside it – is the possibility that Philisides' song might be both 'English' and 'continental' and its archaic diction simultaneously 'idealized' and 'rustical'.

Sidney's experiment with archaic diction in Philisides' poem was apparently overlooked by Ben Jonson, who criticised both Sidney and the Italian dramatist Battista Guarini for breaking decorum in refusing to use rustic language. In his reported conversations with William Drummond, dating from 1619, Jonson repeatedly criticises poets' failure to differentiate people of different class status through the style of their speech, grumbling that 'Sidney did not keep a decorum in making everyone speak as well as himself', that 'Guarini in his *Pastor Fido* kept not decorum in making shepherds speak as well as himself could' and that 'Lucan, Sidney, Guarini make every man speak as well as themselves, forgetting decorum; for Dametas sometimes speaks grave sentences'.[12] Pastoral is only specified once here, in the comments on *Il pastor fido*. Yet Jonson also refers to Dametas – a name given to servile characters in both Sidney and Guarini – and he claims of his own pastoral, *The May Lord*, 'Contrary to all other pastorals, he bringeth the clowns making mirth and foolish sports' (ll. 311–12). His comments to Drummond thus suggest Jonson's preoccupation with the relationship between pastoral and comedy and with the class dynamics of pastoral, an issue to which I will return later in this chapter.

Closely related to the issue of class is one of region. Regional versions of English were often assumed to preserve old words and forms of speech, and generations of early modern commentators viewed them as less adulterated than metropolitan speech. Alexander Gil, for instance, argued in 1619 that the '*Northern dialect*' could legitimately be imitated by writers because it was '*the most delightful, the most ancient, the purest, and approximates most nearly to the speech of our ancestors*'.[13] In composing their pastorals, however, writers often looked not to genuine regional speech, but to older literary texts. Thus, an archaism in a pastoral text might represent a genuine feature of regional speech, but it might equally be a literary import; archaism might therefore be simultaneously a marker of pastoral's rustic authenticity and a marker of its literary artificiality.

Archaic style has dual associations with both grandeur and simplicity; the introduction of archaism in pastoral would be congruent with some versions of pastoral's 'poor', 'coarse' or 'silly' style, but might also risk encroaching on the 'high' style. Even Spenser's pastorals contain considerable variation, and his practice often runs counter to E.K.'s theory. For instance, E.K. somewhat anxiously remarks in his comments on *The Shepheardes Calender* that the October Eclogue differs in its style from the others. Noting its imitation of Theocritus' sixteenth Idyll, 'wherein hee reproued the Tyranne Hiero of Syracuse for his nigardise toward Poetes', he notes that it also mimics its style, 'more loftye then the rest, and applyed to the heighte of Poeticall witte' (*SP*, 132–3). In his last set of stanzas Cuddy exclaims,

> Thou kenst not *Percie* how the ryme should rage.
> O if my temples were distained with wine,
> And girt in girlonds of wild Yuie twine,
> How I could reare the Muse on stately stage,
> And teache her tread aloft in buskin fine,
> With queint *Bellona* in her equipage. ('October', ll. 109–14)

E.K. writes, sourly, 'He seemeth here to be rauished with a Poetical furie. For (if one rightly mark) the numbers rise so ful, and the verse groweth so big, that it seemeth he hath forgot the meanenesse of shepheards state and stile' (*SP*, 136–7). Indeed, the eclogue's distance from a purely pastoral archaism is signalled not only in its emphatic use of alliteration, its invocation of the Muse and its vocative 'O', but also in the last word quoted here, 'equipage', which appears to have been adopted from French only in the 1570s and is glossed by E.K. as a strange or unfamiliar word.[14]

Together with Antonio's attempt to speak like a shepherd, the comments from writers and critics quoted thus far underline the intricate set of linguistic and stylistic factors that went into the writing of pastoral, and the complex problems faced by its authors. In the early seventeenth century these pressures increased as new influences were introduced to English pastoral, notably the Italian plays of Guarini, Torquato Tasso and others in the Jacobean period, and the works of French poets such as Honorat de Bueil, seigneur de Racan, and François le Metel, sieur de Boisrobert, after Charles I's accession in 1625. Their plays largely avoid archaism, they associate pastoral strongly with tragicomic rather than comic forms, and their audiences and preoccupations were generally aristocratic.[15] These innovations inflected the composition and reception of dramatic pastoral, and many who followed their lead – notably Samuel Daniel in *The Queen's Arcadia* (1605) and *Hymen's Triumph* (1614), Mary Wroth in *Love's Victory* (c.1620), Walter Montagu in *The Shepherds' Paradise* (1633), and Joseph Rutter in *The Shepherds' Holiday* (c.1634) – rejected archaism in adopting these up-to-date models.

Italian and French pastoral posed a challenge to playwrights who were unwilling simply to jettison English pastoral's archaising heritage. Indeed, a reluctance to eschew native models can be seen even in texts such as the 1602 English translation of *Il pastor fido*, probably carried out by Tailboys Dymock, in which pastoral archaisms such as 'wight', 'lorn', 'leese' and 'swain' appear.[16] The translation's deliberate 'Englishing' – in more ways than one – can also be seen in Samuel Daniel's dedicatory verses to Sir Edward Dymock, Tailboys' brother. Daniel recounts that when he and Edward Dymock met Guarini in Italy the dramatist criticised English poetry, saying that '*our costes were with no measures grac'd / Nor barbarous tongues could any verse bring forth*'.[17] Instead, Daniel claims, the translation will show Guarini that his play '*now in England can / Speake as good English as Italian*'.[18] In rhetorical terms, to use barbarism is to lack elegance; we recall George Puttenham's remark that the 'foulest vice in language is to speak barbarously', which he classifies it as pronouncing a word incorrectly or writing it 'by wrong orthography'.[19] Guarini's reported comment thus suggests that he viewed English rather as Thomas Nashe saw archaism, as 'the Oouse which ouerflowing barbarisme, withdrawne to her Scottish Northren chanell, had left behind her'.[20] Daniel's comments are therefore double-edged: in the context of pastoral, speaking good English means not only speaking correct English but also adopting the genre's characteristic native mode; however, following English convention and using an archaic style also risks the very 'barbarism' that Guarini apparently associated with English itself. It is this apparent contradiction that Fletcher seeks to negotiate in *The Faithful Shepherdess*.

Missing Whitsun ales: *The Faithful Shepherdess*

It has long been a cliché to assert that *The Faithful Shepherdess*, first performed by the Children of the Revels around 1608, is archaic in its style.[21] For Cyrus Hoy in the 1950s, attempting to distinguish

Fletcher from Beaumont and both from Massinger and others, *The Faithful Shepherdess* was a stylistic anomaly: 'although it is undoubtedly Fletcher's own,' he writes, 'linguistically at least it has nothing in common with any other of his unaided works. Its language is that of pastoral poetry, uncolloquial and somewhat archaic'.[22] Similarly, E. H. C. Oliphant asserted half a century earlier that 'the student desirous of acquainting himself with [Fletcher's] style must pay no attention to The Faithful Shepherdess, for, like the Masque of the Inner Temple, it is less a play than a poem, and is in every way totally unlike every other drama known to belong to Fletcher alone'.[23] *The Faithful Shepherdess* has often been associated with Spenserian models; in 1840 George Darley argued that 'Various thoughts, descriptions, &c., are taken from or imitated from the "Shepherd's Calendar"', while Philip Finkelpearl in 1987 classified Fletcher as a 'Spenserian playwright', arguing that the 'immediate impression of *The Faithful Shepherdess* is of characters from *The Shepheardes Calendar* – some with identical names – placed in the world of Book III of *The Faerie Queene*'.[24]

It is notable, therefore, that Fletcher actively avoids the major stylistic characteristics of Spenserian archaism. Although occasional archaisms such as 'swain', 'wight' and 'tine' figure in *The Faithful Shepherdess*, he uses none of the more extreme markers of Spenserian style, such as 'algate', 'eld', 'gar', 'hent', 'muchel', 'n'ould', 'sith', 'thilk', 'unnethes' or 'whilom'.[25] Nor does he employ other prominent archaising devices used by Spenser and his followers, such as the past participle prefix 'y-' or the uninflected plural form (e.g. 'skyen' for 'skies'). This does not mean that the play is not archaic in its style. Rather, Fletcher eschews Spenserian archaism in favour of an alternative method, manipulating specific linguistic structures in ways that would have rendered his syntax archaic to early seventeenth-century ears. In doing so, he reformulates archaism and its place in pastoral, seeking to reconfigure its place in the high/low binaries set out at the start of this chapter.

Fletcher uses three techniques in particular, some of which will be familiar from the discussion of archaism in religious prose in Chapter 3: he selects less colloquial forms where Early Modern English gives him the choice; uses old-fashioned syntactic forms; and opts for more formal or static verse forms. The speech in Act 3 in which the Sullen Shepherd marvels at Amaryllis' transformation into the form of another shepherdess, Amoret, displays all of these strategies in some measure:

> By yonder moone, but that I heere do stand,
> Whose breath hath thus reformd thee, and whose hand,
> Let thee downe dry, and pluckt thee up thus wet,
> I should my selfe take thee for *Amoret*,
> Thou art in clothes, in feature, voice and hew
> So like, that sence can not distinguish you.[26]

Fletcher opts for '-th' forms such as 'hath' or 'doth' over '-s' forms such as 'has' and 'does'; he also rejects contractions – although some of these choices may be governed by the demands of the verse line – and prefers the more formal and old-fashioned 'you' over 'ye', even though he uses the latter extensively elsewhere.[27] Taken together, these choices mean that the language of *The Faithful Shepherdess* is relatively formal and old-fashioned, and markedly less colloquial than that of most of Fletcher's plays.

Further, Fletcher uses two syntactic forms that were increasingly archaic in the early seventeenth century: he prefers 'thou' to 'you' as the second person singular pronoun, and uses auxiliary 'do' in ways that were becoming outmoded.[28] In the quotation above, the Sullen Shepherd only uses 'you' for the plural, addressing Amaryllis throughout as 'thee' and 'thou'. The choice between 'thou' and 'you' was often conditioned by social factors (polite 'you' forms were traditionally used by social inferiors to social superiors, who would in turn greet them with condescending 'thou' forms) and emotional factors ('you' could signal politeness or remoteness, 'thou' intimacy, rudeness or anger). There was also a convention in literary texts that supernatural figures tended to give and receive 'thou' forms.[29] However, this system was being complicated in the early seventeenth century by the fact that 'thou' forms were increasingly seen as archaic, a tendency on which Protestant translators of the Bible capitalised in their attempt to make liturgical language seem timeless. Fletcher's overwhelming preference for 'thou' forms in *The Faithful Shepherdess*, a strategy that is at odds with his habits in his other plays, therefore looks more like a decision based on style than one based on dramatic situation alone.[30] It is a way of representing both plain speech and the characteristically intimate and informal relationships between shepherds (an issue to which I will return).[31]

In the first line of his speech to Amaryllis, the Sullen Shepherd tells her 'I heere do stand', rather than 'I stand here', and this would likewise have given the impression of archaism to spectators. The use of auxiliary 'do' in Present Day English is highly regulated: it is obligatory in certain sentence types (negative declaratives, positive and negative questions) and absent in others (positive declaratives, for example, where it now automatically carries emphasis). In Early Modern English, it was optional, or unregulated, in all of these contexts, although its use was becoming gradually more regulated over time.[32] However, Charles Barber suggests that unregulated 'do' was preserved to a higher degree in literary usage, suggesting that writers use it – as the biblical translators did – as a stylistic tool.[33] Jonathan Hope's unpublished analysis of *The Faithful Shepherdess* shows that Fletcher again favours the more archaic option: the rate at which he regulates auxiliary 'do' is markedly lower than in his other plays, and its use cannot be wholly accounted for by the demands of metre.[34]

Taken together, these linguistic features suggest that Fletcher aims in *The Faithful Shepherdess* for a form of English that would have struck its original hearers as formal and old-fashioned. He reinforces this impression through other aspects of style. If we look again at the Sullen Shepherd's speech, we can see that it is written in heavily end-stopped heroic couplets, and neither the opening nor closing lines are shared with Amaryllis. This is typical of the play: run-on and shared lines are comparatively infrequent and mostly occur at moments of high emotion, such as the climactic moment at which Perigot wounds his sweetheart Amoret for the first time (3.1.337–46). As George T. Wright notes, shared lines usually have the effect of hurrying dramatic dialogue; a lack of such lines slows the pace.[35] End-stopping had itself become old-fashioned by the early seventeenth century, at odds with late Elizabethan and Jacobean drama's demand for more fluid, colloquial-sounding verse. In addition, the extensive use of tetrameter and trimeter, the songs, and Fletcher's comparative reluctance to use blank verse render *The Faithful Shepherdess* more lyrical and less colloquial than many plays of this period.

Thus, while the poetry of Spenser and, especially, of his followers, used archaism to position pastoral style as humble, 'real' and rustic, Fletcher uses alternative forms of archaism to reposition it as relatively formal, artificial and elevated. Although archaism retains its capacity to create intimacy – here achieved through the preference for 'thou' forms – its emotional and stylistic effects are recalibrated. In this respect, Fletcher follows the example of Italian pastoral poets. In his influential *Aminta*, for example, Tasso creates a calculated impression of simplicity through generally plain language and occasional colloquialism, and against this backdrop his shepherds and nymphs occasionally reach to sophisticated literary expression, ennobled by love. C. P. Brand captures its style neatly when he describes it as 'an illusion of pastoral conversation, a sort of recitative between the styles of lyric aria and prose dialogue'.[36] The second chorus underlines the self-consciousness of Tasso's pastoral aesthetic,

calling for a simple, rustic style, but doing so in a remarkably self-aware
fashion by adopting its own 'coarse' and irregular metrical style:

> Amor, leggan pur gli altri
> le socratiche carte,
> ch'io in due begli occhi apprenderò quest'arte;
> e perderan le rime
> de le penne più saggie
> appo le mie selvaggie,
> che rozza mano in rozza scorza imprime.

[O Love, let others read Socratic writings [i.e. of Plato], for I will learn this
art from two beautiful eyes; and verse from more learned pens will be
judged inferior to my rustic rhymes, which are carved by a coarse hand on
coarse bark.][37]

In the chorus, therefore, Tasso underlines the extent to which his pastoral
diction is less natural than it seems; even when it strives for rusticity, it
cannot help displaying its own artificiality.

Guarini's approach to pastoral is similar. Although he says little on the
specifics of pastoral style, he argues that 'le pastorali sono capaci della
grandezza Tragica, e che de'loro soggetti si possano formare buone Tragedie' ('Pastorals are capable of tragic grandeur, and good tragedies can be
made out of pastoral subjects').[38] Together with his insistence that literary
shepherds are not necessarily humble or poor, these comments suggest
that Guarini sought tragic rather than comic decorum in matters of
style. Moreover, they are intended to counter the accusation made by
Giason Denores that pastoral – as exemplified by Virgil's *Eclogues* and
Theocritus' *Idylls* – was incapable of incorporating noble figures and
tragic narratives.[39] This did not, however, prevent attacks on the style of
Il pastor fido itself: as Lisa Sampson describes, Giovanni Pietro Malacreta
thought that its version of Arcadia was too 'delicato e vago' ('delicate and
delightful') and its shepherds overly 'dotti e sentenziosi' ('learned and
sententious'), while Paolo Beni likewise thought that its setting was overly
sophisticated.[40]

Set alongside *Aminta* and *Il pastor fido*, the linguistic texture and
prosody of *The Faithful Shepherdess* both suggest that Fletcher sought in
this play a delicately archaic formality that would avoid the rusticity of
Spenserian pastoral. His rejection of some elements of English tradition is
underlined in his notorious letter to the reader, printed with the play on its
first publication around 1609, and written in response to its apparent
failure in performance. 'It is', he writes,

a pastorall Tragie-comedie, which the people seeing when it was plaid, having ever had a singuler guift in defining, concluded to be a play of country hired Shepheards, in gray cloakes, with curtaild dogs in strings, sometimes laughing together, and sometimes killing one another: And missing whitsun ales, creame, wassel and morris-dances, began to be angry.[41]

Fletcher sarcastically repositions the pastoral by describing what it is not: it is not about humble, hired shepherds; it does not feature rural festivity. Momentarily prioritising the literary traditions of pastoral over its potential to depict real-life social conditions, he declares that pastoral is 'a representation of shepheards and shephearddesses ... not exceeding former fictions, and vulgar traditions' (ll. 10–13). For Fletcher, in contrast with Turberville or Drayton, 'representation' does not entail creating a verisimilar portrait of reality, but a negotiation with earlier literary tradition. In this, Fletcher echoes Guarini; indeed, the annotations in the 1602 Italian edition of *Il pastor fido* insist 'che'l sito di essa è tutto finto, si come è finta tutta la fauola, & finte tutte le cose, che sono *in* essa' ('that the setting is totally fictional, as is the plot and everything in it').[42]

An intriguing paradox is created through the stylistic choices of *The Faithful Shepherdess*. Fletcher does not appear to have abandoned the oppositional stance of the Spenserian poets – he shared his strong Protestant convictions and scepticism about courtly excess with Drayton, for instance, with whom he also shared important patrons.[43] Moreover, while Fletcher rejects Spenserian archaism in favour of a more elevated and integrated style, he nonetheless retains specific allusions to the older poet's works, quoting from *The Shepheardes Calender* in Act 5 and thereby suggesting that he seeks to 'English' the Italian pastoral play, in more ways that one.[44] He uses specific allusions and combinations of sources to critique some of the assumptions on which pastoral drama rests, and he recasts the material that he inherits along feminocentric lines.

This strategy is clear in the play's opening speech, in which the recently bereaved Clorin takes a vow of chastity:

> thus I free
> My selfe from all ensuing heates and fires
> Of love, all sports, delights and games,
> That Shepheards hold full deare: thus put I off.
> Now no more shall these smooth browes be girt,
> With youthfull coronals, and lead the dance,
> No more the company of fresh faire Maids
> And wanton shepheards be to me delightfull,

> Nor the shrill pleasing sound of merry pipes,
> Under some shady dell, when the coole winde
> Plaies on the leaves: all be farre away,
> Since thou art farre away[.]   (1.1.6–17)

Fletcher marks his distance from recent pastoral tradition by focusing the opening of his play squarely on female experience rather than that of the shepherds. Moreover, just as his shepherds are economically independent agents, so his shepherdesses – no 'nymphs' here – also own their own flocks. His female characters share the status of their male counterparts, a fact drawn forcibly to spectators' attention in Cloe's concern that she is neglected because she has 'not a flocke sufficient great' and her boasting claim, 'My flockes are many, and the downes as large / They feed uppon' (1.3.11, 16–17).

Some of the reasons for this strategy become clear if we look again at the theatrical origin of Fletcher's pastoral. As I have argued elsewhere, a crucial context for *The Faithful Shepherdess* is its place in the repertory of the Children of the Revels – a company well known for its performance of satiric, political drama – and the role of Anna of Denmark as that company's recent patron.[45] Anna was an enthusiast for Italian literature and, especially, drama, and Samuel Daniel – who was briefly appointed the licenser of the Queen's Revels company in the early years of James's reign – wrote two Italianate pastorals for performance before her.[46] The queen's masques appear to critique many of her husband's policies and assumptions, and she was thought a fit patron by the Spenserian poet George Wither, who dedicated his *Abuses Stripped and Whipped* to her in 1614.[47] Thus, where the pastoral plays of Tasso and Guarini – named after their male protagonists – are masculine and aristocratic in their political leanings and aesthetics, Fletcher's instead depends on its complex position in relation to the *courts* of Jacobean England and the demands of his female patron. Written for the company patronised by the pastorally aware Queen Anna, *The Faithful Shepherdess* makes a calculated pitch for her attention through its emphasis on female agency and experience.

Fletcher's refashioning of pastoral aesthetics and the genre's archaising heritage is clear within the play itself, which is far more sly and self-conscious than many commentators have acknowledged.[48] In his letter to the reader, Fletcher complains that the Blackfriars spectators expected 'whitsun ales, creame, wassel and morris-dances' and were enraged when they did not get them. The play's opening speech sets out the play's refusal to provide such pleasures from its outset. This refusal is underlined in Act 5, when the Old Shepherd speculates that the young shepherds have been drawn from their beds by 'some lusty sport, / Or spiced wassel Boule' in a neighbouring town (5.1.28–9), despite their purification at the hands of the Priest in Act 1. The play teases its spectators with conventional pastoral pleasures even as it denies them, imposing the narrative's general frustration of desire onto the playhouse audience itself.[49]

Much of the play's irony settles on the Satyr, a figure who in some respects embodies Fletcher's knowing revision of pastoral tradition. In pastoral plays such as Tasso's *Aminta* and Guarini's *Il pastor fido*, the Satyr is an insurgent figure, the embodiment of disruptive lust.[50] In contrast, Fletcher's Satyr participates in what Anthony Parr terms the 'reformation of the satyr' in English literary culture in the sixteenth and early seventeenth centuries.[51] Clorin and the power of her chastity instantaneously tame him, and uncontrollable desire is displaced onto humans such as the Sullen Shepherd and the manipulative shepherdess Amaryllis. The Satyr also emblematises Fletcher's knowing treatment of pastoral, and the ways in which the dramatist brings together varying traditions, because he is the play's most consistent user of linguistic archaism. Only the Satyr and Clorin use the word 'wight', and where she uses it only once (5.5.106), he uses it repeatedly at the moment at which he finds the wounded Alexis (3.1.192–206). When he finds yet another wounded mortal, this time Amoret, he exclaims 'Yet more blood, / Sure these wanton Swaynes are wood' (4.4.184–5). 'Wood', meaning insane, rabid, senseless or violent (*OED* wood, *adj.* 1–3), appears in both *The Shepheardes Calender* and *The Faerie Queene*; it was comparatively rare in the early seventeenth century, and seems to have been viewed by Fletcher as a word appropriate to pastoral. Like 'wight', it is used in *The Faithful Shepherdess* only by the Satyr and Clorin. Pastoral conventions are used most heavily by those characters who in other respects transgress them, suggesting the sly wit with which Fletcher has constructed his play.

This self-conscious manipulation of 'former fictions' is also evident elsewhere. The names of Fletcher's characters are taken mainly from pastoral tradition, but they are assigned and juxtaposed in intriguing ways. An old shepherd named 'Thenot' appears in the February, April and November Eclogues of *The Shepheardes Calender*, and 'Perigot' appears in the August Eclogue. Amoret features in *The Faerie Queene*, while 'Amaryllis' is the name of a faithful lover in *Il pastor fido*. Alexis is the name of the shepherd wooed by Corydon in Virgil's second Eclogue, and Daphnis and Cloe are the name of the eponymous lovers in Longus' late-classical pastoral romance *Daphnis and Cloe*. The choice of names is not accidental. Fletcher's Thenot may be young, but his desire for Clorin, provoked only by her fidelity to her dead lover, renders him dryly unproductive. Amaryllis is sardonically transformed from faithful lover to an unscrupulous schemer whose lust for Perigot leads her magically to transform herself so as to impersonate the chaste Amoret. Daphnis is here a bashful boy, unsuited to the comically rapacious Cloe, and although the pair wind up together in a hollow tree, Cloe's lust is unsatisfied, Daphnis' chastity remaining 'unspotted' (5.2.84) when he is later tested by Clorin and the Satyr. Alexis is transformed from Virgil's scornful boy into an ardent wooer of Cloe, but he too is denied the consummation of his love, and the wound that he suffers at the hands of the Sullen Shepherd will not heal until he manages to dismiss lustful thoughts. This intertexual play, like Fletcher's use of archaism, aims to undercut spectators' expectations, to leave them unsettled and inclined to question what they know – or think they know – about dramatic pastoral.

In verses printed in the 1647 Folio edition of the works of Fletcher and his collaborators, 'In Memory of Mr. Iohn Fletcher', Henry Howard presents a picture of Fletcher in Elysium, where 'Ancient Laureates' vie to outdo him. Having failed with his epic works, Virgil tries a different front:

> Now lastly for a refuge, Virgill shewes
> The lines where Corydon Alexis woes;
> But those in opposition quickly met
> The smooth tongu'd Perigot and Amoret:
> A paire whom doubtlesse had the others seene,
> They from their owne loves had Apostates beene[.]⁵²

Howard's comments encapsulate the tactics that Fletcher adopts in his dramatic pastoral: it both emulates its predecessors and radically reworks them, fusing influences from native, classical and Italian sources, and creating a delicately yet searchingly ironic play in which pastoral conventions are both admired and questioned. The play's use of archaism is part of a broader attempt to reconfigure the binary relationships between old and new, high and low, elevated and humble, on which earlier pastorals had depended. *The Faithful Shepherdess* uses an old technique to make the pastoral 'new', and it deconstructs the genre in order to reconstruct it for the court of Queen Anna.

Doric delicacy: *A Masque at Ludlow Castle*

Fletcher's pastoral is notorious for its failure on the stage when it was first performed around 1608. Also well known is its new popularity in the early 1630s. A second edition of the play in 1629 was followed in 1634 by one advertising its performance by the King's Men: 'ACTED AT SOMERSET House before the KING and QVEENE on Twelfe night last, 1633. And divers times since with great applause at the Private House in Blacke-Friers, by his Majesties Servants'. The performance of 'Fletchers pastorall called The Faithfull Sheapheardesse' at court on 6 January 1634 was recorded by the Master of the Revels, Henry Herbert, as taking place 'in the clothes the Queene had given Taylor the year before of her own pastorall' – that is, Montagu's *The Shepherds' Paradise*, performed at Somerset House on 9 January and 2 February 1633 – and with scenery designed by Inigo Jones.[53]

I have suggested that in its original context *The Faithful Shepherdess* was closely entwined with the politics and cultural tastes of Anna of Denmark. The play's feminocentric revision of pastoral also made it appealing to Henrietta Maria, her successor as queen consort. Karen Britland suggests that Fletcher's focus on chastity made *The Faithful Shepherdess* adaptable to Charles and Henrietta Maria's project to reform drama and behaviour in the Caroline court through sponsorship of new plays and strategically selected revivals.[54] Nonetheless, the revival of *The Faithful Shepherdess* also takes on particular resonance against the backdrop of Henrietta Maria's cultural activities and her especial fondness for pastoral. As Britland points out, she was in 1625 the dedicatee of Abraham Rémy's pastoral romance *La Galatée et les adventures du Prince Astiagés*, in which she is figured as Galatée (*Courts*, III). Furthermore, the first play that she mounted at court as Queen of England was a 1626 performance of Racan's *Arthénice, ou les bergeries* – first performed at l'Hôtel de Bourgogne in 1619 – in which she played the eponymous Arthénice; this was followed in 1632–3 by Montagu's *The Shepherds' Paradise* and in 1635 by Boisrobert's *Florimène*, both written specifically for her.[55] Just as Italianate pastoral had been strongly associated with Anna of Denmark, so French and French-influenced pastoral was a crucial part of Henrietta Maria's cultural project.

The court performances of *Arthénice*, *The Shepherds' Paradise* and *The Faithful Shepherdess* took place at Somerset House (also known as Denmark House), a key site in the matrix of buildings and spaces that made up the queen's court. It had been rebuilt and refurbished for Anna of Denmark, and Daniel's *Hymen's Triumph* was performed there in 1614, in part in celebration of the palace's completion.[56] As Herbert was at pains to record, the performance of *The Faithful Shepherdess* in 1634 was also in dialogue with that of *The Shepherds' Paradise* a year earlier. In addition to the apparent use of the costumes that queen and courtiers had worn in Montagu's play, Joseph Taylor, the leading actor with the King's Men in the Caroline period, had instructed Henrietta Maria and her ladies in acting technique for their performance of *The Shepherds' Paradise*.[57] The court performance of *The Faithful Shepherdess* was thus part of a broader engagement between King's Men and queen consort, and of a dialogue between the cultural activities of successive queens consort. The revived pastoral looked both backwards and forwards: backwards towards its dual Italian and Spenserian lineages, and their connections with Anna of Denmark's aesthetic activities; and forwards towards the new continental influences associated with the French queen consort.

By the early 1630s it may already have been becoming difficult to separate the archaism of *The Faithful Shepherdess* from that of early Jacobean drama in general. However, it is noticeable that Montagu's play eschews linguistic and stylistic archaism entirely, employing neither Spenser's techniques nor Fletcher's. In fact, *The Shepherds' Paradise* avoids almost all of pastoral's usual touchstones: there are no references to 'swains' or 'nymphs'; not only do genuine shepherds and their flocks not feature, but sheep are not even mentioned in passing. Montagu's pastoral is fundamentally aristocratic, and its preoccupation with narrow refinements of rank is underlined by the fact that while 'thou' forms appear relatively infrequently in this play a large number of them are assigned to the King. Relationships between the shepherds are framed within governing conventions of politeness, and the hierarchical distance between shepherds and monarch is maintained. With its perspective scenery, stylistic decorum and aristocratic edge, Montagu's play reflects both its court production and Caroline pastoral's movement away from Spenserian archaism.[58] In contrast, while both Milton in *A Masque* and Jonson in *The Sad Shepherd* draw on these techniques – notably in their actual or projected use of perspective scenery – they also seek to rework and reinvigorate pastoral's archaising traditions.

Performed in the Great Hall at Ludlow Castle, Shropshire, on 29 September 1634, *A Masque* was produced collaboratively by a group including Milton, the composer Henry Lawes, who also played the Attendant Spirit, various designers of stage and scenery, and its patron, the Earl of Bridgewater. The entertainment responded to Bridgewater's inauguration as Lord President of the Council of the Marches, an important political role in the counties surrounding the border between England and Wales, and it featured in leading roles three of his children: fifteen-year-old Lady Alice Egerton, who played the Lady; eleven-year-old John Egerton, Viscount Brackley, who played the Elder Brother, and nine-year-old Thomas Egerton, who played the Second Brother.[59] Lawes, who was music tutor to the Egerton children, appears to have co-ordinated the project. The political and regional dimensions of *A Masque*, and its position in the development of the Caroline court and provincial masque, have received a good deal of attention from scholars in recent years.[60] Similarly, its mingling of genres – masque and pastoral in particular – has been extensively analysed.[61] However, its use of archaism and the role played by archaic style in its manipulation of pastoral convention have been less extensively considered. I focus here on the ways in which Milton uses archaism as part of a synthesis of pastoral's 'low' and 'high' styles. Scholars have debated the extent to which *A Masque* draws on Italian models, and the extent of its debt to dramatists such as Shakespeare and Fletcher.[62] In contrast, the use of archaic words and grammatical forms allows Milton to reinscribe a very direct link between his new pastoral and earlier traditions, traditions that he can then rework and reformulate.

Readers of the early print editions of *A Masque* would have been cued immediately into the text's interaction with pastoral tradition. The first edition, published in 1637 and prepared by Lawes with Milton's apparent collusion, carries the title-page epigraph '*Eheu quid volui misero mihi! floribus austrum Perditus*' ('[A]las! what hope, poor fool, has been mine? Madman, I have let in the south wind to my flowers'), taken from Virgil's second Eclogue.[63] The epigraph identifies Milton with Corydon, who pursues Alexis in vain in Virgil's eclogue, and it suggests a certain degree of self-depreciation – the speaker's gifts are inadequate and will be rejected – even as it argues that Milton is fit to vie with Virgil on his home ground of the pastoral.[64]

In contrast, the title-page of the 1645 text of *A Masque* does not carry an epigraph, although the title-page to the volume as a whole quotes Virgil's seventh Eclogue, '*Baccare frontem / Cingite, ne vati noceat mala lingua futuro*' ('wreathe my brow with foxglove, lest his evil tongue harm the bard that is to be'), maintaining a connection with Virgilian pastoral.[65] Instead, *A Masque* is prefaced by Henry Lawes's dedication to John Egerton, Viscount Brackley, retained from the 1637 edition, and by a new addition, a letter to Milton from Sir Henry Wotton, written in 1638.[66] In contrast with the Virgilian echoes established by the epigraphs, Wotton foregrounds the pastoral's contemporary resonance. He tells Milton that he received his 'dainty piece of entertainment' with the poet's letter of 6 April 1638, and comments, 'I should much commend the tragical part, if the lyrical did not ravish me with a certain Doric delicacy in your songs and odes, whereunto I must plainly confess to have seen yet nothing parallel in our language: *Ipsa mollities* [delicacy itself].'[67] 'Doric' was often used in the

1620s and 1630s as a synonym for 'simple' or even 'rustic'; Milton himself refers to his archaising elegy 'Lycidas' as a 'Doric lay' sung by an 'uncouth swain' (ll. 189, 186), while a hostile Robert Burton attacks '*Doricke* dialecte' as an example of barbaric style.[68] However, the term could also signal that something was unaffectedly sweet: Francis Quarles, for instance, glosses '*Dorick* straines' in *Argalus and Parthenia* (1629) as 'sweet mollitious ayres . . . *Lyrick* songs, and voyces'.[69] While Wotton's reference to 'Doric delicacy' has sometimes been viewed as an oxymoron,[70] comments later in the letter suggest that he has the latter meaning in mind. He notes that he had already received a copy of *A Masque* from 'Mr R.', enclosed with the poems of the recently deceased Thomas Randolph, 'whereunto it was added (as I now suppose) that the accessory might help out the principal, according to the art of stationers, and to leave the reader *con la bocca dolce* [i.e. with a sweet taste in his mouth]'.[71] Wotton's 'Doric delicacy' hints at simplicity, rusticity, sweetness and delicacy, and it suggests that Milton's pastoral aesthetic should be viewed as a calculated synthesis of different influences and sources.

The use of pastoral archaism in *A Masque* is part of this project. Comparison of the various print and manuscript texts shows that archaisms were part of Milton's original conception of *A Masque*; they appear in the Trinity manuscript, the earliest surviving version, and remain stable across the later revisions.[72] Milton drops in just enough archaic words and syntactic features to establish connections between his pastoral and its Spenserian predecessors. Many of them are given to the Attendant Spirit, who in his disguise as the 'swain' Thyrsis, with his 'rural mistrelsy' (l. 547), is the one of *A Masque*'s principal pastoral voices. The Spirit uses pastoral archaisms even before he takes on his disguise, referring to the Earl of Bridgewater as a 'noble peer of mickle trust and power' (l. 31) and describing the 'perplexed paths of this drear wood' (l. 37); he also occasionally uses grammatical archaism, as in his description of the 'knot-grass dew-besprent' (l. 542). The Spirit is not, however, the only character to use archaism. Even the mortals occasionally draw on this language; the Elder Brother's declaration that Wisdom's wings are 'all to-ruffled' (l. 380) introduces another delicate touch of grammatical archaism, and the Second Brother wishes that he could hear 'The folded flocks, penned in their wattled cotes, / Or sound of pastoral reed with oaten stops' (ll. 345–6). Furthermore, Comus's lyrical attempts on the Lady's chastity include his evocations of the 'swinked [tired] hedger' (l. 293), and he also dips into on Spenserian style in his references to 'the pert fairies and the dapper elves' (l. 118) and the 'Dingle, or bushy dell, of this wild wood, / And every bosky bourn from side to side' (ll. 312–13). In contrast with the Spirit's apparently authentic use of archaism, Comus's appears to be part of his appropriation of pastoral tropes, his desire to turn particular poetic and behavioural modes to his own advantage; Comus is, as Annabel Patterson suggests, 'pretending pastoralism only to betray'.[73] Milton thus suggests that there are right and wrong ways to use pastoral, and that the form and its conventions are open to abuse.

Milton underscores the calculated way in which he uses archaism in *A Masque* with the cluster of examples that surround his references to Spenser.[74] After Comus has been dismissed, the Lady is still not free from his influence, and the Spirit hits upon another solution, one originally told to him by 'Meliboeus old ... The soothest shepherd that e'er piped on plains' (ll. 822–3). As becomes clear, 'Meliboeus' is Spenser, whose description of Sabrina in Book 2 of *The Faerie Queene* (2.10.14–19) is Milton's main source for his presentation of the princess-turned-river-goddess Sabrina, who liberates the captive. But the debt is signalled not only in the use of the pastoral epithet – ultimately drawn from Virgil's first Eclogue – and the description of Meliboeus as the 'soothest [truest or most faithful] shepherd', but in the verbal texture of the following lines, in which the Spirit begins his narrative of Sabrina's history:

> There is a gentle Nymph not far from hence,
> That with moist curb sways the smooth Severn stream:
> Sabrina is her name, a virgin pure;
> Whilom she was the daughter of Locrine ... (ll. 824–7)

As we saw in Chapter 2, Spenser uses 'whilom' in Book 4 of *The Faerie Queene* to underline the moment at which he turns to Chaucer as a narrative source, naming the poet in the lines that follow. Milton reverses this procedure, but the effect is similar: for these poets, to imitate a revered predecessor – here the 'old swain' Spenser (l. 852) – is not only to draw on his works but also to inhabit his style. Milton's negotiations with his predecessor are also – necessarily, it seems – negotiations with the form(s) in which he wrote.[75] In re-establishing pastoral's connection with Spenser, he also reasserts both the genre's Englishness – in the face of Francophile court plays – and its scepticism about the court and royal power.

Milton's revisionary interactions with Fletcher and *The Faithful Shepherdess* – recently appropriated by the queen's court – are also part of this process, especially given that *A Masque* shares the ambivalence of Fletcher's play to 'mirth'. A stage direction describes Comus's crew as '*making a*

riotous and unruly noise' (92.4SD); their master comments that 'Rigour now
is gone to bed' (l. 107), and they dance what the Trinity and Bridgewater
manuscripts describe as 'a wild rude and wanton antic'.[76] The Lady's later
evocation of their aural impact underlines the presentation of rural festivity
as disruptive and potentially threatening:

> methought it was the sound
> Of riot and ill-managed merriment,
> Such as the jocund flute or gamesome pipe
> Stirs up among the loose unlettered hinds,
> When, for their teeming flocks and granges full,
> In wanton dance they praise the bounteous Pan,
> And thank the gods amiss. I should be loath
> To meet the rudeness and swilled insolence
> Of such late wassaillers[.]   (ll. 171–9)

As the representative of chastity, the Lady parallels Fletcher's Clorin, and
her attitudes towards festive ritual are remarkably congruent with those of
her predecessor.[77] Similarly, later in the drama the virgin goddess Sabrina's
liberating invocation (ll. 911–19) also echoes the incantations with which
Clorin and the Satyr free the shepherds from their debilitating lust (see,
in particular, 5.2.60–70). Thus far, it would be fair to argue that Milton's
use of Fletcher's play in his 'reformation of the masque', as David
Norbrook has termed it, is in line with the uses to which Britland sees
Henrietta Maria putting *The Faithful Shepherdess* in reforming behaviour
at the Caroline court.[78] However, Milton's interaction with Fletcher is
more complex than this might suggest, and he is far more alert to the
disruptive undertones of *The Faithful Shepherdess* than the queen appears
to have been. Where Henrietta Maria may have taken Fletcher's chastity
narrative at face value, Milton pays more attention to the ways in which it
is ironised.

We might look, in particular, at Comus's speeches to and about the
Lady. Although he frequently shifts into blank verse, Comus's native mode
of speech is apparently the tetrameter or trimeter couplet favoured by
supernatural beings in *The Faithful Shepherdess* and other Jacobean plays:

> The star that bids the shepherd fold
> Now the top of heaven doth hold;
> And the gilded car of day
> His glowing axle doth allay (ll. 93–6)

At the moment when he sees the Lady, his lyrical expression of desire
mimics her blank verse, as he asks, 'Can any mortal mixture of earth's

mould / Breathe such divine enchanting ravishment?' (ll. 244–5). He then maintains this mode of speech when he addresses the Lady directly:

> I'll speak to her,
> And she shall be my queen. – Hail, foreign wonder!
> Whom certain these rough shades did never breed,
> Unless the goddess that in rural shrine
> Dwell'st here with Pan or Sylvan, by blest song,
> Forbidding every bleak unkindly fog
> To touch the prosperous growth of this tall wood. (ll. 264–70)

This speech epitomises in some respects Comus's linguistic transformations, his decorous and regular iambic pentameter gaining a tinge of pastoralism through his reference to 'Pan or Sylvan'. Fletcher's Satyr makes his first appearance with a similarly opulent evocation of the landscape that surrounds him, and he is similarly struck by the virginal presence of a stranger in the wood:

> Through yon same bending plaine,
> That flings his armes downe to the maine,
> And through these thicke woods have I runne
> . . .
> But behold a fairer sight,   *He stands amazed.*
> By that heavenly forme of thine,
> Brightest faire thou art devine:
> Sprong from great immortall race
> Of the Gods: for in thy face,
> Shines more awfull majesty,
> Then dull weake mortalitie
> Dare with misty eies behould
> And live[.]   (1.1.47–9, 57–65)

Despite the structural and stylistic similarities between the Satyr and Comus's opening speeches, there are important differences. In contrast with Comus's deceptive appropriation of the Lady's style of speech, the Satyr sticks to his trimeter lines. Moreover, while the demi-god Comus enacts the traditional crude, lustful behaviour of the Satyr of Italian drama, Fletcher's civilised, or civilisable, Satyr marks his independence from those sources. Alert to the ironies created by Fletcher's urbane Satyr, Milton draws on all the potential sweetness and delicacy of the Doric mode to present a practised seducer, a figure who combines the effect of Guarini's Satyr and his bawd-like nymph Corisca. The use of *The Faithful Shepherdess* in *A Masque* therefore epitomises Milton's productive use of his source;

he unmakes and remakes the ironies of Fletcher's reshaping of pastoral tradition in order to reinforce the suspicions that knowledgeable spectators will harbour towards Comus and to underline the latter's abuse of pastoral conventions.

Thus far I have focused on Milton's revisionary treatment of pastoral tradition within the text of *A Masque*. Yet, as noted above, *A Masque* combines its deployment of these established modes with a similarly knowing use of innovative techniques and new material, elements that may have been as much the work of Milton's collaborators as the poet himself. Henry Lawes, who composed the songs, was a prominent court musician, and the surviving settings indicate that they were written in fashionable modes.[79] Therefore, auditors may have been struck by the juxtaposition of pastoral archaism in the dialogue and up-to-date strains in the music, encouraging them to consider the status of archaism within the 'new' aesthetic cultures of the early 1630s.[80]

Similarly, *A Masque*'s staging at Ludlow contributed to its mixture of old and new elements. Scholars such as Philip Schwyzer and Julie Sanders have recently set out the particular resonances of this location, Sanders in particular viewing it as a species of site-specific performance, and exploring its connections with the broader locality of the Forest of Dean.[81] Here, I merely wish to point to the final scene, at which '*The Scene changes, presenting Ludlow Town, and the President's Castle: then come in country dancers; after then the* ATTENDANT SPIRIT, *with the two* BROTHERS *and* THE LADY' (l. 957SD). The Trinity manuscript here has the more detailed direction 'enter country dances and such / like gambols etc.'.[82] Following Comus's defeat, it seems, rural festivity – and, perhaps, archaism with it – can be reclaimed as part of the 'right' way of doing pastoral; as Barbara K. Lewalski notes, the shepherds' dances 'recuperate pastoral from its deceptive appropriation by the false masquer, Comus'.[83] However, the Spirit's interruption of the dancing, and his comment 'Back, shepherds, back! Enough your play / Till next sun-shine holiday' (ll. 958–9) suggest the tight control that is nonetheless exercised. Rural jollity may be allowed but, as *The Faithful Shepherdess* also (at least overtly) argues, it must be closely regulated.

The use of scenery also has further implications. In terms of pastoral aesthetics, the ending of *A Masque* suggests a desire to reconnect the Doric mode with the 'real' countryside or, conversely, a desire to reshape that landscape in the mould of literary pastoral. Its use of perspective scenery mimics that of court masques and Henrietta Maria's court pastorals; in particular, the closing direction recalls the end of *Arthénice*, in which

'Quand La pastorell est finist La Seine se change en vng mont desus Lequel sont assis les masques qui dessendent pour danser et puis après se change La seine en la maison de Sourmarcet et sy voit Le fleuue de Tamise qui est La fin' [When the pastoral is finished, the scene changes to a mountain on top of which are seated the masque[r]s, who descend in order to dance and then, after, the scene is changed to Somerset House and the Thames river is seen, which is the end].[84] In *Arthénice*, as John Orrell comments, the conceit draws spectators' attention back to the queen's court itself, 'as if the real world might be tuned with the harmony of what went before', mediated through the intellectual pretensions of pastoral and the sensory immediacy of the masque.[85]

However, in both *Arthénice* and *A Masque* the relationship between the representation and the 'real' is tentative and provisional, as the artificiality of the perspective scenery might itself suggest. The country dancers are the only 'real' rural folk who appear in *A Masque*; elsewhere, shepherds appear only in the disguises that the Spirit and Comus adopt, and Comus does not even put on shepherds' clothes, relying instead on 'magic dust' (l. 165) to deceive the Lady's eyes and his linguistic impersonation – his calculated use of pastoral tropes and modes of expression – to deceive her ears. Milton and his collaborators thus suggest the difficulty of fully inhabiting pastoral forms in the early 1630s, and the effort of impersonation that is required to present them. *A Masque* implicitly comments on both the absence of pastoral convention in Montagu's *The Shepherds' Paradise* – in which the queen and her ladies merely donned the (stylised and sanitised) costume of shepherds and shepherdesses – and the process of courtly appropriation through which Joseph Taylor and his fellow actors appeared in those costumes for their court performance of *The Faithful Shepherdess*. If *A Masque* has difficulty in reconnecting the pastoral with the English landscape, such a manoeuvre is, it implies, impossible at Somerset House, where only 'false' pastoral can be performed.

Rustic play: *The Sad Shepherd*

As we have seen, *A Masque* delicately balances the 'high' and 'low' aspects of pastoral, and Milton softens the potential roughness of Spenserian diction by using archaism sparingly and in combination with a range of other literary effects. In his incomplete fragment *The Sad Shepherd*, seemingly written not long after *A Masque*, Jonson takes on much of the same literary, cultural and political material, but he reformulates it in different ways, simultaneously reconnecting pastoral with 'authentic'

rusticity and suggesting through alternative forms of archaism its funda-
mental artificiality. He also engages in detail with the idea of pastoral
'mirth', seeking to reconnect the genre with comedy. Furthermore, in
doing so he rejects some of pastoral's continental influences, instead
drawing on indigenous material such as the Robin Hood legend. As
I will argue, archaism plays a crucial role in both of these manoeuvres,
underlining pastoral's comic potential and localising it within the physical
and cultural landscape of England.

Some of these negotiations are highlighted in the play's prologue and
paratextual material. When *The Sad Shepherd* was first published in 1640–1,
its title-page bore the epigraph *'Nec erubuit sylvas habitare Thaleia'*, taken
from the second line of Virgil's sixth Eclogue, and translated variously as
'My Muse . . . blushed not to dwell in the woods' and 'Thalia [the muse of
comedy] did not blush to be a forest-dweller'.[86] The epigraph asserts
Jonson's right to write pastoral drama, but it also implicitly asserts his
right specifically to an English pastoral, since the opening two lines of the
sixth Eclogue read, in full, 'Prima Syracosio dignata est ludere versu /
nostra nec erubuit silvas habitare Thalea' ('My Muse first deigned to sport
in Sicilian strains, and blushed not to dwell in the woods'). Where Virgil's
muse condescends to sport or play in Sicily, Jonson's is self-consciously
placed in an indigenous landscape, and this effect would have been
especially striking if the play was performed with the perspective scenery
that he seems to have envisaged. The opening stage direction reads, *'The
scene is Sherwood: consisting of a landscape of forest, hills, valleys, cottages, a
castle, a river, pastures, herds, flocks, all full of country simplicity. Robin
Hood's bower; his well; the witch's dimble; the swineherd's oak; the hermit's
cell'* ('The Persons of the Play', ll. 28–31). The scene thus presents the key
locations of the play, and an epitome of an English pastoral 'landscape',
establishing the setting and the local and national milieu in which the
dramatic action is situated.[87]

The prologue underlines this localising strategy, asking the spectators to
'sit awake' and pay attention to what the playwright has delivered them:

> though he now present you with such wool
> As from mere English flocks his muse can pull,
> He hopes when it is made up into cloth
> Not the most curious head here will be loath
> To wear a hood of it – it being a fleece
> To match or those of Sicily or Greece.   (ll. 9–14)

Like the epigraph, the prologue supports Jonson's attempt to match and
outdo classical pastoral, or native pastorals with Italian or Greek settings

such as *The Faithful Shepherdess*, which is set in Thessaly. Moreover, as Stephen Knight points out, the choice of the word 'hood' here points to the adaptation of the English Robin Hood materials,[88] a subject to which the prologue then turns explicitly:

> His scene is Sherwood, and his play a tale
> Of Robin Hood's inviting from the vale
> Of Belvoir all the shepherds to a feast,
> Where, by the casual absence of one guest,
> The mirth is troubled much, and in one man
> As much of sadness shown as passion can.
> The sad young shepherd, whom we here present

[EGLAMOUR,] *the sad shepherd, passeth silently over the stage.*

> Like his woe's figure, dark and discontent
> For his lost love, who in the Trent is said
> To have miscarried.   (ll. 15–24)

As the prologue suggests, and as Sanders has explained in illuminating detail, the play draws on the Nottinghamshire setting, locating the folk-loric figure of Robin Hood in a carefully delineated environment in which river, forest and village are equally significant.[89] Yet it also hints at the play's revisions to the Robin Hood narrative – particularly in the add-itional figure of the sad shepherd Eglamour – and the ways in which Jonson will inflect it with pastoral conventions. The dialogues in which *The Sad Shepherd* is engaged work both ways, and if pastoral is 'Englished' here, Robin Hood is also pastoralised.

Developing these hints, the second half of the prologue deals directly with questions of genre. Having apparently finished, the prologue '*returns upon a new purpose and speaks on*' (l. 30SD). In doing so, he raises some terms that were – as we have seen – crucial to the cultural place of pastoral in the 1630s:

> But here's an heresy of late let fall,
> That mirth by no means fits a pastoral.
> Such say so who can make none, he presumes;
> Else there's no scene more properly assumes
> The sock. For whence can sport in kind arise
> But from the rural routs and families?
> Safe on this ground then, we not fear today
> To tempt your laughter by our rustic play. (ll. 31–8)

The pun on 'play' in the final line quoted here underlines the tension between convention and dramatic representation, and the changes that pastoral had undergone. While Fletcher in 1608 complained that spectators expected too much 'mirth', Jonson in the mid-1630s apparently fears that courtly productions such as *The Shepherds' Paradise* have rendered comedy and laughter incompatible with pastoral. In countering these views, he asserts that pastoral is more suited to comedy – here represented by the 'sock' worn by personifications of that genre – than any other mode. Comedy, he argues, naturally arises from rural customs and social structures. In view of the urbanism of Jonson's Jacobean comedies, we might view this statement with suspicion; however, some of his other Caroline comedies, such as *The New Inn* (King's Men, 1629) and *The Tale of a Tub* (Queen Henrietta Maria's Men, 1633), also suggest the dramatist's desire at this stage in his career to develop comedy's rural potential.

In reinstating pastoral's links with comedy, Jonson also critiques then-current pastoral aesthetics:

> But that no style for pastoral should go
> Current but what is stamped with 'Ah' and 'Oh',
> Who judgeth so may singularly err,
> As if all poesy had one character
> In which what were not written were not right[.] (ll. 53–7)

In their recent edition of *The Sad Shepherd*, Anne Barton and Eugene Giddens suggest that this comment should be viewed as a critique of 'the languishing style of Caroline pastoral generally', and they point out that the play itself includes occasional exclamations of 'Ah' and 'Oh' (*CBJ*, 7: 430). However, exclamations of this sort appear in Caroline pastoral only infrequently; instead, they were more closely associated with Italianate pastoral than native varieties. The first English translation of Guarini's *Il pastor fido*, reprinted – significantly, for my purposes here – in 1633, contains over ninety examples of 'Oh', more than sixty of 'O', and over thirty of 'Ah'; while Daniel's *Hymen's Triumph* (1614), one of the most Italianate of English pastorals and thought by some commentators to be the target of Jonson's ire,[90] includes over forty examples of 'Ah'. In the context of the prologue's earlier declaration of rivalry with the pastorals of '*Sicily, or Greece*', Jonson's criticism of the languishing style also suggests his desire here to rewrite pastoral along 'English' lines.

The uses to which Jonson puts pastoral genre and style are clear in the surviving fragment of the play itself, in particular in its treatment of mirth and of the characters that most nearly represent what he calls 'rural routs and families'. A number of references to mirth cluster in the opening scenes, linking it with genre, emotion and social custom. Much, who is described as '*Robin Hood's bailiff, or acater*' ('The Persons of the Play', l. 10), declares that the loss of the shepherdess Earine, who has supposedly drowned in the Trent (as the prologue advertises) will 'mar [Robin's] mirth' (1.3.50). Similarly, an extended exchange between Robin and the shepherds Clarion and Lionel later in the same act focuses on the vexed place of festivity within their community. Robin and his companions enter the stage '*with music of all sorts*' (1.4.0SD), but mirth quickly becomes the object of reflection rather than action. Robin comments,

> Why should or you or we so much forget
> The season in ourselves as not to make
> Use of our youth and spirits, to awake
> The nimble hornpipe and the tambourine,
> And mix our songs and dances in the wood,
> And each of us cut down a triumph-bough?
> Such were the rites the youthful June allow. (1.4.11–17)

Robin appears to express nostalgia for a lost age, but the dialogue between Clarion and Friar Tuck that follows suggests that mirth actually faces opposition within the rural community. Other shepherds, dubbed the 'sourer sort' by Clarion (1.4.18), are hostile to pastoral mirth, dubbing rural festivities 'pagan pastimes' that infect the community and breed wantonness and lust (1.4.36–9). Friar Tuck calls these shepherds' motives into question, accusing them of being 'hurried more / With covetise and rage', and keen to exploit their neighbours: among other crimes, 'They add the poor man's eanling and dare sell / Both fleece and carcass, not gi'ing him the fell' (1.4.22–5). The opponents of pastoral festivity also refuse to conform to other accepted models of rural behaviour, suggesting that they are disconnected from the 'real' spirit of the countryside.

The ideological basis of the dispute is then set in a different light as the conversation turns to the recent past:

> ROBIN HOOD I do not know what their sharp sight may see
> Of late, but I should think it still might be
> (As 'twas) a happy age, when on the plains
> The woodmen met the damsels, and the swains
> The neatherds, ploughmen, and the pipers loud,
> And each did dance – some to the kit or crowd,
> Some to the bagpipe, some the tabret moved,
> And all did either love or were beloved.
>   LIONEL The dextrous shepherd then would try his sling,
> Then dart his hook at daisies, then would sing,
> Sometimes would wrestle.

CLARION   Ay, and with a lass,
And give her a new garment on the grass,
After a course at barley-break or base.
    LIONEL And all these deeds were seen without offence
Or the least hazard o' their innocence.
    ROBIN HOOD Those charitable times had no mistrust.
Shepherds knew how to love, and not to lust.   (1.4.40–56)

Pastoral mirth is presented here as something just out of reach, but this is
not precisely nostalgia. Rather, Jonson's painstaking delineation of real
stresses and strains within the rural community – as Sanders notes, this is
'a careful analysis of the operations of woodland communities at the time
of composition'[91] – unsettles pastoral convention, suggesting a potentially
productive gap between representation and reality.

In the 1630s, moreover, pastoral festivity had broader associations. In
1633 Charles reissued one of his father's key statements on rural policy: *The
King's Majesty's Declaration to His Subjects, Concerning Lawful Sports to Be
Used*. The 'Book of Sports', as it is often known, was originally published
in 1618, and it sought to legitimise and co-opt various kinds of festivity by
giving explicit sanction to holiday sports and pastimes such as Morris
dancing, as a means of countering both '*Papists and Puritanes*'.[92] As Leah
Marcus writes, James and Charles 'attempted to extend royal power into
an area of ambivalence and instability, to channel the equivocal status
of popular festival into what we can perhaps call an official "paradox of
state"'.[93] The Caroline 'Book of Sports' is itself the product of a kind of
nostalgia, opening as it does with a recollection of the reasons why James
issued the original proclamation:

> OVr Deare Father of blessed Memory, in his returne from Scotland,
> comming through Lancashire, found that his Subiects were debarred from
> Lawful Recreations vpon Sundayes after Euening Prayers ended, and vpon
> Holy dayes: And Hee prudently considered, that if these times were taken
> from them, the meaner sort who labour hard all the weeke, should haue no
> Recreations at all to refresh their spirits.[94]

Lawful recreation here includes '*dauncing, either men or women, Archery for
men, leaping, vaulting, or any other such harmlesse Recreation . . . May-
Games, Whitson Ales, and Morris-dances, and the setting up of May-poles &
other sports therewith vsed*'; however, '*vnlawfull games*' such as bear- and
bull-baiting, '*interludes*' and bowling are still prohibited (11, 12). The 'Book
of Sports' thus seeks to encourage rural sports as a form of officially
sanctioned safety valve, but it also closely regulates the forms that they
might take.

In their expression of nostalgia for the 'happy age' of rural games, Robin and the shepherds are thus aligned with Caroline political orthodoxy, even though the amorous tone of their pursuits was probably not what Charles had in mind. We might contrast the treatment of festivity here with its portrayal in *A Masque* where, as critics have argued, Comus's rout appears to embody the licentiousness that some associated with the activities encouraged by the 'Book of Sports' and with the court itself.[95] Nonetheless, as Marcus points out, *The Sad Shepherd* also undercuts its apparent support for royal policy in its depiction of Maudlin and her family, who, with their desire for privacy and apparent disdain for the 'coarse rustic mouths' (1.7.6) of their neighbours, most resemble those 'who refuse to acknowledge that pastoral can (and should) be anchored in collective mirth'.[96] While the witch and her children may represent the comic 'rural routs and families' to which Jonson draws attention in his prologue, they also threaten the very collectivity on which rural life is here assumed to depend.

Archaism is part of *The Sad Shepherd*'s carefully poised negotiation with pastoral traditions, but – in contrast with rural festivity – these linguistic revivals of past practices are treated not with wistful longing but with a certain suspicion. With the exception of pastoral markers such as 'swain', which are used more broadly, archaic words and syntactic forms are restricted almost entirely to a small group of characters. Most of them are uttered by Maudlin the witch, her daughter Douce and her son, Lorel the swineherd; some are also given to 'old' Will Scathlocke, one of Robin's huntsmen. These characters use words such as 'mickle', 'dight', 'deft' and 'gar', familiar to us from Spenserian pastoral. Indeed, Lorel's position is emphasised by the fact that his name is itself an archaism, marked as an 'olde word' by John Bullokar in his 1616 dictionary and glossed by him as 'A deuourer'.[97] They also on occasion use '-and' and '-en' verb inflections, and depart from the play's general use of blank verse by dropping into tetrameter couplets. In cursing the loss of the venison that she has tried to cheat from Marion and the huntsmen, for instance, Maudlin declares,

> The swilland dropsy enter in
> The lazy cuke, and swell his skin,
> And the old mortmal on his shin
> Now prick and itch withouten blin. (2.6.62–5)

Archaism is thus linked not only with the play's lower orders but also with aberrant forms of speech such as cursing.

The place of archaism in *The Sad Shepherd* is also complicated by the fact that the words and forms used by Maudlin and her children did not appear in Early Modern English merely as literary archaisms. Instead, they appear to have been part of the living speech of parts of Scotland and northern areas of England, and they feature alongside words drawn from regional dialect and words that are rendered in phonetic spelling. Thus, these characters appear to represent an attempt on Jonson's part to represent regional speech in an authentic manner. A good example of its effect can be seen in the speeches in which Lorel preeningly asserts his status as a master of his own livestock to the disdainful Earine, who is not dead but has been captured by Maudlin to be her son's bride:

> I am na fay, na incubus, na changelin',
> But a good man that lives o' my awn gear.
> This house, these grounds, this stock is all mine awn.
> . . .
> An hundred udders for the pail I have
> That gi' me milk and curds, that make me cheese
> To cloy the mercats; twenty swarm of bees,
> Whilk all the summer hum about the hive
> And bring me wax and honey in by live;
> An agèd oak, the king of all the field,
> With a broad beech there grows afore my dur,
> That mickle mast unto the ferm doth yield;
> A chestnut, whilk hath larded mony a swine,
> Whose skins I wear to fend me fra the cold[.] (2.2.10–12, 15–24)

Terms such as 'gear' (possessions) were strongly associated with Northern and Scottish English at this time, as was the '-lk' ending in 'whilk' (which); 'mickle', on the other hand, appears frequently in literary texts as a pastoral archaism. The linguist Katie Wales describes this as 'a conglomerate Northern/Scots dialect', and suggests that it may be explained in part by the idea of the 'north of the Trent' – a significant political boundary – in the early modern popular imagination.[98]

In giving regional forms to the witch and her family, Jonson potentially uses their language to mark them as 'other' in both social and narrative terms. Yet the fact that Scathlocke also uses these forms complicates this picture; remarkably, Scathlocke's brother, Scarlet, does not use them, and they are perhaps therefore to be associated with the former's age rather than his social or regional status. It is notable that William Denny's later pastoral play *The Shepherds' Holiday* (1651) gives its most concentrated use

of archaism to the old shepherd Geron, who represents age or time.[99]
Moreover, the literary background and implicit inauthenticity of Jonson's
dialogue is suggested in the close paraphrase of Spenser's February Eclogue
in lines 20–3 of the speech quoted above.[100] The use of regional English in
The Sad Shepherd is therefore more nuanced than Blank suggests when she
asserts that 'dialect, for Jonson, is the language of witches, louts, and
thieves' (*Broken English*, 165). Although Maudlin is carefully positioned
as the '*witch of Papplewick*' ('The Persons of the Play', l. 21; see also 3.2.11),
a village in the southern part of Sherwood Forest, her speech and that of
her children is less localised.

Elsewhere in the play, moreover, the use of archaism and regional
dialect is not treated as an essential characteristic, but something that can
be put on or taken off at will. When Earine rejects Lorel's comically
pastoral offering of a baby badger, two baby hedgehogs and a ferret –
'Smooth bauson's cub, the young grice of a grey, / Twa tiny urchins, and
this ferret gay' (2.2.39–40) – in the course of his wooing, she mimics his
accent and dialect terms:

> Oh, the fiend and thee!
> Gar take them hence; they fewmand all the claithes
> And prick my coats. Hence with 'em, limmer lown,
> Thy vermin and thyself! Thyself art one!   (2.2.42–5)

Conversely, Maudlin is able to imitate Marion's mode of speech when she
uses her magic girdle to assume the younger woman's appearance and
deceive Robin and his followers. Archaism and dialect are both unstable,
and they become increasingly difficult to associate securely with one class
or regional group.

The ways in which Jonson aligns archaism and regional dialect also
render complex one of the few moments in the surviving text at which
genuine mirth and glee is expressed. When Maudlin hypocritically thanks
Marion for the venison that she herself has swindled from the huntsmen,
she declares,

> 'Twas such a bounty
> And honour done to your poor beadswoman,
> I know not how to owe it, but to thank you,
> And that I come to do. I shall go round
> And giddy with the toy of the good turn.
> *She turns round [while delivering the following lines], till she falls.*
> Look out, look out, gay folk about,
> And see me spin. The ring I'm in
> Of mirth and glee with thanks for fee

The heart puts on for th'venison
My lady sent, which shall be spent
In draughts of wine to fume up fine
Into the brain and down again.
Fall in a swoon upo' the groun'. (2.6.10–22)

The abandon of the speech and its action is suggested in Robin's comment, 'Look to her! She is mad' (2.6.23). Maudlin's incantatory dance, which occasions an almost total lack of bodily control, does not express the unity and harmony generally associated with pastoral festivity. Instead, it marks her isolation from the other figures on stage and, potentially, from the 'neighbours' to whom she claims to have promised a share in the venison.

Moreover, Maudlin's speech also incorporates another form of literary archaism. Although they are not set out as such in Barton and Giddens' edition, nor in the 1640 folio edition of Jonson's works, the internal rhymes in the lines quoted above mean, as Knight points out, that these lines take the form of a Skeltonic: 'Look out, look out, / Gay folks about, / And see me spin. / The ring I'm in ...'[101] Skeltonics, named after their most famous proponent, the early Tudor poet John Skelton, appear frequently in mid-Tudor poetry but had dropped out of mainstream use by the late Elizabethan period. As Elaine Spina describes, classic Skeltonics take the form of 'Irregular short lines with no predictable number of syllables, rhyme in pairs or runs of three to ten or more, without cross-rhyme, and alliteration and parallelisms of structure'.[102] Maudlin's Skeltonics are actually a little too regular both in metre and rhyme, but they have an authentically helter-skelter quality in their increasing pace.

Like pastoral archaism, the Skeltonic had a set of literary and social associations in the early seventeenth century: with satire, with nonsense, and with particular articulations of English national identity and popular culture.[103] Moreover, it had precise associations within both Jonson's works and the Robin Hood tradition. Jonson had used the Skeltonic in two Jacobean court masques, *The Gypsies Metamorphosed* (1621) and *The Fortunate Isles and their Union* (1625). In the former it is given to the gypsies, and is integrated with their use of thieves' cant; in the latter, Skelton is apparently called from the dead to appear alongside the jest-book stalwart Scogan and other notorious figures such as Howleglass, Long Meg and the alewife Eleanor Rumming, one of Skelton's own characters. Thus Jonson associates the Skeltonic with two forms of marginal culture: the thieves' cant of the gypsies and the outmoded popular literature of the sixteenth century. Moreover, as James Knowles has demonstrated, in *The Gypsies Metamorphosed* the Skeltonic is also associated with Jacobean libelling culture.[104] Skelton's work and his style represent an uncomfortable collision between elite and popular forms of writing, between the centre and the margins, and Jonson makes productive use of both in these masques.

In addition to these Jonsonian associations, the Skeltonic also had strong connections with the Robin Hood tradition. Anthony Munday's *The Downfall of Robert, Earl of Huntingdon*, an influential version of the Robin Hood story first performed by the Admiral's Men in 1598, presents its narrative as a play written by Skelton, which is being performed before either Henry VII or Henry VIII – it is not entirely clear which monarch is intended.[105] Skelton appears in the frame narrative, and he goes on to play Friar Tuck in the main play. However, Skelton's identity is not contained by that of the character that he plays, since the characteristic rhythms of the Skeltonic are always prone to breaking through within his dialogue. In *The Downfall*, the Skeltonic is part of a broader concern with the temporality of language, and it helps to create a complex dialectic between present and past, in which various different time-periods are collapsed into the 'now' of performance.[106]

Jonson is not so interested in the temporal possibilities of the Skeltonic, and his echo of Munday's Skelton may be in part unconscious. However, the connections that the Skeltonic allows between the Robin Hood story and other forms of English popular culture are clearly suggestive. It evokes a form of speech that is forever on the verge of collapse, and, just as Maudlin's lack of bodily control suggests her ambivalent relationship with pastoral festivity and commonality, so does her verbal expression. Moreover, its connection with the thieves' cant of *The Gypsies Metamorphosed* similarly suggests the extent to which Maudlin and her family are positioned as renegade outsiders within the community of the play. Archaism is no longer an intrinsic part of pastoral diction and decorum – as it was for Spenser and, to an even greater extent, his followers – but a symptom of a more disturbing heteroglossia, a tendency for language to slip the bounds of convention and order. Thus, while Jonson breaks down some of the associations between pastoral archaism and regional and class identity, his use of the Skeltonic reinforces not only Maudlin's status as a user of archaism, but also her capacity to disrupt both linguistic and social norms. Here, as elsewhere, archaism's aesthetic possibilities clearly appeal to Jonson, but he finds its potential to undermine conventional aesthetics unsettling.

In *The Sad Shepherd*, archaism and dialect are fused in a powerful reassessment of pastoral's conventions and its potential effects. Although

Blank is right to argue that dialect in *The Sad Shepherd* is not a 'generalized "pastoral diction" at all, but the language of a few chosen characters' (*Broken English*, 163), it is part of a broader consideration of the nature and function of pastoral diction. Archaism is an integral part of this process, Jonson's combination of his refashioned and repurposed pastoral diction with the alternative archaism of the Skeltonic a sign of the potential that pastoral has to overflow the boundaries of the conventional genre. Thus, Jonson's play, with its modish perspective scenery, its unstable 'rustic' dialect and its range of archaic effects, reconstructs the dramatic pastoral as something rich, strange and paradoxically 'English' in its mixed heritage.

Conclusion

As Sir Henry Wotton's term, 'Doric delicacy', suggests, pastoral archaism draws much of its unsettling aesthetic power from its capacity to mediate between the binaries of 'low' and 'high' set out in the introduction to this chapter. It is crude *and* delicate, natural *and* artificial, rustic *and* courtly, and even where a work leans to one side of the spectrum – as in *The Faithful Shepherdess*, with its finely calibrated syntactic and poetic archaism – the other will still be present in implied or nascent form. In the hands of Fletcher, Milton and Jonson, pastoral drama is an especially striking example of the uses to which writers might put archaism in their attempts to negotiate between old and new, and to reshape an old technique for new purposes. Fletcher reshapes pastoral under the aegis of Anna of Denmark, fusing aspects of its Italianate and indigenous heritage in a deft and self-consciously allusive fashion. Milton creates a synthesis of 'high' and 'low', juxtaposing Spenserian diction with fashionable music and staging techniques, and in doing so he alludes to the ways in which pastoral was both used and abused in Caroline court theatre. Drawing on some of the same material, Jonson revisits the question of archaism's links with regional dialect, simultaneously asserting and denying – through his use of the literary artifice of the archaic Skeltonic – the capacity of pastoral to capture or anatomise real-life social conditions.

In *The Knave in Grain*, pastoral archaism is used to make fun of a young man who bases his idea of the countryside on poetry and drama rather than lived experience, and the author of that play appears to view the technique as an exhausted literary trope. This view was shared by Caroline writers such as Walter Montagu, for whom pastoral was a predominantly courtly genre, and pastoral was to become more and more closely aligned with royal and aristocratic experience as the seventeenth century wore on, making it an increasingly inappropriate environment for literary archaism.[107] By the early 1650s, when William Denny wrote his *Shepherds' Holiday*, archaism needed to be thematically justified; with the exception of terms such as 'swain', which had become part of a general poetic discourse, it was no longer an integral part of dramatic pastoral. In contrast, in the Jacobean and Caroline periods the genre was less settled and archaism remained a productive option for pastoral dramatists. The pastorals of Fletcher, Milton and Jonson are not simply the product of apish imitation of current fashions, or of nostalgic yearning for earlier modes, but a vibrant fusion of new and old, produced as part of a conversation between different nations, regions and times.

CHAPTER 6

Archaism and the 'English' epic

In early 1668 the former and future MP Sir John Hobart wrote two excited letters to a cousin in Norwich about a work that he had just read: Milton's epic poem, *Paradise Lost*, recently published in ten books. 'I have been strangely pleas'd in a deleberate & repeated reading of him,' he told his cousin on 22 January, describing his 'delight' as 'soe excessive, That I can say truly I never read any thing more august'.[1] On 1 February he went into more detail about the book and its author,

> a criminall & obsolete person, & many of his words being ye last some moderne creticks will condemne him for being guilty (in this boo[k]e as well as others) of ye first too, But perhaps hee may thinke this continued (& sure extreordinary) Peice may purchase him soe high a place amounge our eminent Poets, That hee may use ye liberty of Homer or Virgill, who resussitated many words (as I have heard) from obscurity, & incorporated them, wth ye the Greeke and Latine (then in use)[.][2]

For Hobart, Milton is a doubly archaic figure: a professed republican in a world in which many former supporters of the Commonwealth – including Hobart himself – have refashioned themselves as supporters of the restored monarchy; and a perpetrator of outmoded forms of writing. Both varieties of obsolescence are liable to render the poet 'criminal', whether in political or aesthetic terms. Yet Hobart is also able to take a step back and to view *Paradise Lost* in its literary context, and he concludes that formal archaism is, ultimately, something that epic poets do, even though political obsolescence is less easily excused.

This chapter takes Hobart's comments on *Paradise Lost* as its starting point for an examination of the ways in which archaic diction and metrical form not only inflected but also helped to structure English responses to classical and modern epic. The use of archaism in epic was not, of course, an English innovation. It dates back at least as far as Homer, and it is obliquely referred to in Aristotle's discussion of what he calls the high style, in which he argues that epic should include, among other features, 'unusual' or 'strange (or rare) words' (*glottan*) and 'that [which] differs from the normal idiom'.[3] Aristotle's *glottan* is generally thought to refer to archaism, and it was understood to mean that by later writers such as Galen, who glossed it as 'an old word that has fallen out of contemporary usage'.[4] As Michael Silk notes, the longevity of the Greek poetic tradition and its authors' respect for that tradition 'ensured a constant supply of obsolete words and a willingness to perpetuate them'.[5] However, as we saw in the introduction to this book, archaism was a more contested area in Latin epic, and some Roman writers opposed its use. Jonson paraphrases Quintilian when he writes in *Discoveries* that 'Words borrowed of antiquity do lend a kind of majesty to style, and are not without their delight sometimes. For they have the authority of years, and out of their intermission do win to themselves a kind of grace like newness'.[6] Yet both writers also place strict limitations on this use of these 'borrowed' words: they argue that that 'the eldest of the present and newest of the past language is the best', as Jonson puts it, and Quintilian also asserts that archaisms must not be drawn from 'remote and now forgotten ages'.[7]

George Puttenham is more precise about the pitfalls that face a writer of epic. While he acknowledges that some 'words and speeches and sentences' are especially suited to the high style, he describes in detail the characteristics that he considers unsuitable, suggesting the reasons why both archaism and neologism might be considered suspect:

> the high style is disgraced and made foolish and ridiculous by all words affected, counterfeit, and puffed up, as it were a wind-ball carrying more countenance then matter, and cannot be better resembled than to these midsommer pageants in London, where to make the people wonder are set forth great and ugly giants marching as if they were alive and armed at all points, but within they are stuffed full of brown paper and tow, which the shrewd boys underpeering, do guilefully discover and turn to a great derision. Also all dark and unaccustomed words, or rustical and homely, and sentences that hold too much of the merry and light, or infamous and unshamefast, are to be accounted of the same sort, for such speeches become not princes, nor great estates, nor them that write of their doings to utter or report and intermingle with the grave and weighty matters.[8]

In practice, writers often found it difficult to gauge whether a word or phrase was majestic or counterfeit, authoritative or affected. In reaching after the high style they risked achieving only bathos, in the manner of the pageant figures that Puttenham describes, with their brown-paper bombast. Archaism in particular might be both 'darke' (obscure) and 'rusticall and homely'. The fact that Spenser, the era's most consistent archaic stylist, wrote major works in pastoral and epic modes, using some of the same archaic vocabulary in both, underlined the problem without suggesting a clear solution.

Translation posed further problems. Writing in the 1630s, John Denham spoke for many when he argued that 'what is most excellent, is most inimitable', suggesting the inability of English to capture the greatness of classical epic.[9] And even if an ancient author were to be translated, what idiom should the translator use? Denham again voiced a common perspective when he argued that 'if *Virgil* must needs speak English, it were fit he should speak not onely as a man of this Nation, but as a man of this age' (A3r–v). However, many translators of epic appear to have decided that the demands of the high style necessitated that they resort to archaism. Paradoxically, therefore, archaism was used as a means of bringing a text in line with contemporary aesthetics, of giving it a 'grace like newness', as Jonson puts it.

In exploring these issues this chapter argues first that archaism played a crucial role in making epic 'English' in this period and, second, that attending to the uses of archaism in epic poetry also reveals the aesthetic and political strains intrinsic to this project. It jutaposes three kinds of texts: original epic poems such as *The Faerie Queene* and *Paradise Lost*; translations of classical and modern epics such as George Chapman's version of Homer's *Iliad* (1598–1611) and Edward Fairfax's version of Torquato Tasso's *Gerusalemme liberata*, *Godfrey of Bulloigne, or The Recovery of Jerusalem* (1600); and texts composed in other genres, which appropriate epic conventions, such as Shakespeare's play *Cymbeline* (King's Men, *c.*1611) and Ben Jonson's poem 'On the Famous Voyage', published in the *Epigrams* in 1616 but written a few years earlier.[10]

The first section focuses on the resonant uses of a single archaic word, 'dight', in *The Faerie Queene* and *Godfrey of Bulloigne*, exploring the ways in which archaic diction helps to render material from continental epic 'English' in both aesthetic and religio-political terms. The second section turns its attention to archaic metrical forms, exploring the epic lineage of the fourteener line and the implications of its use in Chapman's translation of *The Iliad* and Shakespeare's *Cymbeline* in a period when this metre had slipped out of fashion. The latter also helps to show the ways in which questions of epic form and its links with national identity were not merely debated and exploited within the epic itself, but in other genres too. While *Cymbeline* exploits the potential fragility of epic convention, the texts explored in the third section, Jonson's 'On the Famous Voyage' and

Charles Cotton's burlesque versions of Books 1 and 4 of *The Aeneid* (1664–5) thoroughly deconstruct the use of archaic diction in the English epic, parodying it and suggesting that this mode of expression is reaching an aesthetic dead-end. The final section brings together archaic diction and metrical form, exploring their uses in Milton's *Paradise Lost*. It has become a cliché to assert that *Paradise Lost* both summarises and concludes an epic tradition. T. J. B. Spencer puts this case most strongly when he argues that the poem is an 'anti-epic', claiming that it 'closed this history of this poetic genre in England'.[11] Focusing more closely on style, Margaret Doody similarly declares that *Paradise Lost* 'consumes epic styles, devices and narrative formulae, to the point where these become unusable in any other poem'.[12] However, while scholarship has often focused on Milton's revisionary appropriation of epic form and conventions, his use of archaism has been widely neglected. In contrast with Spencer and Doody, I argue that attending to archaism demonstrates how Milton aims not only to dismantle the epic – in the style of Jonson or Cotton – but also to recuperate and refashion it for new purposes.

Fowly dight: Spenser, Ariosto, Fairfax, Tasso

In many respects, Spenser's *Faerie Queene* offers an object lesson in the ways in which the modern epic in the 1590s might incorporate archaic style, and it was to set a potent standard for later writers. Focusing on the uses of a single word, 'dight', and the contexts in which it is employed, suggests some of the ways in which archaism enables Spenser to make the epic 'English', and to establish both its aesthetic and religio-political credentials. The word 'dight' is a particularly significant example of Spenserian archaism owing to its perceived heritage and the range of meanings that were available for it in the late sixteenth century. Early modern dictionaries and glossaries define it as to dress, to make ready, to provide, to appoint, to use, to handle, to cover, and to 'force or indeuour to an acte or doynge'.[13] Sources cited by *OED* also suggest that it could be used to mean to put to death (dight *v.* 4a, 5b). In his Chaucer glossary, Thomas Speght marks it as deriving from 'Some Dialects within this our Country of Brittain, and many of them deriued from the Saxon tongue'.[14] Spenser draws on all of these meanings and associations in the course of *The Faerie Queene*, and many of them coalesce in one especially powerful moment in Book 1.

At the end of the eighth canto, the sorceress Duessa is stripped of her veneer of glamour, and appears in her 'true' form:

Her craftie head was altogether bald,
    And as in hate of honorable eld,
    Was ouergrowne with scurfe and filthy scald;
    Her teeth out of her rotten gummes were feld,
    And her sowre breath abhominably smeld;
    Her dried dugs, like bladders lacking wind,
    Hong downe, and filthy matter from them weld;
    Her wrizled skin as rough, as maple rind,
So scabby was, that would haue loathd all womankind.

Her neather parts, the shame of all her kind,
    My chaster Muse for shame doth blush to write;
    But at her rompe she growing had behind
    A foxes taile, with dong all fowly dight;
    And eke her feete most monstrous were in sight;
    For one of them was like an Eagles claw,
    With griping talaunts armd to greedy fight,
    The other like a Beares vneuen paw:
More vgly shape yet neuer liuing creature saw. (1.8.47–8)

In this 'cruel parody of a blazon', as Andrew Hadfield terms it,[15] Spenser balances old and new words. 'Dug' in stanza 47 appears to have been an early sixteenth-century coinage and 'wrizled' may have been very recently adopted,[16] while 'eld' in stanza 47 and 'dight' and 'eke' in stanza 48 are all archaisms. Spenser calls attention to 'dight' by putting it at the end of the line and alliterating it with 'dong', and the stanzas also play self-consciously with the idea of age. Duessa's mangy scalp is 'as in hate of honorable eld'; stripped of her borrowed clothes and her magical powers, she is a parody of the worst aspects of old age, set against the grandeur of epic's own antiquity.

The mixture of old and new in the description of Duessa's abjection underlines Spenser's negotiations between different materials in his efforts to render the epic 'English'. Or, rather, to make it embody a particular kind of Englishness. In the first place, a mixture of old and new is appropriate to Duessa's role within the poem as an embodiment of the Catholic church, an institution that was viewed by English Protestants as both outmoded and newfangled.[17] Moreover, Spenser brings together a series of new and old texts, holding their various associations in suspension and positioning Duessa as a multi-layered amalgam of various traditions. First, he alludes to biblical texts that had specific resonance for Protestant readers. In Revelation 17:16 'the ten hornes which thou sawest vpon the beast, are they that shal hate the whore, and shal make her desolate and naked', while Isaiah 3:16–24 describes the stripping of the daughters of

Zion: 'in stead of swete sauour, there shalbe stinke, and in stead of a girdle, a rent, & in stead of dressing of ye heere, baldnes, and in stead of a stomacher, a girding of sacke cloth, & burning in stead of beautie' (24).[18] The revelation of Duessa's true character and physicality in *The Faerie Queene* echoes and fuses two biblical prophecies, and the Geneva translators' references to anachronistic items of clothing underline the perceived applicability of these prophecies to current events, a perception that Spenser exploits.

Simultaneously, Spenser's description has specific connections with Reformation polemic. A sequence in which the Whore of Babylon is stripped appears in John Bale's *The Image of Both Churches* (1545), but – as D. Douglas Waters describes – an even stronger association can be drawn between Duessa and Mistress Missa, an allegorical representation of the Roman Catholic mass who appears or is alluded to in many texts of the 1540s and 1550s.[19] In Luke Shepherd's *Pathos* (1548), for example, the Pope mourns his daughter the Mass in vigorous Skeltonics:

> For whan she was newe
> I did her endue
> Wyth clothynge of Gospel
> And of the Epistel
> And nowe they be gon
> She semeth as one
> That is but skin and bon
> As leane as a rake
> As flat as a cake
> As stife as a stake
> Hir lippes be pale
> Hir eyes wexe smale
> Hir checkes thyne
> With a yealowe skine
> And nought wythin
> Hir nose is sharpe
> And a wrye doeth warpe
> As heauy as leade
> She is neare deade[20]

Duessa's nakedness and the revelation of her ugliness thus recall not only the Bible itself, but its more recent polemical offshoots. In addition, despite the obvious differences in style between Spenser's and Shepherd's works, there is an echo of Shepherd's vigour in Spenser's monosyllabic line-endings. Spenser's depiction of Duessa is thus embedded in a network of Protestant, virulently anti-Catholic texts, and it draws some of its force

from the sectarian energies of polemic. Linguistic and literary style combine to associate his epic with articulations of English identity that were
shaped both by biblical tradition and the Protestant polemic that sought to
reshape that tradition.

Spenser never forgets, however, that he is writing epic. The abjection of
Duessa is based not only on polemic, but on the recent history of the epic
itself and, in particular, Ariosto's depiction of the fraudulent witch Alcina
in Book 7 of *Orlando Furioso*:

> Pallido, crespo e macilente avea
> Alcina il viso, il crin raro e canuto,
> sua statura a sei palmi non giungea:
> ogni dente di bocca era caduto;
> che più d'Ecuba e più de la Cumea[.][21]

> [She was whey-faced, wrinkled, and hollow-cheeked; her hair was white and
> sparse; she was not four feet high; the last tooth had dropped out of her jaw;
> she had lived longer than anyone else on earth, longer than Hecuba or the
> Cumaean Sibyl.[22]]

Spenser does not only quote directly Ariosto's description of Alcina's
toothless mouth; his description of Duessa and, in particular, his reference
to old age also clearly mirror the Italian poet's blazon, in a gesture that is
simultaneously parody and homage. Duessa is simultaneously, therefore,
an archetypal figure from the Bible (or, more accurately, a fusion of more
than one figure), a personification drawn from Reformation polemic and a
modern literary witch whose sexuality is a lure and a trap. Peter DeSa
Wiggins argues that the use of Revelation and Isaiah in *The Faerie Queene*
makes the echo of Alcina's exposure here 'pointless' if it is not 'another
polemical demonstration of how much more serious the *Faerie Queene* is
than the *Orlando Furioso*'.[23] However, Melinda Gough has pointed out the
depiction of Alcina itself draws on Revelation, and she argues – I think
correctly – that in taking up the motif of the temptress disrobed Spenser
'turns a weapon of the old church back on itself', asserting 'specifically
geopolitical interests along with literary and hermeneutic ones'.[24] For
Gough, therefore, the allusion to Ariosto in *The Faerie Queene* has a similar
function to that of the allusion to Reformation traditions, and Spenser's
literary and religio-political interests are fused in Duessa's abjection.

So far, I have traced the various traditions that underpin Spenser's
depiction of Duessa, and its mixture of old and new elements. What
interests me particularly, however, is the way in which his fusion of these
traditions comes together in the rawly abusive archaism of his description

of Duessa's 'neather parts' and her fox's tail, 'with dong all fowly dight' (1.8.48.4). The archaic word, 'dight', here emblematises not only the polemical underpinnings of the passage, in its position at the end of the line and its vigorous alliteration with 'dong', but also – as we will see – its uses of epic convention. Moreover, its very Englishness underlines *The Faerie Queene*'s reshaping of continental sources. Spenser evidently liked the phrase 'fowly dight', which appears four times in *The Faerie Queene*: in the description of Duessa; in the evocation of the blood falling onto Guyon from the bleeding truck of his horse after Pyrochles' onslaught (2.5.4.9); in the account of the attack of the Satyrs on Malbecco, whose 'hore beard' is trodden into the dirt (3.10.52.5); and in the description of the headless female corpse near the start of Book 5 (5.1.14.8). In each of these moments 'dight' powerfully evokes the abjection of the human or animal involved, but Spenser also draws on the range of richly contradictory meanings that the term had in the late sixteenth century. Duessa is multiply dighted and undighted in Canto 8: abusively stripped naked, her body is made to reveal itself to the appalled onlookers, but this act of stripping away illusion is itself a form of repair and reparation.

One of *OED*'s alternative meanings for 'dight' is the ironic meaning of 'to dirty, befoul' (dight, *v.* 10d), which it dates to the mid-seventeenth century. However, its earliest citation appears to be indebted to Spenser himself: in Shakerley Marmion's comedy *Holland's Leaguer* (Prince Charles's Men, 1631), the servant Jeffrey complains that if he and his master are not careful 'straight we shall fall / Into a Lake that will fouly dight us'.[25] Marmion was clearly amused by the phrase 'foully dight', and its association with 'dong' lingered in his memory, linking the word to the humiliation to which Duessa is subjected. Moreover, the lingering suggestion of defilement also inflects Spenser's later use of 'dight' in Book 1 of *The Faerie Queene*, when Redcrosse describes Duessa:

> There did I find, or rather I was found
> Of this false woman, that *Fidessa* hight,
> *Fidessa* hight the falsest Dame on ground,
> Most false *Duessa*, royall richly dight[.] (1.12.32.1–4)

Spenser's repetition of another archaic word, 'hight', which is rhymed not only with 'dight' but also, later in the stanza, with 'sight' and 'might', underlines the act of impersonation. In appearing 'royall richly dight', Duessa cloaks herself in an illusion of authority and truth, a disguise that abuses and befouls those who are taken in by it. The word 'dight' thus gathers additional associations and implications as Book 1 progresses.

That the word 'dight' was already considered appropriate to epic when Spenser wrote *The Faerie Queene* is clear from its appearance in the Thomas Phaer/Thomas Twyne translation of Virgil's *Aeneid* (1573) and Arthur Hall's translation of Homer's *Iliad* (1581). In the former, for example, Hecuba spots Priam 'beclad in armes of youth so bold' and asks him 'what minde alas . . . o wofull husband you / In harneis dight: and whither away with wepons run ye now?'.[26] However, the growing archaism of the term is underlined by the fact that it appears only in the Phaer sections of *The Aeneid*, completed in the 1550s. In contrast, in the wake of the publication of the first edition of *The Faerie Queene*, 'dight' made something of a comeback, appearing in the partial or complete translations of Guillaume de Salluste, seigneur Du Bartas's *La Sepmaine; ou, Création du monde* (1578) and *La Seconde Sepmaine* (1584) by William L'Isle (1595 and 1598), Thomas Winter (1603) and Joshua Sylvester (1611), in the translations of Tasso's *Gerusalemme liberata* (1581) by Richard Carew (1594) and Edward Fairfax (1600), and in Chapman's translation of Homer's *Odyssey* (c.1615). Spenser, it appears, successfully reanimated a term that was on the verge of extinction, imbuing it with renewed epic force and with a range of associations on which later writers and translators would build.

The potential of the word 'dight' is particularly evident in Fairfax's translation of *Gerusalemme liberata*, *Godfrey of Bulloigne, or The Recovery of Jerusalem*. The title-page describes the work as '*Done into English heroicall verse*', and Fairfax follows Spenser closely in terms of diction and grammar, adopting such features as the 'y' prefix, '-en' verb inflections, and archaisms such as 'whilom', 'nill', 'ne', 'wight', 'chevisance', 'embay', 'flit', 'reedments', 'yond' and 'yood'.[27] This is, as Colin Burrow describes, a thoroughly 'Spenserian reading' of Tasso.[28] While Burrow reads *Godfrey of Bulloigne* primarily in terms of Fairfax's Spenserian recasting of Tasso's treatment of the key epic motif of sympathy, I am interested here in the three-cornered stylistic relationship between Tasso, Fairfax and Spenser, and in one especially striking moment at which Fairfax resorts to the archaism 'dight'. As scholars have noted, *Gerusalemme liberata* shapes *The Faerie Queene*'s narrative structures, its characterisation and its literary techniques. It provides Spenser with a model for sequences such as Guyon and the Palmer's journey to Acrasia's bower in Book 2, in which some stanzas – for instance, the description of the 'naked Damzelles' in the fountain (2.12.63–9) – are virtual translations of Tasso's poem.[29] Elsewhere, Tasso's depiction of the Amazonian Clorinda, who fights bravely against the crusaders and is eventually killed by Tancredi, the crusader who has fallen in love with her, inflects Spenser's treatment of Britomart, notably in the latter's (false) description of her martial upbringing (3.2.6; compare *Gerusalemme liberata* 2.39) and in the moment at which Britomart's helmet comes off when she is fighting against Artegall (4.6.19–22), which is indebted to the similar moment during Tancredi's battle against Clorinda (*Gerusalemme liberata*, 3.21–2). In addition to providing Spenser with a model for how to reshape the epic to explicitly Christian ends, *Gerusalemme liberata* also gave the English poet hints on how to present the female warriors that would be so crucial to *The Faerie Queene*. Thus, when Fairfax draws on Spenser in translating Tasso, he establishes a complex interaction between the three epic texts, in which matters of style, religious affiliation and national identity are intertwined.

In particular, Fairfax's use of Spenserian archaism renders even more complex Clorinda's place in the religious politics of *Gerusalemme liberata*. Tasso presents her not only as a Muslim, a faith instilled in her by her guardian, the eunuch Arsete, but also as the daughter of the Christian Ethiopian king and queen. In Canto 12, Arsete reveals Clorinda's parentage to her, detailing how her pregnant mother prayed before a picture of St George saving a white virgin from a dragon and, to her surprise and alarm, gave birth to a daughter with white skin. Terrified that her husband would think that she had been unfaithful to him, the queen entrusted the infant Clorinda to Arsete, asking him to have her baptised according to Coptic practice; she also invoked St George's protection for her. Arsete failed to carry out the queen's request, with the result that Clorinda fights on the 'wrong' side at the siege of Jerusalem. As David Quint describes, Tasso's representation of Clorinda thus alludes to recent attempts by the papacy to force the Ethiopian church – with which it had recently re-established contact – to conform to Roman Catholic doctrine.[30] It is, he writes, 'unclear from moment to moment in the poem whether Clorinda emulates the knight, Saint George, the white virgin whom he saves from the dragon and converts to Christianity, or the monster-dragon ... of religious error itself' (*Epic*, 244). In reading Tasso through Spenser, and adopting the latter's archaic diction, Fairfax further complicates the debates surrounding Clorinda's religious identity and, in particular, the nature of the 'religious error' in which she is enmeshed.

Shortly after Arsete's narrative has been completed, Clorinda heads out on an expedition to the crusaders' camp, intending to set fire to their siege tower. In order to pass unnoticed, she eschews her usual armour:

> Depon Clorinda le sue spoglie inteste
> d'argento e l'elmo adorno e l'arme altere,
> e senza piuma o fregio altre ne veste
> (infausto annunzio!) ruginose e nere,
> però che stima agevolmente in queste
> occulta andar fra le nemiche schiere.
>
> [Clorinda doffs her silver-threaded cloak,
> her golden casque and breastplate burnished bright,
> and dons a rusty armour, black as smoke
> (unlucky omen!), plumeless, plain, and light,
> thinking she thus will among hostile folk
> move unperceíved and safely through the night.][31]

Fairfax renders the moment thus:

> *Clorinda* there her siluer armes off rent
> Her helme, her shield, her hawberke shining bright,
> An armour blacke as ieat or cole she hent,
> Wherein withouten plume her selfe she dight;
> For thus disguis'd amid her foes she ment
> To passe vnseene, by helpe of friendly night[.][32]

These lines include a number of Spenserian touches in their language, such as the use of the archaisms 'hent' and 'dight', and the '-en' inflection in 'withouten', suggesting the ways in which Fairfax depends on Spenserian models as a way of making the continental epic 'English'. Moreover, the unsettling quality that can adhere to archaic diction is particularly evident in Fairfax's adoption of the term 'dight', which entangles Clorinda in a network of Spenserian associations.

The word 'dight' is often employed in the scenes of knights arming themselves that stud *The Faerie Queene*, which are themselves indebted to the similar scenes in classical and, especially, continental romance. For instance, when Arthur enters into battle with Maleger in Book 2, Spenser describes how 'in glitterand armes he dight, / And his well proued weapons to him hent' (2.11.17.1–2), while the dragon in Book 1 is a horrible parody of the armed knight, his scales making a noise like 'the clashing of an armour bright' and his crest standing up: 'His aery plumes doth rouze, full rudely dight' (1.11.9.6). Having re-established the martial associations of the word 'dight', Spenser uses it three times in his account of Britomart in Book 3. At the end of the first canto, when the enemies have been dismissed, 'The noble *Britomartis* her arayd, / And her bright armes about her body dight' (3.1.67.2–3). More resonant still are the stanzas at the end of Canto 3, when the nurse Glauce takes Britomart to the armoury, and

decides to accompany the younger woman as her squire: 'Another har-
nesse, which did hang thereby, / About her selfe she dight, that the yong
Mayd / She might in equall armes accompany' (3.3.61.2–4). In the next
canto, immediately before Britomart encounters and summarily defeats
Marinell, Spenser describes her momentary depression, Glauce's 'sharpe
repriefe' (3.4.11.4) and the warrior's response:

> Thus as she her recomforted, she spyde,
>   Where farre away one all in armour bright,
>   With hastie gallop towards her did ryde;
>   Her dolour soone she ceast, and on her dight
>   Her Helmet, to her Courser mounting light:
>   Her former sorrow into suddein wrath,
>   Both coosen passions of distroubled spright,
>   Conuerting, forth she beates the dustie path;
> Loue and despight attonce her courage kindled hath. (3.4.12)

In *The Faerie Queene*, for female warriors to 'dight' themselves in preparation for battle is to enter fully into the male world of violence and
chivalry, and to demonstrate their adaptability to that setting.

Tasso's Clorinda helped to shape Spenser's Britomart, a connection that
Fairfax – intentionally or not – underlines in his translation through his
use of 'dight'. However, the Spenserian intertext complicates the translator's presentation of Clorinda. As we have seen, Tasso's Clorinda is caught
between three religious imperatives: the Muslim faith of her upbringing,
the Coptic church of her parents, and the Catholic doctrine of the
crusaders. In the context of *The Faerie Queene*, however, Clorinda is
potentially a Redcrosse, a Britomart or a Duessa, and her act of 'dighting'
herself in ill-omened black armour is a revelation of her misguided and
violent plans. The Spenserian diction of Fairfax's translation ironically
points to the religious gulf between *Gerusalemme liberata* – perhaps the
ultimate Catholic epic – and *The Faerie Queene*, Spenser's stridently
Protestant refashioning of the genre. Where Tasso positions the Coptic
church as the product of a dangerously mistaken theology, Spenser insists
that the Catholic church is itself a false version of Christianity.

Tracing the use of the archaism 'dight' across Spenser and Fairfax thus
suggests that 'Englishing' continental epic in the 1590s also involved
adapting it to late-Elizabethan religio-political conventions. Archaism
facilitates Spenser's engagement with the epic genre, enabling him both
to connect his work with prior tradition and assert his independence from
it. Epic archaism in *The Faerie Queene* is collusive and competitive;
drawing on writers such as Tasso enables Spenser to position his epic as

part of a grand tradition, but the specific resonances of words such as 'dight' also assist him in deconstructing that tradition. His self-consciously 'English' diction ultimately asserts the superiority of Protestant England over both pagan Greece and Rome and Catholic Europe. Yet, as we have seen, this iconoclastic strategy itself became a tradition, setting a pattern for later translators of epic. Writers such as Fairfax were able to capitalise on the Spenserian echoes of words such as 'dight', setting up peculiarly polytemporal interactions between source and intertext, and implicitly questioning the assumptions on which the continental, Catholic epic was based.

Long verse: Chapman and *Cymbeline*

Archaic diction was not, however, the only means of making the epic 'English' in the late sixteenth and early seventeenth centuries. Another tactic lay in the choice of metre, where poets might choose to imitate the classical hexameter or to explore alternatives such as the pentameter or fourteener. In a poem prefacing his edition of the *Iliad*, first published around 1609, George Chapman defends his choice of the fourteener as a means of rendering Homer's hexameter line:

> The long verse hath by proofe receiu'd applause
> Beyond each other number: and the foile,
> That squint-eyd Enuie takes, is censur'd plaine.
>   For, this long Poeme asks this length of verse;
> Which I my self ingenuously maintaine
> Too long, our shorter Authors to reherse.[33]

Epic, Chapman maintains, needs the roomy fourteener line to expand and develop fully, and other poets' failure to recognise this is founded less in their critical judgement than in their own lack of skill. These comments were perhaps a final attempt to justify the long line – which Chapman was to abandon only a few years later in his translation of the *Odyssey* – but they were far from being the first.

The use of both the fourteener and the alexandrine or hexameter in English verse had been the subject of controversy since the late 1570s. Along with poets such as Philip Sidney and Edmund Dyer, Spenser and his friend Gabriel Harvey explored the possibilities of quantitative measures and classical hexameters; as Richard Helgerson reminds us, Spenser's famous question about the status of the English language reads, in full, 'why a Gods name may not we, as else the Grœkes, haue the kingdome of oure owne Language, and measure our Accentes, by the sounde, reseruing the Quantitie to the Uerse?'[34] For a brief period, unrhymed hexameters, ordered along classical lines, looked like the future of English poetry. However, Thomas Nashe, who attacked the hexameter as part of his feud with Harvey in the early 1590s, sets out their limitations in scornful detail:

> The Hexamiter verse I graunt to be a Gentleman of an auncient house (so is many an english begger) yet this Clyme of ours hee cannot thriue in; our speech is too craggy for him to set his plough in, hee goes twitching and hopping in our language like a man running vpon quagmiers vp the hill in one Syllable and down the dale in another, retaining no part of that stately smooth gate, which he vaunts himselfe with amongst the Greeks and Latins.[35]

Antiquity, for Nashe, is not sufficient precedent, and he casts the hexameter as an elderly immigrant, unsuited to his new linguistic environment. The proponents of hexameters may aim for neo-classical smoothness, but they achieve only a stuttering, uneven roughness. While Spenser fantasises that 'rough words must be subdued with Use',[36] Nashe views these experiments as impractical at best. He attacks one of the few wholesale experiments with the hexameter, Richard Stanihurst's vigorously iconoclastic 1582 translation of *The Aeneid*, as consisting of 'foule lumbring boystrous wallowing measures' (*Strange Newes*, G3r), again criticising the perceived clumsiness of English hexameters.

By the time that Chapman wrote his prefatory poem around 1609, the brief vogue for hexameters and quantitative measures had passed. He instead prefers in his version of *The Iliad* another long line: the fourteener. Used extensively by mid-sixteenth-century poets, the fourteener was – in contrast with the rarely used hexameter – the overwhelming verse-form of choice for translators of classical tragedy and epic. Of the ten Senecan translations produced by Jasper Heywood, Alexander Neville, Thomas Nuce, John Studley, Thomas Newton and others in the 1560s, nine use fourteeners for the dialogue. Similarly, translations of classical poetry using fourteeners proliferated: Phaer's version of *The Aeneid*, first published in seven books in 1558, in nine books in 1562, and in a new edition completed by Twyne in 1573; translations of Ovid's *Metamorphoses* by Arthur Golding (1565) and his *Heroical Epistles* by George Turberville (1567); and Arthur Hall's translation of the *Iliad* (1581). Some of these translations were still current ten, twenty and thirty years after their initial publication: the Phaer/Twyne *Aeneid* was reprinted in 1596, 1600, 1607 and 1620, while the Golding *Metamorphoses* was reprinted in 1593, 1603 and 1612. Jonson may have complained to William Drummond in 1619 that 'the translations of Homer and Virgil in long Alexandrines were but prose',[37] but few in the mid-sixteenth century would have agreed with him.

When Spenser began to write *The Faerie Queene* in the 1570s, the fourteener would have been a real option for him. However, it began to slip out of fashion in the 1580s, perhaps in part as a result of Spenser's decision to opt for pentameters and alexandrines and to allude to the fourteener only in his common measure arguments at the head of each book. Even as Chapman adopted the fourteener in the earliest version of his *Iliad*, published in 1598, it was on the verge of extinction in lyric and epic poetry. This fact may explain his title-page's insistence that the *Iliad* is '*Translated according to the Greeke*', and his comment in a letter to the reader, '*The worth of a skilfull and worthy translator, is to obserue the sentences, figures, and formes of speech, proposed in his author: his true sence and height, and to adorne them with figures and formers of oration fitted to the originall*'.[38] The translator begins to register in an oblique form the pressures that would lead him to explicitly defend the fourteener a decade later.

Chapman's comments in the Jacobean edition of his *Iliad* show him defending his investment in an epic aesthetic that had recently become archaic. And it is striking, in this context, that a play written not long after his expanded translation was published, Shakespeare's *Cymbeline*, capitalises on the fourteener's epic resonance, its associations with the 'Englishing' of classical texts, and its vulnerability to fashion, using these features to complicate the play's vision of national identity and origin and, in particular, its interactions with the question of England's place in Jacobean 'Britain'. In the fifth act of *Cymbeline*, the Briton Posthumus is approached in a dream by the ghosts of his family and the god Jupiter, who enters riding on the back of an eagle. A stage direction describes the entrance of Posthumus' father, mother and two brothers thus:

> *Solemn music. Enter, as in an apparition*, SICILIUS LEONATUS, *father to* POSTHUMUS, *an old man attired like a warrior, leading in his hand an ancient matron, his wife and* MOTHER TO POSTHUMUS, *with music before them. Then after other music, follows the* TWO YOUNG LEONATI, *brothers to* POSTHUMUS, *with wounds as they died in the wars. They circle* POSTHUMUS *round as he lies sleeping*[.][39]

When Sicilius finally speaks, his speech is recognisably different from that which precedes and follows it:

> No more, thou Thunder-master, show thy spite on mortal flies.
> With Mars fall out, with Juno chide, that thy adulteries
> Rates and revenges.
> Hath my poor boy done aught but well, whose face I never saw?
> I died whilst in the womb he stayed, attending nature's law,

Whose father then – as men report, thou orphans' father art –
Thou shouldst have been, and shielded him from this earth-vexing
  smart. (5.3.124–30)

Until the entry of Jupiter, the ghosts speak entirely in fourteeners
apart from three short, dimeter lines: 'Rates and revenges', quoted above,
'A thing of pity' (5.3.133), describing the infant Posthumus immediately
after he was 'ripped' from his mother's womb, and 'Sweet Innogen'
(5.3.141).

Shakespeare had used fourteeners for comic effect in earlier plays,
notably in the play-within-a-play in *A Midsummer Night's Dream*
(Chamberlain's Men, 1595–6), which has often been thought to glance at
Golding's translation of Ovid's *Metamorphoses* and/or Phaer's *Aeneid*.[40]
However, it seems unlikely that they are intended merely to burlesque
earlier traditions here.[41] We might look, for instance, to the harrowing
statement of Posthumus' mother:

Lucina lent not me her aid, but took me in my throes,
That from me was Posthumus ripped, came crying 'mongst his foes,
A thing of pity. (5.3.131–3)

In contrast with the parody fourteeners of *A Midsummer Night's Dream*,
Shakespeare demonstrates here a real attempt to get to grips with the
technical demands of the long line. He drew on Chapman's *Iliad* in
composing *Coriolanus*, probably performed not long before *Cymbeline*,[42]
and it seems that epic poetry, not Elizabethan drama – as earlier scholars
have suggested – is his main inspiration here.[43]

Something of Chapman's technique can be seen in his treatment of
another apparition, the ghost of Patroclus, which comes to Achilles in a
dream in Book 23 of *The Iliad*,

                    a hatefull fate depriu'd
My being here; that at my birth, was fixt; and to such fate,
Euen thou, ô god-like man, art markt; the deadly *Ilion* gate,
Must entertaine thy death. O then, I charge thee now, take care
That our bones part not: but as life, combinde in equall fare,
Our louing beings; so let *Death*. When, from *Opuntas* towres,
My father brought me, to your roofes, (since (gainst my will) my powres
Incenst, and indiscreet, at dice, slue faire *Amphidamas*)
Then *Peleus* entertaind me well; then in thy charge I was
By his iniunction, and thy loue: and therein, let me still
Receiue protection. Both our bones, prouide, in thy last Will,
That one Vrne may containe; and make, that vessell all of gold,
That *Thetis* gaue thee; that rich Vrne.[44]

The fourteener's stereotypical characteristics are suppressed in favour of a restrained grandeur and controlled power. Chapman handles his four-teeners in a virtuoso fashion, suppressing their tendency to lapse into sing-song through means such as breaking the line at places other than after the eighth syllable, using enjambment and internal rhyme to under-mine the end-stopping tendencies of the couplet, and using alliteration to structure and modulate individual lines or groups of lines.[45] Nonetheless, when he wants to emphasise the rhyme he does so by varying the metre and end-stopping successive lines – see, for instance, 'fate . . . gate' above. He also varies the pace and effect of individual lines or runs of lines through his use of monosyllabic and polysyllabic words: contrast 'That our bones part not; but as life, combined in equall fare' with 'my powers / Incenst, and indiscreet, at dice, slue faire *Amphidamas*'.

Shakespeare's use of fourteeners in *Cymbeline*, composed around the same time, suggests that he had paid close attention to Chapman's tech-nique. If we look again at Sicilius' first speech (5.3.124–30), we can see that, although some of the fourteeners divide into the traditional syllable pattern of eight and six, the first line is broken after the second and seventh syllables, while the sixth is broken after the fourth as well as the eighth. Similarly, the second line runs on into the short line, breaking up the fourteener pattern. The speech of Posthumus' mother (5.3.131–3) is largely composed of monosyllables, slowing the rhythm and resisting the tendency of the long line to swing, and the short line 'A thing of pity' disrupts things still further; the placing of 'ripped' on the point at which we would expect the fourteener line to break is particularly deft, calling attention to the unnaturally violent way in which Posthumus was born. Later in the sequence, alliteration is introduced with a Chapman-like touch – for instance, in the balance of 'striking' and 'slain' in line 146 and the First Brother's comment, 'Like hardiment Posthumus hath to Cymbeline per-formed' (5.3.148). Moreover, Shakespeare's inclusion of short lines also has a precedent in the English epic, since dimeter and trimeter lines appear regularly in Phaer's translation of *The Aeneid*.[46] These fourteeners may not be as polished or accomplished as those of Chapman, but they are far from parody or burlesque.

Cymbeline's fourteeners are important because the appropriation of a verse form strongly associated with the 'Englishing' of epic verse argues that the debates about nationhood and national identity found elsewhere in the play are also operating on a stylistic level. Developing Patricia Parker's account of the Virgilian echoes that surround Posthumus and Innogen, Martin Butler suggests that at this moment Posthumus 'looks like a new Aeneas, heading for empire', especially because Jupiter's promise to protect Posthumus echoes what he told Venus, Aeneas' mother, in Book 1 of *The Aeneid*.[47] 'Yet', he continues, 'this trail is false': the prophecy may imply that Posthumus is crucial to Britain's redemption, but the return of Innogen's brothers actually removes him 'from the prospect of rule to the role of a private subject' (*Cymbeline*, 53). Paying attention to the specific resonances of the fourteener shows us that archaic style combines with the theatrical spectacle and the prophecy that Jupiter grants the ghosts in creating the 'false trail' of a political, dynastic role for Posthumus.

Yet the fourteener also muddies the waters because it was not a true classical measure, merely a comparatively modern English stand-in. Translations in fourteeners often stress the insular nature of this metre: for instance, Golding's translation of Ovid is described on successive title-pages as having been '*translated oute of Latin into Englishe meter*'.[48] The fourteener line thus suggests not only the epic's imperial qualities but also more specifically the English nation-building with which it had become associated, and the play debates the place of England and the English in relation to epic formations of empire and national identity. Moreover, its juxtaposition with the conventions of the court masque, invoked when Jupiter enters on his eagle, underlines the specifically Jacobean contexts of this debate. As a number of critics have recently argued, *Cymbeline*, with its conclusion in which a British king voluntarily resumes paying tribute to Rome, is intertwined with the ongoing controversy about King James's plan to unite his two kingdoms.[49] How were the English to react to their new identity as 'Britons'?

Reading *Cymbeline* in relation to competing narratives about national origin and the work of antiquarians such as William Camden and Richard Verstegen, which stressed the Anglo-Saxon heritage of the English, Mary Floyd-Wilson sees in Cymbeline's lost heirs Guiderius and Arviragus models for England's Anglo-Saxon descent, and suggests that the play 'spins out an English historical fantasy in which the Scots submit to Anglo-British rule and the English emerge as a race unaffected by Britain's early history of mingled genealogies and military defeats'.[50] The play thus embodies a then-nascent tendency towards English exceptionalism. The use of the fourteener is another submerged 'English' element within the narrative, yet its mixed English and classical heritage means that it dramatises the tensions between competing narratives about Britain and its past, rather than fully seeking to resolve them. Instead, it signals both the vernacular appropriation of classical material and the ghosts' own liminal position as British or proto-English inhabitants of the Roman empire.

Shakespeare's fourteeners thus function simultaneously on three levels, all enabled through their links with earlier traditions of the 'English' epic. First, they intensify the epic undertones of Posthumus' redemption, capitalising on the archaic grandeur and emotional heft of the established form. Second, they are also able to draw on the very precariousness of the fourteener's status within epic; the ghosts' return to Posthumus in his dream is fragile and provisional, and the verse form underlines this fact. Third, they speak to ongoing tensions between various forms of national and literary heritage: English, British and Roman. Where Spenser's appropriation of epic form in the 1590s spoke to a desire to further the imperial aspirations of late-Elizabethan England, Shakespeare's speaks rather to a self-aware meditation on the Jacobean fracturing of national identity and national purpose.[51]

Yclepèd mud: Jonson and Cotton

Around the same time as Shakespeare was composing *Cymbeline*, Ben Jonson was making his own aesthetic intervention in the uses of archaism in epic. According to William Drummond, Jonson had plans to write an epic of his own: 'he had an intention to perfect an epic poem, entitled *Heroologia* [History of heroes], of the worthies of his country roused by fame, and was to dedicate it to his country. It is all in couplets, for he detesteth all other rhymes' (*CBJ*, vol. 5, ll. 1–3).[52] In the event, Jonson's epic appears never to have been finished, but in 'On the Famous Voyage', the last of the *Epigrams*, he pioneered what was to become a prominent Restoration genre: the mock-epic. The outrageously scatological quest of Sheldon and Heydon to voyage up the river Fleet – in the early Jacobean period little more than an open sewer – relentlessly burlesques many of the conventions of the English epic, and archaism is a crucial means through which epic style is both established and deconstructed.

Basing his narrative on Virgil's account of Aeneas' journey into Hell in Book 6 of *The Aeneid*,[53] Jonson weaves in references to specific proponents of English epic style. The final lines, 'And I could wish for their eternized sakes / My muse had ploughed with his that sung A-JAX' (ll. 195–6),[54] glance not only at Sir John Harington's satirical prose work *A New Discourse of a Stale Subject, Called the Metamorphosis of Ajax* (1596) but also his translation of *Orlando Furioso*, published in 1591 and 1607, which employs archaism consistently as a stylistic tool. Further, as Wesley Trimpi points out, Jonson may also have in mind Joshua Sylvester's version of the episode 'The Furies' in his archaising translation of du Bartas's *Seconde*

Sepmaine.[55] In addition to similarities of style, it is noticeable that in the 1616 folio 'On the Famous Voyage' follows a sonnet 'To Master Joshua Sylvester', originally published in the 1605 edition of Sylvester's translation, which Jonson praises in these terms:

> 'Bartas doth wish thy English now were his.'
> So well in that are his inventions wrought
> As his will now be the translation thought,
> Thine the original, and France shall boast
> No more those maiden glories she hath lost. (ll. 10–14)

Sylvester's translation, the sonnet argues, appropriates the French epic for English purposes. In 1619, Jonson apparently told Drummond that 'Sylvester's translation of Du Bartas was not well done, and that he wrote his verses before it ere he understood to confer' (*CBJ*, vol. 5, ll. 20–1). Thus, although Jonson does not change the sonnet to Sylvester, its position in front of the mock-epic 'On the Famous Voyage' suggests his altered perspective, and his newly sceptical view of English epic's capacity to represent either continental or classical epic faithfully.

The opening lines of 'On the Famous Voyage' echo parodically the terms of the sonnet to Sylvester, claiming that English epic can vie with the best of Greece or Rome:

> No more let Greece her bolder fables tell
> Of Hercules or Theseus going to hell,
> Orpheus, Ulysses; or the Latin muse
> With tales of Troy's just knight, our faiths abuse:
> We have a Sheldon and a Heydon got,
> Had power to act what they to feign had not. (ll. 1–6)

Jonson sets up an ironic dialogue between ancient and contemporary, and between fable and 'truth'. His is a self-consciously modern epic, reduced in scope and scale, and focusing on quotidian events. Yet it parodically claims to rival the achievements of classical epic, and it does so by incorporating many of the elements used by translators such as Sylvester in making epic 'English'. Moreover, through its use of archaism, 'On the Famous Voyage' actively dismantles English epic style, suggesting that the techniques that authors and translators typically employ have become exhausted. This strategy becomes clearer still if we put Jonson's poem in dialogue with a later burlesque epic: Charles Cotton's *Scarronides* (1664–5), a parodic adaptation of Books 1 and 4 of *The Aeneid* inspired by the recent work of the French poet Paul Scarron. In the work of Jonson and Cotton, archaism's epic grandeur is parodied and undermined. However, the target of satire is not epic itself, but the means through which it had been rendered – and, it is implied, reduced – through translation and imitation. These poems ultimately suggest, precisely through their use of archaism, that English poetry needs a new way of writing epic.

Jonson and Cotton strategically incorporate archaism into the crucial opening phases of their narratives. Both poems parody the opening words of Virgil's *Aeneid*, 'Arma virumque cano' ('Arms and the man I sing'). The opening of the main part of 'On the Famous Voyage' begins: 'I sing the brave adventure of two wights, / And pity 'tis I cannot call them knights' (ll. 21–2), balancing the echo of Virgil and the archaic 'wights' against a line in which the notorious Jacobean sales of knighthoods are brought forcibly to mind. The first part of *Scarronides*, similarly, opens with 'I *Sing the man*, (read it who list, / A *Trojan*, true, as ever pist)', and its main narrative begins with these lines:

> A little Town there was of Old,
> Thatcht with good Straw to keep out Cold;
> Hight *Carthage*, which (if not bely'd)
> Was by the *Tyrians* occupy'd;
> The lustiest Carles all thereabouts,
> Rich Chuffs, and very sturdy Louts.[56]

Cotton here translates and burlesques Virgil's 'Urbs antiqua fuit (Tyrii tenuere coloni) / Karthago, Italiam contra Tiberinaque longe / ostia, dives opum studiisque asperrima belli' [There was an ancient city, the home of Tyrian settlers, Carthage, over against Italy and the Tiber's mouths afar, rich in wealth and stern in war's pursuits] (*Aeneid*, 1.12–14). As we have seen, one danger of using archaism in heroic tales is that this style can signal both epic grandeur and pastoral homeliness. Here, Cotton reverses the usual effect of archaism in epic: instead of asserting Carthage's grandeur, archaic diction makes it seem homely and familiar, as the 'rich' and 'stern' Carthaginians are reduced to lower-status 'carles', 'chuffs' and 'louts'.

Jonson and Cotton's criticism of the clichéd strategies of the English epic is also signalled in the way in which each poem juxtaposes archaism with neologism and contemporary reference, suggesting that outmoded style is not authentically ancient but trashily modern. In 'On the Famous Voyage', 'the powerful moon / Makes the poor Bankside creature wet it' shoon' (ll. 29–30), while the 'ugly monster / Yclepèd Mud' discharges its 'merd-urinous load' (ll. 61–2, 65); Sheldon and Heydon ask their rowers 'How hight the place?' (l. 89), and Mercury's pretensions to grandeur are debased by his use 'in pills, and eke in potions' (l. 101). Jonson's self-consciousness about the style that he adopts, and its relationship with epic narrative conventions, is signalled in his comment,

> methinks, 'tis odd
> That all this while I have forgot some god
> Or goddess to invoke, to stuff my verse;
> And with both bombard style and phrase rehearse
> The many perils of this port, and how
> Sans help of Sybil or a golden bough,
> Or magic sacrifice they passed along!   (ll. 43–9)

The affectedly archaic 'sans', with its Spenserian associations, suggests the productive gap between epic style and quotidian subject matter, while the poem's professed rejection of 'bombard style' is comically misplaced in the midst of its own periodic recourse to inflated diction.

Cotton's burlesque of *The Aeneid* critiques epic style and its English modes of expression yet more closely. We might look, for example, to the parodic epic simile in which Neptune is compared with a water-spaniel:

> Have you not seen upon a River
> A Water-dog, that is a diver,
> Bring out his Mallard, and eft-soons
> Be-shake his shaggy Pantaloons?
> So *Neptune* when he first appears,
> Shakes the salt Liquor from his ears,
> And made the winds themselves to doubt him,
> He threw the water so about him: (24)

Where Virgil briefly narrates the appearance of Neptune, Cotton uses Virgil's own technique – the epic simile – to render the god's appearance absurd, and the high style invoked by archaisms such as 'eft-soons' and 'Be-shake' is undercut by the incongruous image of the god shaking the water from his ears in the style of a wet dog.

The effect of these modifications is epitomised towards the end of Book 1, in the moment at which Dido asks Aeneas to tell the story of the fall of Troy:

> tears ran down, her fair long Nose,
> The Queen was *Maudlin* I suppose.
> (Quoth shee) *Æneas* out of Jesting,
> Thou needs must tell at my Requesting,
> All the whole Tale of *Troyes* Condition,
> Since first you troubled were with *Grecian;*
> *Hectors* great Fights, and *Priams* Speeches,

And eke describe *Achilles* Breeches,
How strong he was, when he did grapple,
And if *Tydides* horse were dapple.   (111–12)

While Virgil initially describes Dido's enquiries in the third person (1.749–52), Cotton places the whole passage in direct speech, moving lines around and giving his Dido a comically scattershot set of enquiries. The conjunction of the grandly archaic 'eke' with the quotidian 'breeches' underlines the bathos of Cotton's juxtaposition of great fights, grand oratory and forms of clothing, and it helps to maintain the comic tone also established through the polysyllabic rhyme words. Like Jonson, Cotton thus uses archaism as part of a nuanced critique of the ways in which epic has been made 'English'.

For A. C. Swinburne, writing in 1889, Jonson's scatology in 'On the Famous Voyage' was a matter almost of national scandal: 'coprology should be left to Frenchmen,' he complains. 'It is nothing less than lamentable that so great an English writer as Ben Jonson should ever have taken the plunge of a Parisian diver into the cesspool.'[57] However, comparison with the work of Cotton – another English writer prepared to take such a dive – suggests the techniques through which Jonson's mock-epic intervenes in an ongoing debate about epic style. Both writers attack the ways in which epic has been rendered and reduced by neo-Spenserian translators, implicitly arguing for a new epic aesthetic. However, in the event a new aesthetic was to be based not on an entirely new foundation, but on the willingness of another writer of the 1660s – Milton – to revisit the very materials that Jonson and Cotton reject. Parody is better at criticising existing traditions than establishing new ones; Milton's achievement is that his poem both critiques and reconstructs, setting out a new-old path for the English epic.

Grisly terror and blank verse: Milton

Conversing with Drummond in 1619, Jonson had scarcely a good word to say about the epic pretensions of his fellow poets. Spenser's stanzas annoyed him, Sylvester's translation of du Bartas was 'not well done … Nor that of Fairfax his', translations of Homer and Virgil in 'long alexandrines' were 'but prose' and Harington's Ariosto 'under all translations was the worst' (*Informations*, ll. 20–5). While it is tempting to see these judgements as merely spiteful, they also speak to Jonson's fidgety dissatisfaction with the prevailing aesthetic of the English epic. It is not, therefore, surprising to find that he treats epic archaism in 'On the Famous Voyage' with a mixture of affection and distaste. Nor should it surprise us to find that English epic writers became increasingly ill at ease with archaism as the seventeenth century progressed. While translations continued to employ some outmoded words, original epics such as William Davenant's *Gondibert* (1651) and Abraham Cowley's *Davideis* (1656) both largely eschewed archaism. By the 1660s, its use was becoming restricted to burlesques such as Cotton's *Scarronides* or Samuel Butler's wildly popular satire *Hudibras* (1663–78). However, the most important epic of the Commonwealth and Restoration, Milton's *Paradise Lost*, contains what are perhaps the most significant uses of archaism in an epic context since *The Faerie Queene*. Moreover, as Ann Baines Coiro points out, 'Milton's formal choices . . . are as political as they are artistic.'[58]

With the notable exception of scholars such as Hilda Hume and Sylvia Adamson, criticism has not always dealt well with Milton's use of archaism in *Paradise Lost*.[59] B. A. Wright, for instance, states that 'there are comparatively few obsolete words in Milton, no more than in any other writer whose vocabulary has been kept alive by his being continually read', while Thomas N. Corns argues that '*Paradise Lost* contains very few words which can with certainty be identified as archaisms: the Spenserian impulse has evidently run its course, and another cultural imperative obtains'.[60] To some extent, a long-standing and only recently dispelled assumption that Milton's verse is in some way 'un-English' has blinded scholarship to the ways in which it reworks aspects of the language's own past.[61] The poet has often been viewed as taking an 'anti-antiquarian' stance, to borrow David Weil Baker's phrase; as we saw in Chapter 1, he declined in *The History of Britain* 'to wrincle the smoothness of History with rugged names of places unknown'.[62] His work may therefore seem an unlikely place to find a sustained engagement with literary archaism.

Yet early commentators on *Paradise Lost* were insistent about the extent and impact of the poem's archaism. As we saw at the start of this chapter, Sir John Hobart thought that both the ten-book epic and its author were in some respects 'obsolete', and commentators continued to be unsettled by Milton's temporally dissonant language long after the publication of the twelve-book version. In *Sylvae* (1685), John Dryden asks '*cannot I admire the height of his Invention, and the strength of his expression, without defending his antiquated words, and the perpetual harshness of their sound?*'[63] For Dryden, Milton's 'antiquated words' are a symptom of his overexposure to older English writers such as Spenser and Chaucer; he 'imitated *Spencer*, as *Spencer* did *Chawcer*', clothing his 'lofty thoughts' with 'admirable *Grecisms*, and ancient words, which he had been digging from the Mines of *Chaucer*, and of *Spencer*, and which, with all their rusticity, had somewhat of Venerable in them'.[64] Emphasising Milton's desire to emulate Spenser, Dryden here crystallises the close association between archaism and imitation, framing the poet's selection of archaic words as a 'choice' that begins to look more like a compulsion.

Other writers, in contrast, were more prepared to overlook Milton's supposed fault, and to associate it with the genre in which he wrote. In the preface to his own epic poem, *The Life of Our Blessed Lord & Saviour, Jesus Christ* (1693), Samuel Wesley argues that Milton 'seems rather above the common Rules of *Epic* than ignorant of them', and comments, 'For his antique Words I'm not like to blame him whoever does'.[65] Similarly, Charles Gildon writes in a letter to 'Mr. T.S.':

> Those *Antient*, and consequently *less Intelligible* Words, Phrases, and Similies, by which he frequently, and *purposedly* affects to express his Meaning, in my Opinion do well suit with the *Venerable Antiquity*, and *Sublime Grandeur* of his Subject. And how much soever some *Unthinking* have Condemn'd this his Choice. *You*, who have Maturely weigh'd, how much deeper an Impression *less us'd*, (so they be what you will grant his always are) *Significant words*, make on a *Readers* fancy, than such as are *more common*; (you I say) must pay a vast deference to Mr. *Milton*'s great *Judiciousness* in this particular, no less than to his *entire Manage* of every part of that *Charming Poem*, in which upon every Occasion he discovers himself a perfect, unimitable *Master of Language*.[66]

Echoing Jonson and Quintilian, Gildon finds 'antiquity' and 'sublime grandeur' in the use of archaism, and he views it as part of Milton's 'perfect' command of the linguistic tools at his disposal even though he worries that easy comprehensibility may be lost. In view of this anxiety, it is perhaps unsurprising that Patrick Hume's *Annotations on Milton's Paradise Lost* (1695), a pioneering critical commentary on the poem, glosses and provides etymologies for a number of the 'old words' in it.

As Wesley and Gildon argue, Milton's use of archaism should indeed be attributed to his composition of epic, and his debt to the English epic tradition in particular. As in *A Masque Presented at Ludlow Castle*, Milton's use of archaism appears to have been part of his original conception of *Paradise Lost*: archaic words remain stable across the ten-book and twelve-book versions of the poem, and they enable him to play with the traditions that he inherited from earlier writers and translators. A number of his archaic words appear in *The Faerie Queene*, such as 'bane' (1.692, 2.808, 4.167, 9.123, 10.412), 'buxom' (2.842, 5.270), 'doleful'/'dole' (1.65, 4.894), 'emprise' (11.642), 'griding' (6.329), 'grisly' (1.670, 2.704, 4.821), 'emboss'

(12.180), 'lore' (2.815, 9.1128), 'nathless' (1.299), 'reck' (as a verb: 2.50, 9.173), 'scath' (1.613), 'tine' (10.1076), 'uncouth' (2.408, 2.827, 5.98, 6.362, 8.230, 10.475), 'unweeting' (10.335, 10.916), 'welkin' (2.538), 'weed' (3.479), 'ween' (4.741, 6.86) and 'wight' (1.613). The word 'frore' (2.595) may allude to Spenser's 'frory' (*Faerie Queene*, 3.8.35.2), although Milton could also have come across it elsewhere.[67] Although the Spenserian links are strong, a number of these words – notably 'bane', 'dole'/'doleful', 'grisly', 'hail', 'uncouth', 'weed', 'ween' and 'wight' – are prominent in sixteenth- and seventeenth-century translations of classical epic such as the *Aeneid*s of Phaer/Twyne, Stanihurst, John Vicars, Richard Fanshawe and John Ogilby, and the Homeric translations of Hall, Chapman and Ogilby. Spenserian words are also juxtaposed with some additional archaisms, including 'cresset' (1.728), 'gloze' (3.93, 9.549), 'sheer' (1.742), 'tedded' (9.450) and 'tilth' (11.430), some of which also occur in translations of classical and modern epic.[68]

As this begins to suggest, Milton's archaism in *Paradise Lost* is not merely an unthinking imitation of Spenser, as Dryden thought, but a more sustained critique of the place of outmoded style in English epic tradition. These are '*Significant words*', as Gildon understood, and Milton uses them carefully. With a few notable exceptions – such as the consistent association of the word 'behest' with God, the narrator's comment on the subject of love-making in Eden, 'nor turned, I ween, / Adam from his fair spouse, nor Eve the rites / Mysterious of connubial love refused' (4.741–3), and the various, interlinked, uses of the word 'hail', to which I will return – Milton consistently associates outmoded words with Satan, Hell and the fallen angels, and, later, with the effects of the Fall itself. He thus uses archaism as part of his critical appropriation of classical epic, linking it with a more general critique of Homeric and Virgilian heroism, a feature of the poem that has been remarked upon by many readers.[69]

Books 1 and 2 are much the thickest in their use of archaic words, which cluster around descriptions of Satan and Hell. This is part of the strategy noted by Patrick J. Cook, in which 'much of epic's traditional material ends up in hell'.[70] The narrator relates early in Book 1 that the 'darkness visible' of Hell serves 'only to discover sights of woe, / Regions of sorrow, doleful shades' (1.63, 64–5). Beelzebub describes how the fallen angels are 'astounded and amazed' (1.281) – Hume notes that 'astounded' is 'an old word for astonish'd, confounded'[71] – and their ravaged beauty is compared to the withering effect 'when heaven's fire / Hath scathed the forest oaks or mountain pines' (1.612–13); Satan 'nathless' endures his voyage over the 'burning marl' (1.299, 296). Archaic words cluster around the account of the building of Pandemonium. The hill on which the construction effort focuses has a 'grisly top' (1.670), and when the digging reveals a seam of gold readers are instructed by the narrator 'Let none admire / That riches grow in hell; that soil may best / Deserve the precious bane' (1.690–2). Hume glosses bane by noting that '*Bana*' is 'an old word for Murderer' (*Annotations*, 44), while Elisha Coles in his 1677 dictionary defines 'bane' as a Saxon word meaning 'poyson, destruction'.[72] Through his use of archaism Milton carefully positions Satan and his followers as an ancient and deadly force, and he simultaneously suggests that even English versions of classical epic should be treated with caution and suspicion.

Milton continues to use archaic words in describing the finished palace, lit by 'many a row / Of starry lamps and blazing cressets' (1.727–8). Furthermore, the description of Hell's architect mingles classical allusion and carefully judged archaism:

> Nor was his name unheard or unadorned
> In ancient Greece; and in Ausonian land
> Men called him Mulciber; and how he fell
> From heaven they fabled, thrown by angry Jove
> Sheer o'er the crystal battlements: from morn
> To noon he fell, from noon to dewy eve,
> A summer's day, and with the setting sun
> Dropped from the zenith, like a falling star,
> On Lemnos, the Aegean isle: thus they relate,
> Erring; for he with his rebellious rout
> Fell long before[.]   (1.738–48)

As scholars have noted, Milton draws closely on Homer's description of Zeus throwing Hephaestus (Vulcan or Mulciber in Latin) from heaven (*Iliad*, 1.589–94).[73] In Chapman's English translation this reads:

> tis a taske, too dangerous to take part
> Against *Olympius*. I my selfe, the proofe of this still feele;
> When other Gods would faine haue helpt, he tooke me by the heele
> And hurld me out of heauen: all day, I was in falling downe,
> At length in Lemnos I strooke earth; the likewise falling Sunne,
> And I, together set: my life, almost set too; yet there
> The *Sintij* cheard, and tooke me vp.[74]

Milton draws on classical narrative, but he explicitly undermines it in his comment that writers such as Homer 'err' in their accounts; he thus stakes his claim to a deeper truth. His use of the archaic word 'sheer' intensifies this effect. Hume's note on line 742, 'Quite over the bright Battlements of Heaven: *Sheer*, an old Word signifying Pure, Bright, Clear' (*Annotations*, 48), draws attention to the way in which Milton puns on two meanings of the word: the adverbial meaning of 'completely' or 'absolutely', often used, as *OED* notes, with verbs 'expressing removal, separation, cleavage, etc.' (sheer, *adv.* 1.a); and the archaic adjectival meaning of 'bright' or 'shining' (*OED* sheer, *adj.* 4). In tipping 'sheer' from heaven, the fallen angels have lost their 'sheer' beauty, and with it their claim to divinity. Furthermore, in conjunction with the neologism 'Pandemonium' (1.756) itself constructed from old words, the cluster of archaisms and the critical revision of Homer's description of Hephaestus suggest the fallen angels' usurpation of epic grandeur, their perversion of old models of heroism.[75] Milton thus makes extensive use of the stylistic resources of English epic, but he simultaneously maintains a sceptical distance from it.

Later books reinforce the impression that archaism is to be associated primarily with Satan and his followers. God laments Satan's 'glozing lies' (3.93), while in the description of the war in Heaven the rebellious angels 'weened . . . by fight or by surprise / To win the Mount of God' (6.86–8); Michael's 'griding sword' wounds Satan (6.329) while Moloch's pain is 'uncouth' (6.362). The uses of archaism in Book 9 are especially deft. In the build-up to his assault on Eve, Satan declares that 'all good to me becomes / Bane' (9.122–3), Milton capitalising on his earlier association of the fallen angels with the 'precious bane' of Hell's buried gold, and the irreligious force of revenge is emphasised when Satan claims that he 'reck[s] not' if his vengeance rebounds on him, 'so it light well aimed' (9.173). In addition, archaism signals the ways in which Satan's perspective is filtered through the third-person narration when the narrator refers to 'The smell of grain, or tedded grass, or kine' (9.450) in describing how the serpent spies on Eve. Further archaisms cluster around the Fall itself. God's strictures are recalled in the narrator's intervention after Satan's first appeal to Eve, 'So glozed the tempter' (9.549). Furthermore, Eve's consumption of the apple is book-ended by the only two occurrences of the then-archaic word 'blithe': 'the wily adder' is 'blithe and glad' (9.625) when he persuades Eve to approach the tree, while the fallen Eve has 'countenance blithe' as she in turn tempts Adam (9.886); again – as we also saw in *The Faerie Queene* – an archaic word picks up additional force from its repeated use. After Adam decides to eat, his and Eve's mental disorder is evoked with another archaism: 'For understanding ruled not, and the will / Heard not her lore' (9.1127–8). In all of these ways, Milton suggests that the established techniques of the English epic are a seductive snare, and classical epic itself a poisonous trap.

However, Milton does not only deconstruct the English epic through his use of archaism; he also uses the same technique to suggest the ways in

which the epic might be refashioned for Christian purposes. Crucial here is
the word 'hail', glossed by Hume as 'the old word used in Salutations,
answering to the χαιρε of the Greeks, and the Roman *Salve*, of the Sax.
Hael, Health' (*Annotations*, 96), which appears ten times in the poem.
Initially, it is associated with Satan, who greets his fate with the words 'hail,
horrors, hail, / Infernal world' (1.250–1), in an apparent echo of Aeneas'
exclamation on arriving in Latium, 'salve fatis mihi debita tellus vosque'
(*Aeneid*, 7.120–1), translated by John Vicars in 1632 as 'Faire fate-given
land, all hail'.[76] However, the word 'hail' is not restricted in *Paradise Lost*
to Satan and his followers. Book 3 opens with the words 'Hail, holy light'
(3.1), while the Son is also addressed with 'hail' (3.412); the narrator cries
'Hail, wedded love' in Book 4 (750), and Adam and Eve use the phrase
'Hail universal lord' in their prayer in Book 5 (205). Unlike most of the
archaic words in *Paradise Lost*, 'hail' clearly has multiple associations.

The reasons for the ambiguity of 'hail' become clear when Raphael
greets Eve in Book 5:

> On whom the Angel 'Hail'
> Bestowed – the holy salutation used
> Long after to blest Mary, second Eve:
> 'Hail mother of mankind, whose fruitful womb
> Shall fill the world more numerous with thy sons
> Than with these various fruits the trees of God
> Have heaped this table.'   (5.385–91)

Milton here alludes to Luke 1:28, in the style adopted by successive
generations of translators: 'And the angel came in vnto her, and said, Haile
thou that art highly fauoured, the Lord is with thee: Blessed art thou
among women.'[77] Archaism is thus to be associated not only with the
English epic tradition, but also with the traditions of the Protestant
Bible: it is a tool for both damnation and salvation. Milton reinforces
this impression later in the poem when Michael and Adam salute
Eve and Mary with the word 'hail' (11.158–61, 12.379–85). The action of
the poem thus recuperates the word 'hail' from Satan and, it is implied,
from pagan texts such as *The Aeneid*, enacting in miniature the way in
which Milton directs the epic away from its classical models and towards
its new Christian orientation. By the end of *Paradise Lost*, linguistic
archaism is more closely aligned with Protestant liturgical diction than
the English epic.

Milton's manipulation of archaic diction runs in tandem with his self-
conscious use of another form of archaism: that of verse form. Here
archaism has a directly political impact, as Milton rejects the prevailing

aesthetics of the Restoration regime along with its style of rule. Other important inventions in epic form in the years of the Commonwealth and Restoration, such as Davenant's *Gondibert* and Cowley's *Davideis*, use rhyme; so does Lucy Hutchinson's *Order and Disorder*, apparently written between the late 1650s and the late 1670s, despite its author's unease about what she terms 'elevations of style' and 'charms of language'.[78] Milton's defensiveness about his choice of blank verse is clear in the prefatory comments added to *Paradise Lost* in later issues of the first edition:

> The measure is English heroic verse without rhyme, as that of Homer in Greek, and of Virgil in Latin – rhyme being no necessary adjunct or true ornament of poem or good verse, in longer works especially, but the invention of a barbarous age, to set off wretched matter and lame metre; graced indeed since by some famous modern poets, carried away by custom, but much to their own vexation, hindrance, and constraint to express many things otherwise, and for the most part worse, than else they would have expressed them.[79]

Milton draws comparisons between his use of blank verse and that of Italian and Spanish poets and 'our best English tragedies', rejecting rhyme as a 'trivial' and 'jingling' distraction. He concludes that the 'neglect ... of rhyme so little is to be taken for a defect, though it may seem so perhaps to vulgar readers, that it rather is to be esteemed an example set, the first in English, of ancient liberty recovered to heroic poem from the troublesome and modern bondage of rhyming'. Milton self-consciously positions his use of blank verse as a form of innovative archaism, a renewal of English poetry through a return to ancient convention, and he makes clear his departure from contemporary standards. Here, archaism is a form of classicism, and one that relates directly to Milton's classicised idea of republican virtue. As Barbara K. Lewalski notes, Milton elevates his blank verse 'above the practices of the barbarous gothic age and the vulgar taste of the present', associating it with both ancient poetic liberty and the challenge to Stuart tyranny. Milton, she argues, 'makes his choice of blank verse the aesthetic complement to republican politics and culture'.[80] Thus, archaism in *Paradise Lost* represents both negative and positive aspects of classical heritage, and both archaic diction and outmoded verse forms can be recuperated for the Christian, republican cause.

Milton may have been disappointed or wryly amused by the response to his use of blank verse: far from setting an example to his contemporaries and immediate successors it became a point of dispute.[81] Shortly after *Paradise Lost* was published, Dryden argued that blank verse was not sufficiently elevated for poetry, even though it might be suited to drama.[82]

Translators debated the validity of rhyme as a vehicle for classical epic. In 1683, for instance, the preface to a translation of Anacreon bewailed the prevailing fashion, writing that it *could allmost wish* blank Verse *were much in vogue, knowing very well it would give the Fancy fairer play, being not imprisoned within the* narrow limits *of Rhyme*.[83] Similarly, Thomas Fletcher observed in 1692 on the subject of translating Virgil's *Aeneid*,

> Methinks blank Verse carries in it somewhat of the Majesty of *Virgil*; when Rhimes, even the most happy of them (after tedious pumping for them, and having good Expressions balk'd for want of them) do but emasculate Heroick Verse, and give it an unnatural Softness. In Songs, Pastorals, and the softer sorts of Poetry, Rhimes may perhaps be not unelegantly retain'd; but an Heroe drest up in them looks like *Hercules* with a Distaff.[84]

Fletcher chafes within the prevailing aesthetic, uneasy with the effects rhyme has on epic style – in particular what he thinks of as its effeminising qualities – but unable finally to bring himself to challenge its cultural dominance. Translators may have been uneasy with the effects of rhyme, but they were not sufficiently convinced by the alternative.

Others, however, clung to rhyme for more positive reasons. Dryden maintained his stance boldly, commenting in 1693, 'whatever Causes [Milton] alledges for the abolishing of Rhyme ... his own particular Reason is plainly this, that Rhyme was not his Talent; he had neither the Ease of doing it, nor the Graces of it'.[85] For Dryden, the only explanation for Milton's reluctance to use rhyme is his lack of aptitude for it. Six years later, in 1699, John Hopkins published the earliest of a string of versions of *Paradise Lost* in rhyme. Echoing Fletcher but reversing the terms of his argument, he alleges that Milton's work *'like the Tree of Knowledge is Forbidden to the Ladies, to those I mean, who would Tast the Apples, but care not for Climbing to the Bough, and I have heard some say* Mr. Milton *in Rhyme would be a Fine thing'*.[86] For such writers, Milton's use of blank verse was part of his archaic roughness, his refusal to 'allure' his readers with 'tinkling rhyme', as Andrew Marvell put it in a (rhyming) poem first published with the twelve-book version of *Paradise Lost* in 1674, himself – as he admits within the poem – 'transported by the mode' (ll. 46, 51).[87]

Milton appears to have absorbed from Spenser, Jonson and Fairfax a lesson about the aesthetic capital that can be made from playing with the precise effects of a single word or a cluster of words, and from Chapman and Shakespeare the impact that neglected verse forms could have. Reshaping his inherited material, he gives archaism two interrelated functions in *Paradise Lost*. First, in the shape of archaic diction, archaism allows Milton to critique and, finally, to recuperate the ossified conventions of English epic writing. Second, in the shape of an unfashionable verse style, it enables him to underscore his rejection of current literary trends and, implicitly, the political regime in which they have proliferated. Archaism thus provides him with the means to mount a politicised attack on the rhyming, royalist epic of writers such as Davenant and Cowley, underlining his status as 'criminal and obsolete', in both aesthetic and political terms.

Conclusion

All of the writers examined in this chapter draw on the strong relationship that traditionally existed between epic poetry and outmoded style. They do so in ways that are both imitative and innovative, using long-standing techniques to establish the generic credentials of their work but simultaneously revising, critiquing and, in many cases, reinvigorating those techniques. Spenser in *The Faerie Queene* is able to use individual words such as 'dight' both to establish and to deconstruct the connections between his poem and prior tradition; archaic diction is part of a network of different forms of indebtedness, the combination of which finally allows him to match and outdo the 'antique Poets historicall' – Homer, Virgil, Ariosto and Tasso – on which he draws.[88] In doing so, he renders the epic 'English', marking his distance from both classical and continental influence; however, this is a very particular – and very Protestant – form of Englishness, as the presentation of Duessa 'fowly dight', with its allusions to anti-Catholic polemic, reminds us. Similar opportunities and problems are faced by Fairfax in *Godfrey of Bulloigne*, as he attempts to render the Italian Catholic Tasso's religious epic in 'English heroicall verse', and they inflect his presentation of figures such as Clorinda through the archaism that – thanks in no small part to Spenser himself – remained at the heart of the English epic tradition.

In contrast, when they write in fourteeners, Chapman and Shakespeare negotiate with a form that had recently fallen out of fashion, attempting either to restate its credentials or to capitalise on the very precariousness of its epic status. Drawing on the archaic aesthetic and the affective qualities of the fourteener in Chapman and Phaer's translations, Shakespeare manipulates the associations between the fourteener and English epic style, using it to underline the fragility of national identity within his play. The precariousness of epic convention is also suggested in Jonson's 'On the Famous Voyage' and Cotton's *Scarronides*. However, in contrast with

Chapman and Shakespeare – both of whom make productive use of archaic style – Jonson and Cotton use archaism to probe the weaknesses of the conventional 'English' epic. In doing so, they suggest that the tricks used by writers and translators of epic – archaism prominent amongst them – have become exhausted clichés, desperately in need of renewal.

Milton's experiments in *Paradise Lost* can thus be seen to be part of a line from Spenser onwards, as succeeding generations of poets play with epic's conventional association with outmoded style. However, he also responds to contemporary anxieties about the place of archaic style in the epic. While the way in which Milton dismantles archaic diction through its association with Satan and the fallen angels echoes Jonson and Cotton's critique of English epic style, his use of words such as 'hail' recuperates linguistic archaism and, together with the use of blank verse, suggests the ways in which epic might be renewed as an aesthetic and political force. If writing epic is a means of writing the nation, as generations of writers and critics have argued, the uses of archaic style in the 'English' epic suggest both the importance of literary and national tradition and the ways in which these traditions might be deconstructed and reconstructed.

Coda: looking backward, looking forward

> A wight he was, whose very sight wou'd
> Entitle him *Mirrour of Knighthood* . . .
>
> Samuel Butler[1]

I end this book where I began it, with a knight setting out on a journey at the start of an epic poem in which archaism is a crucial aspect of literary style. This is not, however, Spenser's *Faerie Queene*, but Samuel Butler's *Hudibras*, the first part of which appeared on bookstalls late in 1662. *Hudibras* carries many of the trappings of epic romance, including its six-line arguments at the head of each canto, its martial protagonist and his attendant, Ralpho, and its archaic diction. However, in contrast with Spenser's remarkably straight-faced treatment of knightly endeavour, Butler remorselessly burlesques Hudibras's exploits:

> A wight he was, whose very sight wou'd
> Entitle him *Mirrour of Knighthood*;
> That never bent his stubborn knee
> To any thing but Chivalry,
> Nor put up blow, but that which laid
> Right Worshipfull on shoulder-blade:
> Chief of Domestick Knights and Errant,
> Either for Chartel or for Warrant:
> Great on the Bench, Great in the Saddle,
> That could as well bind o're, as swaddle:
> Mighty he was at both of these,
> And styl'd of *War* as well as *Peace*.
> (So some Rats of amphibious nature,
> Are either for the Land or Water.)
> But here our Authors make a doubt,
> Whether he were more wise, or stout.
> Some hold the one, and some the other:
> But howsoe're they make a pother,

The difference was so small, his Brain
Outweigh'd his Rage but half a grain:
Which made some take him for a tool
That Knaves do work with, call'd a Fool. (1.1.15–36)

Butler's language is multi-temporal, balancing archaisms such as 'wight'
against more recent coinages such as 'pother' and neologisms such as
'amphibious'.² He refers to earlier romances such as the Spanish *Del espejo
de principes y caballeros* (1578–1601), translated into English as *The Mirror of
Knighthood*, but reduces their narratives to the modern activities of a
Justice of the Peace, and creates confusion about precisely what it is that
his sources tell him. Moreover, Butler draws attention to his warped digest
of archaic style in his comments on Hudibras's own mangled style of
speech, lofty in sound and consisting of '*English* cut on *Greek* and *Latin*, /
Like Fustian heretofore on Sattin' (1.1.97–8).

   Butler's calculated use of archaism resembles in some respects Charles
Cotton's in *Scarronides*, discussed in Chapter 6, but there is a greater
degree of political force behind his use of outmoded style. The first book
of *Hudibras* was composed, its title-page claims, '*in the Time of the Late
Wars*', and this context is highlighted in the opening lines of Canto 1,
which situate the narrative at a time 'WHEN *civil* Fury first grew high, /
And men fell out they knew not why', when they fought 'like
mad or drunk, / For Dame *Religion* as for Punk' (1.1.1–2, 5–6).³ Much
of *Hudibras*'s satire is directed at the religious radicals of the Civil War
and Commonwealth, and Butler's systematic refusal to take epic and its
aesthetic shapes seriously is intertwined with his similar refusal to give
any credence to the Parliamentarian cause. Old words are mocked as
part of a broader attack on the Good Old Cause; as Richard Terry has
argued, 'the heroic vein enters the poem already pre-discounted'.⁴
Although the first part of *Hudibras* was published half a decade before
Paradise Lost, the mock-epic feels like a pre-emptive response to Milton's
poem. Where Milton attempts to mould a new epic aesthetic that
proclaims the 'ancient' liberties of writer and country, Butler conversely
seeks to push the exhausted tradition beyond its reasonable limits.
Both texts are, as Alvin Snider suggests, Janus-faced;⁵ they look back at
a long tradition and forward to a literary future that each configures in
different ways.

   Scholars have suggested that *Hudibras* and *Paradise Lost* between them
destroyed the epic as a serious force in English literature.⁶ These works
may also have deterred later writers from exploring archaism's varied

potential as a form of literary expression. Between 1590 and the early 1660s, archaism appeared in a multitude of forms, enabling writers to experiment with a range of aesthetic and thematic effects, and to explore the productively confused temporality produced by the imitation of outmoded style. As we have seen, the publication of *The Faerie Queene* in 1590, and archaism's shift from pastoral to epic, was followed by a series of rapid changes in literary fashion and taste, meaning that archaism was re-established as a major literary technique at precisely the time at which a new set of modes and styles became archaic. Poetic forms such as the fourteener and common measure, theatrical forms such as the morality play and the 1560s Senecan translation, and the increasingly ossified style adopted in liturgical prose all presented themselves to writers as models for imitation, revision and parody. Simultaneously, developments in Anglo-Saxon scholarship made the Old English language available to literary writers, leading to its use in quotation and, in time, original writing; changing attitudes towards medieval literary style made the cultural position of writers such as Chaucer and Gower productively unstable. The result was a proliferation of archaic styles and modes, as successive generations of writers capitalised on the aesthetic and cultural opportunities that archaism offered them.

By the early 1670s, in contrast, it seems that the only way to play with archaism in the mainstream of literary culture was simply that: to play with it. Pleasure and playful irony had always been a large part of archaism's appeal, but in the late seventeenth century its other qualities were gradually forgotten. Moreover, while some of the experiments of the early and mid-seventeenth century – such as the composition of poems in Old English[7] or in common measure – persisted into the early years of the eighteenth century, many others were lost or rejected. In contrast with the engagements with Chaucerian or Gowerian style of Spenser, Cartwright or Shakespeare and Wilkins, writers such as Dryden or Davenant preferred to rehabilitate their medieval predecessors by translating them into modern English, and to update the work of Elizabethan writers rather than capitalising on the aspects of their style that had become outmoded.[8]

The late seventeenth century even saw an attempt to update *The Faerie Queene* in Edward Howard's *Spenser Redevivus* (1687), in which Spenser's 'Essential Design' was preserved, 'but his obsolete Language and manner of Verse totally laid aside', and his stanzas exchanged for heroic couplets.[9] The opening of Howard's version of Book 1, Canto 1, reads:

The Patron of true Piety
Foul Error doth Defeat,
But Snares of vile Hipocrisy
His Virtue next do Cheat.

A Worthy Knight was Riding on the Plain,
In Armour Clad, which richly did Contain
The Gallant Marks of many Battels fought,
Tho' he before no Martial Habit sought;
How Warlike ere his Person seem'd to Sit
On a Bold Steed, that scarce obey'd the Bit[.] (1)

The only remnants of Spenserian archaism that linger in *The Fairie Queene* can be found in the arguments, which retain the common measure of the original, and words such as 'swain', which had become part of accepted poetic convention, archaic in everyday usage but current in verse. Howard's conviction that the style of *The Faerie Queene* *'seems no less unintelligible at this Day, than the obsoletest of our* English *or* Saxon *Dialect'* (A3r) may seem overstated, but it was apparently sincere. For such Restoration readers, Spenser's temporally dissonant language was not part of his poetic achievement but a distraction from it. Indeed, Howard professes himself unable to comprehend Spenser's motivation in his choice of language *'that he could not but know, was of too antiquate a Date, if not generally exploded by all Writers in the time he liv'd'*, unless he was determined to imitate Chaucer or *'affected it out of design to restore our* Saxon English' (A7v). Wilful archaism, by this time, could only be either the product of unmerited respect for one's predecessors or mere affectation. Not only was the archaic aesthetic of the earlier age to be rejected, it was to be written out of the texts entirely.

In addition to the exhaustion of some of its main generic vehicles, two interrelated factors seem to lie behind the Restoration's unease with archaism as a literary strategy. The first is a prevailing taste for neo-classical decorum in language, evident in Howard's claim elsewhere that imitating 'the expressions of obsolete Authors ... renders even Wit barbarous, and looks like some affront to the present Age'.[10] The second relates to the link that writers such as William Camden and Kenelm Digby drew between linguistic and national stability, an association that appears to have intensified in the turbulent decades of the mid-seventeenth century. Writing in 1660, Thomas Tomkins attacked those who sought to mount any challenge to the authority of the restored monarchy, contending,

If the King is the onely Supream Governour of this Realm, and the two
Houses are equal with him in the Government, and we may swear this, and
yet believe that, it is time to change not onely our law, but our language;
and the Houses should make us new Dictionaries that we may know, what
English words signifie.[11]

The 'tension between the decomposing effects of time and the desire for
monumental stability', as Alok Yadav terms it, is particularly evident in
this period, and it seems to have fuelled a general desire for stability of style
in literary works, and hostility towards linguistic extravagance or
experimentation.[12]

Many Restoration writers seem to have viewed literary history as a
linear narrative of progress. We recall from the introduction to this book
Dryden's remark 'We must be Children before we grow Men', and his line
of literary descent: 'after *Chaucer* there was a *Spencer*, a *Harrington*, a
Fairfax, before *Waller* and *Denham* were in being'.[13] Archaism, which
resists such teleologies, was largely inimical to late seventeenth-century
tastes, the subject of mockery rather than a source of inspiration. However,
later decades and centuries have shown that writers do not merely build,
step by step, on the works of their immediate predecessors, but cut back
and forth between distant past, immediate past and a host of intermediate
pasts, drawing on established classics and rediscoveries alike. Gathering
and recasting his 'fragments' of earlier works, T. S. Eliot writes at the end
of his modernist, archaist masterpiece *The Waste Land*:

> These fragments I have shored against my ruins
> Why then Ile fit you. Hieronymo's mad againe.
> Datta. Dayadhvam. Damyata.
> Shantih shantih shantih[14]

Literary archaism recurs whenever writers are attentive to the precise detail
of the voices of the past and are determined to build on their aesthetic and
cultural potential. In their works, Hieronymo's mad againe. And againe.

Notes

Introduction: conceptualising archaism

1 I borrow this term from Geoffrey B. Waywell, 'The Sculptors of the Mausoleum at Halicarnassus', in Ian Jenkins and Geoffrey B. Waywell (eds.), *Sculptors and Sculpture of Caria and the Dodecanese* (London: British Museum Press, 1997), 58–67 (66), quoted in Erich S. Groen, *Cultural Borrowings and Ethnic Appropriation in Antiquity* (Stuttgart: Franz Steiner Verlag, 2005), 159. *OED* refers to the 'retention or imitation of what is old or obsolete' (archaism, *n.* 1).

2 On the problems that Spenser's language poses, or is assumed to pose, see Andrew Zurcher, *Spenser's Legal Language: Law and Poetry in Early Modern England* (Cambridge: D. S. Brewer, 2007), 7–8.

3 Claire McEachern, *The Poetics of English Nationhood, 1590–1612* (Cambridge University Press, 1996), 3.

4 John Dryden, *Fables Ancient and Modern Translated into Verse from Homer, Ovid, Boccace, & Chaucer, with Original Poems* (London, 1700), *B2v. As I describe in Chapter 2, Chaucer had already been translated – albeit into Latin, not modern English – in the 1630s; this was, however, an early example of a practice that increased as the seventeenth century went on.

5 Carolyn Dinshaw, Lee Edelman, Roderick A. Ferguson, Carla Freccero, Elizabeth Freeman, Judith Halberstam, Annamarie Jagose, Christopher Nealon and Nguyen Tan Hoang, 'Theorizing Queer Temporalities: A Roundtable Discussion', *GLQ: A Journal of Lesbian and Gay Studies* 13 (2007), 177–95 (186–7).

6 On queer temporalities see Carolyn Dinshaw, *Getting Medieval: Sexualities and Communities, Pre- and Post-Modern* (Durham, NC: Duke University Press, 1999); Judith Halberstam, *In a Queer Time and Place: Transgender Bodies, Subcultural Lives* (New York University Press, 2005); Carla Freccero, *Queer/ Early/Modern* (Durham, NC: Duke University Press, 2006); Dinshaw et al., 'Theorizing Queer Temporalities'; Madhavi Menon, *Unhistorical Shakespeare: Queer Theory in Shakespearean Literature and Film* (Basingstoke: Palgrave Macmillan, 2008).

7 See Veré L. Rubel, *Poetic Diction in the English Renaissance* (New York: Modern Language Association, 1941); Noel Osselton, 'Archaism', in *The Spenser*

Encyclopedia, gen. ed. A. C. Hamilton (Toronto University Press, 1990), 52–3; Paula Blank, *Broken English: Dialects and Politics of Language in Renaissance English* (London: Routledge, 1996), 100–4.

8 Thomas Wilson, *The Arte of Rhetorique* (London, 1553), Y2v.

9 Rubel, *Poetic Diction,* 47.

10 Dryden, *Fables,* *C2v.

11 Peggy A. Knapp, *Time-Bound Words: Semantic and Social Economies from Chaucer's England to Shakespeare's* (Basingstoke: Macmillan, 2000), 8. For another example of a 'single words' approach to early modern literature see also Annabel Patterson, *Milton's Words* (Oxford University Press, 2009).

12 Alison Shell, *Oral Culture and Catholicism in Early Modern England* (Cambridge University Press, 2007), 104.

13 Andrew Zurcher, 'Spenser's Studied Archaism: The Case of "Mote"', *Spenser Studies* 21 (2006), 231–40 (238). Other useful linguistic approaches to archaism include Terttu Nevalainen, 'Motivated Archaism: The Use of Affirmative Periphrastic *do* in Early Modern Liturgical Prose', in Dieter Kastovsky (ed.), *Historical English Syntax* (Berlin: Mouton de Gruyter, 1991), 303–20; Kathleen M. Wales, 'Thou and You in Early Modern English: Brown and Gilman Re-Appraised', *Studia Linguistica* 37 (1983), 107–25; Charles Barber, *Early Modern English,* 2nd edn (Edinburgh University Press, 1997), 53, 67–70; Manfred Görlach, *Introduction to Early Modern English* (Cambridge University Press, 1991), 25–7, 139–45; and essays by Görlach, Nevalainen, Matti Rissanen and Sylvia Adamson in Roger Lass (ed.), *The Cambridge History of the English Language: 1476–1776* (Cambridge University Press, 1999).

14 For a range of important recent approaches see Kathleen Biddick, *The Shock of Medievalism* (Durham, NC: Duke University Press, 1998); Dinshaw, *Getting Medieval*; Chris Jones, *Strange Likeness: The Use of Old English in Twentieth-Century Poetry* (Oxford University Press, 2006); Michael Alexander, *Medievalism: The Middle Ages in Modern England* (New Haven, Conn.: Yale University Press, 2007); Deanne Williams, 'Medievalism in English Renaissance Literature', in Kent Cartwright (ed.), *A Companion to Tudor Literature* (Oxford: Wiley Blackwell, 2010), 213–27. Williams' 'Shakespearean Medievalism and the Limits of Periodization in *Cymbeline*', *Literature Compass* 8 (2011), 390–403 offers a useful overview.

15 Valuable recent work on literary style includes Blank, *Broken English*; Russ McDonald, *Shakespeare's Late Style* (Cambridge University Press, 2006); Sylvia Adamson, Gavin Alexander and Katrin Ettenhuber (eds.), *Renaissance Figures of Speech* (Cambridge University Press, 2007); Carla Mazzio, *The Inarticulate Renaissance: Language Trouble in an Age of Eloquence* (Philadelphia: University of Pennsylvania Press, 2009); and two recent essays by Jeff Dolven, 'Reading Wyatt for the Style', *Modern Philology* 105 (2007), 65–86, and 'Tudor Versification and the Rise of Iambic Pentameter', in Cartwright, *Companion to Tudor Literature,* 365–80.

16 Richard Helgerson, *Forms of Nationhood: The Elizabethan Writing of England* (University of Chicago Press, 1992); McEachern, *Poetics*; Mary Floyd-Wilson,

English Ethnicity and Race in Early Modern Drama (Cambridge University Press, 2003); John Kerrigan, *Archipelagic English: Literature, History, and Politics, 1603–1707* (Oxford University Press, 2008). On the development of English national identity see also Liah Greenfeld, *Nationalism: Five Roads to Modernity* (Cambridge, Mass.: Harvard University Press, 1992); Colin Kidd, *British Identities Before Nationalism: Ethnicity and Nationhood in the Atlantic World, 1600–1800* (Cambridge University Press, 1999), esp. 75–122; Krishan Kumar, *The Making of English National Identity* (Cambridge University Press, 2003). Chapters on 'Literature and National Identity' by Claire McEachern, Johann P. Sommerville and Derek Hirst in David Loewenstein and Janel Mueller (eds.), *The Cambridge History of Early Modern Literature* (Cambridge University Press, 2002), 313–42, 459–86, 633–63 provide useful overviews of the Elizabethan, early Stuart and Civil War/Commonwealth periods.

17 For a range of current approaches to historiography and notions of the past see Daniel Woolf, *Reading History in Early Modern England* (Cambridge University Press, 2000); Philip Schwyzer, *Archaeologies of English Renaissance Literature* (Oxford University Press, 2007); Paulina Kewes (ed.), *The Uses of History in Early Modern England* (San Marino, Calif.: Huntington Library Press, 2006); Brian Walsh, *Shakespeare, the Queen's Men, and the Elizabethan Performance of History* (Cambridge University Press, 2009). On early modern understandings of time see Ricardo Quinones, *The Renaissance Discovery of Time* (Cambridge, Mass.: Harvard University Press, 1972); Alison Chapman, 'Making Time: Astrology, Almanacs, and English Protestantism', *Renaissance Quarterly* 60 (2007), 1257–90; Alexandra Walsham, 'Introduction: Relics and Remains', *Past and Present*, Supplement 5 (2010), 9–36; David Houston Wood, *Time, Narrative and Emotion in Early Modern England* (Aldershot: Ashgate, 2009). Important recent work on the interactions between medieval and early modern literary cultures includes James Simpson, *Reform and Cultural Revolution, The Oxford English Literary History*, vol. 2, *1350–1547* (Oxford University Press, 2002); David Wallace, *Premodern Places: Calais to Surinam, Chaucer to Aphra Behn* (Oxford: Blackwell, 2004); Gordon McMullan and David Matthews (eds.), *Reading the Medieval in Early Modern England* (Cambridge University Press, 2007); Brian Cummings and James Simpson (eds.), *Cultural Reformations: Medieval and Renaissance in Literary History* (Oxford University Press, 2010); Williams, 'Shakespearean Medievalism'.

18 Schwyzer, *Archaeologies*, 26.

19 See Menon, *Unhistorical Shakespeare*, esp. 3.

20 Linell B. Wisner, 'Archaism, or Textual Literalism in the Historical Novel', PhD thesis, University of Tennessee, Knoxville, 2010, 26.

21 For a stimulating account of the representation of the past in historical fiction see Alex Davis, *Renaissance Historical Fiction: Sidney, Deloney, Nashe* (Cambridge: Boydell and Brewer, 2011), esp. 15–27.

22 Margaret Rose, 'Extraordinary Pasts: Steampunk as a Mode of Historical Representation', *Journal of the Fantastic in the Arts* 20 (2009), 319–33 (322);

Fredric Jameson, *Postmodernism, or, the Cultural Logic of Late Capitalism* (Durham, NC: Duke University Press, 1991), 20.

23 *OED*'s first citation, and the earliest I have traced, is William Slatyer's *The Psalmes of David in 4 Languages and in 4 Parts Set to ye Tunes of our Church* (London, 1643), A5r. in which he refers to the *'Archaisme, or Circumlocution'* of previous translations. See *OED* archaism, *n.* 1.

24 Nicholas Udall, *Floures for Latine Spekynge Selected and Gathered Oute of Terence* (London, 1534), K7v. For uses of the term 'archaismos' see also Philemon Holland (trans.), *The Roman Historie . . . Written First in Latine by Ammianus Marcellinus* (London, 1609), a4v; John Brinsley, *The Posing of the Parts. Or, A Most Plaine and Easie Way of Examining the Accidence and Grammar* (London, 1615), C3r (the note is not included in the 1612 first edition).

25 *The Art of English Poesy by George Puttenham: A Critical Edition*, ed. Frank Whigham and Wayne A. Rebhorn (Ithaca, NY: Cornell University Press, 2007), 337. See also *OED* caco-zeal, *n.*

26 *The Dictionary of Syr Thomas Eliot Knyght* (London, 1538), 2H6r.

27 The earliest known use of the term appears in Thomas Nashe's *Strange Newes, of the Intercepting Certaine Letters* (London, 1592), A2r, and he may have coined it. See also George Sydenham's dedicatory verse in Thomas Coryate, *The Odcombian Banquet* (London, 1611), I1v.

28 Jonson, *Discoveries*, ed. Lorna Hutson, in *CBJ*, vol. 7, ll. 1379–80; Fuller, *The History of the Worthies of England* (London, 1662), 219.

29 Terence Cave, *The Cornucopian Text: Problems of Writing in the French Renaissance* (Oxford: Clarendon Press, 1979), 35.

30 Thomas M. Greene, *The Light in Troy: Imitation and Discovery in Renaissance Poetry* (New Haven, Conn.: Yale University Press, 1982), 19.

31 Jonson, *Discoveries*, ll. 1274–83. See Donald A. Russell (ed. and trans.), *The Orator's Education*, 5 vols., Loeb Classical Library (Cambridge, Mass.: Harvard University Press), vol. 1, 2.5.19–23. For discussions of the passage in *Discoveries* see Wesley Trimpi, *Ben Jonson's Poems: A Study of the Plain Style* (Stanford University Press, 1962), 3–40; Margaret Tudeau-Clayton, *Jonson, Shakespeare and Early Modern Virgil* (Cambridge University Press, 1998), 40–1, 179–80; Willy Maley, 'Spenser's Languages: Writing in the Ruins of English', in Andrew Hadfield (ed.), *The Cambridge Companion to Spenser* (Cambridge University Press, 2001), 162–79 (163–4); and Hutson's notes in her edition.

32 Sander M. Goldberg, 'Antiquity's Antiquity', in Wim Verbaal, Yanick Maes and Jan Papy (eds.), *Latinitas Perennis*, vol. 1, *The Continuity of Latin Literature* (Leiden: Brill, 2007), 17–29 (18). On literary and cultural archaism in Greek texts see E. L. Bowie, 'Greeks and their Past in the Second Sophistic', in Moses I. Finley (ed.), *Studies in Ancient Society* (London: Routledge and Kegan Paul, 1974), 166–209; Olav Hackstein, 'The Greek of Epic', and Michael Silk, 'The Language of Greek Lyric Poetry' in Egbert J.

Bakker (ed.), *A Companion to the Ancient Greek Language* (Oxford: Blackwell, 2010), 401–23, 424–40.

33 See Goldberg, 'Antiquity's Antiquity', 118–19; John Bryan Hainsworth, *The Idea of Epic* (Berkeley: University of California Press, 1991), 79–80.

34 Russell, *Orator's Education*, 10.1.88. On Ennius and his reputation see also David Scott Wilson-Okamura, *Virgil in the Renaissance* (Cambridge University Press, 2010), 121–4.

35 Russell, *Orator's Education*, 8.3.29–30. See also Suetonius, *De Grammaticis et Rhetoribus*, 10, 15, in J. C. Rolfe (ed. and trans.), *Suetonius*, 2 vols. (London: William Heinemann, 1914), 2: 410–15, 418–21.

36 See also E.K.'s preface to *The Shepheardes Calender*, ll. 34–6, quoted in Chapter 2.

37 Anne Barton, 'Jonson, Ben', in Hamilton, *Spenser Encyclopedia*, 411–12 (412). On Chaucer as Ennius see also Barnabe Googe, *The Zodiake of Life Written by the Godly and Zealous Poet Marcellus Pallingenius Stellatus*, 2nd edn (London, 1565) (‡)3v; Charles Fitzgeoffrey, 'Ad Edmundum Spenserum', in *Caroli Fitzgeofridi affaniae: sive epigrammatum libri tres ejusdem cenotaphia* (Oxford, 1601), D5r; Aston Cokain, 'A Remedy for Love', in *Small Poems of Divers Sorts* (London, 1658), 8.

38 Wilson-Okamura, *Virgil in the Renaissance*, 122 (quoting Cassiodorus, *De institutione divinarum scripturatum*, 1.1.8), 124.

39 William Hawkins, *Apollo Shroving* (London, 1627), E5r.

40 Linda Hutcheon, *A Theory of Parody: The Teachings of Twentieth-Century Art Forms* (London: Methuen, 1985), 6.

41 Margaret Rose, *Parody: Ancient, Modern, and Post-Modern* (Cambridge University Press, 1993), 90. (This is a different Margaret Rose from that cited above.) For further useful recent accounts of parody see also Simon Dentith, *Parody* (London: Routledge, 2000); Richard Dyer, *Pastiche* (London: Routledge, 2007).

42 Samuel Daniel, 'Sonnet L', in *Delia* (London, 1592), H1v.

43 Görlach, *Introduction to Early Modern English*, 25.

44 On anachronism in Shakespeare see, among others, Sigurd Burckhardt, *Shakespearean Meanings* (Princeton University Press, 1968), 4–11; John W. Velz, 'The Ancient World in Shakespeare: Authenticity or Anachronism? A Retrospect', *Shakespeare Survey* 31 (1978), 1–12; Phyllis Rackin, *Stages of History: Shakespeare's English Chronicles* (Ithaca, NY: Cornell University Press, 1990), 86–145; Clifford Ronan, *'Antike Roman': Power Symbology and the Roman Play in Early Modern England, 1585–1635* (Athens: University of Georgia Press, 1995), 11–35. On Dante see Greene, *Light in Troy*, 19, 28–9.

45 Jeremy Tambling, *On Anachronism* (Manchester University Press, 2010), vii; Thomas Blount, *Glossographia: Or A Dictionary* (London 1656), C6r.

46 Thomas Greene, 'History and Anachronism', in Gary Saul Morson (ed.), *Literature and History: Theoretical Problems and Russian Case-Studies* (Stanford

University Press, 1986), 205–20 (208, 209). See also Greene, *Light in Troy*, 28–53.

47 Greene, 'History and Anachronism', 210–11.

48 We might also look to the perceived connection between a sense of anachronism and Elizabethan antiquarianism: see Patrick Collinson, 'One of Us? William Camden and the Making of History', *Transactions of the Royal Historical Society*, 6th series, 8 (1998), 139–63.

49 See, in particular, Peter Burke's four central works in this area: 'The Sense of Historical Perspective in Renaissance Italy', *Journal of World History* 11 (1968), 615–32; *The Renaissance Sense of the Past* (London: Edward Arnold, 1969); 'The Renaissance Sense of the Past Revisited', *Culture and History* 13 (1994), 42–56; and 'The Sense of Anachronism from Petrarch to Poussin', in Chris Humphrey and W. M. Ormrod (eds.), *Time in the Medieval World* (Woodbridge: York Medieval Press/Boydell Press, 2001), 157–74.

50 Margreta de Grazia, 'Anachronism', in Cummings and Simpson, *Cultural Reformations*, 13–32 (26).

51 Tambling, *On Anachronism*, 4.

52 Christopher S. Wood and Alexander Nagel, *Anachronic Renaissance* (New York: Zone Books, 2010), 9. For further comments on anachrony and temporal confusion in early modern texts see Linda Charnes, *Hamlet's Heirs: Shakespeare and the Politics of a New Millennium* (London: Routledge, 2006); Marjorie Garber, 'Shakespeare's Laundry List', in *Profiling Shakespeare* (London: Routledge, 2008), 195–215. 'Timely Meditations', a special issue of *Early Modern Culture: An Electronic Seminar* 6 (2007): http://emc.eserver.org/1-6/issue6.html, includes useful essays by Charnes, Harris, Huw Griffiths, Shankar Raman and Sadia Abbas.

53 For further discussion of the implications of *Anachronic Renaissance* for our understanding of early modern literary works see Williams, 'Shakespearean Medievalism', 395.

54 Jonathan Gil Harris, *Untimely Matter in the Time of Shakespeare* (Philadelphia: University of Pennsylvania Press, 2009), 8.

55 Michel Serres and Bruno Latour, *Conversations on Science, Culture, and Time*, trans. Roxanne Lapidus (Ann Arbor: University of Michigan Press, 1995), 60.

56 Jane Donawerth, *Shakespeare and the Sixteenth-Century Study of Language* (Urbana and Chicago: University of Illinois Press, 1984), 30–1; on this topic see also Margreta de Grazia, 'Words as Things', *Shakespeare Studies* 28 (2000), 231–5.

57 Elizabeth Fay, 'Archaic Contamination: Hegel and the History of Dead Matter', *Publications of the Modern Language Association of America* 118 (2003), 581–90 (581).

58 Svetlana Boym, 'Nostalgia and its Discontents', *The Hedgehog Review: Critical Reflections on Contemporary Culture* 9.2 (Summer 2007), 7–18 (8–9); see also Boym, *The Future of Nostalgia* (New York: Basic Books, 2001); Fredric Jameson, 'Nostalgia for the Present' (1989), repr. in Jameson, *Postmodernism*, 279–96.

59 Renée R. Trilling, *The Aesthetics of Nostalgia: Historical Representation in Old English Verse* (University of Toronto Press, 2009), 5.

60 Harry Berger Jr, 'Archaism, Immortality and the Muse in Spenser's Poetry' (1969), repr. in his *Revisionary Play: Studies in the Spenserian Dynamic* (Berkeley: University of California Press, 1998), 36–50 (38).

61 Henri Bergson, *Matter and Memory* (London: Allen & Unwin, 1911), 80.

62 Michael Rothberg, *Multidirectional Memory: Remembering the Holocaust in the Age of Decolonization* (Stanford University Press, 2009), 35–6; Rothberg draws on the model of memory set out by Richard Terdiman in *Present Past: Modernity and the Memory Crisis* (Ithaca, NY: Cornell University Press, 1993).

63 See Jerome McGann, 'Keats and the Historical Method in Literary Criticism', *Modern Language Notes* 94 (1979), 988–1032 (1001).

64 Charles Dickens, *Bleak House* (London: Bradbury and Evans, 1853), 155.

65 Blank, *Broken English*, 100.

66 On archaism in medieval texts see, for example, Derek Brewer, 'The Paradox of the Archaic and the Modern in Laȝamon's *Brut*', in Malcolm Godden, Douglas Gray and Terry Hoad (eds.), *From Anglo-Saxon to Early Middle English* (Oxford: Clarendon Press, 1994), 188–205; Tadao Kubouchi, 'A Note on Modernity and Archaism in Ælfric's *Catholic Homilies* and Earlier Texts of *Ancrene Wisse*', *Leeds Studies in English* 37 (2006), 379–90; R. D. Fulk, 'Archaisms and Neologisms in the Language of *Beowulf*', in Christopher M. Cain and Geoffrey Russom (eds.), *Studies in the History of the English Language III: Managing Chaos: Strategies for Identifying Change in English* (Berlin: Mouton de Gruyter, 2007), 267–87.

67 On this debate see Rubel, *Poetic Diction*; Richard Foster Jones, *The Triumph of the English Language: A Survey of Opinions Concerning the Vernacular from the Introduction of Printing to the Restoration* (London: Oxford University Press, 1953), esp. 68–141; Blank, *Broken English*, esp. 100–4; Barber, *Early Modern English*, 42–102; Cathy Shrank, *Writing the Nation in Reformation England, 1530–1580* (Oxford University Press, 2004); Jenny C. Mann, *Outlaw Rhetoric: Figuring Vernacular Eloquence in Shakespeare's England* (Ithaca, NY: Cornell University Press, 2012), esp. 1–54.

68 Io. Gower *De Confessione Amantis* (London, 1532), aa2v.

69 'A Letter of Syr I. Cheekes', in *The Courtyer of Count Baldessar Castilio*, trans. Edward Hoby (London, 1561), 3A1r.

70 See Blank, *Broken English*, 101–2.

71 Jones, *Triumph*, 120.

72 See, among others, Bruce R. McElderry, 'Archaism and Innovation in Spenser's Poetic Diction', *Publications of the Modern Language Association of America* 47 (1932), 144–70; Paula Blank, 'The Dialect of *The Shepheardes Calender*', *Spenser Studies* 10 (1989), 71–94; Dorothy Stephens, 'Spenser's Language(s): Linguistic Theory and Poetic Diction', in Mike Pincombe and Cathy Shrank (eds.), *The Oxford Handbook of Tudor Literature, 1485–1603* (Oxford University Press, 2009), 367–84.

73 Epistle to *The Shepheardes Calender*, ll. 19–27.
74 See *OED* roundness 4.
75 Shrank, *Writing the Nation*, 222. On Spenser's creation of an 'English' visual and verbal style in *The Shepheardes Calender* see also 226–32.
76 John Baret, 'To the Reader', in *An Alvearie, or Triple Dictionarie, in Englishe, Latin, and French* (London, 1574), *5v.
77 Kevin Pask reads E.K.'s reference to Evander's mother in the context of Virgil's *Aeneid* and argues that the epistle 'converts the condemnation of archaisms into a covert insistence upon their importance to Virgil's representation of political (and linguistic) *imperium*' (*The Emergence of the English Author: Scripting the Life of the Poet in Early Modern England* (Cambridge University Press, 1996), 103).
78 James VI and I, *Basilicon Doron*, in Johann P. Sommerville (ed.), *Political Writings* (Cambridge University Press, 1994), 59.
79 'An Essay: Endeavouring to Ennoble our English Poesie by Evidence of Latter Qvills; and Reiecting the Former', in *The Poems of George Daniel . . . From the Original MSS in the British Museum: Hitherto Unprinted*, ed. Alexander B. Grosart, 4 vols. (Boston, Lincs.: Privately Printed, 1878), vol. 1, ll. 134–9. Grosart's edition is based on BL Add. MS 19255.
80 See Sean Keilen, *Vulgar Eloquence: On the Renaissance Invention of Literature* (New Haven, Conn.: Yale University Press, 2006) for a lively account of 'the literary history that the English Renaissance fabled for itself' (12) from the 1580s onwards through its engagements with classical literature.
81 Helgerson, *Forms of Nationhood*, 23.
82 Jonathan Hope, *Shakespeare and Language: Reason, Eloquence and Artifice in the Renaissance* (London: Arden Shakespeare, 2010), 6.
83 McEachern, *Poetics of English Nationhood*, 6.
84 William Davenant, *A Discourse upon Gondibert. An Heroick Poem* (Paris, 1650), 12.
85 Susan Stewart, *On Longing: Narratives of the Miniature, the Gigantic, the Souvenir, the Collection* (Durham, NC: Duke University Press, 1993), 23.
86 Francesco Orlando, *Obsolete Objects in the Literary Imagination: Ruins, Relics, Rarities, Rubbish, Uninhabited Places, and Hidden Treasures* (New Haven, Conn.: Yale University Press, 2006), 11. For a linguist's perspective on early modern obsolescence see Terttu Nevalainen, 'Early Modern English Lexis and Semantics', in Lass, *Cambridge History of the English Language*, 332–458 (347–9).
87 *No Wit/Help Like a Woman's*, ed. John Jowett, in Thomas Middleton, *The Collected Works*, gen. eds. Gary Taylor and John Lavagnino (Oxford University Press, 2007), 4.79–82.
88 Anne Norris Michelin, *Euripides and the Tragic Tradition* (Madison: University of Wisconsin Press, 1987), 96–7.
89 Dinshaw, *Getting Medieval*, 12.
90 Roland Barthes, *Camera Lucida: Reflections on Photography*, trans. Richard Howard (London: Vintage, 2000), 26–7, 43.

91 Thomas Nashe, *Strange Newes*, K1r.
92 Henry More, *Psychodia Platonica* (Cambridge, 1642), 1 (Book 1, Stanza 1).
93 More, *Philosophical Poems* (Cambridge, 1647), A2v. On Spenser, and More's other literary influences see Alexander Jacob (ed.), *A Platonick Song of the Soul* (London: Associated University Presses, 1998), xi–xii, 1–15.
94 Thomas Vaughan, *The Man-Mouse Taken in a Trap, and Tortur'd to Death for Gnawing the Margins of Eugenius Philalethes* (London, 1650), 35. On the contexts of this quarrel see F. B. Burnham, 'The More–Vaughan Controversy: The Revolt Against Philosophical Enthusiasm', *Journal of the History of Ideas* 35 (1975), 33–95.

1 Within our own memory: Old English and the early modern poet

1 Matthew Parker, 'Præfatio ad Lectorum', in John Asser, *Ælfredi regis res gestæ* (London, 1574), ¶1r, translated by Michael Murphy in 'Anglo-Saxon at Tavistock Abbey', *Duquesne Review* 11 (1966), 119–24 (122). Parker's Latin text reads: '*Quem in finem superioribus sæculis a maioribus nostris monialium quædam Collegia instituta sunt, in quibus essent quæ & huius linguæ scientia imbuerentur, & eandem (cum alijs communicando) ad posteros transmitterent. Quod quidem in Cænobio monialium Tauenstokensi in comitatu Deuoniæ, & multis alijs conuenticulis (nostra memoria) receptum fuit, credo, ne eius sermonis peritia, ob linguæ insolentiam penitus obsolesceret.*' On Parker's statement and the later tradition see also Eleanor N. Adams, *Old English Scholarship in England from 1566–1800* (New Haven, Conn.: Yale University Press, 1917), 21–3.
2 William Camden, *Britain*, trans. Philemon Holland (London, 1610), 199–200.
3 Camden, *Britannia* (London, 1607), 144.
4 See H. P. R. Finberg, *Tavistock Abbey: A Study in Social and Economic History of Devon* (Cambridge University Press, 1951), 224 n., 285.
5 *Camden's Britannia Newly Translated into English, with Large Additions and Improvements* (London, 1695), 38. For an intermediate account, which links the Tavistock narrative with a similar story about another Anglo-Saxon foundation, Croyland (or Crowland) in Lincolnshire, see William Somner, *A Treatise of the Roman Ports and Forts in Kent* (London, 1693), 28. Somner draws on Camden and on the Latin chronicle supposedly composed by Ingulf, Abbot of Croyland, printed in *Rerum Anglicarum scriptorum veterum*, ed. Thomas Gale and William Fulman (Oxford, 1684), 98.
6 For a summary of evidence see Fred C. Robinson, *The Tomb of Beowulf and Other Essays on Old English* (Oxford: Blackwell, 1993), 277–9.
7 On the monastery's manuscripts and its printing press see Finberg, *Tavistock Abbey*, 223–4, 290–3. The surviving manuscripts are Cambridge University Library MS Ii.4.6 and BL Cotton Vitellius C.v.
8 See 'Smectymnuus, *or the Club-Divines*', in *The Character of a London-Diurnall with Severall Select Poems by the Same Author* (London, 1647), 30.

9 Chris Jones, *Strange Likeness: The Use of Old English in Twentieth-Century Poetry* (Oxford University Press, 2006), 7.

10 Hannah Crawforth, 'Strangers to the Mother Tongue: Spenser's *Shepheardes Calender* and Early Anglo-Saxon Studies', *Journal of Medieval and Early Modern Studies* 41 (2011), 293–316 (296, 310).

11 For background see Francis Lee Utley, 'Two Seventeenth-Century Anglo-Saxon Poems', *Modern Language Quarterly* 3 (1942), 243–61; Alberta Turner, 'Another Seventeenth-Century Anglo-Saxon Poem', *Modern Language Quarterly* 9 (1948), 389–93; Michael Murphy, 'Scholars at Play: A Short History of Composing in Old English', *Old English Newsletter* 15.2 (1982), 26–36; Murphy and Edward Barrett, 'Abraham Wheelock, Arabist and Saxonist', *Biography* 8 (1985), 163–85; Robinson, *Tomb*, 275–303.

12 Camden, *Britannia* (1607), 144.

13 Camden, *Britannia* (London, 1586), 80; *Britannia* (London, 1590), 128.

14 On scholarship in Old English see, among others, Adams, *Old English Scholarship*; David C. Douglas, *English Scholars 1660–1730*, 2nd edn (London: Eyre and Spottiswoode, 1951); C. E. Wright, 'The Dispersal of Monastic Libraries and the Beginnings of Anglo-Saxon Studies', *Transactions of the Cambridge Bibliographical Society* 1 (1949–53), 208–37; Carl T. Berkhout and Milton McC. Gatch (eds.), *Anglo-Saxon Scholarship: The First Three Centuries* (Boston, Mass.: G. K. Hall, 1982); Timothy Graham (ed.), *The Recovery of Old English: Anglo-Saxon Studies in the Sixteenth and Seventeenth Centuries* (Kalamazoo, Mich.: Medieval Institute Publications, 2000); Graham, 'Anglo-Saxon Studies: Sixteenth to Eighteenth Centuries', in Philip Pulsiano and Elaine M. Treharne (eds.), *A Companion to Anglo-Saxon Literature* (Oxford: Blackwell, 2001), 415–33.

15 For useful accounts see Christopher Hill, *Puritanism and Revolution: Studies in Interpretation of the English Revolution of the 17th Century* (London: Secker & Warburg, 1958), 52–68; Theodore H. Leinbaugh, 'Ælfric's Sermo de Sacrificio in Die Pascæ: Anglican Polemic in the Sixteenth and Seventeenth Centuries', in Berkhout and Gatch, *Anglo-Saxon Scholarship*, 51–68; Allan J. Frantzen, *Desire for Origins: New Language, New Style, and Teaching the Traditions* (New Brunswick, NJ: Rutgers University Press, 1990), esp. 35–50, 130–67; Colin Kidd, *British Identities Before Nationalism: Ethnicity and Nationhood in the Atlantic World, 1600–1800* (Cambridge University Press, 1999), esp. 99–122; Graham, 'Anglo-Saxon Studies'; Benedict S. Robinson, 'John Foxe and the Anglo-Saxons', in Christopher Highley and John N. King (eds.), *John Foxe and his World* (Aldershot: Ashgate, 2001), 54–72; Donna B. Hamilton, 'Catholic Use of Anglo-Saxon Precedents, 1565–1625', *Recusant History* 26 (2003), 537–55; Felicity Heal, 'Appropriating History: Catholic and Protestant Polemics and the National Past', *Huntington Library Quarterly* 68 (2005), 109–32; Jessica Dyson, 'Staging Legal Authority: Ideas of Law in Caroline Drama', PhD thesis, University of Stirling, 2007, esp. 147–65; Christopher Highley, *Catholics Writing the Nation in Early Modern Britain and Ireland* (Oxford University Press, 2008), 84–91.

16 *The New Inn*, ed. Julie Sanders, in *CBJ*, vol. 6, 4.2.16–17. See *OED* wapentake, *n*.

17 Angus Vine describes Drayton as 'the most antiquarian of seventeenth-century poets' (*In Defiance of Time: Antiquarian Writing in Early Modern England* (Oxford University Press, 2010), 169). On the interaction between the two writers see *ibid*., 169–99; Anne Lake Prescott, 'Drayton's Muse and Selden's "Story": The Interlacing of Poetry and History in *Polyolbion*', *Studies in Philology* 87 (1990), 128–35, and 'Marginal Discourse: Drayton's Muse and Selden's "Story"', *Studies in Philology* 88 (1991), 307–28.

18 See Ode 7, 'Of Hengist', in *The History of Great Britanie From the First Peopling of this Island to this Present Raigne of or Happy and Peacefull Monarke K: Iames* (London, 1621), 165. Slatyer salutes *Polyolbion* as his model in a dedicatory poem in an unpaginated section at the end of the volume (2D4r).

19 On Spenser and Milton see Crawforth, 'Strangers'; William E. Engel, 'John Milton's Recourse to Old English: A Case-Study in Renaissance Lexicography', *LATCH: A Journal for the Study of the Literary Artefact in Theory, Culture, or History* 1 (2008), 1–29; Crawforth, *Etymology and the Invention of English in Early Modern Literature* (Cambridge University Press, 2013). On 'Saxon' monosyllables in English poetry see Sandra A. Glass, 'The Saxonists' Influence on Seventeenth-Century English Literature', in Berkhout and Gatch, *Anglo-Saxon Scholarship*, 91–105 (99–101) and the discussion in Chapter 3.

20 Graham, 'Anglo-Saxon Studies', 418.

21 See Danielle Cunniff Plumer, 'The Construction of Structure in the Earliest Editions of Old English Poetry', in Graham, *Recovery*, 243–79 (Appendix: 'Printed Editions of Old English Poetry 1574–1799' (274–9)). The other poems printed before 1655 are: 'A Proverb from Winfred's Time' in Nicolaus Serarius' *Epistolæ s. Bonifacii martyris* (Mainz, 1605); 'Thureth' in Henry Spelman's *Concilia* (London, 1639); 'Cædmon's Hymn' and poems from the Anglo-Saxon *Chronicle* in Wheelock's *Historiæ ecclesiasticæ gentis Anglorum* (Cambridge, 1643); and the Old English 'Durham' in Roger Twysden's *Historiæ Anglicanæ scriptores X* (London, 1652).

22 These appear at years 937 ('The Battle of Brunanburh' (the victory of Athelstan over the Scots and Norse)), 942 (the capture of the Five Boroughs), 973 (the coronation of Edgar), 975 (the death of Edgar), 1036 (the death of Alfred) and 1065 (the death of Edward the Confessor).

23 Wheelock, *Historiæ*, 555. The Latin 'horridum' might also be translated as 'rough' or 'barbarous'.

24 Plumer, 'Construction', 254.

25 The letter is dated 4 March 1643. See B. J. Timmer, 'De Laet's Anglo-Saxon Dictionary', *Neophilologus* 41 (1957), 199–202; John Considine, *Dictionaries in Early Modern Europe: Lexicography and the Making of Heritage* (Cambridge University Press, 2008), 159.

26 Phillip Pulsiano, 'William L'Isle and the Editing of Old English', in Graham, *Recovery*, 173–206 (194–5), transcribing Bodleian MS Laud Misc. 636 (L'Isle's own copy of the Peterborough Chronicle), fols. 96v, 97r.

27 On the date and composition of *The History of Britain* see Nicholas von Maltzahn, *Milton's History of Britain: Republican Historiography in the English Revolution* (Oxford: Clarendon Press, 1991), 22–47, 168–74; Barbara K. Lewalski, *The Life of John Milton: A Critical Biography* (Oxford: Blackwell, 2000), 212–16, 346–7.

28 Milton, *The History of Britain, That Part Especially Now Call'd England* (London, 1670), 225. See Huntingdon, *Historia Anglorum*, in Henry Savile, *Rerum Anglicarum scriptores post Bedam præcipvi* (London, 1596), fol. 203r–v (misnumbered 204), who refers to the poem as a kind of song ('quasi carminis') and foregrounds the faithfulness of his translation ('translatione fida donandi sunt') (203r).

29 See Lewalski, *Life of John Milton*, 346–7.

30 On *Paradise Lost* and Old English versions of Genesis see W. F. Bolton, 'A Further Echo of the Old English Genesis in Milton's *Paradise Lost*', *Review of English Studies*, ns 25 (1974), 58–61; J. Martin Evans, *Paradise Lost and the Genesis Tradition* (Oxford: Clarendon Press, 1968), 143–67; Glass, 'Saxonists' Influence', 96–7. For further discussion of Milton and Anglo-Saxon history see von Maltzahn, *Milton's History of Britain*, 166–97.

31 See Plumer, 'Construction', 260.

32 See T. A. Birrell, 'The Society of Antiquaries and the Taste for Old English 1705–1840', *Neophilologus* 50 (1966), 107–17; Plumer, 'Construction', 260. On the edition's influence on scholars see Peter J. Lucas (ed.), *Caedmonis monachi paraphrasis poetica* (Amsterdam: Rodopi, 2000), xxvi–xxviii.

33 See Kenneth Sisam, 'The Authenticity of Certain Texts in Lambard's *Archaionomia* 1568', in *Studies in the History of Old English Literature* (Oxford: Clarendon Press, 1953), 232–58 (conflates essays originally published in 1923 and 1925); Robin Flower, 'Laurence Nowell and the Discovery of England in Tudor Times', *Proceedings of the British Academy* 21 (1935), 47–73 (73 n. 6); Robinson, *Tomb*, 279–81; Stuart Lee, 'Oxford, Bodleian Library, MS Laud Misc. 381: William L'Isle, Ælfric, and the *Ancrene Wisse*', in Graham, *Recovery*, 207–42 (esp. 225–31); Graham, 'Anglo-Saxon Studies', 424–5.

34 William L'Isle, 'To the Readers', in *A Saxon Treatise Concerning the Old and New Testament* (London, 1623), fol. 3r–v. In L'Isle's text the Old English phrase is printed in Old English types.

35 Siân Echard, *Printing the Middle Ages* (Philadelphia: University of Pennsylvania Press, 2008), 44.

36 See below for Middleton and Cartwright. For the other uses see Rastell, *The Pastyme of People* (London, 1530), Civ; Hardyng, *The Chronicle of Jhon Hardyng in Metre* (London, 1543), h1v; Foxe, *Actes and Monuments* (London, 1583), 108; Holinshed, *Chronicles of England, Scotlande, and Irelande* (London, 1577), 81; Verstegan, *A Restitution of Decayed Intelligence:*

In Antiquities (Antwerp, 1605), 130; Speed, *The History of Great Britaine under the Conquests of ye Romans, Saxons, Danes and Normans* (London, 1611), 285; Heywood, *The Life of Merlin* (London, 1641), 15; Jones, *The Most Notable Antiquity of Great Britain, Vulgarly called Stone-Heng on Salisbury Plain* (London, 1655), 20; Milton, *History of Britain*, 117; Stillingfleet, *Origines Britannicae* (London, 1685), 325; Brady, *A Complete History of England* (London, 1685), 96.

37 Speed, *History*, 285.

38 On this issue see also Paula Blank, *Broken English: Dialects and Politics of Language in Renaissance English* (London: Routledge, 1996), 101–2.

39 Camden, *Remaines of a Greater Worke, Concerning Britaine* (London, 1605), C3r.

40 Verstegan, *Restitution*, 1.

41 For the early modern spelling of 'mote' as 'moth' see *OED* mote, *n.*¹.

42 I discuss the figure of the antiquary in more detail in Chapter 2.

43 See Holinshed, *Chronicles*, 81. For discussion of the sources see R. C. Bald (ed.), *Hengist, King of Kent; or The Major of Queenborough* (New York: Scribner's, 1938), 127–36; Julia Briggs, 'New Times and Old Stories: Middleton's *Hengist*', in Donald Scragg and Carole Weinberg (eds.), *Literary Appropriations of the Anglo-Saxons from the Thirteenth to the Twentieth Century* (Cambridge University Press, 2000), 107–21 (112–14).

44 Thomas Middleton, *The Mayor of Queenborough [or Hengist King of Kent]*, ed. Howard Marchitello (London: Nick Hern Books, 2004), 4.3.21–3. Marchitello's text is based on the first quarto edition of 1661 (and he follows its title); the two manuscript versions, the 'Portland Manuscript' (Nottingham University Library MS PwV20) and the 'Lambarde Manuscript' (Folger Shakespeare Library MS J.b.6) do not differ substantially here. See Grace Ioppolo (ed.), *Hengist, King of Kent*, in Thomas Middleton, *The Collected Works*, gen. eds. Gary Taylor and John Lavagnino (Oxford University Press, 2007) (based on the Lambarde Manuscript), and Ioppolo (ed.), *Hengist, King of Kent, or the Mayor of Queenborough* (Oxford: Malone Society, 2003) (reproduces the Portland Manuscript). All citations are to Marchitello's edition; any major variations in the manuscript texts are indicated in the notes.

45 In her Oxford edition, Ioppolo inserts the stage direction '*Vortiger and Hengist embrace*' here (4.4.49SD).

46 The manuscripts have minor variations, such as 'nenp your sexes' at l. 2116 in the Portland version. See Ioppolo's Oxford edition, 4.4.33–6, 40–52, and her transcript of the Portland manuscript, ll. 2096–9, 2104–20.

47 See Julia Briggs, 'Middleton's Forgotten Tragedy: *Hengist, King of Kent*', *Review of English Studies* 41 (1990), 479–95 (489); Gordon McMullan, 'The Colonisation of Early Britain on the Jacobean Stage', in Gordon McMullan and David Matthews (eds.), *Reading the Medieval in Early Modern England* (Cambridge University Press, 2007), 119–40 (129).

48 Camden, *Remaines*, C3r; Verstegan, *Restitution*, 188.

49 For further discussion in this context of *Hengist* and other Jacobean plays set in Anglo-Saxon England see Lucy Munro, '"Nemp your sexes!": Anachronistic Aesthetics in *Hengist, King of Kent* and the Jacobean "Anglo-Saxon" Play', *Modern Philology*, forthcoming.

50 James F. Larkin and Paul L. Hughes (eds.), *Stuart Royal Proclamations*, 2 vols. (Oxford: Clarendon Press, 1973–83), I: 94–5.

51 Edward Sharpham, *The Fleer*, ed. Lucy Munro (London: Nick Hern Books, 2006), 2.1.284–6.

52 The play was probably performed at Christ Church, Oxford. On its date and auspices see G. Blakemore Evans (ed.), *The Plays and Poems of William Cartwright* (Madison: University of Wisconsin Press, 1951), 259.

53 An allusion to a performance of *Hengist* in *The Book of Bulls* (London, 1636), fol. 9r–v, suggests that it was current on the stage; it was among the plays protected for the King's Men on 7 August 1641 (see G. E. Bentley, *The Jacobean and Caroline Stage*, 7 vols. (Oxford: Clarendon Press, 1941–68), I: 66).

54 *The Ordinary*, in Evans, *Plays and Poems of William Cartwright*, l. 1697. All citations are to this edition.

55 The Old English phrases appear in the original text in Anglo-Saxon types.

56 Huntingdon, *Historia Anglorum*, in Savile, *Rerum Anglicarum*, fol. 208r (Edric's exclamation is printed in black letter). For Holinshed's version see *Chronicles*, 254. The episode appears, minus the archaic phrase, in another early modern play, *Edmond Ironside*, written around 1595 but apparently revived in the early 1630s. See Bentley, *Jacobean and Caroline Stage*, I: 323.

57 That is, in the name of twenty devils. The oath appears three times in Chaucer's *The Canterbury Tales*: see *The Miller's Tale*, l. 3713, *The Reeve's Tale*, l. 4257, *The Canon Yeoman's Tale*, l. 782.

58 See Judith Halberstam, *In a Queer Time and Place: Transgender Bodies, Subcultural Lives* (New York University Press, 2005).

59 John 6:12, quoted by William L'Isle on a draft title-page for his projected edition of 'Saxon-english / Remaines of the Pentateuch, / Iosua, Iudges, &ct. / out of S[r]. Robert Cottons / Manuscripts, of most reuerend antiquity' (Lee, 'MS Laud Misc. 381', 213, quoting Bodleian MS Laud 381, fol. I(a)r).

60 For details see Pulsiano, 'William L'Isle'; Lee, 'Oxford'.

61 On L'Isle's authorship of the translation, published under the initials 'W.L.', see G. W. Pigman III, 'William Lisle's Translation of Virgil's Eclogues', *Notes & Queries*, ns 54 (2007), 389–91.

62 On L'Isle's use of Vives see Andrew Wallace, *Virgil's Schoolboys: The Poetics of Pedagogy in Renaissance England* (Oxford University Press, 2010), 106–10.

63 See Maley, 'Spenser's Irish English: Language and Identity in Early Modern Ireland', *Studies in Philology* 91 (1994), 417–31; 'Spenser's Languages'. See also Crawforth, 'Strangers'.

64 Richard Stanihurst, *The Historie of Irelande* in *The Firste Volume of the Chronicles of England, Scotlande, and Irelande*, ed. Raphael Holinshed (London, 1577), A3r (the section has separate signatures).

65 *Virgils Eclogues Translated into English by W. L. Gent.* (London, 1628), A8v, B1r, D6r, F6r.

66 L'Isle, 'To the Prince his Highnes, Welcome-home and Dedication, by Way of Eclogue, Imitating the Fourth of Virgil', in *A Saxon Treatise*, ¶1r, ¶2v, ¶2r.

67 See, for instance, Pulsiano, 'William L'Isle', 180 ('The *Aeneid* "Scotished" would have benefited L'Isle little, if at all, in his studies'). On the relationships between Middle Scots, Old English and Early Modern English see J. Derrick McClure, 'English in Scotland', in R. W. Burchfield (ed.), *The Cambridge History of the English Language*, vol. 5 (Cambridge University Press, 1994), 23–93; C. I. Macafee, 'Older Scots Lexis', in Charles Jones (ed.), *The Edinburgh History of the Scots Language* (Edinburgh University Press, 1997), 182–212. As Blank points out, early modern scholars and commentators frequently argued that Old English was preserved in Northern English (*Broken English*, 106–8); L'Isle is more unusual in his desire to single out Scotland.

68 Adapted from Martial, *Epigrams*, 14.220 ('A cook should have the taste of his master'); see *Martial: Epigrams*, ed. and trans. D. R. Shackleton Bailey, Loeb Classical Library, 3 vols. (Cambridge, Mass.: Harvard University Press, 1993), 3: 312–13.

69 Wallace, *Virgil's Schoolboys*, 229.

70 See *OED*, homely, *adj.* 2a, 4, 5.

71 For an overview of Roman, Medieval and Early Modern commentaries on Virgil's style in the *Eclogues* see David Scott Wilson-Okamura, *Virgil in the Renaissance* (Cambridge University Press, 2010), 73–6. The stylistic oddities of L'Isle's version become clear when it is compared with the two versions of Abraham Fleming's Elizabethan translation, *The Bucolics of Pulius Virgilius Maro* (London, 1575 and 1589); the earlier version is described on its title-page as '*Drawn into Plaine and Familiar Englishe*'.

72 The hurtle, or bilberry, is glossed as 'a wilde berry, black as Iet' (C1v). L'Isle may have been familiar with the 1575 version of Fleming's translation, in which the plants are 'White Dasyes' and 'Violets, purple blewe' (C3r); in the 1589 version they are 'White priuet [flowers]' and 'black violets' (B2v; the square brackets are Fleming's own).

73 *OED*'s earliest use in an English text dates from 1675 (galore, *adv.*).

74 See Richard A. McCabe, *Spenser's Monstrous Regiment: Elizabethan Ireland and the Poetics of Difference* (Oxford University Press, 2002), 193–6; Maley, 'Spenser's Languages', 165, 166–7.

75 See Murphy and Barrett, 'Abraham Wheelock'; J. C. T. Oates, *Cambridge University Library: A History: From the Beginnings to the Copyright Act of Queen Anne* (Cambridge University Press, 1986), 173–92; Graham, 'Anglo-Saxon Studies', 425–6; Alastair Hamilton, 'Wheelocke, Abraham (*c.*1593–1653)', *ODNB*: www.oxforddnb.com/view/article/29191 (accessed 10 August 2011).

76 See Peter J. Lucas, 'William Retchford, Pupil of Abraham Wheelock in Anglo-Saxon: "He Understands the Saxon as well as myself"', *Transactions of the Cambridge Bibliographical Society* 12 (2003), 335–61.

77 See Turner, 'Another'; Alan Marshall, 'Williamson, Sir Joseph (1633–1701)', *ODNB*: www.oxforddnb.com/view/article/29571 (accessed 10 August 2011).

78 On the Caroline university miscellany and the contexts of its production see James Loxley, *Royalism and Poetry in the English Civil Wars: The Drawn Sword* (Basingstoke: Macmillan, 1997), 9–57, 68–71; Robert Wilcher, *The Writing of Royalism 1628–1660* (Cambridge University Press, 2001), 99–104. On *Musarum Oxoniensium* see Edward Holberton, *Poetry and the Cromwellian Protectorate: Culture, Politics, and Institutions* (Oxford University Press, 2008), 61–86.

79 See Loxley, *Royalism*, 21–8.

80 *Ibid.*, 27.

81 See Lucas, 'From Politics to Practicalities: Printing Anglo-Saxon in the Context of Seventeenth-Century Scholarship', *The Library*, 7th series, 4.1 (March 2003), 28–48 (41); David McKitterick, *A History of Cambridge University Press*, 3 vols. (Cambridge University Press, 1992–2004), I: 190. Williamson's poem is printed in a standard type. An earlier set of Old English types had been produced for Parker in the 1560s.

82 Wheelock was possibly misled by his reading in the late thirteenth-century chronicle attributed to Robert of Gloucester, written in rhyming couplets, which he quotes in his notes to Bede's *Historia* (25).

83 For analyses see Utley, 'Two', 246–61; Turner, 'Another', 391–3; Robinson, *Tomb*, 282–3; Plumer, 'Construction', 251–3.

84 For a chronology of the major events of 1640–2 see David Cressy, *England on Edge: Crisis and Revolution 1640–1641* (Cambridge University Press, 2006), 427–31. On the poetry produced in reaction to these events see Loxley, *Royalism*, 58–79.

85 *Irenodia Cantabrigiensis* (Cambridge, 1641), L1r. On the treatment of this theme see Wilcher, *Writing*, 100–3.

86 I am very grateful to Tanya Pollard and William Stenhouse for their help with the Latin translations in this section.

87 Retchford adds a note here: 'sc. *Britannico*'. See Figure 3.

88 Retchford's note: 'Ceorl. *maritus. sponsus.*'.

89 Retchford's note: 'D. Hen Spelm in Concil. pag. 623. Lambard. in ἀρχαιονομ fol. 128'. He refers to Sir Henry Spelman's *Concilia, decreta, leges, constitutiones, in re ecclesiarum orbis Britannici* (London, 1639), 622 (not 623), and William Lambarde's *Archaionomia, siue de priscis anglorum legibus libri sermone Anglico* (London, 1568), fol. 128v.

90 Retchford's note: '*Carol. Magn.*'.

91 Retchford's note: '*Hibernia.*'.

92 An alternative translation would be 'stills' or 'silences'.

93 See, for instance, John Hayward, *An Answer to the First Part of a Certain Conference Concerning Succession* (London, 1603), O2v.

94 See Wilcher, *Writing*, 99–100.

95 Henry Peacham, for instance, glosses the phrase 'Earth-bounding Orkney' with 'The Isles of Orkney beyond Scotland – Ultima Thule, Virg.' (*Thestylis Atrata: Or A Funeral Elegie vpon the Death of the Right Honourable, Most Religious and Noble Lady, Frances, Late Countesse of Warwick* (London, 1634), B1v).

96 See K2r–v, K4r, L1v–2r. For discussion see Wilcher, *Writing*, 101–3.

97 See n. 89 above.

98 Dyson, 'Staging', 125.

99 James Maxwell, *Admirable and Notable Prophesies, Uttered in Former Times by 24. Famous Romain-Catholickes* (London, 1615), 32–3. See also John Carion, *The Thre Bokes of Cronicles ... Gathered wyth Great Diligence of the Beste Authours that have Written in Hebrue, Greke or Latine* (London, 1550), fol. cxc.

100 On Charles as Charlemagne see, for instance, the poem appended to J.H., *King Charles his Entertainment, and Londons Loyaltie* (London, 1641), 5–6 which opens with the words 'Brave *Charlemains* return'd' (5).

101 John Selden, *Titles of Honor* (London, 1614), 225.

102 Oates, *Cambridge University Library*, 181, quoting BL Harley MS 374, fol. 144.

103 Wheelock glosses these lines 'Hen. Huntingdon. lib. 6. in principio lib. hic cum pseudopropheta suo refellitur.' See Figure 2.

104 The allusion is to Genesis 25:26: 'And after that [i.e. the birth of Esau] came his brother out, and his hand took holde on Esaus heele; and his name was called Jacob.' I am very grateful to Andrew King for discussing this allusion with me.

105 Huntingdon, *Historia Anglorum*, in Savile, *Rerum Anglicarum*, fol. 206r.

106 John Weever, *Ancient Funerall Monuments within the United Monarchie of Great Britain, Ireland, and the Ilands Adiacent* (London, 1631), 358.

107 As Utley points out, 'These lines are conclusive evidence that the Hebrew [poem] is the original, for in the Anglo-Saxon the pun which gives point to the compliment is lost, and the result is complete ambiguity' ('Two', 252).

108 Untitled poem, in *Rex redux, sive Musa Cantabrigiensis voti damnas de incolumitate & felici reditu Regis Caroli post receptam coronam, comitiáq[ue] peracta in Scotia* (Cambridge, 1633), F2v. I am extremely grateful to Tanya Pollard and Tania Demetriou for translating and commenting on this poem for me.

109 See 1 Kings 12:1–24.

110 Henry Parker, *A Discourse Concerning Puritans* (London, 1641), 49. Parker developed the parallel between Charles and Rehoboam in *The Contra-Replicant, His Complaint to his Majestie* (London, 1643), 24–5, and *The Oath of Pacification* (London 1643), 4–5. See Michael Mendle, *Henry Parker and the English Civil War: The Political Thought of the Public's 'Privado'* (Cambridge University Press, 1995), 120–2.

111 John Taylor, *The Whole Life and Progresse of Henry Walker the Ironmonger* (London, 1642), A2v. For Walker's defence and denial that he either printed

the pamphlet or threw it see *The Modest Vindication of Henry Walker* (London, 1642), 2–3. See also Cressy, *England on Edge*, 294.

112 This paragraph draws on Steven C. A. Pincus, *Protestantism and Patriotism: Ideology and the Making of Foreign Policy, 1650–68* (Cambridge University Press, 1996), 83–191; Timothy Venning, *Cromwellian Foreign Policy* (Basingstoke: Macmillan, 1996), 153–71; Barry Coward, *The Cromwellian Protectorate* (Manchester University Press, 2002), 125–8; and Allan T. Macinnes, *The British Revolution, 1629–1660* (Basingstoke: Palgrave Macmillan, 2005), 195–211.

113 David Norbrook, *Writing the English Republic: Poetry, Rhetoric and Politics, 1627–1660* (Cambridge University Press, 1999), 302.

114 For varying interpretations of these actions see Kevin Sharpe, '"An image doting rabble": The Failure of Republican Culture in England', in Kevin Sharpe and Steven N. Zwicker (eds.), *Refiguring Revolutions: Aesthetics and Politics from the English Revolution to the Romantic Revolution* (Berkeley: University of California Press, 1998), 25–56 (47–8); Norbrook, *Writing*, 301–2; Coward, *Cromwellian Protectorate*, 33–4; Laura Lunger Knoppers, *Constructing Cromwell: Ceremony, Portrait, and Print, 1645–1661* (Cambridge University Press, 2000), 69–106.

115 Holberton, *Poetry*, 62.

116 *Musarum Oxoniensium* (Oxford, 1654), K2r–v.

117 I am very grateful to Karen Britland for her help in translating the French section.

118 See Considine, *Dictionaries*, 193–4.

119 *The Poems of Andrew Marvell*, ed. Nigel Smith, rev. edn (London: Pearson Education, 2007), ll. 1–2.

120 John Kerrigan, *Archipelagic English: Literature, History, and Politics, 1603–1707* (Oxford University Press, 2008), 240.

121 Considine, *Dictionaries*, 194.

122 Knoppers, *Constructing Cromwell*, 93.

123 See Marshall, 'Williamson'; Blair Worden, *God's Instruments: Political Conduct in the England of Oliver Cromwell* (Oxford University Press, 2012), 100 n.

124 For context see Vivienne Larminie, 'Smectymnuus (*act.* 1641)', in *ODNB*: www.oxforddnb.com/view/theme/94600 (accessed 22 August 2011).

125 Cleveland, *Character*, 30.

126 For this identification see Henry B. Woolf, 'John Cleveland's "West Saxon Poet"', *Philological Quarterly* 30 (1951), 443–7.

2 Chaucer, Gower and the anxiety of obsolescence

1 *Troilus and Criseyde*, 2.22–8.

2 John Bullokar, *An English Expositor Teaching the Interpretation of the Hardest Words Used in our Language* (London, 1616), L3v.

3 *OED* nice, *adj.*, 1.b.; strange, *adj.*, 7, 1.

4 'The Garland of Laurel', in *Pithy Plesaunt and Profitable Workes of Maister Skelton, Poete Laureate* (London, 1568), A7v. On early Tudor attitudes towards Chaucer see also Caroline F. E. Spurgeon, *Five Hundred Years of Chaucer Criticism and Allusion, 1357–1900*, 3 vols. (New York: Russell & Russell, 1960 [1925]); Veré L. Rubel, *Poetic Diction in the English Renaissance* (New York: Modern Language Association, 1941), 14–30; Derek Brewer, *Chaucer: The Critical Heritage*, vol. 1, *1385–1837* (London: Routledge and Kegan Paul, 1978), 81–106; Stephanie Trigg, *Congenial Souls: Reading Chaucer from Medieval to Postmodern* (Minneapolis: University of Minnesota Press, 2001), 109–29.

5 Angus Vine, *In Defiance of Time: Antiquarian Writing in Early Modern England* (Oxford University Press, 2010), 3.

6 John Marston, 'To those that seeme Iudiciall Perusers', in *The Scourge of Villanie: Three Bookes of Satyres* (London, 1598), B4v.

7 Samuel Daniel, 'Musophilus: Containing a Generall Defence of All Learning', in *The Poeticall Essayes of Sam. Danyel* (London, 1599), B3r.

8 Philip Sidney, *An Apology for Poetry*, ed. Geoffrey Shepherd, rev. R. W. Maslen (Manchester University Press, 2002), 82.

9 R. M. Cummings, *Edmund Spenser: The Critical Heritage* (London: Routledge and Kegan Paul, 1971), 149, quoting BL MS Harleian 4153, 'A Discourse Concerning Edmund Spenser', addressed to Thomas May and apparently written around 1628.

10 *The Poems of George Daniel . . . From the Original MSS in the British Museum: Hitherto Unprinted*, ed. Alexander B. Grosart, 4 vols. (Boston, Lincs.: Privately Printed, 1878), vol. 1, ll. 31–3, 75–8.

11 See *OED* antic, *adj.* 2.

12 See *OED* authentic, *adj.* 1, 3, 4. Perhaps appropriately, Daniel's use of 'in-authenticke' pre-dates *OED*'s earliest citation by more than two centuries.

13 Aston Cokain, 'Of Chaucer', in *A Chain of Golden Poems* (London, 1658), 155.

14 *The Art of English Poesy by George Puttenham: A Critical Edition*, ed. Frank Whigham and Wayne A. Rebhorn (Ithaca, NY: Cornell University Press, 2007), 336–7.

15 On the publication of Chaucer in the early modern period see H. G. Wright, 'Thomas Speght as Lexicographer and Annotator of Chaucer's Works', *English Studies* 40 (1959), 194–208; A. S. G. Edwards, 'Observations on the History of Middle English Editing', in Derek Pearsall (ed.), *Manuscripts and Texts: Editorial Problems in Later Middle English Literature* (Cambridge: D. S. Brewer, 1987), 34–48; Tim William Machan, 'Speght's *Works* and the Invention of Chaucer', *Text* 8 (1995), 145–70; Kevin Pask, *The Emergence of the English Author: Scripting the Life of the Poet in Early Modern England* (Cambridge University Press, 1996), 9–52; Clare R. Kinney, 'Thomas Speght's Renaissance Chaucer and the Solaas of Sentence in *Troilus and Criseyde*', in Theresa M. Krier (ed.), *Refiguring Chaucer in the Renaissance* (Gainesville: Florida University Press, 1998), 66–84; Trigg, *Congenial Souls*, 129–34; David Matthews, 'Public Ambition, Private Desire and the Last Tudor Chaucer',

in Gordon McMullan and David Matthews (eds.), *Reading the Medieval in Early Modern England* (Cambridge University Press, 2007), 74–88; Megan L. Cook, 'Making and Managing the Past: Lexical Commentary in Spenser's *Shepheardes Calender* (1579) and Chaucer's *Works* (1598–1602)', *Spenser Studies* 26 (2011), 179–222.

16 'F.B. to his Very Loving Friend, T.S.', in *The Workes of our Antient and Learned English Poet Geffrey Chaucer, Newly Printed* (London, 1598), [a]4v. For further commentary on this epistle see Cook, 'Making', 199–205.

17 Chaucer, *Works* (1598), 4A1r–4B1v; *The Workes of our Ancient and Learned English Poet, Geffrey Chaucer, Newly Printed* (London, 1602), 3T1r–3U6r. For a comparison of the 1598 and 1602 glossaries see Wright, 'Speght as Lexicographer', 197–207. See also Trigg, *Congenial Souls*, 137; Tim William Machan, *Textual Criticism and Middle English Texts* (Charlottesville: University Press of Virginia, 1994), 42; Cook, 'Making'.

18 See, for instance, *Ancient Funerall Monuments within the United Monarchie of Great Britain, Ireland, and the Ilands Adjacent* (London, 1631), 60–1, 63–4. For a detailed account of Weever's textual interactions see Jennifer Summit, *Memory's Library: Medieval Books in Early Modern England* (University of Chicago Press, 2008), 183–96.

19 On these editorial strategies see Machin, 'Speght's Works', 167.

20 See John N. King, *English Reformation Literature: The Tudor Origins of the Protestant Tradition* (Princeton University Press, 1982), 329–30; Charlotte Brewer, *Editing Piers Plowman: The Evolution of the Text* (Cambridge University Press, 1996), esp. 15–16; Sarah A. Kelen, *Langland's Early Modern Identities* (Basingstoke: Palgrave Macmillan, 2007), esp. 57–8; James Doelman (ed.), *Early Stuart Pastoral: The Shepherd's Pipe by William Browne and Others and The Shepherd's Hunting by George Wither* (Toronto: CRRS Publications, 1999), 10, 27–8.

21 Thomas Malory, *The Most Ancient and Famous History of the Renowned Prince Arthur King of Britaine* (London, 1634), ¶3v.

22 See Tsuyoshi Mukai, 'Stansby's 1634 Edition of Malory's *Morte*', *Poetica* 36 (1992), 38–54; David R. Carlson, 'Arthur Before and After the Revolution: The Blome–Stansby Edition of Malory (1634) and *Brittains Glory* (1684)', in Martin B. Shichtman and James P. Carley (eds.), *Culture and the King: The Social Implications of the Arthurian Legend* (Albany: State University of New York Press, 1994), 234–53.

23 See Pask, *Emergence*, 45–6.

24 See Caroline F. E. Spurgeon (ed.), *Richard Brathwait's Comments in 1665, Upon Chaucer's Tales of the Miller and the Wife of Bath* (London: Chaucer Society, 1901).

25 *A Comment upon the Two Tales of our Ancient, Renovvned, and Ever Living Poet Sr. Jeffray Chaucer, Knight* (London, 1665), 46–7; bold text here represents the original's use of black letter for quotations from Chaucer.

26 BL Add. MS 29494, quoted from Herbert G. Wright (ed.), *A Seventeenth-Century Modernisation of the First Three Books of Chaucer's 'Troilus and*

Criseyde' (Berne: Francke Verlag, 1960), 89. On the translation see also Barry
A. Windeatt (ed.), *Troilus and Criseyde* (Oxford: Clarendon Press, 1992),
379–80; Clare R. Kinney, 'Lost in Translation: The Vicissitudes of the
Heroine and the Emasculation of the Reader in a Seventeenth-Century
Paraphrase of *Troilus and Criseyde*', *Exemplaria* 5 (1993), 343–62.
27 Wright, *Seventeenth-Century Modernisation*, 238.
28 On Kynaston's translation see Lawrence Ryan, 'Chaucer's Criseyde in Neo-
Latin Dress', *English Literary Renaissance* 17 (1987), 288–302; J. W. Binns,
*Intellectual Culture in Elizabethan and Jacobean England: The Latin Writings of
the Age* (Leeds: Francis Cairns, 1990), 253–7; Richard Beadle, 'The Virtuoso's
Troilus', in Ruth Morse and Barry Windeatt (eds.), *Chaucer Traditions: Studies
in Honour of Derek Brewer* (Cambridge University Press, 1990), 213–33; Tim
William Machan, 'Kynaston's *Troilus*, Textual Criticism, and the Renaissance
Reading of Chaucer', *Exemplaria* 5 (1993), 161–83; Machan, *Textual Criticism*,
44–7.
29 *Amorum Troili et Cresidae libri duo priores Anglico-Latini*, trans. Francis
Kynaston (Oxford, 1635), A3v; translation from Machan, *Textual Criticism*, 45.
30 Machan, *Textual Criticism*, 45.
31 William Cartwright, 'To the Worthy Author on this his *Approved Translation*',
in *Amorum Troili et Cresidae*, 2*r.
32 Francis James, 'Vpon Noble Sir *Francis Kinastons* Translation of the Excellent
Poem of *Troilus* and *Creseide*', in *Amorum Troili et Cresidae*, 3*r.
33 On the use of black letter in Speght's edition of Chaucer see Trigg, *Congenial
Souls*, 130. Speght's publisher, George Bishop, uses black letter for older
writers elsewhere. For example, Richard Hakluyt's *The Principal Navigations,
Voyages, Traffiques and Discoveries of the English Nation* (London, 1599–1600),
printed by Bishop, Ralph Newberry, and Robert Barker, includes a quotation
from the opening of *The Knight's Tale*, printed in black letter, and this type
is also used for quotations from Tacitus' *Annals*, Bede's Latin *Historia*,
and William of Malmesbury's *Gesta Regum Anglorum* (*Principal Navigations*,
124–5).
34 Zachary Lesser, 'Typographic Nostalgia: Playreading, Popularity and the
Meanings of Black Letter', in Marta Straznicky (ed.), *The Book of the Play:
Playwrights, Stationers, and Readers in Early Modern England* (Amherst:
University of Massachusetts Press, 2006), 99–126.
35 Sidney, *Apology*, 110.
36 Bodleian Rawlinson MS Misc. 1, cited from Joseph Haslewood, *Ancient
Critical Essays upon English Poets and Poesy*, vol. 2 (London: Ralph Triphook,
1815), 249.
37 Haslewood, *Ancient Critical Essays*, 247.
38 *Discoveries*, ed. Lorna Hutson, in *CBJ*, vol. 7, ll. 1281–2.
39 Cummings, *Edmund Spenser*, 147.
40 Kenelm Digby, 'A Discourse Concerning Edmund Spenser', *ibid.*, 148.
41 Craig Berry, '"Sundrie Doubts": Vulnerable Understanding and Dubious
Origins in Spenser's Continuation of the *Squire's Tale*', in Krier, *Refiguring*

Chaucer, 106–27 (107). On this issue see also William J. Kennedy, 'Spenser's Squire's Literary History', in Patrick Cheney and Lauren Silberman (eds.), *Worldmaking Spenser: Explorations in the Early Modern Age* (Lexington: University Press of Kentucky, 2000), 45–62.

42 *OED* cankerworm, *n.* 1.

43 See *Polimanteia, or The Meanes Lawfull and Unlawfull, to Judge of the Fall of a Common-wealth* (Cambridge, 1595), R3r.

44 *OED* cankerworm, *n.* 1–2. *OED*'s earliest usage is from 1580, but it appears in a figurative sense in Thomas Norton's *Orations of Arsanes against Philip the Treacherous Kyng of Macedone* (London, 1560), D2r ('an enemy of vertue, a stayne and canker woorme of princely maiestie'). The use of 'canker' itself is older: see *OED* canker, *n.* 3, 4.

45 See David A. Lawton, *Chaucer's Narrators* (Woodbridge: Boydell and Brewer, 1985), 107; William Kamowski, 'Trading the "Knotte" for Loose Ends: The *Squire's Tale* and the Poetics of Chaucerian Fragments', *Style* 31 (1997), 391–412 (391).

46 *Chaucer's Piller, Being his Master Peece, Called the Squiers Tale; Wch Hath Binn Given Lost, for Almost Thease Three Hundred Yeares: But Now Found Out, and Brought to Light by John Lane*, Bodleian MS Ashmole 53, fol. iʸ. This is a 1630 revision of a continuation of *The Squire's Tale* originally written in 1616; the earlier version is preserved as Bodleian MS Douce 170. The manuscripts were published by F. J. Furnivall in *John Lane's Continuation of The Squire's Tale* (London: Chaucer Society, 1887), most of the editorial work having been carried out by Angelina F. Parker.

47 For detailed discussion of this point see Berry, 'Sundrie Doubts', 116.

48 See *ibid.*, 118. Elizabeth Scala, *Absent Narratives, Manuscript Textuality and Literary Structure in Late Medieval England* (Basingstoke: Palgrave Macmillan, 2002), 83, summarises editorial attempts to 'gloss over' this problem in *The Squire's Tale*.

49 See Jonathan Goldberg, *Endlesse Worke: Spenser and the Structures of Discourse* (Baltimore, Md.: Johns Hopkins University Press, 1981), 43.

50 See, for instance, ll. 35–41, 103–9, 283–7, 401–8. On narration in *The Squire's Tale* see Lawton, *Chaucer's Narrators*, 106–29; Shirley Sharon-Zisser, 'The *Squire's Tale* and the Limits of Non-Mimetic Fiction', *Chaucer Review* 26 (1992), 377–94; Kamowski, 'Trading the "Knotte"'; Goldberg, *Endlesse Worke*, 35–41; Scala, *Absent Narratives*, 71–98.

51 'Trading the "Knotte"', 403.

52 See Ariosto, *Orlando Furioso in English Heroical Verse*, trans. John Harington (London, 1591), 1.78–9 and 42.34–5; Boiardo, *Orlando Inamorato ... Done into English Heroicall Verse*, trans. R.T. (London, 1598), G4v–H1r. For discussion see Peter V. Marinelli, 'Ariosto, Lodovico' and Charles Ross, 'Boiardo, Matteo Maria', in *The Spenser Encyclopedia*, gen. ed. A. C. Hamilton (University of Toronto Press, 1990), 56–7, 100–1.

53 Berry, '"Sundrie Doubts"', 121.

54 *Ibid.*

55 On attitudes towards Chaucer's 'racier accomplishments' see also Lars Engle, *Shakespearean Pragmatism: Market of his Time* (University of Chicago Press, 1993), 135–7.

56 Harrington, 'A Preface, or Rather a Briefe Apologie of Poetrie, and of the Author and Translator of this Poem', in *Orlando Furioso*, ¶7r.

57 J. B. Leishman (ed.), *The Three Parnassus Plays, 1598–1601* (London: Nicholson and Watson, 1949), ll. 934–40. All references are to this edition. The play survives in Bodleian MS Rawlinson D 398; variations from the manuscript in Leishman's edition are footnoted below.

58 'Against' is supplied by Leishman from Chaucer.

59 Leishman here substitutes Chaucer's 'scriuenly' for the manuscript's 'scrivener'.

60 Leishman argues that this insertion 'improves both the sense and the metre' but notes that 'the author has deliberately loosened it in places, to suggest what he and most of his contemporaries regarded as the "rudeness" of Chaucer' (190–1).

61 See *Horace: Satires, Epistles, Ars Poetica*, ed. and trans. H. Rushton Fairclough, Loeb Classical Library (London: William Heinemann, 1926), 450–1; Windeatt, *Troilus*, iii.

62 *OED* jape, *n.* i.a, *n.* 2; Norman Davis et al., *A Chaucer Glossary* (Oxford: Clarendon Press, 1979), 81.

63 See *OED* jape, *n.* i.c; jape, *v.* 2.a, 2.b. Searches of *LION* and *EEBO* suggest that the word was current in non-sexual contexts until the 1540s, but that it fell rapidly out of use in the following decades. On its sexual uses see Gordon Williams, *A Dictionary of Sexual Language and Imagery in Shakespearean and Stuart Literature*, 3 vols. (London: Athlone Press, 1994), 2: 730, who – like *OED* – cites a poem dated to the 1380s.

64 *The Passionate Morrice*, in *Tell-Trothes New-Yeares Gift and The Passionate Morrice*, ed. F .J. Furnivall (London: New Shakespeare Society, 1896), 94–5.

65 For discussion and examples see Engle, *Shakespearean Pragmatism*, 136; Williams, *Dictionary*, 2: 734.

66 Thomas Ravenscroft, *Melismata. Musicall Phansies. Fitting the Court, Citie, and Countrey Humours* (London, 1611), Div. The poem is found, for example, in Rosenbach Museum and Library, Philadelphia, MS 1083/15, p. 3. I am very grateful to Joel Swann for this reference.

67 *Brittons Bowre of Delights* (London, 1591), C4r.

68 Paula Glatzer, *The Complaint of the Poet: The Parnassus Plays. A Critical Study of the Trilogy Performed at St. John's College, Cambridge, 1598/99–1601/2* (Salzburg: Institut für Englische Sprache und Literatur, Universität Salzburg, 1977), 151.

69 As Sasha Roberts argues in *Reading Shakespeare's Poems in Early Modern England* (Basingstoke: Palgrave Macmillan, 2003), both Gullio and Shakespeare 'are assumed to have a taste for light literature that differentiates them from "schollers"' (68).

70 On Gower's reputation see John Fisher, *John Gower: Moral Philosopher and Friend of Chaucer* (New York University Press, 1964), 1–36; Neil Gilroy-Scott,

'John Gower's Reputation: Literary Allusions from the Early Fifteenth Century to the Time of *Pericles*', *The Yearbook of English Studies* 1 (1971), 30–47; Derek Pearsall, 'The Gower Tradition', in *Gower's Confessio Amantis: Responses and Reassessments*, ed. Alastair J. Minnis (Cambridge: D. S. Brewer, 1983), 179–97; Siân Echard, 'Introduction: Gower's Reputation', in Siân Echard (ed.), *A Companion to Gower* (Cambridge: D. S. Brewer, 2004), 1–22.

71 Barbara Mowat, 'The Theater and Literary Culture', in John D. Cox and David Scott Kastan (eds.), *A New History of Early English Drama* (New York: Columbia University Press, 1997), 213–30 (221). For useful accounts of Gower in *Pericles* see Gilroy-Scott, 'John Gower's Reputation'; F. David Hoeniger, 'Gower and Shakespeare in *Pericles*', *Shakespeare Quarterly* 33 (1982), 461–79; Richard Hillman, 'Shakespeare's Gower and Gower's Shakespeare: The Larger Debt of *Pericles*', *Shakespeare Quarterly* 36 (1985), 427–37; Stephen Dickey, 'Language and Role in *Pericles*', *English Literary Renaissance* 16 (1986), 550–6; Helen Cooper, '"This Worthy Olde Writer": *Pericles* and Other Gowers', 1592–1640', in Echard, *A Companion to Gower*, 99–113; Stephen J. Lynch, *Shakespearean Intertextuality: Studies in Selected Sources and Plays* (Westport, Conn.: Greenwood Press, 1998), 61–82; Kelly Jones, '"The Quick and the Dead": Performing the Poet Gower in *Pericles*', in Martha W. Driver and Sid Ray (eds.), *Shakespeare and the Middle Ages: Essays on the Performance and Adaptation of the Plays with Medieval Sources or Settings* (Jefferson, NC: McFarland, 2009), 201–14; R. F. Yeager, 'Shakespeare as Medievalist: What it Means for Performing *Pericles*', in Driver and Ray, *Shakespeare and the Middle Ages*, 215–31. On the play's 'medievalism' see also Howard Felperin, 'Shakespeare's Miracle Play', *Shakespeare Quarterly* 18 (1967), 363–74; Cooper, *Shakespeare and the Medieval World* (London: Arden Shakespeare, 2010), esp. 196–203.

72 Summit, *Memory's Library*, 190.

73 Hoeniger, 'Gower and Shakespeare', 464.

74 See Graham Parry, *The Trophies of Time: English Antiquarians of the Seventeenth Century* (Oxford: Clarendon Press, 1995); Stuart Piggott, *Ancient Britons and the Antiquarian Imagination: Ideas from the Renaissance to the Regency* (London: Thames and Hudson, 1989), 13–35; Vine, *In Defiance of Time*, esp. 1–21; Summit, *Memory's Library*.

75 John Earle, *Micro-cosmographie, or, A Peece of the World Discovered in Essayes and Characters* (London, 1628), C1v–C2r.

76 Vine, *In Defiance of Time*, 3, 5.

77 John Aubrey, 'An Essay Towards the Description of the North Division of Wiltshire', in John Edward Jackson (ed.), *Wiltshire: The Topographical Collections of John Aubrey* (Devizes: Wiltshire Archaeological and Natural History Society, 1862), 4.

78 Richard Bauman and Charles L. Briggs, *Voices of Modernity: Language Ideologies and the Politics of Inequality* (Cambridge University Press, 2003), 74.

79 Suzanne Gossett (ed.), *Pericles* (London: Arden Shakespeare, 2004), 1.0.1–16. All citations are to this edition.

80 The phrase also occurs in John Bridges, *A Defence of the Government Established in the Church of Englande* (London, 1587), 126 and George Abbot, *The Reasons Which Doctour Hill hath Brought, for the Upholding of Papistry* (London, 1604), 4.

81 John Gower, *Confessio Amantis*, ed. Russell A. Peck, 3 vols. (Kalamazoo, Mich.: Medieval Institute Publications, Western Michigan University, 2000), 1: 203; M. P. Tilley, *A Dictionary of the Proverbs in England in the Sixteenth and Seventeenth Centuries* (Ann Arbor, Mich.: University of Michigan Press, 1950), C934.

82 *Greenes Vision Written at the Instant of his Death* (London, 1592); for a recent account of this work, and its engagements with late-medieval literary culture, see Jeremy Dimmick, 'Gower, Chaucer and the Art of Repentance in Robert Greene's *Vision*', *Review of English Studies*, ns 57 (2006), 456–73.

83 George Wilkins, 'The Argument of the Whole Historie', in *The Painfull Adventures of Pericles Prince of Tyre* (London, 1608), A3r. For discussion of Gower's picture see Hoeniger, 'Gower and Shakespeare', 463; Yeager, 'Shakespeare as Medievalist', 220.

84 See, for instance, Felperin, 'Shakespeare's Miracle Play', 365; Yeager, 'Shakespeare as Medievalist', 218–19, both of whom overlook or downplay the use of dumb shows in plays contemporaneous with *Pericles*.

85 On the tournament and the changes made to the source narrative see Cooper, *Shakespeare's Medieval World*, 200–1.

86 'Ode to Himself', ed. Colin Burrow, in *CBJ*, vol. 6, ll. 21–5.

87 *Pericles* was revived at the Globe on 10 June 1631. See N. W. Bawcutt (ed.), *The Control and Censorship of Caroline Drama: The Records of Sir Henry Herbert, Master of the Revels 1623–73* (Oxford: Clarendon Press, 1996), 173. On the play in the 1630s see Lucy Munro, 'A Neglected Allusion to *Pericles* and *Hengist King of Kent* in Performance', *Notes & Queries* ns 51 (2004), 307–10.

88 See also Earle's character of 'A Criticke' in the same volume: 'His owne Phrase is a Miscellanie of old words, deceas'd long before the *Caesars*, and entoomb'd by *Varro*, and the modern'st man hee followes is *Plautus*' (G5v–G6r).

89 'An Antiquary', in *The Genuine Remains in Verse and Prose of Mr. Samuel Butler*, 2 vols. (London, 1759), 2: 95.

90 G. Blakemore Evans (ed.), *The Plays and Poems of William Cartwright* (Madison: University of Wisconsin Press, 1951), ll. 462, 466–7.

91 See l. 560. For detailed summaries of Moth's borrowings from Chaucer see Friedrich Gerber, *The Sources of William Cartwright's Comedy The Ordinary: A Complementary Study to the Earlier Stuart-Drama* [*sic*] (Berne: Gustav Grunau, 1909); Erma R. Gebhardt, 'An Edition of William Cartwright's *The Ordinary*. With Critical Introduction and Notes', unpublished B.Litt. thesis, Oxford, 1932.

92 See *OED* liking, *adj.*¹ 1.

93 Bartholomew Robertson, 'To the Reader', in *Adagia in Latine and English Containing Five Hundred Proverbs* (London, 1621), A3v.

3 Archaic style in religious writing: immutability, controversy, prophecy

1 Thomas Nashe, *Strange Newes, of the Intercepting Certaine Letters* (London, 1592), K1v.

2 See *OED* horrisonant, *adj.*

3 James Holstun, *Ehud's Dagger: Class Struggle in the English Revolution* (London: Verso, 2000), 189.

4 Sebastian Franck, *The Forbidden Fruit or A Treatise of the Tree of Knowledge of Good & Evill* (London, 1640), 128–9.

5 For general accounts of archaism in the Protestant Bible see A. C. Partridge, *English Biblical Translation* (London: André Deutsch, 1973), 115–38; Gerald Hammond, *The Making of the English Bible* (Manchester: Carcanet New Press, 1982), 25–6, 175–6; Manfred Görlach, *Introduction to Early Modern English* (Cambridge University Press, 1991), 25; Matti Rissanen, 'Syntax', in Roger Lass (ed.), *The Cambridge History of the English Language: 1476–1776* (Cambridge University Press, 1999), 187–331 (224, 276); Stephen Prickett, 'Language Within Language: The King James Steamroller', in Hannibal Hamlin and Norman W. Jones (eds.), *The King James Bible After 400 Years: Literary, Linguistic, and Cultural Influences* (Cambridge University Press, 2010), 27–44 (esp. 30–3).

6 See Partridge, *English Biblical Translation*, 118; Görlach, *Introduction to Early Modern English*, 80.

7 On the receding use of 'thou' in Early Modern English, and its use in liturgical texts, see Roger Brown and Albert Gilman, 'The Pronouns of Power and Solidarity', in Thomas A. Sebeok (ed.), *Style in Language* (Cambridge, Mass.: MIT Press, 1960), 253–76; Kathleen M. Wales, 'Thou and You in Early Modern English: Brown and Gilman Re-Appraised', *Studia Linguistica* 37 (1983), 107–125; Jonathan Hope, *The Authorship of Shakespeare's Plays: A Socio-Linguistic Study* (Cambridge University Press, 1994), 54–66; Charles Barber, *Early Modern English*, 2nd edn (Edinburgh University Press, 1997), 154–6; Penelope Freeman, *Power and Passion in Shakespeare's Pronouns: Interrogating 'You' and 'Thou'* (Aldershot: Ashgate, 2007), 13–15. For further discussion see also Chapter 5.

8 SP, 114; Hammond, *Making of the English Bible*, 22–9. Hammond notes that the King James Bible not only retains but actually augments the use of 'and' to translate *waw* (25).

9 See Terttu Nevalainen, 'Motivated Archaism: The Use of Affirmative Periphrastic *do* in Early Modern Liturgical Prose', in Dieter Kastovsky (ed.), *Historical English Syntax* (Berlin: Mouton de Gruyter, 1991), 303–20.

10 Compare Miles Coverdale's translation, *Biblia: The Byble, that is, the Holy Scrypture of the Olde and New Testament, Faithfully Translated in to Englyshe* (London, 1535).

11 See Richard Baxter, *Reliquiæ Baxterianæ, or, Mr. Richard Baxters Narrative of the Most Memorable Passages of his Life and Times* (London, 1696), 272, 314, 318.

12 William Barton, *A View of Many Errors and Som Gross Absurdities in the Old Translation of the Psalms in English Metre* (London, 1656), A4r–v. Barton lists both the 'Improper, unseemly and non-sensical passages in the old *Psalm-book*' and its 'Old, obsolete, clip't & coined words, bald words, and botches' (see B1r–v). See also the prefatory material to his *Psalms and Hymns Composed and Fitted for the Present Occasion of Publick Thanks-giving, October 24, 1651* (London, 1651), A2r–A6r.

13 Beth Quitslund, *The Reformation in Rhyme: Sternhold, Hopkins and the English Metrical Psalter, 1547–1603* (Aldershot: Ashgate, 2008), 71. Quitslund prefers a 1547 date for the first, undated, edition of the Psalms (see 27–8); others have dated them as late as 1549 and therefore question whether the metre originated with Sternhold, given that Robert Crowley's metrical *Psalter of David* appeared in the same year. See, for instance, Hannibal Hamlin, 'Piety and Poetry: English Psalms from Miles Coverdale to Mary Sidney', in Mike Pincombe and Cathy Shrank (eds.), *The Oxford Handbook of Tudor Literature, 1485–1603* (Oxford University Press, 2009), 203–21 (207).

14 Edward Doughtie, *Lyrics from English Airs* (Cambridge, Mass.: Harvard University Press, 1970), 17 (his emphasis). For a summary of the debate see Hannibal Hamlin, *Psalm Culture and Early Modern English Literature* (Cambridge University Press, 2004), 24; on the sixteenth-century Psalm tradition see also Rivkah Zim, *English Metrical Psalms: Poetry as Praise and Prayer, 1535–1601* (Cambridge University Press, 1987).

15 On these attacks see Ramie Targoff, *Common Prayer: The Language of Public Devotion in Early Modern England* (University of Chicago Press, 2001), 82–4.

16 Joseph Hall, *Holy Observations. Lib. 1. Also Some Fewe of Davids Psalmes Metaphrased, for a Taste of the Rest* (London, 1607), G4v.

17 George Wither, *A Preparation to the Psalter* (London, 1619), 3.

18 Joseph Hall, *Epistles: The First Volume* (London, 1608), L2r.

19 David Norton, *A Textual History of the King James Bible* (Cambridge University Press, 2005), 7, quoting (in modern spelling), BL MS Add. 28721, fol. 24r.

20 Responding to Tyndale's translation, the hostile Robert Ridley, chaplain to the Bishop of London, complained, 'By this translation shal we losse al thies Christian wordes, penance, charite, confession, grace, prest, chirche, which he alway calleth a congregation' (A. W. Pollard, *Records of the English Bible* (London: Oxford University Press, 1911), 124, quoting BL MS Cotton Cleopatra E.v.362[b]). See also Thomas More's attack on Tyndale in *A Dialogue Concerning Heresies* (1529), and the subsequent exchange of pamphlets between More and Tyndale. On these disputes see, among others, Partridge, *English Biblical Translation*, 40–7; David Daniell, *William Tyndale: A Biography* (New Haven, Conn.: Yale University Press, 1994), 261–80; David Norton, *A History of the English Bible as Literature* (Cambridge University Press, 2000), 22–6; Ilona N. Rashkow, 'The Renaissance', in John F. A. Sawyer (ed.), *The Blackwell Companion to the Bible and Culture* (Oxford: Blackwell, 2006), 54–68 (56–62); Gergely Juhász, 'Antwerp Bible Translations

in the King James Bible', in Hamlin and Jones, *King James Bible*, 100–123 (108–9).

21 Pollard, *Records*, 339.

22 On this point see Gerald Hammond, 'Translations of the Bible', in Michael Hattaway (ed.), *A Companion to English Renaissance Literature and Culture*, 2nd edn (Oxford: Blackwell, 2008), 165–75 (169).

23 Pollard, *Records*, 297, quoting what is now NA, SP 12/48, fol. 9.

24 Matthew Parker, *The Whole Psalter Translated into English Metre* (London, 1567), B3v. 'Seache' appears to be a variant spelling of 'seek', here meaning to harass or afflict (*OED* seek, v. 6.a).

25 Gregory Martin, 'The Preface to the Reader', in *The New Testament of Jesus Christ, Translated Faithfully into English, out of the Authentical Latin* (Rheims, 1582), c3r.

26 *The Text of the New Testament of Jesus Christ, Translated out of the Vulgar Latine by the Papists of the Traiterous Seminarie at Rhemes* (London, 1589), *4r, C4v–C5r.

27 James Hyatt, *The Preachers President, or, The Master and Scholler* (London, 1625), 13.

28 For a summary of controversial terms see Partridge, *English Biblical Translation*, 41–2.

29 William Rainolds, *A Refutation of Sundry Reprehensions, Cavils, and False Sleightes, by which M. Whitaker Laboureth to Deface the Late English Translation, and Catholike Annotations of the New Testament* (Rheims, 1583), 277–8.

30 *A Treatise of Gods Effectual Calling*, trans. Henry Holland (London, 1603), 125.

31 Barton, *View*, A4r.

32 Richard Baxter, *An Accompt of all the Proceedings of the Commissioners . . . for the Review of the Book of Common Prayer* (London, 1661), 6.

33 *Reliquiae Baxterianae*, 314.

34 E.W. [Edward Whiston?], *The Life and Death of Mr. Henry Jessy* (London, 1671), 55; the square brackets around 'occupy' are Whiston's.

35 Norton, *History*, 109.

36 Hall, *Epistles*, L2r; Wither, *Preparation to the Psalter*, 68, 9; see also John Donne's complaint in 'Upon the Translation of the Psalmes by Sir *Philip Sydney*, and the Countess of Pembroke his Sister' that 'these Psalmes are become / So well attyr'd abroad, so ill at home' (*The Complete English Poems of John Donne*, ed. C. A. Patrides (London: Dent, 1985), ll. 37–8).

37 King, *The Psalmes of David, from the New Translation of the Bible Turned into Meter* (London, 1651), A2v, A3r. See also Richard Goodridge, *The Psalter, or, Psalms of David Paraphras'd in Verse Set to New Tunes* (Oxford, 1684), a6v–a7r, who quotes King in his rejection of 'the Verse of *seven* Feet' (a7r).

38 I. M. Green, *Print and Protestantism in Early Modern England* (Oxford University Press, 2000), 549.

39 Christopher Highley, *Catholics Writing the Nation in Early Modern Britain and Ireland* (Oxford University Press, 2008), 1. On English Catholicism and

national identity see also Arthur F. Marotti (ed.), *Catholicism and Anti-Catholicism in Early Modern English Texts* (London: Macmillan, 1999); Highley, '"The Lost British Lamb": English Catholic Exiles and the Problem of Britain', in David J. Baker and Willy Maley (eds.), *British Identities and English Renaissance Literature* (Cambridge University Press, 2002), 37–50; Frances E. Dolan, 'Gender and the "Lost" Spaces of Catholicism', *Journal of Interdisciplinary History* 32 (2002), 641–65; Ethan Shagan (ed.), *Catholics and the 'Protestant Nation': Religious Politics and Identity in Early Modern England* (Manchester University Press, 2005); Felicity Heal, 'Appropriating History: Catholic and Protestant Polemics and the National Past', *Huntington Library Quarterly* 68 (2005), 109–32; Ronald Corthell, Frances E. Dolan, Christopher Highley and Arthur F. Marotti (eds.), *Catholic Culture in Early Modern England* (Notre Dame, Ind.: University of Notre Dame Press, 2007).

40 See Chapter 1.

41 See Nancy Pollard Brown, 'Southwell, Robert [St Robert Southwell] (1561–1595)', *ODNB*: www.oxforddnb.com/view/article/26064 (accessed 19 February 2012); Anne Sweeney, *Robert Southwell: Snow in Arcadia: Redrawing the English Lyric Landscape, 1586–95* (Manchester University Press, 2006).

42 See Dorothy L. Latz, 'Neglected Writings by Recusant Women, Part I – Poetry: 17th Century English Metaphysical Poetesses Gertrude More, Clementina Cary, Gertrude Aston Thimelby and Katherine Thimelby Aston', in Dorothy L. Latz (ed.), *Neglected English Literature: Recusant Writings of the 16th–17th Centuries: Papers from the Recusant Sessions of the International Medieval Congresses at Western Michigan University, Kalamazoo, Michigan (USA), 1990–1994* (Salzburg: Institut für Anglistik und Amerikanistik Universität Salzburg, 1997), 11–24 (14); Julia Bolton Holloway, 'More, Helen (1606–1633)', *ODNB*: www.oxforddnb.com/view/article/19178 (accessed 19 February 2012); Heather Wolfe, 'Reading Bells and Loose Papers: Reading and Writing Practices of the English Benedictine Nuns of Cambrai and Paris', in Victoria E. Burke and Jonathan Gibson (eds.), *Early Modern Women's Manuscript Writing* (Aldershot: Ashgate, 2004), 135–56; Arthur F. Marotti (ed.), *Gertrude More* (Aldershot: Ashgate, 2009), ix–xviii. For a helpful overview of the English convents see Caroline Bowden, 'The English Convents in Exile and Questions of National Identity *c.*1600–1688', in David Worthington (ed.), *British and Irish Emigrants and Exiles in Europe, 1603–1688* (Leiden: Brill, 2010), 297–314.

43 *An Humble Supplication to her Majestie to Answere to the Late Proclamation* ([English Secret Press], 1600), A5r. The tract was written in 1591, is dated 1595, and was not printed until 1600.

44 I quote the 1582 Rheims translation, cited above (n. 25).

45 Sweeney, *Robert Southwell*, 4–5.

46 On Southwell's reputation see Scott R. Pilarz, *Robert Southwell and the Mission of Literature, 1561–1595: Writing Reconciliation* (Aldershot: Ashgate, 2004), xvii–xxi; Alison Shell, *Catholicism, Controversy and the English Literary Imagination, 1558–1660* (Cambridge University Press, 1999), 58–99.

47 Sweeney, *Robert Southwell*, 12.

48 Bodleian Rawlinson MS Misc. 1; I quote the edition in Joseph Haslewood, *Ancient Critical Essays upon English Poets and Poesy*, vol. 2 (London: Ralph Triphook, 1815), 250.

49 Robert Southwell, *Collected Poems*, ed. Peter Davidson and Anne Sweeney (Manchester: Carcanet, 2007), 45.

50 Alison Shell, *Oral Culture and Catholicism in Early Modern England* (Cambridge University Press, 2007), 84.

51 On Southwell's publication in manuscript see Davidson and Sweeney, *Collected Poems*, 147–9.

52 *Ibid.*, 12.

53 *The Art of English Poesy by George Puttenham: A Critical Edition*, ed. Frank Whigham and Wayne A. Rebhorn (Ithaca, NY: Cornell University Press, 2007), 168.

54 For further discussion see Sandra A. Glass, 'The Saxonists' Influence on Seventeenth-Century English Literature', in Carl T. Berkhout and Milton McC. Gatch (eds.), *Anglo-Saxon Scholarship: The First Three Centuries* (Boston, Mass.: G. K. Hall, 1982), 91–105 (99–101).

55 John Beaumont, 'To his Late Maiesty, Concerning the True Forme of English Poetry', in *Bosworth-field with a Taste of the Variety of Other Poems* (London, 1629), 109.

56 William Loe, *Songs of Sion* ([Hamburg], 1620), A3r.

57 Sadia Abbas, 'Polemic and Paradox in Robert Southwell's Lyric Poems', *Criticism* 45 (2003), 453–82 (457–8). On Southwell's style see also F. W. Brownlow, *Robert Southwell* (New York: Twayne, 1996), esp. chaps. 4 and 5; Brian Oxley, 'The Relation Between Southwell's Neo-Latin and English Poetry', *Recusant History* 17 (1985), 201–17; Oxley, '"Simples are by Compounds Farre Exceld": Southwell's Longer Latin Poems and St. Peter's Complaint', *Recusant History* 17 (1985), 330–40.

58 Bowden, 'English Convents', 297, 309. On the convents and national identity see also Marie-Louise Coolahan, 'Identity Politics and Nuns' Writing', *Women's Writing* 14 (2007), 306–20.

59 Wolfe, 'Reading', is particularly helpful on Baker's instructions; see also Holloway, 'More'; Bowden, 'English Convents', 308–9.

60 See Wolfe, 'Reading', 143.

61 See *The Spiritual Exercises of the Most Vertuous and Religious D. Gertrude More of the Holy Order of S. Bennet and English Congregation of Our Ladies of Comfort in Cambray* (Paris, 1658), part 1, 7–112; part 2, 1–237 (the confessions have separate pagination).

62 *Ibid.*, 2: 5–6.

63 Marotti, *Gertrude More*, xvi.

64 Elizabeth Clarke and Jonathan Gibson, Introduction to Jill Seal Millman and Gillian Wright (eds.), *Early Modern Women's Manuscript Poetry* (Manchester University Press, 2005), 7. This tradition stretches into the later seventeenth century in the work of poets such as Julia Palmer: see *ibid.*, 169–81.

65 A note claims 'This Booke was written at Chelsey in the yeare 1625' (*A Ladies Legacy to her Daughters* (London, 1645), 3).

66 M^{ris}. *Cookes Meditations* (London, 1650), 14–16.

67 Dolan, 'Gender'; Milton, 'A Qualified Intolerance: The Limits and Ambiguities of Early Stuart Anti-Catholicism', in Marotti, *Catholicism and Anti-Catholicism*, 85–115.

68 Dolan, 'Gender', 646, 647.

69 Angus Fletcher, *The Prophetic Moment: An Essay on Spenser* (University of Chicago Press, 1971), 4, 5.

70 Sue Wiseman, 'Unsilent Instruments and the Devil's Cushions: Authority in Seventeenth-Century Women's Prophetic Discourse', in Isobel Armstrong (ed.), *New Feminist Discourses: Critical Essays on Theories and Texts* (London: Routledge, 1992), 176–96 (189).

71 Erica Longfellow, *Women and Religious Writing in Early Modern England* (Cambridge University Press, 2004), 172.

72 The best account of Hawkins and her prophecies is that of Longfellow in *Women and Religious Writing*, 155–8.

73 John Williams, Bishop of Lincoln, to Dudley Carleton, Viscount Dorchester, 28 April 1629, SP 16/141, no. 63.

74 John Hacket, *Scrina Reservata: A Memorial Offer'd to the Great Deservings of John Williams, D.D.* (London, 1693), 2: 47.

75 Williams to Carleton, 5 May 1629, NA, SP 16/142, no. 19. Hacket provides a detailed summary of Tookey's retraction (*ibid.*, 2: 47–8).

76 NA, SP 16/142, no. 19. The sample is on a different stock of paper and appears to be written in a different hand.

77 Hacket, *Scrina Reservata*, 2: 47.

78 See David Como, 'Women, Prophecy, and Authority in Early Stuart Puritanism', *Huntington Library Quarterly* 61 (1998), 203–22.

79 The most important accounts include Phyllis Mack, *Visionary Women: Ecstatic Prophecy in Seventeenth-Century England* (Berkeley: University of California Press, 1992); Diane Purkiss, 'Producing the Voice, Consuming the Body: Women Prophets of the Seventeenth Century', in Isobel Grundy and Susan Wiseman (eds.), *Women, Writing, History, 1640–1740* (London: Batsford, 1992), 139–58; Megan Matchinske, 'Holy Hatred: Formations of the Gendered Subject in English Apocalyptic Writing, 1625–1651', *English Literary History* 60 (1993), 349–77; Kate Chedgzoy, 'Female Prophecy in the Seventeenth Century: The Instance of Anna Trapnel', in William Zunder and Suzanne Trill (eds.), *Writing the English Renaissance* (London: Longman, 1996), 239–54; Hilary Hinds, *God's Englishwomen: Seventeenth-Century Radical Sectarian Writing and Feminist Criticism* (Manchester University Press, 1996); Diane Watt, *Secretaries of God: Women Prophets in Late Medieval and Early Modern England* (Woodbridge: D. S. Brewer, 1997).

80 See NA, SP 16/248, no. 93, verses beginning 'God of the Earth'.

81 Collins, *Divine Songs and Meditacions* (London, 1653), 63.

82 See Trapnel, *The Cry of a Stone* (London, 1654), a2r. On Trapnel and the Fifth Monarchists see Susannah B. Mintz, 'The Specular Self of *Anna Trapnel's Report and Plea*', *Pacific Coast Philology* 25 (2000), 1–16; Pamela S. Hammons, *Poetic Resistance: English Women Writers and the Early Modern Lyric* (Aldershot: Ashgate, 2001), 58, 88–90; David Loewenstein, *Representing Revolution in Milton and his Contemporaries: Religion, Politics, and Polemics in Radical Puritanism* (Cambridge University Press, 2001), 116–17; Ann Hughes, '"Not Gideon of Old": Anna Trapnel and Oliver Cromwell', *Cromwelliana* Series 2 (2005), 77–96.

83 *Ehud's Dagger*, 274 (Holstun's emphasis); see also Bernard Capp, *The Fifth Monarchy Men: A Study in Seventeenth-Century English Millenarianism* (London: Faber, 1972) and 'The Fifth Monarchists and Popular Millenarianism', in J. F. McGregor and Barry Reay (eds.), *Radical Religion in the English Revolution* (Oxford University Press, 1984), 165–89.

84 Richard Flecknoe, *Aenigmaticall Characters* (London, 1658), 28; for comment see Capp, *Fifth Monarchy Men*, 180; Holstun, *Ehud's Dagger*, 275.

85 *The Journal of George Fox*, ed. Norman Penney, 2 vols. (Cambridge University Press, 1911), 1: 54. See also the reference to a Quaker's 'signal termes as *thou* and *thee*' in John Deacon, *An Exact History of the Life of James Naylor* (London, 1657), 18. The Quakers' use of thou is also discussed in Richard Farnworth, *The Pure Language of the Spirit of Truth . . . Or, Thee & Thou, in its Place, is the Proper Language to any Single Person Whatsoever* (London, 1655); William Caton, *The Moderate Enquirer* (London, 1658), 51–2; George Fox, *A Battledoor for Teachers & Professors to Learn Singular & Plural; You to Many, and Thou to One: Singular One, Thou; Plural Many, You* (London, 1660) and George Bishop, *New England Judged, not by Man's, but the Spirit of the Lord* (London, 1660), 195–6.

86 Capp, *Fifth Monarchy Men*, 143, citing Historical Manuscripts Commission, *Fifth Report*, Appendix, Part 1 (London: HMSO, 1876), MSS of the Duke of Sutherland, 163.

87 See Barber, *Early Modern English*, 155–6; Capp, *Fifth Monarchy Men*, 143.

88 See Brown and Gilman, 'Pronouns', 265–6; Stephen Howe, *The Personal Pronouns in the Germanic Languages: A Study of Personal Pronoun Morphology and Change in the Germanic Languages from the First Records to the Present Day* (Berlin: de Gruyter, 1996), 172.

89 See, for instance, the final couplet of Herbert's 'The Collar' (analysed in insightful detail by Targoff in *Common Prayer*, 102) and Vaughan's apocalyptic 'Day of Judgement'. On Vaughan and the Fifth Monarchists see Nigel Smith, *Literature and Revolution in England, 1640–1660* (New Haven, Conn.: Yale University Press, 1994), 268–75; Philip G. West, *Henry Vaughan's Silex Scintillans: Scripture Uses* (Oxford University Press, 2001), 153–8, 170–4, 181–6; John Kerrigan, *Archipelagic English: Literature, History, and Politics, 1603–1707* (Oxford University Press, 2008), 196–210.

90 John Reading, *The Ranters Ranting* (London, 1650), 1, 2, 3–4.

91 Winstanley includes poems in common measure in *The Breaking of the Day of God* (1649), *Truth Lifting up his Head* (1649) and *A New Year's Gift for the Parliament and Army* (1650); poems in fourteeners and poulter's measure appear in *The Law of Freedom* (1651). See Thomas N. Corns, Ann Hughes and David Loewenstein (eds.), *The Complete Works of Gerrard Winstanley*, 2 vols. (Oxford University Press, 2009), 1: 188–9, 453–4; 2: 128, 148–9, 312, 359. On the style of Winstanley's poetry see 1: 68–9.

92 *Works*, 1: 189.

93 On Trapnel's use of Ezekiel and Elisha see Achsah Guibbory, 'England's "Biblical" Prophets, 1642–60', in Roger D. Sell and Anthony W. Johnson (eds.), *Writing and Religion in England, 1558–1689: Studies in Community-Making and Cultural Memory* (Aldershot: Ashgate, 2009), 305–26 (314).

94 See Powell, *Tsofer Bepah, or The Bird in the Wing* (London, 1661), sect. 2, 1–26 (H1r–I5v); Llwyd, *Gweithiau Morgan Llwyd o Wynedd*, ed. Thomas E. Ellis, vol. 1 (Bangor: Jarvis and Foster / London, J. M. Dent, 1889), 52–4. All references to Llwyd's works are to this edition unless noted otherwise.

95 See Powell's metrical paraphrase of Jeremiah in *Tsofer Bepah*, sect. 2, 1–26 (H1r–I5v); 'Mr. Powels Hymne', dated 8 October 1650, in *Three Hymnes, or Certain Excellent New Psalms* (London, 1650), 6–8; and 'His Hymn at Christ-Church', dated 18 December 1653, which is printed, with a savage response poem, in Alexander Griffith's *Strena Vavasoriensis, a Nevv-Years-Gift for the Welch Itinerants, or a Hue and Cry after Mr. Vavasor Powell* (London, 1654). Powell's other poems include 'Of ye Late K. Charles of Blessed Memory' (National Library of Wales MS HM2.14/7a, b), to which Katherine Philips wrote a response. See Capp, 51 (with a quotation from the poem); Elizabeth Hageman and Andrea Sununu, '"More copies of it abroad than I could have imagin'd": Further Manuscript Texts of Katherine Philips, "the Matchless Orinda"', *English Manuscript Studies* 5 (1995), 127–69 (with the full text and discussion of its relationship with Philips' poem). A manuscript copy of 'Mr. Feakes Hymne: ~ August ye 11: 1653' is preserved among the Thomason Tracts in the British Library (E710/13).

96 See Hammons, *Poetic Resistance*, 55–99; Longfellow, *Women and Religious Writing*, 149–79; Smith, *Literature and Revolution*, 268–75; Kerrigan, *Archipelagic English*, 202–10. It should be noted that Llwyd's reputation as a writer of Welsh and, in particular, Welsh prose, has always been high.

97 NA, SP 18/66, no. 20.

98 The book was purchased by the Bodleian Library in December 1901 and is catalogued as Bodleian Library S 1.42 Theology; it is hereafter cited as 'Folio'. It was first described by Bertram Dobell in 'A Unique Book', *Notes & Queries*, 9th ser., 8 (Oct. 1901), 319–21; Trapnel is identified as the author in Champlin Burrage, 'Anna Trapnel's Prophecies', *English Historical Review* 26 (1911), 526–35. See also Dobell, 'A Unique Book: Anna Trapnel', *Notes & Queries* 11th ser. 9 (March 1914), 221–2.

99 The prophecies are carefully dated: see Burrage, 'Anna Trapnel's Prophecies', 527.

100 See *ibid.*, 534–5; Longfellow, *Women and Religious Writing*, 171.
101 Matthew Prineas, 'The Discourse of Love and the Rhetoric of Apocalypse in Anna Trapnel's Folio Songs', *Comitatus* 28 (1997), 90–110 (93).
102 Ramona Wray, '"What Say You to [This] Book? ... Is it Yours?": Oral and Collaborative Narrative Trajectories in the Mediated Writings of Anna Trapnel', *Women's Writing* 16 (2009), 408–24. See also Wiseman, 'Unsilent Instruments'; Maria Megro, 'Spiritual Autobiography and Radical Sectarian Women's Discourse: Anna Trapnel and the Bad Girls of the English Revolution', *Journal of Medieval and Early Modern Studies* 34 (2004), 405–37; Marcus Nevitt, *Women and the Pamphlet Culture of Revolutionary England, 1640–1660* (Aldershot: Ashgate, 2006), esp. 1–19.
103 See, for instance, 'An Appendix of the Letter Sent to the Differing Brethren'; among Llwyd's papers in National Library of Wales MS 11433B are a list of names with a cancelled note reading 'who should have the booke of my verse' (pp. 19–20).
104 The final couplet translates as 'O heavy cry we would have made, hadst not thou, O God, / Killed the three who killed thee, to enable us to live': see Raymond Garlick and Roland Mathias (eds.), *Anglo-Welsh Poetry, 1480–1980* (Bridgend: Seren Books, 1984), 72.
105 Longfellow, *Women and Religious Writing*, 172. On Trapnel's 'singing' see also Smith, *Perfection Proclaimed: Language and Literature in English Radical Religion 1640–1660* (Oxford: Clarendon Press, 1989), 50–1; Hammons, *Poetic Resistance*, 56–8, 83–99.
106 See 637, 644, 859.
107 See also Trapnel's use of 'hallelujah' in *Cry of a Stone*, 35.
108 See also Folio, 842, and the attack on 'the National Clergy' in *Cry of a Stone*, 42–3. On Fifth Monarchist attacks on university-educated clergy see Capp, *Fifth Monarchy Men*, 188–9; for a broader account of sectarian attacks see Smith, *Perfection Proclaimed*, 289–95. Winstanley similarly uses the Psalm form to attack the established clergy in *A New Year's Gift*. See *Works*, 2: 140–1.
109 M. H. Abrams, 'Apocalypse: Theme and Variations', in C. A. Patrides and Joseph Wittreich (eds.), *The Apocalypse in English Renaissance Thought and Literature* (Ithaca, NY: Cornell University Press, 1984), 342–68 (343).
110 H. W. Robinson, *Inspiration and Revelation in the Old Testament* (Oxford: Clarendon Press, 1946), 166, 171.
111 Williams to Carleton, NA SP 16/141, no. 63; letter of 21 December 1654, Bodleian Library Rawlinson MS A.21.325, quoted in Burrage, 'Anna Trapnel's Prophecies', 532.
112 Morgan Llwyd, *An Honest Discourse Between Three Neighbours, Touching the Present Government in These Three Nations: Viz. Between Goodman Past, Goodman Present, & Goodman Future* (London, 1655), 2.
113 Capp, *Fifth Monarchy Men*, 136.
114 Folger MS V.a.421, in Nancy Pollard Brown (ed.), *Robert Southwell, S.J., Two Letters and Short Rules of a Good Life* (Charlottesville: University of Virginia Press for the Folger Shakespeare Library, 1973), 81.

4 Staging generations: archaism and the theatrical past

1 Edward Guilpin, 'Satyra Sexta', in *Skialetheia* (London, 1598), E1r.
2 *Hamlet*, ed. Ann Thompson and Neil Taylor (London: Arden Shakespeare, 2006), 1.2.89–90.
3 For a useful overview of Elizabethan dramatists' uses of earlier forms of theatre see Michael O'Connell, 'Continuities Between "Medieval" and "Early Modern" Drama', in Michael Hattaway (ed.), *A New Companion to English Renaissance Literature and Culture*, 2 vols. (Oxford: Wiley Blackwell, 2010), 2: 60–9.
4 See Middleton, *The Roaring Girl*, ed. Coppélia Kahn, in Thomas Middleton, *The Collected Works*, gen. eds. Gary Taylor and John Lavagnino (Oxford University Press, 2007), Epistle, 1–9; Heywood, 'The Epilogue to the Reader', in *The Royall King, and the Loyall Subject* (London, 1637), K3v; Fletcher, *The Noble Gentleman*, ed. L. A. Beaurline, in *The Dramatic Works in the Beaumont and Fletcher Canon*, gen. ed. Fredson Bowers, vol. 3 (Cambridge University Press, 1976), Prologue.
5 Epistle to *The Shepheardes Calender*, ll. 94–5.
6 Harold Bloom, *The Anxiety of Influence: A Theory of Poetry*, 2nd edn (Oxford University Press, 1997), xxiv.
7 Judith Burnett, *Generations: The Time Machine in Theory and Practice* (Aldershot: Ashgate, 2010), 1–2.
8 Sigrid Weigel, 'Familienbande, Phantome und die Vergangenheitspolitik des Generationsdiskurses: Abwehr von und Sehnsucht nach Herkunft', in Ulrike Jureit and Michael Wildt (eds.), *Generationen: Zur Relevanz eines wissenschaftlichen Grundbegriffs* (Hamburg: Hamburger Edition, 2005), 108–26 (117), quoted and translated in Susanne Vees-Gulani and Laurel Cohen-Pfister, 'Introduction: A Generational Approach to German Culture', in *Generational Shifts in Contemporary German Culture* (Rochester, NY: Camden House, 2010), 1–23 (3, 18).
9 On this tradition see Alan B. Spitzer, 'The Historical Problem of Generations', *American Historical Review* 78 (1973), 1353–85; Jane Pilcher, *Age and Generation in Modern Britain* (Oxford University Press, 1995), 22–5, 134–45; June Edmunds and Bryan S. Turner, 'Introduction', in Edmunds and Turner (eds.), *Generational Consciousness, Narrative, and Politics* (Lanham, Md.: Rowman and Littlefield, 2002), 1–12; Vees-Gulani and Cohen-Pfister, 'Introduction'.
10 Karl Mannheim, 'The Problem of Generations', in *Essays on the Sociology of Knowledge* (London: Routledge, 1997), 276–322 (293). For useful discussion of generations in a cultural context see also Vees-Gulani and Cohen-Pfister, *Generational Shifts*; Michael Corsten, 'The Time of Generations', *Time and Society* 8 (1999), 249–72.
11 For recent reappraisals of the date see MacDonald P. Jackson, 'Deciphering a Date and Determining a Date: Anthony Munday's *John a Kent and John a Cumber* and the Original Version of *Sir Thomas More*', *Early Modern Literary Studies* 15.3 (2011), 1–24: www.purl.org/emls/15-3/jackdate.htm (accessed 10

April 2012); John Jowett (ed.), *Sir Thomas More* (London: Arden Shakespeare, 2011), 424–33. For a summary of evidence relating to the authorship see Jowett, *Sir Thomas More*, 415–60.

12 *Bartholomew Fair*, ed. John Creaser, in *CBJ*, vol. 4, Induction, ll. 79–82.

13 On developments within the morality tradition see T. W. Craik, *The Tudor Interlude: Stage, Costume and Acting* (University of Leicester Press, 1958); David Bevington, *From Mankind to Marlowe: Growth of Structure in Popular Drama of Tudor England* (Cambridge, Mass.: Harvard University Press, 1962); Robert A. Potter, *The English Morality Play: Origins, History and Influence of a Dramatic Tradition* (London: Routledge and Kegan Paul, 1975); Darryll Grantley, 'Morality and Interlude Drama', in Peter Brown (ed.), *A Companion to Medieval English Literature and Culture, c.1350–c.1500* (Oxford: Wiley Blackwell, 2009), 473–87; Paul Whitfield White, 'Interludes, Economics, and the Elizabethan Stage', in Mike Pincombe and Cathy Shrank (eds.), *The Oxford Handbook of Tudor Literature, 1485–1603* (Oxford University Press, 2009), 555–70; Ineke Murakami, *Moral Play and Counterpublic: Transformations in Moral Drama, 1465–1599* (New York: Routledge, 2011).

14 Much of this work has centred on Shakespeare, where some of the most influential works include John Dover Wilson, *The Fortunes of Falstaff* (Cambridge University Press, 1943); Bernard Spivack, *Shakespeare and the Allegory of Evil: The History of a Metaphor in Relation to his Major Villains* (New York: Columbia University Press, 1958); Alan C. Dessen, *Shakespeare and the Late Moral Plays* (Lincoln: University of Nebraska Press, 1986). The most thorough examination of Jonson's debt to the morality tradition is Dessen's *Jonson's Moral Comedy* (Evanston, Ill.: Northwestern University Press, 1971); see also Jonathan Haynes, *The Social Relations of Jonson's Theater* (Cambridge University Press, 1992), 8–10, 13–23; Janette Dillon, 'The Blackfriars Theatre and the Indoor Theatres', in Julie Sanders (ed.), *Ben Jonson in Context* (Cambridge University Press, 2010), 124–33 (129–30).

15 *The Staple of News*, ed. Joseph Loewenstein, in *CBJ*, vol. 6, Induction, 0.1SD, 7–8.

16 Thomas Lodge, 'To the Reader of Either Sort', in *Wits Miserie, and the Worlds Madnesse* (London, 1596), A4r.

17 John Gee, *The Foot out of the Snare with a Detection of Sundry Late Practices and Impostures of the Priests and Jesuits in England* (London, 1624), 62–3.

18 Dillon, 'Blackfriars Theatre', 130.

19 *The Devil is an Ass*, ed. Anthony Parr, in *CBJ*, vol. 4, 1.1.43.

20 See Peter Happé (ed.), *The Devil is an Ass* (Manchester University Press, 1994), 59. On the date and auspices of *Histriomastix*, and the appearance of Iniquity in this play, see below. Shakespeare mentions Iniquity in *Richard III*, 3.1.82, and *1 Henry IV*, 2.4.458–9.

21 See Dillon, 'Blackfriars Theatre', 129.

22 Jan Frans van Dijkhuizen, *Devil Theatre: Demonic Possession and Exorcism in English Renaissance Drama* (Cambridge: D. S. Brewer, 2007), 174.

23 On the censorship see Scott McMillin, *The Elizabethan Theatre and The Book of Sir Thomas More* (Ithaca, NY: Cornell University Press, 1987), 74–95; William B. Long, 'The Occasion of *The Book of Sir Thomas More*', in T. H. Howard-Hill (ed.), *Shakespeare and Sir Thomas More: Essays on the Play and its Shakespearean Interest* (Cambridge University Press, 1989), 45–56; Richard Dutton, *Mastering the Revels: The Regulation and Censorship of English Renaissance Drama* (London: Macmillan, 1991), 81–6; Janet Clare, *Art Made Tongue-Tied by Authority: Elizabethan and Jacobean Dramatic Censorship*, 2nd edn (Manchester University Press, 1999), 51–7; Tracey Hill, 'Marked Down for Omission: Censorship and *The Booke of Sir Thomas More*', *Parergon* 17 (1999), 48–65; Jowett, *Sir Thomas More*, 26–9.

24 All references are to Jowett, *Sir Thomas More*.

25 See Giorgio Melchiori and Vittorio Gabrieli (eds.), *Sir Thomas More* (Manchester University Press, 2002), 9–10, 242. For more detailed discussion of the sources of the inset play see Melchiori, 'The Contexualization of Source Materials: The Play within the Play in "Sir Thomas More"', *Le forme del teatro* 3 (Rome: Edizioni di storia e letteratura, 1984), 59–94; Jowett, *Sir Thomas More*, 55–6, 63–8. For further discussion of the role of the acting troupe see Bevington, *Mankind to Marlowe*, 18–19; Charles R. Forker and Joseph Candido, 'Wit, Wisdom and Theatricality in *The Book of Sir Thomas More*', *Shakespeare Studies* 13 (1980), 85–104; Tom Rutter, 'The Actors in *Sir Thomas More*', *Shakespeare Yearbook* 16 (2007), 223–40; Donna B. Hamilton, *Anthony Munday and the Catholics, 1560–1633* (Aldershot: Ashgate, 2005), 120–2; Jowett, *Sir Thomas More*, 84–8.

26 Hamilton, *Anthony Munday*, 121.

27 See 9.72–7, in which More questions the player about the composition of the troupe and their use of doubling.

28 For commentary see Melchiori and Gabrieli, *Sir Thomas More*, 143; Jowett, *Sir Thomas More*, 245.

29 Melchiori and Gabrieli, *Sir Thomas More*, 9. See also Melchiori, 'Contextualization'. On the manuscript (BL Add. MS 26782) and the possibility of a print edition see Trevor N. S. Lennam (ed.), *The Marriage Between Wit and Wisdom* (Oxford: Malone Society, 1971), v–xi.

30 See W. W. Greg (ed.), *The Book of Sir Thomas More* (Oxford: Malone Society, 1911), xix.

31 J. M. Nosworthy (ed.), *Lusty Juventus* (Oxford: Malone Society, 1971), v–xxv.

32 Peter Happé (ed.), *The Trial of Treasure* (Manchester: Malone Society, 2010), esp. xviii–xxii.

33 See Spivack, *Shakespeare*, 136–40; John D. Cox, *The Devil and the Sacred in English Drama, 1350–1642* (Cambridge University Press, 2000), 76–7, 85–6, 101–4.

34 See *Lusty Juventus*, ll. 774–820.

35 See *ibid.*, ll. 774–5, 776–8, 781–8. See also Melchiori, 'Contextualization'.

36 See Melchiori and Gabrieli, *Sir Thomas More*, 151; Jowett, *Sir Thomas More*, 256. Melchiori and Gabrieli argue that 'prithee' is also an archaism intended to conform with the 'deliberate artlessness' of the new sections.

I am less convinced, given that 'prithee' is ubiquitous in late sixteenth-
and early seventeenth-century drama.

37 For Ogle's activities in the 1570s and 1580s see Albert Feuillerat, *Documents
Relating to the Office of the Revels in the Time of Queen Elizabeth* (Louvain:
A. Uystpruyst, 1908). Philip Henslowe records a loan of 10 shillings given to
Thomas Downton of the Admiral's Men on 10 February 1600 'for the company
to geue *v*nto father ogell & other thinges'; see *Henslowe's Diary*, ed. R. A. Foakes
[and R. T. Rickert], 2nd edn (Cambridge University Press, 2002), 131.

38 James Simpson, 'Rhetoric, Conscience, and the Playful Positions of Sir
Thomas More', in Pincombe and Shrank, *Oxford Handbook*, 121–36 (130–1).

39 Robert Weimann, *Shakespeare and the Popular Tradition in the Theater: Studies
in the Social Dimension of Dramatic Form and Function*, ed. Robert Schwartz
(Baltimore, Md.: Johns Hopkins University Press, 1978), 98.

40 *Histrio-mastix: Or, The Player Whipt* (London, 1610), H2v. All references are
to this edition. For an acute analysis of the play's structure and major thematic
concerns see Haynes, *Social Relations*, 22–4.

41 For arguments in favour of an Inns of Court Performance see Philip
Finkelpearl, 'John Marston's *Histrio-Mastix* as an Inns of Court Play:
A Hypothesis', *Huntington Library Quarterly* 29 (1966), 223–34; Roslyn Lander
Knutson, *Playing Companies and Commerce in Shakespeare's Time* (Cambridge
University Press, 2001), 82–96. For a counter-argument in favour of Paul's see
James P. Bednarz, 'Writing and Revenge: John Marston's *Histriomastix*',
Comparative Drama 36 (2002), 21–51.

42 1590s words that appear in *Histriomastix* include: ''slid' (1598: *Every Man in his
Humour; The Merry Wives of Windsor*); 'russeting' (1597: Hall's *Virgide-
miarum*); 'helter-skelter' (1592: Nashe's *Strange News*); 'ingle' as a noun
(1592: Nashe's *Strange News*); 'home-spun' (*c.*1589: Nashe's *An Almond for a
Parrot*); 'coney-catchers' (1591: Greene's *A Notable Discovery of Cozenage*);
'penurious' (1590: Richard Harvey's *Theological Discourse*). Two words,
'autumnian' (Dekker's *Magnificent Entertainment*) and 'transparently'
(Thomas Winter's translation of Du Bartas' *The Third Day's Creation*), are
first recorded in 1604; this might suggest revision – something posited by
Bednarz on the basis of an apparent reference to *Eastward Ho*: see 'Writing
and Revenge', 43–4 – or the author(s) of *Histriomastix* may have coined them.
My references here are drawn from *OED*, *EEBO* and *LION*.

43 See '*Histriomastix, Hamlet*, and the "quintessence of Duckes"', *Notes &
Queries*, ns 50 (2003), 427–30.

44 For arguments in favour of Marston's authorship see David Lake, '*Histriomastix*: Linguistic Evidence for Authorship', *Notes & Queries* 226 (1981),
148–52; Bednarz, 'Writing and Revenge', esp. 33–5; John Peachman, 'Previously Unrecorded Verbal Parallels Between *Histrio-Mastix* and the Acknowledged Works of John Marston', *Notes & Queries*, ns 51 (2004), 304–6;
Charles Cathcart, *Marston, Rivalry, Rapprochement and Jonson* (Aldershot:
Ashgate, 2008), 8–13. For arguments against see Knutson, *Playing Companies*,
77–82. Cathcart concludes that 'the available evidence indeed indicates

a probable composing role for Marston … though by no means a sole agency, nor a composition certainly intended for Paul's' (*Marston*, 37).

45 Knutson, *Playing Companies*, 163 (n. 15).

46 Ian Lancashire (ed.), *The Interlude of Youth*, in *Two Tudor Interludes: The Interlude of Youth; Hick Scorner* (Manchester University Press, 1980), ll. 210–11. Later editions date from *c*.1557–9 and *c*.1566–9. For discussion of the play's printing and performance dates see *ibid*., 1–5, 17–22.

47 A number of allusions suggest the existence of a play about Dives and Lazarus, notably the player's declaration in *Greene's Groatsworth of Wit*: 'I can serue to make a pretie speech, for I was a countrey Author, passing at a Morrall, for twas I that pende the Morrall of mans witte, the Dialogue of Diues' (*Greenes, Groats-worth of Witte, Bought with a Million of Repentance* (London, 1592), E1r). Other allusions to a Dives and Lazarus play can be found in Jonson's *Poetaster* (Chapel Children, 1601), Fletcher's *The Noble Gentleman* (King's Men, 1626) and T.B.'s non-dramatic version of *The Life and Death of the Merry Devill of Edmonton* (1631).

48 Bevington, *Mankind to Marlowe*, 191.

49 Thomas Nashe, *Pierces Supererogation or A New Prayse of the Old Asse* (London, 1593), 2A3v. *OED*'s earliest citation dates from 1602 (huffing, *adj.*), although the work cited is *How a Man May Choose a Good Wife from a Bad*, a play which was printed in that year and may have been performed earlier.

50 Margreta de Grazia, *'Hamlet' without Hamlet* (Cambridge University Press, 2007), 7, 9.

51 See Jessica Winston, 'Seneca in Early Elizabethan England', *Renaissance Quarterly* 59 (2006), 29–58 and 'English Seneca: Heywood to *Hamlet*', in Pincombe and Shrank (eds.), *Oxford Handbook*, 472–87. While Winston cites *Hamlet* in the latter essay, she does not make the precise connections that I argue for here. For a general account of Seneca's influence on Shakespeare see Robert Miola, *Shakespeare and Classical Tragedy: The Influence of Seneca* (Oxford: Clarendon Press, 1992); on Senecan tragedy in England in the sixteenth century see also Bruce R. Smith, *Ancient Scripts and Modern Experience on the English Stage, 1500–1700* (Princeton University Press, 1988), esp. 199–215, 240–8.

52 Madeleine Doran, 'The Language of *Hamlet*', *Huntington Library Quarterly* 27 (1963–4), 259–78 (260).

53 For a recent reappraisal and summary of earlier arguments see Thompson and Taylor, *Hamlet*, 51–2, 58–9.

54 *Ibid*., 2.2.399–402. This edition reproduces the second quarto text; all references are to this text/edition unless otherwise stated. The first quarto here reads: '*Baked and imparched in coagulate gore, / Rifted in earth and fire – old grandsire Priam seeks*' (7.349–50). All references to the first quarto and folio texts are taken from Ann Thompson and Neil Taylor (eds.), *Hamlet: The Texts of 1603 and 1623* (London: Arden Shakespeare, 2006). Important variations between the three texts are noted here in the footnotes.

55 Marston, *Antonio's Revenge*, ed. G. K. Hunter (London: Edward Arnold, 1965), 1.1.17–20.

56 *OED*'s earlier citations date from the fifteenth and early sixteenth centuries, with a large gap before *Hamlet* and *Timon of Athens*, and *EEBO* does not suggest more widespread use. The word also appears in Webster and Heywood's *Appius and Virginia* (auspices uncertain, *c.*1625–7), and Heywood's *The Royal King and the Loyal Subject* (?Worcester's Men, 1602).

57 G. R. Hibbard (ed.), *Hamlet* (Oxford University Press, 1987), 257.

58 The first quarto's version of *The Murder of Gonzago* provides a variant (and much shorter) text in which the opening lines are almost entirely different (9.98–110); this version lacks the second quarto and Folio version's abundance of classical allusion, and its reduced length means that it is not as circumlocutory as the longer version, but it includes the dumb show and the end-stopped couplets and even adds the conventional archaism 'whilom' (9.102).

59 Philip Edwards (ed.), *Hamlet* (Cambridge University Press, 1985), 10.

60 O. B. Hardison Jr, *Prosody and Purpose in the English Renaissance* (Baltimore, Md.: Johns Hopkins University Press, 1989), 254.

61 'Influence of the Court Tragedy on the Play Scene in *Hamlet*', *Journal of English and Germanic Philology* 32 (1933), 44–50. Childs' characterisation of these plays as 'court tragedy' is unreliable, given that they had their origins in the Inns of Court.

62 On Queen Elizabeth's Men's medley style see Scott McMillin and Sally-Beth MacLean, *The Queen's Men and Their Plays* (Cambridge University Press, 1998), esp. 124–7, 143–54.

63 *The Ninth Tragedie of Lucius Anneus Seneca Called Octavia. Translated out of Latine into English* (London, [1566]), C2v.

64 Dieter Mehl, *The Elizabethan Dumb Show: The History of a Dramatic Convention* (London: Methuen, 1965), 114. Dumb shows appear, with little sense of anxiety, in Heywood's *The Four Prentices of London* (Admiral's Men, *c.*1594), *Captain Thomas Stukeley* (Admiral's Men, 1596), Munday and Chettle's *Huntingdon* plays (Admiral's Men, 1598) and *A Warning for Fair Women* (Chamberlain's Men, 1599).

65 See George Chapman, *The Gentleman Usher*, ed. John Hazel Smith (London: Edward Arnold, 1970), 2.1.195–298.

66 'Telmah', in Patricia Parker and Geoffrey Hartman (eds.), *Shakespeare and the Question of Theory* (London: Methuen, 1985), 310–32 (316).

67 Richard Dyer, *Pastiche* (London: Routledge, 2007), 69.

68 On *Hamlet* and religious tradition see, among others, Stephen Greenblatt, *Hamlet in Purgatory* (Princeton University Press, 2001). On Hecuba see Tanya Pollard, 'What's Hecuba to Shakespeare?', *Renaissance Quarterly* 65.4 (Winter 2012), 1060–93.

69 See Foakes and Rickert, *Henslowe's Diary*, 21.

70 The most thorough review of the evidence is Lukas Erne, *Beyond the Spanish Tragedy: A Study of the Works of Thomas Kyd* (Manchester University Press, 2001), 146–50. On the scholarly narratives surrounding the Ur-*Hamlet* see also Emma Smith, 'Ghost Writing: *Hamlet* and the Ur-Hamlet', in *The Renaissance Text: Theory, Editing, Textuality* (Manchester University Press,

2000), 177–90; James J. Marino, *Owning William Shakespeare: The King's Men and their Intellectual Property* (Philadelphia: University of Pennsylvania Press, 2011), 75–106.

71 Thomas Nashe, 'To the Gentlemen Students of both Universities', in Robert Greene, *Menaphon: Camillas Alarum to Slumbering Euphues* (London, 1589), **3r.

72 Marino, *Owning*, 80.

73 David Scott Kastan, '"His semblable is his mirror": *Hamlet* and the Imitation of Revenge', *Shakespeare Studies* 19 (1987), 111–24 (122).

74 See first quarto 7.266–73, and Folio 2.2.328–360.

75 In an important essay Roslyn Lander Knutson suggests that the folio passage refers to the political disruption caused by the Queen's Revels company (formerly the Chapel Children) in 1608, rather than the commercial threat posed by the children's companies *c*.1600. See 'Falconer to the Little Eyases: A New Date and Commercial Agenda for the "Little Eyases" Passage in *Hamlet*', *Shakespeare Quarterly* 46 (1995), 1–31.

76 The lines are 'The screeking Rauen sits croking for reuenge. / Whole heads of beasts comes bellowing for reuenge', taken from a soliloquy uttered by the murderous King Richard. See *The True Tragedie of Richard the Third* (London, 1594), H1v.

77 These lines do not appear in the first quarto; the Folio text has 'breathes' instead of 'breaks' and the penultimate line appears as 'And do such bitter business as the day' (3.2.379, 381).

78 This moment was used to great effect in the RSC's 2008 production of *Hamlet*, directed by Gregory Doran and featuring David Tennant as Hamlet, in which the interval was taken after these words, with Hamlet holding his dagger above Claudius' head. For the space of the interval, therefore, Hamlet was Pyrrhus, standing like a 'painted tyrant' and doing nothing.

79 Middleton, *The Roaring Girl*, ed. Kahn, Epistle, ll. 2–9.

5 Shepherds' speech: archaism and Stuart pastoral drama

1 For a recent reappraisal of the date see Matthew Steggle, '*The Knave in Grain* Puts Holland's Leaguer on Stage', *Notes & Queries*, ns 51 (2004), 355–6.

2 *The Knave in Graine, New Vampt. A Witty Comedy* (London, 1640), G1v.

3 See *SP*, 102, 50, 105.

4 George Turberville, *The Eglogs of the Poet B. Mantuan Carmelitan, Turned into English Verse* (London, 1567), A3v.

5 *Poems by Michael Drayton Esquire* (London, 1619), 432.

6 See David Scott Wilson-Okamura, *Virgil in the Renaissance* (Cambridge University Press, 2010), 73, 89; Kathryn J. Gutzwiller, *Theocritus' Pastoral Analogies: The Formation of a Genre* (Madison: University of Wisconsin Press, 1991), 184–5.

7 Wilson-Okamura, *Virgil*, 74.

8 Philip Sidney, *An Apology for Poetry*, ed. Geoffrey Shepherd, rev. R. W. Maslen (Manchester University Press, 2002), 110.

9 Sidney, *The Countess of Pembroke's Arcadia (The Old Arcadia)*, ed. Katherine Duncan-Jones (Oxford University Press, 1985), 221–2. The poem appears in the eclogues at the end of Book 1 in the 1590 edition, but is placed in this position in the 1593 text.

10 For insightful readings of the use of beast fable and its links with Spenser see Annabel Patterson, *Censorship and Interpretation: The Conditions of Writing and Reading in Early Modern England* (Madison: Wisconsin University Press, 1984), 45–8; David Norbrook, *Poetry and Politics in the English Renaissance: Revised Edition* (Oxford University Press, 2002), 87–8; Erica Fudge, *Perceiving Animals: Humans and Beasts in Early Modern English Culture* (Basingstoke: Macmillan, 1999), 77–81.

11 Robert E. Stillman, *Philip Sidney and the Poetics of Renaissance Cosmopolitanism* (Aldershot: Ashgate, 2008), 113; Paula Blank, *Broken English: Dialects and Politics of Language in Renaissance English* (London: Routledge, 1996), 118; Blair Worden, *The Sound of Virtue: Philip Sidney's Arcadia and Elizabethan Politics* (New Haven, Conn.: Yale University Press, 1996), 269; Norbrook, *Poetry and Politics*, 87.

12 *Informations to William Drummond of Hawthornden*, ed. Ian Donaldson, in *CBJ*, vol. 5, ll. 12–13, 45–6, 490–1.

13 Alexander Gil, *Logonomia Anglica*, part 2, trans. Robin C. Alston, ed. Bror Danielsson and Arvid Gabrielson (Stockholm: Almquist and Wiksell, 1972), 104. See also *The Art of English Poesy by George Puttenham: A Critical Edition*, ed. Frank Whigham and Wayne A. Rebhorn (Ithaca, NY: Cornell University Press, 2007), 229.

14 See *SP*, 137. The earliest citation I have found is in George Gascoigne's *A Hundreth Sundrie Flowres Bound up in One Small Poesie* (London, 1573), Giv.

15 For a recent reappraisal of the development of Italian pastoral drama see Lisa Sampson, *Pastoral Drama in Early Modern Italy: The Making of a New Genre* (London: Legenda, 2006); on France see John S. Powell, *Music and Theatre in France, 1600–1680* (Oxford University Press, 2000), 160–87.

16 See, for instance, *Il Pastor Fido: Or The Faithfull Shepheard. Translated out of Italian into English* (London, 1602), C2r, G2v, B1r. On the identity of the translator see Elizabeth Story Donno (ed.), *Three Renaissance Pastorals: Tasso. Guarini. Daniel* (Binghamton, NY: Medieval and Renaissance Texts and Studies, 1993), xii–xiv.

17 Samuel Daniel, 'To the Right Worthy and Learned Knight . . . Syr *Edward Dymock*, Champion to her Maiestie, Concerning This Translation of *pastor fido*', in *Il pastor fido*, A1v.

18 On the implications of Daniel's poem and his broader engagement with Italian literature see Jason Lawrence, *'Who the Devil Taught Thee So Much Italian?': Italian Language Learning and Literary Imitation in Early Modern England* (Manchester University Press, 2005), 62–117. See also Raphael Lyne, 'English Guarini: Recognition and Reception', *The Yearbook of English Studies* 36 (2006), 90–102 (92–3).

19 Puttenham, *Art*, 336–7.
20 Thomas Nashe, *Strange Newes, of the Intercepting Certaine Letters* (London, 1592), K1r.
21 On the date see Lucy Munro, *Children of the Queen's Revels: A Jacobean Theatre Repertory* (Cambridge University Press, 2005), 172–3.
22 Cyrus Hoy, 'The Shares of Fletcher and his Collaborators in the Beaumont and Fletcher Canon (I)', *Studies in Bibliography* 8 (1956), 129–46 (142).
23 E. H. C. Oliphant, 'The Works of Beaumont and Fletcher', *Englischen Studien* 14 (1890), 53–94 (57). The lack of italics is Oliphant's own.
24 George Darley (ed.), *The Works of Beaumont and Fletcher*, 2 vols. (London: Edward Moxon, 1840), 1: xii; Finkelpearl, 'John Fletcher as Spenserian Playwright: *The Faithful Shepherdess* and *The Island Princess*', *Studies in English Literature* 27 (1987), 285–302 (285–6). For a critique of this line of argument see also Gordon McMullan, *The Politics of Unease in the Plays of John Fletcher* (Amherst: University of Massachusetts Press, 1994), 56–8.
25 See Charles Barber, *Early Modern English*, 2nd edn (Edinburgh University Press, 1997), 67–70; Noel Osselton, 'Archaism', in *The Spenser Encyclopedia*, gen. ed. A. C. Hamilton (London: Routledge, 1990), 52–3.
26 Cyrus Hoy (ed.), *The Faithful Shepherdess*, in *The Dramatic Works in the Beaumont and Fletcher Canon*, gen. ed. Fredson Bowers, vol. 3 (Cambridge University Press, 1976), 3.1.45–50. All references are to this edition.
27 In Fletcher's 'solo' canon as a whole Hoy calculates that the dramatist uses 'ye' 322 times per play; in *The Faithful Shepherdess* it occurs 32 times. Conversely, 'hath' occurs 3 times per play in the solo canon, and 47 times in *The Faithful Shepherdess*. The colloquial ''em' occurs 59 times on average in the other plays, but only once in *The Faithful Shepherdess*. The more formal 'them' is used 8 times in the other plays, but 34 times in *The Faithful Shepherdess*. The figures for Fletcher's plays are listed in Hoy, 'Shares', 145–6; the *Faithful Shepherdess* counts are my own, taken from the first quarto edition, *The Faithful Shepheardesse* (London, [?1609]).
28 On these features see Jonathan Hope, *The Authorship of Shakespeare's Plays: A Socio-Linguistic Study* (Cambridge University Press, 1994). Hope draws on the work of socio- and sociohistorical linguists such as William Labov and Suzanne Romaine.
29 See *ibid.*, 62.
30 In other 'solo' plays, his use of 'you' forms ranges from 55 per cent (in *Bonduca*) to 78 per cent (in *Monsieur Thomas*): see Hope, *Authorship*, 59 (Table 4.2). In contrast, in *The Faithful Shepherdess* 'you' forms are used only 22 per cent of the time. In carrying out this analysis I followed the method used by Hope. Figures for all forms of 'thou' and 'you' were collected (i.e. 'thou', 'thy', 'thine', 'thee', 'you', 'ye', 'your', etc.). Forms such as 'prithee' were omitted, as were pronouns used in personification and apostrophe. Self-address, aside, and address in absence were included where the addressed was a person.
31 As Katie Wales suggests, use of 'thou' later became linked with Northern English, but it does not seem to be so strongly marked in the seventeenth

century. See *Northern English: A Social and Cultural History* (Cambridge University Press, 2006), 181–5.

32 This is a simplified account of a vexed question in historical sociolinguistics. See David Denison, *English Historical Syntax: Verbal Constructions* (London: Longman, 1993); Hope, *Authorship*, 11–15; Barber, *Early Modern English*, 193–6; Matti Rissanen, 'Syntax', in Roger Lass (ed.), *The Cambridge History of the English Language: 1476–1776* (Cambridge University Press, 1999), 187–331. A useful recent reassessment can be found in Anthony Warner, 'Why DO Dove: Evidence for Register Variation in Early Modern English Negatives', *Language Variation and Change* 17 (2005), 257–80.

33 Barber, *Early Modern English*, 196.

34 In the ten Fletcher plays sampled by Hope, the average rate of regulation was 93 per cent; the lowest rate was 90 per cent (*The Wild Goose Chase*) and the highest 94 per cent (*The Humorous Lieutenant*) (*Authorship*, 157). In contrast, Hope found that the rate of regulation in *The Faithful Shepherdess* was only 84 per cent (personal correspondence, 30 July 1999). I am very grateful to Professor Hope for sharing his unpublished research with me.

35 See George T. Wright, 'Hearing Shakespeare's Dramatic Verse', in David Scott Kastan (ed.), *A Companion to Shakespeare* (Oxford: Blackwell, 1999), 256–76 (270–2).

36 C. P. Brand, *Torquato Tasso: A Study of the Poet and his Contribution to English Literature* (Cambridge University Press, 1965), 51.

37 Marco Ariani (ed.), *Il teatro italiano II: La tragedia del Cinquecentro* (Turin: Einaudi, 1977), Chorus II, 36–42; translation from Sampson, *Pastoral Drama*, 79.

38 *Il Verrato Contra M. Jason Denores*, in *Opere*, ed. G. A. Barotti and A. Zeno, 5 vols. (Verona, 1737–8), 2: 291, translation from Robert Henke, 'Pastoral as Tragicomedic in Italian and Shakespearean Drama', in Michele Marrapodi (ed.), *The Italian World of English Renaissance Drama: Cultural Exchange and Intertextuality* (Cranbury, NJ: Associated University Presses, 1998), 282–301 (290).

39 On the debate between Denores and Guarini see Sampson, *Pastoral Drama*, 137–41.

40 *Ibid.*, 143, quoting and translating Malacreta, *Considerazioni intorno al Pastor fido*, in Guarini, *Opere*, 4: 38–9; see also Beni, *Risposta alle considerazioni o dubbi dell'eccellentissimo Signor Dottor Malacreta accademico ordito sopra il Pastorfido, ibid.*, 4: 125–300.

41 John Fletcher, 'To the Reader', in Hoy, *The Faithful Shepherdess*, 497 (ll. 3–8).

42 Guarini, *Il Pastor Fido, Tragicommedia Pastorale* (Venice, 1602), 6v; Sampson, *Pastoral Drama*, 145.

43 See McMullan, *Politics of Unease*, 62–5. On the politics of the Spenserian poets see also Norbrook, *Poetry and Politics*, 173–98; Michelle O'Callaghan, *The 'Shepheards Nation': Jacobean Spenserians and Early Stuart Political Culture* (Oxford: Clarendon Press, 2000), 88–91.

44 See 5.5.215–17, 230–1.

45 See *Children of the Queen's Revels*, 33–4, 102–3, 124–33.
46 See John Pitcher (ed.), *Hymen's Triumph by Samuel Daniel* (Oxford: Malone Society, 1994), v–xix; Leeds Barroll, *Anna of Denmark, Queen of England: A Cultural Biography* (Philadelphia: University of Pennsylvania Press, 2001), 139–42; Clare McManus, *Women on the Renaissance Stage* (Manchester University Press, 2002), 100–1.
47 See Barbara K. Lewalski, *Writing Women in Jacobean England* (Cambridge, Mass.: Harvard University Press, 1993), 15–43; Barroll, *Anna*, 36–73; McManus, *Women*.
48 Notable exceptions are Gordon McMullan and Lee Bliss, whose groundbreaking reassessment of *The Faithful Shepherdess*, 'Defending Fletcher's Shepherds', *Studies in English Literature* 23 (1983), 295–310, remains the single most important essay on the play.
49 The treatment of chastity and virginity in *The Faithful Shepherdess* has received much critical attention. See, in particular, Nancy Cotton Pearse, *John Fletcher's Chastity Plays: Mirrors of Modesty* (Lewisburg, Pa.: Bucknell University Press, 1973); James J. Yoch, 'The Renaissance Dramatization of Temperance: The Italian Revival of Tragicomedy and *The Faithful Shepherdess*', in Nancy Klein Maguire (ed.), *Renaissance Tragicomedy: Explorations in Genre and Politics* (New York: AMS Press, 1987), 115–23; Philip J. Finkelpearl, *Court and Country Politics in the Plays of Beaumont and Fletcher* (Princeton University Press, 1990), 101–14; Marie H. Loughlin, *Hymeneutics: Interpreting Virginity on the Early Modern Stage* (Cranbury, NJ: Associated University Presses, 1997), esp. 53–73; Sandra Clark, *The Plays of Beaumont and Fletcher: Sexual Themes and Dramatic Representation* (London: Harvester Wheatsheaf, 1994), 27–33.
50 See Sampson, *Pastoral Drama*, 77–9; Ornella Garraffo, 'Il satiro nella pastorale ferrarese del Cinquecento', *Italianistica* 14 (1985), 185–201.
51 See Anthony Parr, 'Time and the Satyr', *Huntington Library Quarterly* 68 (2005), 429–65, esp. 450–5.
52 *Comedies and Tragedies Written by Francis Beaumont and John Fletcher, Gentlemen* (London, 1647), a1v.
53 N. W. Bawcutt, *The Control and Censorship of Caroline Drama: The Records of Sir Henry Herbert, Master of the Revels 1623–73* (Oxford: Clarendon Press, 1996), 186; Sarah Poynting (ed.), *The Shepherds' Paradise* (Oxford: Malone Society, 1997), xii.
54 See Karen Britland, *Drama at the Courts of Queen Henrietta Maria* (Cambridge University Press, 2006), 137–9; see also Britland, 'Queen Henrietta Maria's Theatrical Patronage', in Erin Griffey (ed.), *Henrietta Maria: Piety, Politics and Patronage* (Aldershot: Ashgate, 2008), 57–73.
55 On *Arthénice* see Britland, *Drama*, 35–52; Kasey Marie Mattia, 'Crossing the Channel: Cultural Identity in the Courts of Queen Henrietta Maria, 1625–1640', PhD thesis, Duke University, 2007, 161–79. On the performance and reception of *The Shepherds' Paradise* see Poynting, *Shepherds' Paradise*, vii–xv, and '"The Rare and Excellent Partes of Mr. Walter Montague"':

Henrietta Maria and Her Playwright', in Griffey, *Henrietta Maria*, 73–88. For the identification of Boisrobert as the author of *Florimène*, the text of which is now lost, and a reappraisal of the play's cultural contexts, see Britland, *Drama*, 150–67.

56 See Pitcher, *Hymen's Triumph*, esp. v–xvii.

57 See Poynting, *Shepherds' Paradise*, viii; Mattia, 'Crossing the Channel', 180–2.

58 For reproductions of the designs for the scenes and costumes see Stephen Orgel and Roy Strong, *Inigo Jones: The Theatre of the Stuart Court*, 2 vols. (London: Sotheby Parke Bernet, 1973), 2: 505–35.

59 On the performance and its contexts see John Creaser, '"The present aid of this occasion": The Setting of *Comus*', in David Lindley (ed.), *The Court Masque* (Manchester University Press, 1984), 111–34; Cedric C. Brown, *John Milton's Aristocratic Entertainments* (Cambridge University Press, 1985), 26–40.

60 See Creaser, 'Present Aid'; David Norbrook, 'The Reformation of the Masque', in Lindley, *The Court Masque*, 94–110 (esp. 104–6); Barbara K. Lewalski, 'Milton's *Comus* and the Politics of Masquing', in David Bevington and Peter Holbrook (eds.), *The Politics of the Stuart Court Masque* (Cambridge University Press, 1998), 296–320. See also Jeanne S. Martin, 'Transformations of Genre in Milton's *Comus*', *Genre* 10 (1977), 195–213.

61 See, in particular, Nancy Lindheim, 'Pastoral and Masque at Ludlow', *University of Toronto Quarterly* 67 (1998), 639–68; Heather Dubrow, 'The Masquing of Genre in *Comus*', *Milton Studies* 44 (2005), 62–83. Sue P. Starke, *The Heroines of English Pastoral Romance* (Cambridge: D. S. Brewer, 2007), 142–79, explores the influence of tragicomedy on *A Masque*.

62 See Anthony Mortimer, 'The Italian Influence on *Comus*', *Milton Quarterly* 6 (1972), 8–16; John M. Major, '*Comus* and *The Tempest*', *Shakespeare Quarterly* 10 (1959), 177–83; Finkelpearl, 'John Fletcher'; Maggie Kilgour, '*Comus*'s Wood of Allusion', *University of Toronto Quarterly* 61 (1992), 316–33; Stephen Orgel, 'The Case for Comus', *Representations* 81 (2003), 31–45; Ann Baynes Coiro, '"A thousand fantasies": The Lady and the *Maske*', in Nicholas McDowell and Nigel Smith (eds.), *The Oxford Handbook of Milton* (Oxford University Press, 2009), 89–111 (95).

63 *A Maske Presented at Ludlow Castle, 1634* (London, 1637); Virgil, 'Eclogue II', ll. 58–9.

64 Patterson suggests the importance of the 'self-deprecatory' allusion to Corydon (*Pastoral and Ideology: Virgil to Valéry* (Oxford: Clarendon Press, 1988), 158 n. 34); Norbrook regards it as 'indicating that the work was coming to the light prematurely' (*Poetry and Politics*, 252).

65 *Poems of Mr. John Milton, both English and Latin* (London, 1645); Virgil, 'Eclogue VII', ll. 27–8.

66 On these texts and their implications for our understanding of *A Masque* see Ann Baynes Coiro, 'Anonymous Milton, or "a maske" Masked', *English Literary History* 71 (2004), 609–29.

67 'The Copy of a Letter Written by Sir Henry Wotton to the Author upon the Following Poem', in *CEP*, 59–61 (59–60).
68 Robert Burton, *The Anatomy of Melancholy* (Oxford, 1621), 9.
69 Francis Quarles, *Argalus and Parthenia* (London, 1629), 104.
70 See Lindheim, 'Pastoral', 656–7.
71 *CEP*, 60. See Coiro, 'Anonymous Milton', 612–25 for an insightful consideration of Randolph's influence on Milton; see also Brown, *Aristocratic Entertainments*, 63–4.
72 On the relationship between the texts see John S. Diekhoff, 'The Text of *Comus*, 1634–45', *Publications of the Modern Language Association of America* 52 (1937), 705–27; John T. Shawcross, 'Certain Relationships of the Manuscripts of *Comus*', *Papers of the Bibliographical Society of America* 54 (1960), 35–56; S. E. Sprott, *John Milton: A Maske. The Earlier Versions* (University of Toronto Press, 1973).
73 Patterson, *Pastoral and Ideology*, 158.
74 For further discussion of Milton's interactions with Spenser in *A Masque* see Joan Larson Klein, 'Some Spenserian Influences on Milton's *Comus*', *Annuale Mediaevale* 5 (1964), 27–47; A. Kent Hieatt, 'Milton's *Comus* and Spenser's False Genius', *University of Toronto Quarterly* 38 (1969), 313–18; Kilgour, '*Comus*'s Wood of Allusion'.
75 See also the use of Spenser in ll. 998–1011, which draw on *Faerie Queene* 3.6.43–50; Milton signals his debt through the archaic word 'welkin'.
76 See John Carey (ed.), *John Milton: Complete Shorter Poems*, 2nd edn (London: Longman, 1997), 188.
77 For detailed discussion see Starke, *Heroines*, 142–79.
78 See Norbrook, 'Reformation', esp. 104–6; Britland, *Drama*, 136–9. See also Lewalski, 'Milton's *Comus*', where she argues that *A Masque* implies 'that the moral health of the nation depends upon the formation of such young aristocrats [i.e. the Egertons], not upon the suspect court reformation promoted by the Queen' (307).
79 The songs are preserved in Lawes' autograph manuscript, BL Add. MS 53723, and in BL Add. MS 11518, written in an unknown hand. On variations between these sources see John T. Shawcross, 'Henry Lawes's Settings of Songs for Milton's *Comus*', *Journal of the Rutgers University Libraries* 28 (1964), 22–8. On the songs see also Peter Walls, *Music in the English Courtly Masque 1604–1640* (Oxford: Clarendon Press, 1996), 289–303; Ian Spink, *Henry Lawes: Cavalier Songwriter* (Oxford University Press, 2000), 55–61.
80 Fletcher's songs for *The Faithful Shepherdess* were updated with new settings written by William Lawes, Henry's brother, and possibly composed specifically for the 1634 court performance. See Julia H. Wood, 'William Lawes's Music for Plays', in Andrew Ashbee (ed.), *William Lawes (1602–1645): Essays on his Life, Times and Work* (Aldershot: Ashgate, 1998), 11–67 (44).
81 See Schwyzer, 'Purity and Danger on the West Bank of the Severn: The Cultural Geography of *A Masque Presented at Ludlow Castle, 1634*',

Representations 60 (1997), 22–48; Sanders, 'Ecocritical Readings and the Seventeenth-Century Woodland: Milton's *Comus* and the Forest of Dean', *English* 50 (2001), 1–18, and *The Cultural Geography of Early Modern Drama, 1620–1650* (Cambridge University Press, 2011), 46–7, 75–84; Susan Bennett and Julie Sanders, 'Rehearsing Across Space and Place: Rethinking *A Masque Presented at Ludlow Castle*', in Joanne Tompkins and Anna Birch (eds.), *Performing Site-Specific Theatre: Politics, Place, Practice* (Basingstoke: Palgrave Macmillan, 2012), 37–53.

82 Carey, *Shorter Poems*, 228.

83 Barbara K. Lewalski, 'How Radical was the Young Milton?', in Stephen B. Dobranski and John P. Rumrich (eds.), *Milton and Heresy* (Cambridge University Press, 1998), 49–72 (57).

84 Annotations in a copy of *Arthénice* now owned by the Houghton Library, Harvard University (callmark STC 4016.5), apparently printed and prepared for use in the court production, quoted from Orgel and Strong, *Inigo Jones*, I: 385; translation from Mattia, 'Crossing the Channel', 173–80. See also John Orrell, *The Theatres of Inigo Jones and John Webb* (Cambridge University Press, 1985), 81–4.

85 Orrell, *Theatres*, 82.

86 'Eclogue VI', l. 2; Anne Barton and Eugene Giddens (eds.), *The Sad Shepherd*, in *CBJ*, 7: 425. All references to *The Sad Shepherd* are to this edition. The same line appears as the epigraph to the 1635 printed text of Joseph Rutter's *The Shepherds' Holiday*, to which Jonson contributed dedicatory verses.

87 For discussion see Sanders, *Cultural Geography*, 85; Barton and Giddens, *Sad Shepherd*, 422, 427. As Barton and Giddens point out, the few theatrical venues with the resources necessary for perspective sets were the court theatres and the Salisbury Court playhouse, which produced Thomas Nabbes's spectacular *Microcosmus: A Morall Maske* in 1637.

88 Stephen Knight, '"Meere English flockes": Ben Jonson's *The Sad Shepherd* and the Robin Hood Tradition', in Helen Phillips (ed.), *Robin Hood: Medieval and Post-Medieval* (Dublin: Four Courts Press, 2005), 129–44 (131).

89 See Sanders, *Cultural Geography*, esp. 48–50, 84–99. See also Anne Barton's pioneering reading of the play in *Ben Jonson, Dramatist* (Cambridge University Press, 1984), 300–20; Sanders, 'Jonson, *The Sad Shepherd* and the North Midlands', *Ben Jonson Journal* 6 (1999), 49–68; Knight, 'Meere'; Mary Ellen Lamb, *The Popular Culture of Shakespeare, Spenser and Jonson* (London: Routledge, 2006), 214–28.

90 W. W. Greg, *Pastoral Poetry and Pastoral Drama* (London: A. H. Bullen, 1906), 262 accuses Daniel's pastorals in general; C. H. Herford, Percy Simpson and Evelyn Simpson (eds.), *Ben Jonson*, 11 vols. (Oxford: Clarendon Press, 1925–63), 10: 365, single out *Hymen's Triumph*.

91 Sanders, *Cultural Geography*, 85.

92 *The King's Majesty's Declaration to His Subjects, Concerning Lawful Sports to Be Used* (London, 1633), 5. On the 'Book of Sports' see Leah Marcus, *The Politics*

of Mirth: Jonson, Herrick, Milton, Marvell, and the Defense of Old Holiday Pastimes (University of Chicago Press, 1986); McMullan, *Politics of Unease*, 120–6.

93 Marcus, *Politics of Mirth*, 3.

94 *The Kings Majesties Declaration to his Subjects*, 1–2.

95 See Marcus, *Politics of Mirth*, 187–97; Lewalski, 'How Radical', 55–7.

96 Marcus, *Politics of Mirth*, 138. Lamb sees *The Sad Shepherd* as more straight-forwardly nostalgic and conservative, although she also reads the play as a critique of court pastoral: see Lamb, *Popular Culture*, 214–21.

97 John Bullokar, *An English Expositor Teaching the Interpretation of the Hardest Words vsed in our Language* (London, 1616), K2v. See also *OED*, lorel, n.

98 Wales, *Northern English*, 77. On Northern English in the early modern period see also Blank, *Broken English*, 100–25; Javier Ruano-García, *Early Modern Northern English Lexis: A Literary Corpus-Based Study* (Berne: Peter Lang, 2010), esp. 76–8.

99 BL Add. MS 34065, published in Henry Huth (ed.), *Inedited Poetical Miscellanies 1584–1700* (London: Chiswick Press, 1870).

100 See Thomas P. Harrison, Jr, 'Jonson's *The Sad Shepherd* and Spenser', *Modern Language Notes* 58 (1943), 257–62 (257–8); Spenser, 'Februarie', ll. 113–15.

101 See Knight, 'Meere', 139.

102 Elaine Spina, 'Skeltonic Meter in *Elynour Rummyng*', *Studies in Philology* 64 (1967), 665–84 (665 n. 2).

103 On Skelton's posthumous reputation see Anthony S. G. Edwards, *Skelton: The Critical Heritage* (London: Routledge and Kegan Paul, 1981); Jane Griffiths, *John Skelton and Poetic Authority: Defining the Liberty to Speak* (Oxford: Clarendon Press, 2006), 158–84.

104 James Knowles, '"Songs of Baser Alloy": Jonson's *Gypsies Metamorphosed* and the Circulation of Manuscript Libels', *Huntington Library Quarterly* 69 (2006), 153–73.

105 On the performance and revision of *The Downfall* see R. A. Foakes [and R. T. Rickert] (eds.), *Henslowe's Diary*, 2nd edn (Cambridge University Press, 2002), 86–7, 102; John C. Meagher (ed.), *The Downfall of Robert, Earl of Huntingdon* (Oxford: Malone Society, 1965), vii.

106 On the treatment of temporality in the play see Liz Oakley Brown, 'Framing Robin Hood: Temporality and Textuality in Anthony Munday's Hunting-ton Plays', in Phillips, *Robin Hood*, 113–28.

107 For an overview of pastoral drama in this period see Dale B. Randall, *Winter Fruit: English Drama, 1642–1660* (Lexington: University Press of Kentucky, 1995), 184–207.

6 Archaism and the 'English' epic

1 James Rosenheim, 'An Early Appreciation of *Paradise Lost*', *Modern Philology* 75 (1978), 280–2 (281), quoting Bodleian MS Tanner 45, fol. 258.

2 *Ibid.*, 282, quoting Bodleian MS Tanner 45*, fol. 271.
3 *The Poetics of Aristotle*, ed. and trans. S. H. Butcher, 4th edn (London: Macmillan, 1907), 83 (XXII.1–5).
4 Karl Gottlob Kühn (ed.), *Claudii Galeni opera omnia*, 22 vols. (Leipzig, 1821–33), 19: 66; translation from Michael Silk, 'LSJ and the Problem of Poetic Archaism: From Meanings to Iconyms', *Classical Quarterly*, ns 33 (1983), 303–30 (303).
5 Silk, 'LSJ', 303. See also Silk, 'The Language of Greek Lyric Poetry', and Olav Hackstein, 'The Greek of Epic', in Egbert J. Bakker (ed.), *A Companion to the Ancient Greek Language* (Oxford: Blackwell, 2010), 424–40 (435), 401–23; Olav Hackstein, *Die Sprachform der homerischen Epen. Faktoren morphologischer Variabilität in literarischen Frühformen: Tradition, Sprachwandel, Sprachliche Anachronismen* (Wiesbaden: Reichert, 2002).
6 *Discoveries*, ed. Lorna Hutson, in *CBJ*, vol. 7, ll. 1369–71; see Donald A. Russell, ed. and trans., *The Orator's Education*, 5 vols., Loeb Classical Library (Cambridge, Mass.: Harvard University Press, 2001), 1.6.39. For similar comments see also E.K.'s Epistle to *The Shepheardes Calender*, ll. 52–7, and Cicero's *de Oratore*, 3.38.153, on which it draws.
7 *Discoveries*, ll. 1371–2; *Orator's Education*, 1.6.40–1.
8 *The Art of English Poesy by George Puttenham: A Critical Edition*, ed. Frank Whigham and Wayne A. Rebhorn (Ithaca, NY: Cornell University Press, 2007), 237–8.
9 John Denham, *The Destruction of Troy, an Essay upon the Second Book of Virgils Æneis. Written in the Year, 1636* (London, 1656), A2v.
10 On the date of *Cymbeline* see Martin Butler (ed.), *Cymbeline* (Cambridge University Press, 2005), 3–6; on that of 'On the Famous Voyage' see *CBJ*, vol. 5, 190.
11 T. J. B. Spencer, '*Paradise Lost*: The Anti-Epic', in C. A. Patrides (ed.), *Approaches to Paradise Lost* (University of Toronto Press, 1968), 81–98 (98).
12 Margaret Doody, *The Daring Muse: Augustan Poetry Reconsidered* (Cambridge University Press, 1985), 64.
13 See Richard Huloet, *Huloets Dictionarie Newly Corrected, Amended, Set in Order and Enlarged* (London, 1572), N4v (from which the quotation comes); Thomas Speght (ed.), *The Workes of our Antient and Learned English Poet Geffrey Chaucer, Newly Printed* (London, 1598), 4A2v, and *The Workes of our Ancient and Learned English Poet, Geffrey Chaucer, Newly Printed* (London, 1602), 3T4r; John Rider, *Riders Dictionarie Corrected and Augmented* (London, 1606), H5v; John Bullokar, *An English Expositor* (London, 1616), F2r.
14 *Workes* (1602), 3T1r.
15 Andrew Hadfield, *Shakespeare, Spenser and the Matter of Britain* (Basingstoke: Palgrave Macmillan, 2004), 130.
16 *OED*'s earliest citation for 'dug' dates from 1530 (dug, *n.*¹); the earliest I have been able to find is in Robert Copland's *Here Begynneth the Complaynte of them that ben too Late Married* (London, 1518), A4v; 'wrizled' (see *OED*

wrizzled, *adj.*) appears in Austin Saker's *Narbonus: The Labyrynth of Libertie* (London, 1580), 107 (*OED*'s earliest citation is the passage from *The Faerie Queene*).

17 See Andrea Hume, *Edmund Spenser: Protestant Poet* (Cambridge University Press, 1984), 92–6, and 'Duessa', in A. C. Hamilton (ed.), *The Spenser Encyclopedia* (University of Toronto Press, 1990), 229–30.

18 I quote the Geneva translation: *The Bible and Holy Scriptures Conteyned in The Olde and Newe Testament* (Geneva, 1560).

19 See D. Douglas Waters, *Duessa as Theological Satire* (Columbia: University of Missouri Press, 1970). On Mistress Missa see also John N. King, *English Reformation Literature: The Tudor Origins of the Protestant Tradition* (Princeton University Press, 1982), 284–9; Antoinina Bevan Zlater, *Reformation Fictions: Polemical Protestant Dialogues in Elizabethan England* (Oxford University Press, 2011), 50–3.

20 Luke Shepherd, *Pathose, or an Inward Passion of the Pope for the Losse of hys Daughter the Masse* (London, 1548), B5r–v.

21 Lanfranco Caretti (ed.), *Orlando furioso* (Milan and Naples: Riccardo Ricciardi, 1954), 7.73.1–5.

22 *Orlando Furioso*, trans. Guido Waldman (Oxford University Press, 1974), 69.

23 Peter DeSa Wiggins, 'Spenser's Use of Ariosto: Imitation and Allusion in Book I of *The Faerie Queene*', *Renaissance Quarterly* 44 (1991), 257–79 (273).

24 Melinda Gough, '"Her filthy feature open showne" in Ariosto, Spenser, and *Much Ado About Nothing*', *Studies in English Literature* 39 (1999), 41–67 (47).

25 Shakerley Marmion, *Hollands Leaguer* (London, 1632), B4r.

26 *The Whole. xii. Bookes of the Æneidos of Virgill* (London, 1573), E2v.

27 On Fairfax's use of Spenserian diction see Charles G. Bell, 'Fairfax's Tasso', *Comparative Literature* 6 (1954), 26–52; C. P. Brand, *Torquato Tasso: A Study of the Poet and his Contribution to English Literature* (Cambridge University Press, 1965), 244; Kathleen M. Lea and T. N. Gang (eds.), *Godfrey of Bulloigne: A Critical Edition of Edward Fairfax's Translation of Tasso's Gerusalemme liberata, Together with Fairfax's Original Poems* (Oxford: Clarendon Press, 1981), 53–4; D. N. C. Wood, 'Tasso in England', in Hamilton, *Spenser Encyclopedia*, 679–80; Andrew Zurcher, *Spenser's Legal Language: Law and Poetry in Early Modern England* (Cambridge: D. S. Brewer, 2007), 77–85.

28 Colin Burrow, *Epic Romance: Homer to Milton* (Oxford: Clarendon Press, 1993), 180.

29 See David Quint, 'Tasso, Torquato', in Hamilton, *Spenser Encyclopedia*, 678–9.

30 See David Quint, *Epic and Empire: Politics and Generic Form from Virgil to Milton* (Princeton University Press, 1993), 234–47.

31 Lanfranco Caretti (ed.), *Torquato Tasso: Gerusalemme liberata* (Turin: Einaudi, 1971), 12.18; *The Liberation of Jerusalem*, trans. Max Wickert, ed. Mark Davie (Oxford University Press, 2009), 12.18.

32 Lea and Gang, *Godfrey of Bulloigne*, 12.18.

33 George Chapman, *Homer Prince of Poets: Translated According to the Greeke, in Twelve Bookes of his Iliads* (London, [?1609]), A5r.

34 *Three Proper, and Wittie, Familiar Letters: Lately Passed Betweene Two Universitie Men* (London, 1580), 6. See Richard Helgerson, *Forms of Nationhood: The Elizabethan Writing of England* (University of Chicago Press, 1992), 25–40; see also Jeff Dolven, 'Tudor Versification and the Rise of Iambic Pentameter', in Kent Cartwright (ed.), *A Companion to Tudor Literature* (Oxford: Wiley Blackwell, 2010), 365–80.

35 Thomas Nashe, *Strange Newes, of the Intercepting Certaine Letters* (London, 1592), G3r.

36 *Letters*, 6.

37 *Informations to William Drummond of Hawthornden*, ed. Ian Donaldson, in *CBJ*, vol. 5, ll. 23–4.

38 Chapman, *Seauen Bookes of the Iliades of Homere, Prince of Poets* (London, 1598), A6r.

39 Butler, *Cymbeline*, 5.3.123SD. All references are to this edition.

40 See, among others, R. F. Wilson, 'Golding's *Metamorphosis* and Shakespeare's Burlesque Method in *A Midsummer Night's Dream*', *English Language Notes* 7 (1969), 18–25; Anthony Brian Taylor, 'Bottom's "Hopping" Heart and Thomas Phaer: The Influence of the Early Translators on "Pyramus and Thisbe"', *Notes & Queries*, ns 42 (1995), 309–15; Taylor, 'Golding's Ovid, Shakespeare's "Small Latin", and the Real Object of Mockery in "Pyramus and Thisbe"', *Shakespeare Survey* 42 (1990), 53–64; Madeleine Forey, '"Bless thee Bottom, bless thee! Thou art translated!": Ovid, Golding, and *A Midsummer Night's Dream*', *Modern Language Review* 93 (1998), 321–9.

41 I thus depart from Ros King, who argues in *Cymbeline: Constructions of Britain* (Aldershot: Ashgate, 2005), 34–5, that the appearance of Jupiter, 'an audibly creaking *deus ex machina*', is Shakespeare's joking solution to intractable problems of plot construction, 'the notion of an archaic device' reinforced by 'some distinctly old-fashioned poetry from the Sicilius family ghosts'. For other interpretations of the use of fourteeners here see Roger Warren, *Staging Shakespeare's Late Plays* (Oxford: Clarendon Press, 1990), 78; Maurice Hunt, 'Fourteeners in Shakespeare's *Cymbeline*', *Notes & Queries*, ns 47 (2000), 458–61; Butler, *Cymbeline*, 14.

42 On the date of *Coriolanus* see R. B. Parker (ed.), *Coriolanus* (Oxford University Press, 1994), 2–7; Lee Bliss (ed.), *Coriolanus* (Cambridge University Press, 2000), 1–5.

43 See Butler, *Cymbeline*, 14.

44 Chapman, *The Iliads of Homer Prince of Poets* (London, 1611), 310–11.

45 On Chapman's style see O. B. Hardison Jr, *Prosody and Purpose in the English Renaissance* (Baltimore, Md.: Johns Hopkins University Press, 1989), 206–10; Charles and Michelle Martindale, *Shakespeare and the Uses of Antiquity: An Introductory Essay* (London: Routledge, 1990), 97; Burrow, *Epic Romance*, 203.

46 See, for instance, *Æneidos*, E4r.

47 See Parker's 'Romance and Empire: Anachronistic *Cymbeline*', in George M. Logan and Gordon Teskey (eds.), *Unfolded Tales: Essays on Renaissance Romance* (Ithaca, NY: Cornell University Press, 1989), 189–207. On *Cymbeline* and *The Aeneid* see also Heather James, *Shakespeare's Troy: Drama, Politics, and the Translation of Empire* (Cambridge University Press, 1997), 151–88.

48 Golding, *The Fyrst Fower Bookes of P. Ovidius Nasos Worke, Intitled Metamorphosis* (London, 1565).

49 See, in addition to works cited thus far, Jodi Mikalachki, 'The Masculine Romance of Roman Britain: *Cymbeline* and Early Modern English Nationalism', *Shakespeare Quarterly* 46 (1995), 301–22; Michael Redmond, '"My Lord, I fear, has forgot Britain": Rome, Italy, and the (Re)construction of British National Identity', *Shakespeare Yearbook* 10 (1999), 297–316; Mary Floyd-Wilson, 'Delving to the Root: *Cymbeline*, Scotland, and the English Race', in David J. Baker and Willy Maley (eds.), *British Identities and English Renaissance Literature* (Cambridge University Press, 2002), 101–15; Peter Parolin, 'Anachronistic Italy: Cultural Alliances and National Identity in *Cymbeline*', *Shakespeare Studies* 30 (2002), 188–215; Gordon McMullan, 'The Colonisation of Early Britain on the Jacobean Stage', in Gordon McMullan and David Matthews (eds.), *Reading the Medieval in Early Modern England* (Cambridge University Press, 2007), 119–40; Willy Maley, '*Cymbeline*, the Font of History, and the Matter of Britain: From Times New Roman to Italic Type', in Diana E. Henderson (ed.), *Alternative Shakespeares 3* (London: Routledge, 2008), 119–37.

50 Floyd-Wilson, 'Delving', 102.

51 On Spenser and Elizabethan imperium see, among others, Jeffrey Knapp, 'Error as a Means of Empire in *The Faerie Queene* 1', *ELH* 54 (1987), 801–34; David Norbrook, *Poetry and Politics in the English Renaissance*, rev. edn (Oxford University Press, 2002), 97–139; Patricia Palmer, *Language and Conquest in Early Modern Ireland: English Renaissance Literature and Elizabethan Imperial Expansion* (Cambridge University Press, 2001); Hadfield, *Shakespeare, Spenser and the Matter of Britain*.

52 On this project see Wesley Trimpi, *Ben Jonson's Poems: A Study of the Plain Style* (Stanford University Press, 1962), 96–7.

53 See Victoria Moul, *Jonson, Horace, and the Classical Tradition* (Cambridge University Press, 2010), 187–93.

54 All references are to *The Epigrams*, ed. Colin Burrow, in *CBJ*, vol. 5.

55 Trimpi, *Ben Jonson's Poems*, 98–9.

56 Charles Cotton, *Scarronides: or, Virgile Travestie. A Mock-Poem. Being the First Book of Virgils Æneis in English, Burlesque* (London, 1664), 1, 3–4.

57 A. C. Swinburne, *A Study of Ben Jonson* (London: Chatto and Windus, 1889), 95.

58 Ann Baines Coiro, 'Drama in the Epic Style: Narrator, Muse, and Audience in *Paradise Lost*', *Milton Studies* 51 (2010), 63–100 (65).

59 See Hume, 'On the Language of *Paradise Lost*: Its Elizabethan and Early Seventeenth-Century Background', in Ronald David Emma and John T. Shawcross (eds.), *Language and Style in Milton* (New York: Frederick Ungar, 1976), 65–101; Adamson, 'Literary Language', in Roger Lass (ed.), *The Cambridge History of the English Language*, vol. 3, *1476–1776* (Cambridge University Press, 1999), 539–653 (579).

60 B. A. Wright, *Milton's Paradise Lost* (London: Methuen, 1962), 72; Thomas N. Corns, *Milton's Language* (Oxford: Blackwell, 1990), 111.

61 Notable exceptions are those scholars who have been interested in the Saxon influence on Milton's work: see, for instance, William E. Engel, 'John Milton's Recourse to Old English: A Case-Study in Renaissance Lexicography', *LATCH: A Journal for the Study of the Literary Artefact in Theory, Culture, or History* 1 (2008), 1–29. Hannah Crawforth's *Etymology and the Invention of English in Early Modern Literature* (Cambridge University Press, 2013) includes a groundbreaking reassessment of Milton's uses of etymology, which she views in the context of the English language as well as Latin and Greek. On debates concerning the 'Englishness' of Milton's verse from the eighteenth century onwards see Anne-Julia Zwierlein, 'Milton Epic and Bucolic: Empire and Readings of *Paradise Lost, 1667–1837*', in Nicholas McDowell and Nigel Smith (eds.), *The Oxford Handbook of Milton* (Oxford University Press, 2011), 669–86; F. R. Leavis, 'Milton's Verse', in *Revaluation: Tradition and Development in English Poetry* (Oxford University Press, 1933), 42–67; Christopher Ricks, *Milton's Grand Style* (Oxford University Press, 1963), ch. 1; John K. Hale, *Milton's Languages: The Impact of Multilingualism on Style* (Cambridge University Press, 1997).

62 See David Weil Baker, '"Dealt with at his owne weapon": Anti-Antiquarianism in Milton's Prelacy Tracts', *Studies in Philology* 106 (2009), 207–34; Milton, *The History of Britain, That Part Especially Now Call'd England* (London, 1670), 178.

63 Dryden, 'The Preface', in *Sylvae, or, The Second Part of Poetical Miscellanies* (London, 1685), a7v.

64 Dryden, 'To the Right Honourable Charles, Earl of Dorset and Middlesex', in *The Satires of Decimus Junius Juvenalis Translated into English Verse by Mr. Dryden and Several Other Eminent Hands* (London, 1693), viii, l.

65 Samuel Wesley, 'The Preface', in *The Life of our Blessed Lord & Saviour, Jesus Christ. An Heroic Poem* (London, 1693), b1r.

66 Charles Gildon, *Miscellaneous Letters and Essays on Several Subjects Philosophical, Moral, Historical, Critical, Amorous, &c., in Prose and Verse* (London, 1694), 41.

67 Elias Ashmole, *Theatrum Chemicum Britannicum. Containing Severall Poeticall Pieces of our Famous English Philosophers* (London, 1652), 3S2r.

68 See, for instance, 'cresset' in Phaer and Stanihurst's *Aeneids*, Golding's *Metamorphoses* and Chapman's *Iliads* and *Odyssey*, and 'sheer' and 'tilth' in Golding's *Metamorphoses*.

69 The literature here is vast. See, in addition to works cited below, John M. Steadman, *Milton and the Renaissance Hero* (Oxford: Clarendon Press, 1967); Joan M. Webber, *Milton and His Epic Tradition* (Seattle: University of Washington Press, 1979); Barbara K. Lewalski, *Paradise Lost and the Rhetoric of Literary Forms* (Princeton University Press, 1993); Kenneth Borris, *Allegory and Epic in English Renaissance Literature: Heroic Form in Sidney, Spenser, and Milton* (Cambridge University Press, 2000); Neil Forsyth, *The Satanic Epic* (Princeton University Press, 2002); Christopher Bond, *Spenser, Milton, and the Redemption of the Epic Hero* (Newark: University of Delaware Press, 2011).

70 Patrick J. Cook, *Milton, Spenser and the Epic Tradition* (Aldershot: Ashgate, 1996), 136.

71 Patrick Hume, *Annotations on Milton's Paradise Lost* (London, 1695), 17.

72 Elisha Coles, *An English Dictionary* (London, 1677), D3r. See *OED* bane, *n.*[1].

73 See Charles Martindale, *John Milton and the Transformation of Ancient Epic* (London: Croom Helm, 1986), 72–4; Cook, *Milton*, 135.

74 *Iliads* (1611), 13.

75 On 'Pandemonium' see Corns, *Milton's Language*, 91; Crawforth, *Etymology*, chap. 4.

76 John Vicars, *The XII Aeneids of Virgil, the Most Renowned Laureat-Prince of Latine-Poets; Translated into English Deca-Syllables* (London, 1632), 193.

77 The use of 'hail' in this context had been established at least as early as the Tyndale Bible of 1534.

78 David Norbrook (ed.), *Order and Disorder* (Oxford: Blackwell, 2001), 5. On the date see Norbrook, 'Lucy Hutchinson and *Order and Disorder*: The Manuscript Evidence', *English Manuscript Studies* 9 (2000), 257–91 (274–6).

79 *CEP*, 148. On the background to Milton's use of blank verse see O. B. Hardison Jr, 'Blank Verse before Milton', *Studies in Philology* 81 (1984), 253–74.

80 '*Paradise Lost* and Milton's Politics', *Milton Studies* 38 (2000), 141–68 (147). See also Steven N. Zwicker, 'Lines of Authority: Politics and Literary Culture in the Restoration', in Kevin Sharpe and Steven N. Zwicker (eds.), *Politics of Discourse: The Literature and History of Seventeenth-Century England* (Berkeley: University of California Press, 1987), 230–70, on which Lewalski draws.

81 On the developing response see Nicholas von Maltzahn, 'Milton: Nation and Reception', in David Loewenstein and Paul Stevens (eds.), *Early Modern Nationalism and Milton's England* (Toronto University Press, 2008), 402–42.

82 Dryden, *Of Dramatick Poesie, an Essay* (London, 1668), 58.

83 *Anacreon Done into English out of the Original Greek* (Oxford, 1683), a4v–b1r.

84 Thomas Fletcher, 'The Preface', in *Poems on Several Occasions and Translations Wherein the First and Second Books of Virgil's Æneis are Attempted in English* (London, 1692), A6r–v.

85 Dryden, *Satires*, ix.

86 John Hopkins, 'The Preface', in *Milton's Paradise Lost Imitated in Rhyme* (London, 1699), A4r. For further comments on Milton's use of blank verse see John Dennis, 'The Preface', in *The Passion of Byblis Made English* (London, 1692), C1r; Wesley, *Life*, b1r.

87 I cite the text in *CEP*, 146–7.

88 'A Letter of the Authors', in *FQ*, 737.

Coda: looking backward, looking forward

1 Samuel Butler, *Hudibras*, ed. John Wilders (Oxford: Clarendon Press, 1967), 1.1.15–16.

2 See *OED*, amphibious, *adj.* The earliest use I have traced is in John King, *A Sermon Preached at White-Hall the 5. Day of November. Ann. 1608* (Oxford, 1608), 27.

3 On the date of composition see Wilders, *Hudibras*, xliv–xlviii.

4 Richard Terry, *Mock-Heroic from Butler to Cowper: An English Genre and Discourse* (Aldershot: Ashgate, 2005), 38. On the style of *Hudibras* see also Ian Jack, *Augustan Satire: Intention and Idiom in English Poetry, 1660–1750* (Oxford: Clarendon Press, 1952), 15–42.

5 Alvin Snider, *Origins and Authority in Seventeenth-Century England: Bacon, Milton, Butler* (University of Toronto Press, 1994), 163.

6 See, among others, Michael Wilding, 'The Last of the Epics: The Rejection of the Heroic in *Paradise Lost* and *Hudibras*', in Harold Love (ed.), *Restoration Literature: Critical Approaches* (London: Methuen, 1972), 91–120; Margaret Doody, *The Daring Muse: Augustan Poetry Reconsidered* (Cambridge University Press, 1985), 63–5.

7 See Michael Murphy, 'Scholars at Play: A Short History of Composing in Old English', *Old English Newsletter* 15.2 (1982), 26–36.

8 On these processes see David Fairer, 'Creating a National Poetry: The Tradition of Spenser and Milton', in John Sitter (ed.), *The Cambridge Companion to Eighteenth-Century Poetry* (Cambridge University Press, 2001), 177–202; Gary Taylor, *Reinventing Shakespeare: A Cultural History, from the Restoration to the Present* (Oxford University Press, 1991), 7–51; Michael Dobson, *The Making of the National Poet: Shakespeare, Adaptation and Authorship, 1660–1769* (Oxford: Clarendon Press, 1992).

9 Edward Howard, *Spencer Redivivus Containing the First Book of the Fairy Queen* (London, 1687), title-page. On Howard's authorship see Leicester Bradner, 'The Authorship of *Spenser Redivivus*', *Review of English Studies* 14 (1938), 323–6. The fullest scholarly analysis is Clare R. Kinney, 'What S/he Ought to Have Been: Romancing Truth in *Spenser Redivivus*', *Spenser Studies* 16 (2002), 125–37.

10 Howard, 'The Preface to the Reader', in *The Brittish Princes: An Heroick Poem* (London, 1669), A6r.

11 Thomas Tomkins, *The Rebels Plea, or, Mr. Baxters Judgment Concerning the Late Wars* (London, 1660), 11.

12 Alok Yadav, 'Fractured Meanings: *Hudibras* and the Historicity of the Literary Text', *ELH* 62 (1995), 529–49 (535).

13 Dryden, *Fables Ancient and Modern Translated into Verse from Homer, Ovid, Boccace, & Chaucer, with Original Poems* (London, 1700), *B2v.

14 T. S. Eliot, *The Waste Land and Other Poems*, ed. Joseph Black and Leonard Conolly (Peterborough, ON: Broadview Press, 2011), ll. 433–6.

Index